A Declaration and Constitution for a Free Society

Capitalist Thought: Studies in Philosophy, Politics, and Economics

Series Editor: Edward W. Younkins, Wheeling Jesuit University

Mission Statement

This book series is devoted to studying the foundations of capitalism from a number of academic disciplines including, but not limited to, philosophy, political science, economics, law, literature, and history. Recognizing the expansion of the boundaries of economics, this series particularly welcomes proposals for monographs and edited collections that focus on topics from transdisciplinary, interdisciplinary, and multidisciplinary perspectives. Lexington Books will consider a wide range of conceptual, empirical, and methodological submissions, Works in this series will tend to synthesize and integrate knowledge and to build bridges within and between disciplines. They will be of vital concern to academicians, business people, and others in the debate about the proper role of capitalism, business, and business people in economic society.

Advisory Board

Doug Bandow, Samuel Gregg, Douglas B. Rasmussen
Walter Block, Stephen Hicks, Chris Matthew Sciabarra
Douglas J. Den Uyl, Steven Horwitz, Aeon J. Skoble
Richard M. Ebeling, Stephan Kinsella, C. Bradley Thompson
Mimi Gladstein, James Otteson, Thomas E. Woods

Books in Series

Freedom, Eudaemonia, and Risk: An Inquiry into the Ethics of Risk-Taking by Kathleen Touchstone
On the Private and Public Virtues of an Honorable Entrepreneur by Felix R. Livingston
The Ontology and Function of Money: The Philosophical Fundamentals of Monetary Institutions by Leonidas Zelmanovitz
Andrew Carnegie: An Economic Biography by Samuel Bostaph
Water Capitalism: Privatize Oceans, Rivers, Lakes, and Aquifers Too by Walter E. Block and Peter Lothian Nelson
Capitalism and Commerce in Imaginative Literature: Perspectives on Business from Novels and Plays edited by Edward W. Younkins
Pride and Profit: The Intersection of Jane Austen and Adam Smith by Cecil E. Bohanon and Michelle Albert Vachris
The Seen, the Unseen, and the Unrealized: How Regulations Affect Our Everyday Lives by Per L. Bylund
Global Economics: A Holistic Approach by Clifford F. Thies
On the Private and Public Virtues of an Honorable Entrepreneur: Preventing a Separation of the Honorable and the Useful by Felix R. Livingston
Perspectives on Ayn Rand's Contributions to Economic and Business Thought by Edward W. Younkins.
The Dialectics of Liberty: Exploring the Context of Human Freedom by Roger E. Bissell,

A Declaration and Constitution for a Free Society

Making the Declaration
of Independence and
U.S. Constitution Fully
Consistent with the Protection
of Individual Rights

Brian P. Simpson

LEXINGTON BOOKS
Lanham • Boulder • New York • London

Published by Lexington Books
An imprint of The Rowman & Littlefield Publishing Group, Inc.
4501 Forbes Boulevard, Suite 200, Lanham, Maryland 20706
www.rowman.com

6 Tinworth Street, London SE11 5AL, United Kingdom

British Library Cataloguing in Publication Information Available

Library of Congress Cataloging-in-Publication Data

Library of Congress Control Number: 2020950414

To Annaliese, my wife, and Sparkle, our cat. Sparkle deserves special mention because he was a faithful companion sitting on my lap while I wrote much of this book.

Contents

Preface

I conceived of this project in late 2014, shortly after I finished my two-volume book on the business cycle titled *Money, Banking, and the Business Cycle*. I thought it would be a great way to learn more about the U.S. Constitution and Declaration of Independence, which is something I had always wanted to do. I also thought it would be a great way to teach people about the nature of rights and freedom. I learned more than I ever thought I would in writing this book. I hope you will find reading this book as enlightening an experience as I found writing it.

Writing this book required knowledge in a number of areas. My background is in economics, so I had a great deal to learn about the Constitution, Declaration, and related issues to write this book. The key knowledge that I possessed when I thought of this project, and that I knew would be indispensable to writing the book, was knowledge of the nature of rights and freedom, including their philosophical justification. Unfortunately, far too few people have knowledge of these subjects. That is one of the reasons why this book is desperately needed.

My knowledge of economics has been extremely important in writing this book as well. If one is arguing for a country to move to a free society, one cannot hold up a free society as a moral ideal and expect people to believe, based on moral arguments alone, that that is the direction we must head. One must also be able to show that the free market is practical. Fortunately, there is no break between theory and practice (or between morality and economics). The moral *is* the practical (if one embraces a valid moral code). My background in economics has provided me with a great ability to show that the free market enables people to succeed in practice. That is, laissez-faire capitalism is the only political and economic system that is consistent with the requirements of human life. It enables people to further their lives and well-being and leads to the highest standard of living that is possible. In fact, it achieves both peace and prosperity. This book helps to illustrate the union that exists between theory and practice by providing an important integration of constitutional law, knowledge of freedom and rights, the application of this knowledge to defending specific rights, the philosophical justification for rights, and knowledge of economics to show the practical consequences of protecting rights and freedom (and what happens economically when rights are not protected).

This book is intended for readers who want to understand the fundamental legal requirements of a free society. In addition, one will learn about the philosophical justification for a free society. This book is directed at not only lawyers and constitutional law experts but also economists, political scientists, and philosophers. It is directed at anyone who is interested in arguing for and creating greater freedom in a society.

The book is not written in a technical manner, so it is accessible to intelligent lay readers who are interested in the subject. However, I reference many scholarly works and Supreme Court cases—see the bibliography and list of cases at the end of the book—so legal and other scholars can gain something from the book as well. The book would serve as a good source for individuals in any academic field who want to gain a better understanding of the application and protection of rights.

Even though it is written for advocates of freedom, opponents of freedom can also gain something from the book. To the extent that they want to learn about the ideas of their intellectual adversaries, the book has a great deal to offer them. It will help them better understand the nature of freedom and what it requires. This can aid them in attempting to refute arguments in favor of freedom. Of course, my hope is that the opponents of freedom, after having read this book, will no longer be its enemy but will, in fact, be supporters of freedom . . . and thus supporters of human life.

Brian P. Simpson
La Jolla, CA
December 2020

Acknowledgments

I thank National University for providing me with a sabbatical in the fall of 2020. While on sabbatical, I was a visiting scholar at the Ayn Rand Institute. I thank the Ayn Rand Institute as well. In addition, I thank fellows from the institute who participated in a webinar on a chapter of the book for the feedback they provided. I also thank Gary Lawson of the Boston University School of Law for providing valuable feedback on a chapter of the book. Despite the support I have received while completing this project, I alone am responsible for the views expressed in this book.

Introduction

Given the current philosophical and political climate, the main intention of this book is not to revise the Declaration of Independence and U.S. Constitution in the hope that they will be used as templates to create new versions of these documents any time soon, although I certainly would not object to such an endeavor. The main purpose is to revise these documents as an educational endeavor. It is to help readers understand how these documents must be modified so that they consistently uphold and protect the values of individual rights and freedom. In the process, it will help readers understand the nature of rights and freedom and the importance of protecting them.

I have enormous respect for the Declaration and Constitution. They represent gigantic steps forward in creating a government that performs its appropriate function of protecting individual rights. The Constitution may not have protected rights consistently when it was created (or even at all for black people). Unfortunately, the Constitution still does not protect individual rights consistently (e.g., due to Amendment XVI on the income tax and the Takings Clause of Amendment V). Nonetheless, the establishment of the United States still represented a huge step forward. For the first time in history a government was established for the purpose of protecting individual rights. This was an enormous achievement and should not be ignored, evaded, denounced, or even disrespected. It should be admired and respected for the great achievement that it was.

I also have enormous respect for the men who created these documents, especially the one who wrote the Declaration, Thomas Jefferson. He among all the Founding Fathers understood best what individual rights are and what they require.

It is not my intention to denigrate these men or the documents they created by revising them. However, the documents are not completely consistent with the protection of individual rights and freedom. The defense of rights and freedom that they provide can be improved. As I will show in chapter 1, protecting individual rights and freedom is the only proper purpose of government. Freedom is a fundamental intellectual, moral, political, and economic requirement of human life. Hence, it is an extremely important and useful exercise to revise these documents so that one can see what is necessary for them to be fully consistent with these crucial values. The fact that they can be revised in this endeavor—and not completely scrapped—is indicative of the achievement they represent and the respect for them that I have.

The Constitution, in particular, needs to be revised to make it harder for those who want to violate rights to do so. We need to eliminate the holes in the armor that is protecting freedom to create a stronger defense of freedom. A part of creating a stronger defense of freedom is providing a better understanding of freedom. To this end, one thing that readers will notice is that I often use the terms "individual rights" and "freedom" together. I use them together to emphasize that the two go together. Individual rights are the legal means we use to protect freedom. As one reads the book, one will gain a greater understanding of how these two concepts are linked.

It is not a valid objection to revising the Constitution to say that the document is outdated. The Constitution is still an extremely important document to human life. Technology, fashion trends, fads, and so forth may change, but the fundamental nature of human life does not, including the need for individuals to have their rights protected. The way in which rights are protected in some cases may need to change, such as with regard to the protection of property rights over the airwaves given that radio, television, telephones, and so on did not exist at the founding of the nation. But changing technology makes it that much more important to understand and properly apply the Constitution. Without this, rights will be violated on a greater scale, which I would argue often occurs today in areas of new technology due to a lack of understanding of rights and the Constitution. By helping people better understand how and why rights need to be protected, this book will help people properly apply the Constitution to advancing technology and in other areas where changes occur in society.

One can also learn about the nature of rights and freedom by modifying the Declaration. It does not require the substantial number of changes that the Constitution requires, but important insights into what rights and freedom are can be gained by going through the process of changing it. Particularly, one can understand what the fundamental rights are and gain knowledge of the philosophical underpinning of rights.

Such an endeavor is not merely academic. The Declaration is a part of the laws of the United States and could be changed (or a new Declaration created).[1] The changes I propose would help solidify the protection of rights not only in U.S. law but in the minds of American citizens and individuals around the globe, since the Declaration is widely known for protecting freedom. Making the proper changes to this document could help spawn greater freedom throughout the world by showing in clearer terms what rights and freedom require.

At this point, some might ask the question: Instead of revising the Declaration and Constitution, why not write equivalent documents from scratch to show what is necessary to establish a government that consistently protects individual rights and freedom? While that would be extremely beneficial to me in terms of my learning from such an endeavor, it would not have the impact of revising such important and well-known documents that defend rights. It would also not have as much educational value to readers. Using documents that are well-known for defending rights serves as a good pedagogical device for teaching people about the nature and importance of rights, as well as how to protect them. It will be much more worthwhile for readers to see where these documents go wrong, why they go wrong, and what is needed to correct them. That is invaluable in moving us closer to being able to protect rights consistently.

Moreover, it makes no sense to start from scratch because the documents take us a very long way toward protecting rights consistently. In essence, we do not need to reinvent the wheel. We just need to complete the task of creating the best wheel we possibly can. If we make the necessary revisions, the job will be complete.

Of course, showing how to revise these documents will make it easier to perform the task of revising them and protecting freedom in practice. I will show in detail where, how, and why they need to be changed. In some cases, I even discuss why some provisions of the Constitution do not need to be changed, even though some might think they need to be changed to protect freedom. This will also help in moving the nation toward freedom.

A part of making these documents fully consistent with the protection of rights and freedom includes not only revising their legal and political components, as one would expect, but revising their more fundamental—if only implied in some cases—philosophical content. I discuss in chapter 1 what metaphysical, epistemological, and ethical ideas are consistent with the protection of rights and freedom. I also discuss what ideas in these areas are inconsistent with these indispensable values. I show that only Objectivist philosophy—the philosophy of Ayn Rand—is fully consistent with the protection of rights and freedom. Hence, I will revise these documents from an Objectivist perspective. That is, I will make them consistent with a philosophy that says that absolutes exist, reason is our only means to knowledge, and it is a moral virtue for one to act in his or her rational self-interest.

Although my revision of the Declaration and Constitution is based on Objectivist philosophy, I will not be providing a detailed exposition or defense of this philosophy. That would be a different book. Other writers have written on this topic.[2] My purpose in this book is to apply Objectivist philosophy to revise the Declaration and Constitution. Hence, I provide enough discussion of Objectivist philosophy so that the reader can understand what changes to the Declaration and Constitution are necessary and why they are necessary based on that philosophy. I also discuss fundamental alternative viewpoints to that philosophy so the reader can see where these alternatives go wrong. However, the discussion of the underlying philosophical ideas used to modify the documents is necessarily abbreviated. The book would be too long otherwise. The primary focus is on the changes to the documents themselves.

In revising the Constitution, I am not endorsing the idea that the Constitution is a "living document" as liberals do. However, I also do not accept the validity of the idea that we should base our interpretations of the Constitution on the conservative idea of original intent or meaning. Both of these methods of interpretation are wrong. They are wrong because the first is subjective and the second is intrinsic. The proper method of interpreting (and amending) the Constitution is the objective approach. That is, one must recognize, based on a logical analysis of the facts of reality, that the only proper purpose of government is to protect individual rights. Based on this, the Constitution should always be interpreted to provide the maximum protection of rights that is possible, given the text and meaning of the document. What this means is that given that the Constitution does not consistently protect rights, it may not be possible in all cases to interpret the Constitution in a way that protects rights. That is one reason why it needs to be revised. However, in these cases, interpretations should protect rights as much as the text of the Constitution (or its implied meaning) will allow. I will have more to say on the subjective, intrinsic, and objective in chapter 1.

Here I will only mention that it is obvious that the subjective interpretation of the Constitution is invalid because it implies that words have no meaning (or they have any meaning that one wants them to have) and thus that there is no objective meaning to words and concepts. Hence, the Constitution can be interpreted to mean anything one wants it to mean (or nothing at all). This implies that there are no restraints on government. Governments can violate rights in any way they want. I will show in chapter 1 that this is a contradictory and dangerous position.

It might appear based on the above paragraph that the interpretation based on original intent or meaning is valid. However, this is not true. To see why, imagine if the Founding Fathers wanted to violate rights and created a constitution to do that in a consistent and violent way. Going by the original meaning would be disastrous in this case. This would create a government thoroughly opposed to human life, such as that of North Korea, the former USSR, or Nazi Germany. Here, the "living document" approach to interpreting such a constitution would be a better approach than attempting to consistently interpret the document based on its original meaning. It only appears to some advocates of freedom that the method of interpretation based on original meaning is better because the Founding Fathers wanted to protect rights and today's liberals want to violate rights, such as through the creation of socialized medicine, "free" university education, Social Security, welfare, "living" wages, the antitrust laws, and more. Hence, interpreting the Constitution based on original meaning is put forward as a way of protecting rights. Nonetheless, both of these approaches must be rejected. The rejection of both subjectivism and intrinsicism involves performing an objective analysis of the facts of reality based on the laws of logic to see that protecting individual rights and freedom is a fundamental requirement of human life and thus constitutes the only proper function of government.

I must make it clear that my analysis and revision of the Declaration and Constitution are not based on conservative political ideas, as my rejection of originalism should indicate. Unfortunately, conservatives are not much better than the liberals, since they also want to violate rights in many ways, such as through Social Security, restrictions on immigration and international trade, the antitrust laws, outlawing abortion, and more. Liberals offer us essentially a watered-down version of socialism, which in the case of some liberals is quite concentrated (and the overall concentration among liberals is currently growing). Conservatives offer us a mix of some, very limited, aspects of a free-market economy with various degrees of theocracy and national socialism (conservatives' opposition to free immigration and free international trade is a part of their national socialist elements). My analysis is a purely secular approach that rejects both conservative and liberal principles because both stand in opposition to the protection of individual rights and, therefore, both are fundamentally antithetical to human life.

I must also emphasize that I do not perform an historical analysis of the Declaration, Constitution, and rights. I analyze them—as previously stated—based on a logical analysis of the facts, including the requirements of human life. Of course, many writers throughout history have provided valid analyses of rights. I will turn to these writers on occasion to make certain points. I also draw extensively on the literature in the fields of law, economics, and other fields, as well as relevant Supreme Court cases, to make my arguments. I will also turn to writers who have opposed rights to address criticisms of rights theory. See the bibliography and list of Supreme Court cases for the works drawn upon and cases referenced.

My analysis starts in chapter 1 with a presentation of what rights and freedom are, why they are important, and how to protect them. Then, in chapter 2, I apply the ideas developed in chapter 1 to revise the Declaration. In chapters 3–5, I revise (amend) the original Constitution. In chapters 6 and 7, I revise the current amendments to the Constitution. In chapters 8 and 9, I complete the revision of the Constitution by offering amendments to the Constitution that protect additional freedoms that, for the most part, cannot be protected by modifying existing portions of the Constitution. Finally, in chapter 10, I address proposals that have been suggested as a part of efforts to revise the Constitution or create whole constitutions in an attempt to protect freedom but that fail to do so. I show why these attempts to protect freedom go wrong.

Beyond the educational objectives already mentioned, this exercise will serve a number of additional purposes. By showing what is necessary for a government to consistently protect rights, the book will obviously serve as a guide to what changes need to be made to the current U.S. Constitution so that it can consistently uphold the protection of individual rights. In addition, the revised Constitution can be used as a guide by judges in making rulings that are consistent with the protection of individual rights based on the current, albeit flawed, Constitution. Moreover, it can serve as a guide in the proposal and passage of legislation that more consistently protects rights. Furthermore, it can serve as a guide for the creation from scratch of constitutions in other countries that consistently protect rights. Finally, it can serve as a guide for judges and legislators in other countries in making rulings, passing legislation, and revising constitutions to protect individual rights more consistently. This, among other things, will help countries respond appropriately to crises, including the COVID-19 pandemic, which is discussed in chapter 4. Hence, this exercise is not merely academic. It has a practical purpose whose goal is to influence for the better the functioning of governments around the world.

Such an exercise is vitally important because of the lack of understanding today regarding the proper function of government and the nature of rights and freedom. Freedom is a fundamental requirement of human life because we need freedom to use our minds to think, act on our rational judgment, and produce the values our lives require. In other words, freedom is a fundamental requirement of human life because it is a fundamental requirement of the mind. If we are to understand the world and be able to apply the knowledge we gain to furthering our lives and well-being, we must have the freedom protected that is necessary to investigate the world and make the logical conclusions to which the evidence leads. We must also possess the freedom to apply this knowledge in productive endeavors, such as producing food, clothing, and shelter, as well as lifesaving medicines or the latest electronic device. How can one use one's mind for this end if the freedom of the pursuit and application of knowledge is not protected? How can we further our lives and well-being if the freedom to use our knowledge and property is not protected? For example, how could a pharmaceutical company develop new drugs if its profits and capital are taxed away? How could it use the knowledge it gains about the ability of different combinations of chemicals to fight disease if some government agency makes it prohibitively costly to develop and bring new drugs to the marketplace? How can individuals open new businesses to support themselves if there is a litany of regulations and taxes that make it much harder, if not impossible, to do so? How are wage earners supposed to support themselves if taxes and regulations make it difficult for employers to expand their businesses and hire workers, and thus make it much harder for workers to get jobs, gain skills, and improve their ability to earn higher wages?

The government regulates virtually all aspects of the individual's life today. It regulates everything from what size soda we can purchase and what kind of oil we can use to cook our food, to the fuel we can use in our automobiles, what our children learn in school, and what is on the school lunch menu. The government also regulates the type of health care we can purchase and the racial, gender, and age makeup of workplaces, as well as how long workers can work in a day and what they can be paid. It regulates how we build our homes, how we use our land, the types of bathrooms available in our businesses and schools, and much, much more.

The violations of freedom in these examples occur—and will continue to grow—because rights are not consistently protected. The fundamental political means to ensure that rights are protected is to make the supreme law of the land fully consistent with the protection of individual rights and freedom. But the Constitution, while a great document that took enormous steps forward in protecting rights and freedom relative to what had existed prior to its creation, does not do this.

This does not justify abandoning the Constitution or interpreting or modifying it in a way that would lead to further violations of individual rights, as it appears many legal scholars, politicians, and, unfortunately, Supreme Court justices want to do.[3] What is needed is a strengthening of the protections of freedom that the Constitution affords. The best way to do this is to repeal or modify the parts of the Constitution that are inconsistent with freedom and add provisions that are necessary to make the protection of individual rights that such a document provides as strong as possible.

Another crucial aspect of this endeavor is to ensure that the beacon of freedom—the Declaration of Independence—shines as brightly as possible so that it can guide us in a better fashion toward freedom. This will help prevent the country from heading down the road to a police state; it will help protect in a lasting manner the ability of individuals to further their own lives and well-being and achieve greater and lasting economic prosperity. This is the ultimate goal of this book.

Let us now begin this extremely important undertaking.

NOTES

1. On the fact that the Declaration is a part of the laws of the United States, see Timothy Sandefur, *The Conscience of the Constitution: The Declaration of Independence and the Right to Liberty* (Washington, DC: Cato Institute, 2014), pp. 14–15 and p. 163, note 35. On the influence of the Declaration on the law, see Mark Graber, "The Declaration of Independence and Contemporary Constitutional Pedagogy," *Southern California Law Review* vol. 89, no. 3 (March 2016), pp. 509–39. See, in particular, pp. 516–18 and 520–32.

2. For some examples, see Leonard Peikoff, *Objectivism: The Philosophy of Ayn Rand* (New York: Meridian, 1991); Harry Binswanger, *How We Know: Epistemology on an Objectivist Foundation* (New York: TOF Publications, Inc., 2014); and Allan Gotthelf and Gregory Salmieri, editors, *A Companion to Ayn Rand* (Chichester, UK: Wiley Blackwell, 2016).

3. For some examples, see Mark R. Levin, *The Liberty Amendments: Restoring the American Republic* (New York: Threshold Editions, 2013), pp. 60–63. Also, see John Paul Stevens, *Six Amendments: How and Why We Should Change the Constitution* (New York: Little, Brown and Company, 2014), pp. 79 and 132.

Chapter 1

Rights and Freedom

What Are They and Why Do They Matter?

WHAT ARE RIGHTS AND FREEDOM?

To protect individual rights and freedom, one must understand what they are. First, let us focus on freedom. When one speaks of a free society, what is one referring to? What is one free from? Freedom refers to the absence of the initiation of physical force, the absence of compulsion and coercion.[1] What does it mean to initiate force? It means to start or be the first one to use force. So, to be free from the initiation of physical force means to be free from first users of force. This implies, for example, that murder, rape, and armed robbery are prohibited in a free society. A murderer is a first user of force. He initiates physical force against his victim. This can be seen more clearly in comparison to the police, who arrest the murderer. They use force but do not initiate physical force. They retaliate with force; that is, they are second users of force. They do not violate freedom but protect one's freedom from being violated by criminals or apprehend those who have violated one's freedom.

Most importantly, in a free society, we are free from the government's initiation of physical force. This means government policies such as price controls, the redistribution of wealth and income, and tariffs and quotas are prohibited in a free society. Why? When the government implements, say, a tariff it is initiating physical force and thus violating the freedom of those who are forced to pay the tariff. When someone wants to buy an automobile from a foreign manufacturer, for example, but is forced to pay a tax (i.e., a tariff) to import it into the country, the government is the first user of force. No force is used by the person who wants to import the car, and the foreign manufacturer does not use force to make the person buy it. Both respect the freedom of the other party, and both engage in voluntary trade. It is the government that forces the buyer to pay a tax to be able to bring the car into

9

the country. Further, since neither party to the transaction has used force, the government *initiates physical force* and thus *violates the freedom* of both parties to engage in the trade.

The same is true when the government forces producers to obey regulations. For example, when it forces pharmaceutical companies to abide by safety and efficacy standards in the development of drugs, imposed by the Food and Drug Administration (FDA), it initiates force and thus violates the freedom of pharmaceutical companies. If a pharmaceutical company produces a drug and gets people to buy it voluntarily—without the use of force or fraud—no one's freedom has been violated and therefore when the government forces them to obey its dictates, the government is a first user of force.

Some might think that protecting the freedom of pharmaceutical companies would lead to unsafe drugs being produced and people being harmed or killed as a result. However, as I discuss in my book *Markets Don't Fail!*, FDA regulations cause more harm and death than they prevent because, among other reasons, the FDA has incentives to be overly cautious and delay the approval of beneficial drugs that could save or improve lives. The over cautiousness is due to the FDA facing a great deal of disapprobation if it approves a drug that turns out to be harmful, since those cases tend to receive a lot of attention in the media and elsewhere, but will tend to receive little or no condemnation if it fails to approve (or delays the approval) of a beneficial drug, since those cases generally do not receive much attention. In addition, the delays in approval—it can take eight years to get a drug approved—lead to higher development costs and, as a result, some beneficial drugs never being developed. Estimates show that the morbidity and deaths caused by the FDA outweigh the lives saved and harm prevented by its actions.[2] I will have more to say about regulation in chapter 4 in the discussion on the Commerce Clause and in other chapters as well.

The government also initiates physical force when it taxes the rich to give the money to the poor. The rich have engaged in voluntary trade to earn their income. For example, a wealthy industrialist produces a product and sells it through voluntary trade to buyers who freely pay for the product. When the government takes some of his money to give it to the poor, it is using force to do so. Since neither the industrialist nor the people with whom he trades have used force, the government is the first user of force and thus violates the freedom of the wealthy individual to do with his money what he wants.

If one thinks that the government does not use force when taking money from the rich to give to the poor, one should think about how the government obtains the taxes from the rich to redistribute the money to the poor. Does the government merely ask people to voluntarily pay taxes? No. It forces people to pay them. If people refuse to pay, the government will obtain a court order to take the money from their bank accounts. If they hide their money, the government will seize other assets. If they still refuse to pay, the government will send armed agents to drag the people to jail if it has to. If the people refuse to surrender, the government will kill them if necessary. In all of these cases, the government initiates force against individuals; it uses force to penalize the wealthy—and all individuals—if they do not obey the tax laws.

What does freedom *not* refer to? It does not mean people are free to do whatever they want. For instance, no one is free to commit murder in a free society. Why? Murder is a violation of freedom. Since a free society bans the initiation of physical force, being prevented from committing murder does not violate the murderer's freedom. It prevents the murderer from violating the freedom of his victims.

A free society does not mean goods are free. Goods belong to those who have produced them. To obtain goods, one must respect the freedom of producers and get them to provide you the goods voluntarily. If one does not obtain the goods through voluntary means, force must be used against the owner of the goods to obtain them. Here, either criminals must initiate force to steal the goods or the government must pass laws to forcibly take the goods from the owners. Either way, this is a violation of the freedom of the owners of the goods to use their property as they see fit.

Freedom also does not mean freedom from hunger or need or pain. To provide the things necessary to eliminate hunger or pain or fulfill one's needs—if a person cannot obtain them through trade or charity—force must be initiated either by the government or by an individual. Either an individual must steal the objects or the government, acting, in essence, like a criminal, must tax people to take money from them to be able to provide the objects.[3] In other words, people must be forced to provide food to the hungry person or to do whatever else is claimed will fulfill a person's needs or eliminate his pain.

How do we protect freedom? Rights are the tools used to do this. Rights are moral principles that define and sanction a person's freedom of action in a social context.[4] They not only establish what the sphere of our freedom is but also say we have a moral right to exercise our freedom. For example, the right to life says that your life is your own and you are free to take the necessary actions to further your life and well-being, so long as you do not initiate physical force against others.[5] Rights not only say you have the freedom to do this, but it is moral for you to do this. That is, it is consistent with the fundamental requirements of human life.

In addition, property rights establish that a man is free to use his property to further his life and well-being. For example, a man is free to build a home on his property to protect himself from the elements, and he is morally justified engaging in such an activity. He is also free to produce goods, sell them in the marketplace, and keep the money he earns to achieve his own happiness.

The goods and money are his by right, and he is morally justified in using them for his own benefit.

It would be a contradiction to say that one has a right to his life but no right to property. Property is the means by which we further our lives. How can we further our lives if we do not have a right to keep what we produce? If we grow food but others can legally take it from us, we would starve. Property rights derive from the fact that we have a right to our own lives.

In fact, all the other rights derive from the right to life. For example, the right to liberty protects the freedom to think, choose, and act to further one's life. The right to the pursuit of happiness protects the freedom to enjoy the results of using one's property and exercising one's liberty to successfully further one's life.

It is important to understand that many things that are thought to be rights, in fact, are not rights. For example, it is often thought that people have a right to health care. But this is actually a violation of rights because it is a violation of freedom. Why is this the case?

Saying that someone has a right to health care means there is an obligation to provide the person with health care. But what if no one is willing to voluntarily provide the person with health care? This implies that others must be forced to provide the health care, such as taxpayers being taxed to provide health care to those who cannot afford it. Since taxpayers have not used force against anyone to earn their income, when they are forced to pay for the health care with their income, force is initiated against them and thus their freedom and rights are violated. Hence, a so-called right to health care is actually a violation of the rights and freedom of those forced to provide it. It is a misuse of the concept "rights" to say that someone has a right to health care.

In fact, there is no right to any object that others must provide, such as a job, a wage of a certain level, an education, three meals a day, and so on. In all these cases, force must be initiated against those who are to provide these things to those who do not have them. This is a contradiction. It says, in essence, that some people have the right to violate the rights of others. Some people are to be enslaved to the needs and desires of others. However, slavery is a gross violation of individual rights and freedom.

In addition, rights are not privileges given to individuals by the government that can be taken away by the government at any time. It is also not arbitrary that humans possess rights. The identification that humans need rights is based on the facts of reality that we can objectively identify. Rights are requirements of human life. They are necessary for a rational being to be able to use his basic tool of survival—his reason—to serve his own life. More specifically, rights protect the ability of a person to use his mind to think, act on his own rational judgment, produce the values his life requires, and thus further his life and well-being. Hence, rights are objective necessities of human life, and if the government does not protect the rights of the individual, it is wrong.

One can see based on the view of rights presented here that rights are derived from the nature of human beings. In this sense, it is consistent with natural rights theorists' conception of rights, such as that of John Locke.[6] However, it is not consistent with the natural rights theorists' view that rights are inherent in human beings or that they have a divine source. Rights do not exist innately in human beings. They are a product of reason but based on man's nature. That is, we use our mind to develop the concept "rights," but this development is based on the facts pertaining to human existence. Moreover, rights have their source in the natural world, not the supernatural. More discussion will be provided on these topics in this chapter.

THE MORAL BASIS FOR RIGHTS AND FREEDOM

The moral justification for rights derives from the moral requirements of human life. Morality provides a code of values to further one's life and well-being. Morality determines, at a fundamental level, what it is right and wrong for humans to do.

What determines what humans must do to further their lives and well-being? The answer: the nature of human life. Human life requires each individual to further his own life and well-being. It requires that individuals produce and pursue values, such as food, clothing, shelter, knowledge, friendship, and so on. It requires that they act in their rational self-interest. This means they must use their mind—their rational faculty—and act in a long-range manner to promote their own well-being. If they do not do these things, they put their survival, and ability to flourish, in jeopardy.

To act contrary to one's self-interest is to act in contradiction to the requirements of human life. For example, since life requires the pursuit and attainment of values, giving up or sacrificing one's values is self-destructive. If life requires that I produce food and eat it in order to survive and flourish, then giving to others the food I produced and need to further my life undermines my ability to survive and flourish. Such an action is immoral by the standard of the requirements of human life.

Further, think of the contradiction to which this leads. If virtue consists in giving up one's food, then what does that say about the person who receives and consumes the food? He does not sacrifice himself to others. If he did, he would give it up. So here, virtue consists in serving vice. That is, those who are virtuous sacrifice themselves to those who are immoral. Is this what morality is intended to do? No. Certainly not a rational morality.

By the standard of the requirements of human life, it is immoral to sacrifice oneself to others. That is, it is immoral to act altruistically. Acting altruistically means sacrificing values; it means giving up a greater value for a lesser value or a non-value.[7]

Sacrificing does not consist in merely incurring an expense or having to put forth great effort to achieve a value, such as investing money to earn income or spending years in school and working hard to become a doctor. If the result is worth more to the person than the cost of obtaining the result, as determined by a rational assessment of what is in one's self-interest, then the effort leads to a net gain, not a loss.

A sacrifice would consist in not pursuing a career in medicine to have children instead, even though one would rather pursue the medical career and one does not want to have children. If a woman gets married and has children to, for example, satisfy her parents' desire to be grandparents, instead of pursuing a career she is passionate about, *that* would be a sacrifice.[8]

Rights provide the means to legally recognize the moral requirements of human life. Humans must pursue what is in their own self-interest to survive and flourish. Rights protect each individual's ability to do this. Rights, in essence, acknowledge that your life belongs to you and that your ability to pursue what you deem as best for your own life, based on your rational judgment, must be recognized and protected.

Note that the standard here is not just the bare survival of human life. Rights protect an individual's ability to survive, but they also protect an individual's ability to flourish. They protect the individual's ability to pursue everything he might want out of life: knowledge, fame, fortune, happiness, love, peace-of-mind, and so on. So long as the activity or goal does not involve a violation of the rights of others, one is free to pursue it.

Note also, though, that rights do not guarantee success. Since reality does not guarantee one success in one's endeavors, one is free to pursue whatever one wants but one cannot be guaranteed success, happiness, and so on. Furthermore, rights do not force others to help one achieve one's goals and desires. One must obtain others' cooperation through voluntary means, whether the cooperation comes in the form of engaging in voluntary trade with others, getting others to provide charity, getting others to be one's friend, and so on. One must recognize the principle that *every individual's* life requires that all people be free to use their minds to think, act on their own rational judgment, and pursue the values their lives require. That is, they must be free to gain knowledge, get a job, earn income, and keep the money and wealth they have earned. To forcibly prevent *any person* from doing these things is wrong; it thwarts the ability of individuals to further their lives and well-being.

Related to this point is the fact that acting in one's self-interest does not mean sacrificing others to oneself. For example, stealing from others to obtain wealth is not in one's self-interest. It is in one's self-interest to act on rational principles, which includes respecting the rights of others. This is both moral and practical. It is moral because it recognizes the fundamental requirements of human life: that each individual must be free to further his own life and happiness. It is practical because humans must produce and trade to survive and flourish, not loot. In fact, there is a harmony of rational self-interests among people, where the success of each person promotes the well-being of all people. We can all grow richer and benefit from each other's talents and abilities by producing wealth and engaging in voluntary trade. In contrast, a society of looters would lead to poverty and death, since everyone would be focused on stealing from others and no one would focus on producing the wealth people need to survive and flourish.

Some might claim that individuals automatically act to further their lives and well-being. What we really need to do, these people might claim, is protect the weak and help those who are incapable of helping themselves. This is a destructive belief.

People do not automatically further their lives and well-being. The fact that people commit suicide is the most obvious proof of this. However, the fact that people become alcoholics and engage in drug abuse is also proof. The fact that people sometimes stay in abusive relationships, commit crimes, or act altruistically is proof as well. In addition, the fact that forms of government are created that lead to misery, poverty, and death on a massive scale, such as socialist governments, theocracies, military dictatorships and so on, is further proof that people do not automatically act to further their lives and well-being. People need guidance to understand what it is proper for them to do. At a fundamental level, they need moral guidance. Morality provides individuals with a code of values and guide to action so they can determine the course and purpose of their lives,[9] and people need rational moral guidance to avoid destructive choices and guide them toward beneficial, life-supporting choices.

As for protecting the weak, individual rights do this. Rights protect all people from the initiation of physical force: weak, strong, rich, poor, men, women, black, white, and so on. However, rights also protect individuals from being forced to help others. In a free society, if one wants to help the weak, one is free to do so. But one has no right to force others to help the weak. That would be a violation of rights and, therefore, is morally wrong.

THE EPISTEMOLOGICAL BASIS FOR RIGHTS AND FREEDOM

Epistemology is the field in philosophy that answers questions regarding whether we can gain knowledge and, if so, how. A rational epistemology answers the former question affirmatively. As to the how: humans gain knowledge through the use of reason. As stated by Ayn Rand, "Reason is the faculty that identifies and integrates the material provided by man's senses."[10] It is what enables humans to think at the conceptual level, in terms of ideas and principles. Without reason, humans would be like the lower animals, capable of acting only at the perceptual level.

How is this relevant to rights and freedom? Humans have rights because of their possession of reason. To see why this is true, let us first briefly focus on the lower animals.

The lower animals—dogs, cats, lions, snakes, gazelles, apes, dolphins, and so on—do not possess reason and thus cannot think at the conceptual level. They are not capable of integrating the vast array of perceptual-level data they observe to form concepts. Therefore, they cannot think in terms of principles, including moral principles. Since rights are moral principles and animals cannot understand them, animals fall outside the realm of morality and rights. Animals are neither moral nor immoral beings. They are amoral. This means that animals do not possess rights.

This conclusion is not changed by the fact that animals can feel pain. Pleasure and pain are felt at the perceptual level. It does not provide a basis for having rights because it does not afford animals the ability to understand and act on moral principles, including the principle of rights. Only the possession of reason provides the ability to understand principles and thus serves as the basis for possessing rights.[11]

Think of how one would attempt to apply rights to animals. For example, we would have to respect the alleged rights of a mountain lion that wanders into our neighborhood from the foothills; however, it would not have to respect our rights. It is incapable of understanding what a right is and thus cannot respect our rights. It acts on perceptual-level stimuli. If it sees a person or someone's pet, it may attack if it is hungry or feels threatened. When it attacks, we do not condemn it as immoral. We deal with it in the only manner one can deal with it: by killing, caging, or relocating it.

At this point, there is an important topic related to the validity of reason that I want to address. Above I mention that reason uses information obtained by the senses to form concepts. Some might question the validity of the senses and, based on this, the validity of reason. Some claim the senses are invalid because, for instance, straight sticks can appear to be bent when partially submerged in water. Also, some people are color-blind and thus allegedly do not obtain accurate information about reality from their senses.

The question to ask here is: How is it known that the stick that appears to be bent is actually straight? Likewise, how is it known that objects that appear to be black and white to some people actually possess color? The answer: it is known based on information we obtain from the senses. Those who claim that the senses are invalid use sensory data to attempt to invalidate them. This means they have to accept the validity of the senses in the very attempt to deny their validity.

In fact, the senses are necessarily valid.[12] They do not interpret or filter reality. They provide us raw data about the world. It is at the conceptual level that we interpret the information provided by the senses to determine what it means. So, we discover conceptually that a straight stick can appear to be bent when placed in different mediums because light travels at different speeds through different mediums. We also discover that sensory organs with different capabilities perceive different aspects of reality. For example, bats perceive aspects of reality by bouncing sound waves off objects. Eyes that cannot perceive color provide people with different information about reality than eyes that can perceive color. However, it is all information *about reality*. It is up to humans to determine at the conceptual level what the information tells us about the world. So, this attempt to invalidate reason fails.

Focusing back on reason and rights, reason makes rights both necessary and possible. Rights are possible because our possession of reason gives us the ability to understand principles, including moral principles. Hence, we can form the concept "rights" and devise means to protect them. Reason makes rights necessary because freedom is a fundamental requirement of reason. To use our reason, we need the freedom to think, follow the evidence, and act on our knowledge so that we can use it to further our lives and well-being. We need the freedom to perform experiments, produce goods and services, read books, write books, have a conversation about the importance of rights, and so on. Without freedom, a *human* life is impossible.

Rights are the way to protect the ability of humans to exercise their basic means of survival in a social context. Rights enable humans to apply their reason to the task of survival. Through the respect for rights in the division of labor, the use of reason has enabled humans to survive in a far better manner than was achieved or even dreamed of in past eras. The *average person* today lives in a manner that surpasses the standard of living of kings and queens from past eras in many ways, thanks to the application of reason to production. There is no reason why if rights continue to be respected that the standard of living of the average person cannot rise far higher, thanks to further discoveries and economic progress based on the application of reason.

The importance of protecting rights and freedom to raising the standard of living can be seen in comparisons of governments in the former East and West Germany and the current North and South Korea. The socialist country (the former country in each case) was or is much poorer relative to the freer country. The importance can also be seen in a comparison of the former USSR and the United States. The United States, a much freer nation than the socialist USSR, was much richer when the latter still existed (and still is much richer than the country that remains after the collapse of the USSR, which is still an extremely statist country). In addition, the importance is seen in the rankings of countries around the world, based on how free they are, in the *Economic Freedom of the World* annual reports. These reports consistently show year after year that within freer countries there exist higher incomes, higher rates of economic progress, higher life expectancies, and higher incomes for poor individuals.[13] Freedom and the protection of rights are crucially important to economic progress and the standard of living *because* they are fundamental requirements of human life.

If reason, and thus rights, are rejected, as is occurring more and more today, economic progress will be harder, and eventually impossible, to achieve. In fact, if the trend of the abandonment of reason goes far enough, economic regression will occur. Respect for reason as our only means to knowledge and guide to action, and thus respect for rights, must be restored and maintained.[14]

THE METAPHYSICAL BASIS FOR RIGHTS AND FREEDOM

Metaphysics is the field in philosophy that studies the fundamental nature of reality. It answers such questions as: What is existence? Do absolutes exist? Do cause and effect exist?

It is an axiom that existence exists and that we possess consciousness. Existence is that which is. It is the world we perceive or the "stuff" out there. Consciousness is our faculty of awareness.[15] It is our means of perceiving the world. One has to accept existence and consciousness, even in any attempt to deny that they exist. For instance, if I believe that nothing exists, then who is the being doing the believing if nothing exists? If nothing exists, then I do not exist. Furthermore, what about the concepts I am using to formulate my thought that nothing exists? They exist as well, and they are something.

What if I claim that I am not conscious? This means that I am not aware of anything, since consciousness is the faculty of awareness. This raises the question of how I could form concepts to formulate my thoughts if I am not aware of anything. Concepts are formed by organizing and integrating the material provided by man's senses, and our senses are our primary means of being aware of things. If one is not conscious, one could not be aware of anything and thus one could not formulate thoughts. The very utterance of a thought implies that one must be conscious.

One might claim that we are not conscious and that what we experience is just a dream. In other words, nothing is real. However, a dream is a form of consciousness that is contrasted with existence. How could one know that everything is just a dream if there is nothing that exists to compare it to? We would not be able to identify it as a dream.

More specifically, a dream is generated by information in the subconscious. This is clearly seen in the fact that we dream when we are asleep and thus are not conscious. Knowledge is integrated to the subconscious through the conscious mind. For instance, we automatize the use of words and thus are able to use them without even consciously thinking about them. The meaning of the words is integrated into our subconscious by first consciously learning the definitions of the words and what they refer to. Through repeated use, we can use them without consciously thinking about them.

If nothing exists and everything is just a dream, then what were we conscious of to begin with that led to our possession of knowledge at the subconscious level? What we are conscious of is existence. More specifically, we are conscious of many different concrete aspects of existence. We are conscious of many different existents and their attributes. We are conscious of all kinds of persons, places, and things and the characteristics they possess. This is the knowledge that provides the information on which dreams are based.

I will grant that our knowledge at the subconscious level is often rearranged in bizarre ways in dreams, but the rearrangement of knowledge still implies the existence of such knowledge and a reality that is knowable. The existence of a reality capable of being known and a consciousness capable of knowing it cannot be logically denied if one is going to claim that dreams exist.

Above I make reference to the fact that reality is knowable. This is also inescapable and is a corollary of the law of identity, that is, that everything has a specific nature. If one is going to claim that reality is unknowable, how does one know this? It is a contradictory claim and is thus invalid. If reality was, in fact, unknowable, then one could not know it.

The law of identity says things in the world have certain characteristics and are capable of certain actions or producing certain effects based on their nature (this latter is the law of causality, which is a corollary of the law of identity). So, the Sun can melt a Popsicle based on the Sun's and the Popsicle's characteristics, but it cannot melt a bridge made of steel. One billiard ball will move when struck by another based on their characteristics. However, when the cue ball strikes an anvil, there is a different effect based on the characteristics of the anvil. Likewise, based on the characteristics of man, he can use his free will to focus his mind to understand what a speaker is saying at a lecture or he can let his mind become unfocused, not pay attention to what the speaker is saying, and thus not understand the content of the speech. All of these are examples of cause and effect.

Based on the law of identity (and the law of causality), everything has a specific nature and acts according to its nature. A man can lift one-hundred pounds over his head based on his nature but cannot lift one-million pounds. Roads are not roads one day and serpents the next. The Sun cannot freeze a glass of water based on its characteristics. Freedom is a fundamental requirement of human life and rights protect our freedom.

The law of identity is an axiom; it is at the base of all knowledge. As a result, one must accept it in any attempt to deny it. For example, if one is going to say that nothing has identity, then how could one communicate that viewpoint? One is counting on the identity of the words and concepts one uses to be able to formulate and convey that thought. If nothing had an identity, even words and concepts would not have an identity. This includes the fact that they would not have any specific meaning. A word might have one meaning at one point, another meaning at another point, and might be babbling in the next instance. The world would be chaos.

* * *

So, metaphysically, absolutes exist. This is easily observable. It must be accepted in any attempt to deny it (i.e., if one claims that there are no absolutes, one is claiming that it is an absolute that there are no absolutes). The law of identity is what makes the world knowable. This is the most fundamental law of existence. It enables us to make sense of and apply concepts such as rights and freedom. If the law of identity were not valid, the world would truly be an unknowable, kaleidoscopic flux where up could be down, in could be out, black could be white, day could be night, right could be wrong, and many more contradictions could exist. We would not be able to gain knowledge or survive in such a world. Fortunately, however, such a place cannot exist.

Epistemologically, we gain knowledge about the world through the use of reason. Reason is the means by which we gain knowledge at the conceptual level, in terms of ideas and principles. Our conceptual knowledge is ultimately based, directly or indirectly, on the information we acquire about reality through our senses. Our ability to know the world includes the ability to understand the nature of human beings. We can understand their capabilities and requirements, including their moral and political requirements. We can understand that the most fundamental social requirement of humans is freedom—the absence of the initiation of physical force. We can understand that to protect freedom, rights must be recognized and protected.

Not only can we understand these things and achieve them in reality, morally they are the right thing to do because humans must act in their own rational self-interest to survive and flourish—in other words, because it is a moral virtue to be selfish. Rights are the political and legal means of protecting the ability of humans to act in a moral manner—a manner that their lives require. Hence, we see how an objective reality, reason as our means to knowledge, and the morality of rational self-interest provide the basis for rights.

ALTERNATIVE VIEWS AND THEIR INVALIDITY

There are many alternative arguments to the ones discussed above in the fields mentioned. However, they are all invalid. Some I have shown to be false, such as the altruist code of morality, the belief that reality is unknowable, and the belief that there are no absolutes. The present section will address a number of additional arguments that are not valid, including the beliefs that morality and knowledge in general are subjective and the belief in mystical beings and realities (such as the belief in God). Because of their invalidity, they cannot provide a valid basis for rights and they cannot undercut the argument for rights that says they are an objective necessity of human life.

Subjectivism

Subjectivism is the view that individuals do not merely observe the nature of reality, but that one's consciousness affects the nature of reality. In essence, the nature of a thing is dependent on the consciousness (i.e., the person) observing or considering it. This implies that the truth of an issue, including moral truth, is dependent on the person considering the issue. Truth is based on one's feelings, attitudes, wishes, or preferences. For example, based on subjectivism, if one feels that an idea is true or wants it to be true, it is true. As a result, based on subjectivism, it is believed that truth can vary from person to person. For instance, some believe that what is morally right for one person is not morally right for another person.

Two specific subjectivist ideas are post-truth political theory and postmodern philosophy. Postmodernism rejects the idea that there is an objective reality or objective methods of determining truth. Postmodernism claims that truth is socially conditioned or conditioned in other ways. Following the lead of postmodernism, post-truth political theory says there are no objective standards for determining what is right and wrong in politics. What is true is based on one's feelings or emotions.

Subjectivism is invalid. To illustrate this in the clearest terms, imagine if I feel that two plus two equals five. Will that make it true? Obviously not. If a majority of people or even the entire world believe two plus two equals five, it does not make it true.

Some might claim that I am creating a strawman argument against subjectivism. They might claim that subjectivism does not say it is possible for people to make logical inconsistencies valid just by believing they are valid. However, I am merely drawing out the logical implications of subjectivism. If one's consciousness can affect the nature of reality, it would be possible for logical inconsistencies to be logically valid based on one's wishes or desires. Subjectivists who deny this ignore or evade the logical implications of their viewpoint. They do so in an attempt to make it appear that subjectivism is plausible, both to themselves and others.

Before seeing the implications of subjectivism in morality, let us first consider the nature of morality. As mentioned, morality is a field of philosophy that determines what is right or good for humans to do; it establishes a code of values to guide human action. What is right or good implies the need for a standard of value. If one is going to have a moral code that enables people to further their lives and well-being, that standard must be the individual human life. The morality of rational self-interest does this. It says that an individual's life is one's own; one's life does not belong to the race, the nation, the gender, God, and so on. The good, according to this code of morality, is to live one's life for one's own selfish benefit using the fundamental human tool of survival: reason. This means one lives one's life based on rational standards and validates one's thoughts and actions through a logical analysis of the facts.

In contrast to this, if the good is subjective, then anything goes. This is the result of consciousness being able to affect the nature of reality in the field of morality; it is the logical and consistent end of subjectivism applied to morality. If I believe, feel, or want something to be morally good, then, according to subjectivism, it is morally good. This means, for example, that if I feel murder is morally right, then it must be good and thus I am morally justified in committing murder. If I believe rape and child molestation are morally good, then they are good also. If I want it to be morally proper to sacrifice myself to others or sacrifice others to myself, then I am morally justified in engaging in these types of activities.

Subjectivism is a license to believe in the arbitrary. That is, I can believe something is true regardless of logic, facts, and rational standards. Arbitrary beliefs are beliefs held without evidence. If people acted consistently on such a viewpoint, it would lead to a war of all against all: one person's or group's desires, whims, feelings, wants, or wishes against another's. People would battle for the supremacy of their view of the world, and the ones who could amass the biggest and strongest gang and impose their views on others would rule.

However, if absolutes exist and we gain knowledge of reality through the use of reason, then we have to determine what is morally proper based on the facts that give rise to morality, including the nature of reality, the nature of man, and man's relationship to reality. One cannot (validly) arbitrarily assert whatever one wants and claim that it is true. One must adduce evidence to show why what one is saying is true, and this includes what one is saying about morality. That is, one must show how what one is claiming to be true corresponds to the facts of reality. The nature of reality and the nature of human beings dictate the requirements for doing this.

As is indicated above, what applies to the field of morality applies to knowledge in general. There is no field in which just because someone believes an idea to be true, it must be true. Wishing does not make it so.

This is true both for the individual and for the majority of people. Often in politics people believe that because a majority of voters approve of a measure that it must be morally good and politically beneficial. However, reality does not bend to the will of the majority either. Such a viewpoint can be dubbed the lynch-mob theory of morality. A lynch mob has a clear majority. However, that does not make the lynch mob's actions morally proper. Lynch mobs initiate physical force and violate the rights of their victims. Their actions are therefore morally wrong and politically destructive.

One important function of a proper government is to protect the minority from the tyranny of the majority. That is, it must protect the rights of the minority of voters from being violated by the majority of voters. Most importantly, it must protect the rights of the smallest minority—not black people, the poor, the "underserved," or the "underprivileged," but the individual, regardless of race, gender, nationality, income level, and so on. The individual is always the smallest minority, and today the rights of the individual are constantly under attack.

Social contract theory is a specific political theory to which the above discussion applies. This theory says that a government is legitimate if a large number of people agree that it is or, in a slightly different version, that people consent to the authority of the government, whether explicitly or tacitly, and this gives legitimacy to the government. This is obviously subjectivist. If a government violates individual rights, it does not become legitimate just because many or all people agree, whether explicitly or tacitly, that it is.[16]

A government is legitimate if it protects individual rights. This legitimacy is determined based on the facts of reality, including the requirements of human life. That is, the legitimacy of a government is determined based on the fact that rights and freedom are fundamental requirements of human life. This is true regardless of whether a majority of people (or no people) believe that it is true. Moreover, individuals are obligated to obey the laws of a rights-respecting government not because a majority says that they should but because such a government is consistent with the moral and political requirements of human life.

The epistemological status of majorities applies not only to morality and politics but to knowledge more generally. That is, in general, one does not determine truth by majority vote. If that were true, then at one time the earth must have been flat and it must have been the center of the universe as well, because at one time many people (and probably a majority) believed in these ideas.

What is true, including what is morally true, is objective, not subjective. That is, one determines what is true through a logical analysis of the facts, regardless of what people (including the majority) may feel, wish, or want to be true. One's consciousness cannot affect the nature of reality.

Note that when I say that one's consciousness cannot alter things in reality, I am not saying that humans cannot affect facts that exist in the world. Humans can change things in the world by, for instance, building homes, diverting rivers, and baking a cake. However, humans cannot change the fundamental nature of reality. The appropriate distinction here is between the metaphysical and the manmade. Humans can affect certain facts, but they cannot change the metaphysical nature of reality.

Intrinsicism

Subjectivism says that something is right or morally good merely because a person feels it is or wants it to be. In other words, it says that what is good or right is based on what the subject who is doing the thinking believes or feels is right, regardless of the facts pertaining to the object of one's thinking. An intrinsic view of what is right or morally good says that the "rightness" or "goodness" is contained within the object being considered, regardless of its relation to the subject who is doing the thinking or regardless of other relevant facts. For example, environmentalists consider a wolf to be of value by the mere fact that it exists. It does not matter that the wolf might kill a rancher's livestock. The wolf has intrinsic value—value in and of itself—regardless of its effect on human beings. Thus, the wolf is not to be killed (at least not by humans) regardless of the harm it causes. As another example, the Bible for many people is to be considered the proper source of knowledge and what is morally good because of the mere fact that it was written, regardless of whether what is written in the Bible makes sense logically or agrees with the facts of reality. The Bible has intrinsic validity.

The mystical aspects of the Bible will be dealt with shortly. At this point, let's focus on the idea that what is true or good is intrinsic. The truth of a statement certainly is not based on the fact that the statement was written (or spoken). Humans are capable of gaining knowledge of reality, but they are not omniscient. The view that the validity of a statement is intrinsic ignores the fact that what was written might not agree with the facts of reality and thus might be wrong. For a statement to be true, it must correspond to the facts of reality. This recognizes the objectivity of truth. Truth is neither subjective nor intrinsic. That is, something is not true merely because someone wants it to be true (subjective) and it is not true merely because it was written in some ancient text or passed down as "wisdom" from generation to generation (intrinsic). Truth is an identification of the facts of reality by a conceptual being; it is a thought formulated by the subject about an object that corresponds to the facts pertaining to the object.

What is morally good is not intrinsic to an object either. A wolf is not of value simply because it exists. A wolf is harmful to man if it kills his livestock. What would be of value in this case would be to eliminate the threat to man's source of food.

The value or disvalue of something is determined by the relationship of the object to the being doing the valuing. For example, food is valuable to humans because it sustains their lives. Poison is harmful to humans because it kills them.

A wolf may be of value to humans as an object of curiosity in a zoo, to study to improve their knowledge of the fauna that populate the earth, or to enjoy it as a part of the aesthetic beauty of nature. However, this still is not an intrinsic value. The wolf is not valuable in and of itself. It is of value *to humans*. Even the aesthetic beauty of nature is not an intrinsic value. It is a value that *individuals* can enjoy.

The fact that a wolf may be of value to humans in certain contexts should not be taken to mean that value is subjective or arbitrary. Value is still objective; that is, whether something is of value or not is always based on the relationship of the object to the subject. The value is never in the object apart from the subject or determined by the subject apart from the object. However, the relationship between the object and the subject can change based on the context with which one is dealing. Moreover, knowledge of the value of an object is always obtained through a logical analysis of the facts.

As another example, take the case of poison. Poison in the typical context is a disvalue because it can kill you. However, if one is at war with a country that is attempting to violate one's rights, poison might be of value as a weapon to defend oneself. But again, the value of the poison is not intrinsic. It is still based on the relationship between the poison and the person defending his own rights. Moreover, the context within which the poison is of value is not subjective or arbitrary. Poison is not of value merely because I want it to be of value. It is of value in the context of a certain set of facts.

Some might wonder in my example of the wolf, what about the value of the natural habitat to the wolf? Am I not forgetting about the lower animals when I write of the value of animals to humans?

Of course, certain things can be of value to a wolf. Protection from cold weather and the existence of another animal that it can kill and eat are examples of values to a wolf. However, wolves, and all animals except for humans, cannot think at the conceptual level and thus cannot distinguish between the objective, subjective, and intrinsic. Therefore, such concepts (and all concepts) are useless to them. It is only a conceptual being that can identify that value is objective, not intrinsic or subjective. Nonetheless, the wolf and other animals do determine what is of value to them based on the facts. They merely do so based on the use of their perceptual faculties (ears, eyes, etc.), not based on a conceptual faculty since they do not possess a conceptual faculty.

The senses, whether for humans or the other animals, work automatically; they involve no element of volition. It is only conceptual thinking that requires people to exercise free will and choose to think or not, to choose to use their conceptual faculty or not, to be rational or not. It is this choice that makes it possible for humans to think objectively (or not).[17]

Moreover, one must remember that only humans possess rights. Animals have no rights because of the fact that they are not conceptual beings. Because they are not conceptual beings, they cannot understand any principles, including moral principles. Therefore, moral values, including rights, do not apply to animals.

Objectively, the values of humans take precedence over the values of animals because humans possess reason. Reason enables humans to understand the world and use the resources in the world to meet their needs in a far superior and more comprehensive manner than the animals. Since the animals do not possess reason, they must be considered as resources like any material resources that exist in nature. Animals cannot be reasoned with and, since they do not possess reason, any attempt to elevate the animals to the level of human beings by recognizing their "rights" would end up violating the rights of humans and forcing humans to survive at the level of the animals, without the use and benefit of reason. The superiority of humans to the animals and the precedence of their needs and desires over the needs and desires of the animals is based on the nature of humans, reason, and the animals.

* * *

Claiming that values and knowledge are subjective or intrinsic contradicts the facts of reality. A person must identify values and gain knowledge through a logical analysis of the facts. Both consciousness and existence are involved in gaining knowledge, including identifying values. Neither knowledge nor values can exist or be identified without consciousness and existence.

All of this means that people's possession of rights and the importance of freedom to humans are neither intrinsic nor subjective or arbitrary. Humans do not possess rights and need freedom merely because I want them to possess rights and need freedom. Likewise, humans do not possess rights and need freedom because it has been written somewhere, such as the Declaration of Independence or U.S. Constitution. People's possession of rights and need of freedom are derived from the facts of reality, including the nature of human beings. We can identify objectively why humans possess rights and need freedom. Hence, it is appropriate to declare their rights in the Declaration of Independence and protect their freedom in the Constitution.

Mysticism

Mysticism refers to any non-sensory, non-rational view of knowledge and existence.[18] Mysticism encompasses but is not limited to the belief in the validity of Ouija boards, fortune-telling, faith as a means to knowledge, astrology, religion, numerology, and voodoo. It embraces the idea that mystical realms and means to knowledge exist that are beyond this world, the senses, and reason. All such viewpoints contradict the axioms of existence, consciousness, and identity. Here I am going to primarily focus on religion because this is the form of mysticism that the Declaration of Independence and U.S. Constitution refer to.

Mystics claim that there are tools beyond reason and the senses that can be used to gain knowledge. This knowledge is beyond the comprehension of anyone who does not possess the mystical power to see what some claim they see. Mysticism, from an epistemological standpoint, is a form of the arbitrary. It represents claims to knowledge put forth without evidence. Anything goes based on arbitrary assertions and mysticism. One can claim anything is true because no proof, validation, or evidence is necessary to support one's claim. How does one know? It cannot be explained. One just knows. The ultimate "defense" of the mystic (or those in general who resort to arbitrary assertions) is: to those who understand, no explanation is necessary, to those who don't, no explanation is possible. This is the method mystics use to avoid having to provide evidence for their claims and thus evade the baseless nature of their claims.

Faith is a specific means of allegedly gaining knowledge used by religious mystics. Faith in this context means believing in something without evidence. In fact, it refers to believing in something despite the fact that such a belief contradicts the evidence. For example, how do I know God exists? I do not have any evidence. I have faith. I "just know" he exists.

But the burden of proof is on the person who makes the claim that something exists or is true. This burden requires that anyone claiming something to be true must present at least some evidence for the claim to be elevated on to the continuum of proof. The continuum of proof says that before the truth or validity of a claim can be considered a possibility, at least an iota of evidence is needed in support of the claim. Something being a possibility is the first step on the continuum of proof. The second step (or portion of the continuum) constitutes something being a probability. There is a greater likelihood that a claim is true as it moves from being a possibility to a probability, and correspondingly more evidence is required for it to move from being a possibility to a probability. The third and final step is certainty. For one to be certain regarding a claim to knowledge, definitive evidence is required.

As an example, the day before the big football game one may believe that it is possible that one's favorite team will win. This may be based on its performance in previous games and one's knowledge of the quality of the players on both teams, among other knowledge. If one's team is ahead by twenty points with five minutes left in the fourth quarter, it would be appropriate to say one's team will probably win. One has more evidence about the outcome of the game given the time that is left and the lead the team possesses. If the team gets the ball with a fresh set of downs at their opponent's twenty-yard line, forty seconds remaining on the clock, and still has the twenty-point lead, their victory is certain.

There is absolutely no evidence for mystical beliefs. They are based on what people merely want to be true or feel is true. They do not even make it on to the continuum of proof. Hence, like any arbitrary assertion, they can be dismissed without consideration.[19] One does not have to address the claims made by mystics—one does not need to refute them—because there is nothing to refute. It is as if nothing has been said because, from a cognitive standpoint, nothing, in fact, has been said. There is no reference to logic and facts or to any rational evidence whatsoever.

In addition, mysticism contradicts the fact that absolutes exist. Mystics might say that this is not true because God creates the absolutes. He dictates the laws of logic, the laws of physics, and other absolutes. However, if such a being exists and creates the laws of reality, he could have created different laws or no laws at all. One day force could equal mass multiplied by acceleration and the next it could equal mass divided by acceleration or something even more bizarre if he decides the "absolutes." This means there are no absolutes, and, as I have shown, that is a contradiction.

The above means that mysticism contradicts the law of identity and that it contradicts the fact that existence exists and *only* existence exists. Existence and the law of identity are inseparable. It is not that existence possesses identity. Identity is not an attribute of existence that can be separated from existence. The proper relationship is, in the immortal words of Ayn Rand, "Existence *is* Identity"[20] (emphasis added). They are just two different perspectives on the same fact. One cannot say "it is" without the "it" and the "is." The "it" identifies that what exists is a specific existent (with a specific identity). The "is" identifies that the specific existent exists.

The invalidity of mysticism can also be seen in the many puzzles to which such beliefs lead. For instance, a puzzle often discussed by religious mystics is the idea that if God is omnipotent, then he should be able to create a rock that even he cannot lift. However, if he cannot lift the rock then he is not omnipotent. But, if he cannot create such a rock, he is also not omnipotent.

Another contradiction if God exists is that existence does not exist. If God is omnipotent, he could eliminate existence and bring it back. He could turn something into nothing and vice versa. He could even eliminate himself and bring himself back. He can both exist and not exist. He can both have identity and not have identity. He can be both A and non-A (at the same time and in the same respect).

The solution to such contradictions is to reject the entire premise that mysticism is valid. It is riddled with contradictions, both logical fallacies and contradictions of the facts. The contradictions to which mysticism leads are a part of the evidence that demonstrates its invalidity.

Based on the above, we can conclude that rights do not come from God. First, God does not exist. Moreover, if they did come from such a being, they could be taken away by him at any time because with God there are no absolutes. What is true today might not be true tomorrow.

In addition, the source of rights, morality, does not have its source in God. Some believe that without God there is no morality and thus anything goes with regard to morality. There will be no restraints on what people can do without God, they claim. This represents the false alternative of intrinsicism versus subjectivism. Sound thinking rejects both alternatives. Sound thinking says that absolutes exist, that human life has a specific nature, and that people must act according to their nature to further their lives and well-being. Rational egoism is what human life requires morally. Other codes of morality, such as altruism, hedonism, and utilitarianism (among others), stand in opposition to the requirements of human life. Hence, they are destructive, vicious, and irrational.

Since God does not exist, we do not have to worry about him taking our rights away. However, what does happen is that those who convince others that they are God's representatives end up determining whether rights will be respected or violated. Based on this, rights are not moral and political requirements based on the nature and characteristics of human beings. They are turned into privileges provided by God's representatives that can be taken away at any moment based on their alleged communications with him and their claim that they are enacting God's will.

How are we to determine that these people communicate with God and know what is right? We are to take what they tell us on faith. What if one disagrees with what these "representatives" say? Can a fellow religious mystic present evidence to make his case and convince them of the rightness of his own mystical viewpoint and the invalidity of their position? Absolutely not. Faith allegedly transcends reason and evidence, which means that it is superior to reason and thus that evidence is irrelevant in matters of faith. The only recourse to "convince" others to believe in one's ideas regarding matters of faith, is force. As Ayn Rand has shown, faith and force are corollaries.[21] There are no logical arguments and no facts to which one can point to back up one's claims in matters of faith. That is why, today, radical Muslims murder people who do not submit to their views. That is why contemporary Christians have bombed abortion clinics and murdered doctors who work at such clinics. That is why Christians during the Crusades and the Inquisition murdered people who did not bow to their ideas.

While it is true that the great majority of Muslims and Christians (and, of course, all religious people more generally) do not commit murder in the name of their beliefs, the important point to remember is that such ideas are consistent with murder. Many people do not take the ideas they believe in seriously or act on them consistently. In addition, many religious people have also been influenced by rational ideas. This is especially true of Christians since the Renaissance and the Enlightenment, which have led to a reduction in the influence of Christian ideas. Both periods were products of growing respect for reason.

Some might claim that my argument that rights and freedom are based on the embracement of reason and rationality is contradicted by the fact that it is sometimes said that communists and Nazis were advocates of reason and communists and Nazis were most certainly not advocates of freedom and the protection of individual rights. While it is true that it is sometimes claimed that communists and Nazis were advocates of reason, these claims are invalid. Neither group embraced reason. Nazis judged people not by the ability to use their minds (their reason) but by race and nationality. The alleged superiority of the Aryan race was their claim. Communists believed that the ideas one accepts as true are determined by one's economic class, not by a logical analysis of the facts through the use of reason.

Moreover, both the Nazis and communists claimed the moral superiority of collectivism and altruism. The communists also claimed that socialism was economically superior to capitalism. They claimed that socialism provided a scientific method of organizing production through the central planning of the state and would lead to a much greater productive capability and higher standard of living than capitalism. I have shown elsewhere the false nature of these claims, as well as the vicious and destructive nature of altruism, collectivism, and socialism (and have briefly discussed the destructive nature of altruism above). I have also shown elsewhere both the economic and the moral superiority of capitalism over socialism.[22] Ludwig von Mises predicted that socialism would be an economic disaster shortly after it was implemented in Russia.[23] If the communists and Nazis embraced reason, they would have rejected altruism, collectivism, and socialism for rational egoism, individualism, and capitalism. They adhered to altruism, collectivism, and socialism despite the destructive nature of these ideologies precisely because they abandoned reason.[24]

Some might also claim, in contradiction to what I argue, that religion can provide support for freedom and the protection of rights. In support of this claim, they might point to the fact that the American Founding Fathers created a government to protect rights and freedom, and most of the founders were Christians. While most of the founders were Christians, this does not deny the incompatibility of religion with freedom, as I have shown. The growing respect for freedom and individual rights embraced by the Founding Fathers was a product of the Enlightenment, which, as I have mentioned, was a period that saw a rising influence of reason. It was Enlightenment ideas embraced by the founders, not their religion, that led to their embracement of freedom and individual rights. If Christian ideas were what was necessary to establish a free society, one would expect a free society to have arisen during the centuries of Christian influence prior to the Enlightenment. This did not happen. Instead, Christianity led to the Crusades, the Inquisition, and centuries of stagnation and poverty during the Dark and Middle Ages. This is a significant point. Christianity had *centuries* to lead to a free society, but it led to less freedom not more freedom.

CONCLUSION

Individual rights and freedom are fundamental requirements of human life. Rights are the means by which we protect freedom. That is why it is so important to understand what changes need to be made to the Declaration and Constitution to make them fully consistent with the protection of rights.

Man possesses rights because of his nature. He is a being that possesses reason, and in order to be able to use his reason to further his life and well-being, he needs the freedom to think and act on his knowledge. He needs the freedom to apply his reason to the task of pursuing his own rational self-interest. He needs freedom to produce the values his life requires. This is why free societies are the most prosperous and innovative societies. We see here that if one embraces and consistently applies a proper code of morality—the morality of rational self-interest—one will conclude that freedom is both moral and practical.

In addition, rights do not come from the state. We possess them independently of the state, based on our nature as rational beings. However, government is needed to protect rights. The protection of rights is the only proper function of the government; that is, it is the only function of the government that is consistent with the fundamental requirements of human life. In order for the government to protect rights, it must use force only in a retaliatory manner. It must use force against those who initiate physical force, such as rapists, murderers, pickpockets, con artists, terrorists, and totalitarian regimes—anyone that threatens our rights.

Rights are also not given to us by the majority of voters. Individuals need rights to protect them *from* the majority. That is, they need rights to protect them from a majority of voters who, for example, want to expropriate their money through higher taxes or government bond initiatives (the latter of which taxpayers could be required to pay off). Rights also do not come from God because there is no God. God—and mysticism in general—contradicts the metaphysical facts of reality.

Rights are also not subjective rules we establish just because we happen to like them. They are objective necessities of human life. That is, they can be shown to be necessities of human life based on the facts of reality and a logical analysis of those facts.

Now that we have established what rights and freedom are and why they are so crucial to human life, let us move on to the task of determining what changes need to be made to the Declaration and Constitution to strengthen the protection of these extremely important values that these documents provide.

NOTES

1. Ayn Rand, *Capitalism: The Unknown Ideal* (New York: Signet, 1967), p. 46.

2. On the FDA, see Brian P. Simpson, *Markets Don't Fail!* (Lanham, MD: Lexington Books, 2005), pp. 108–10.

3. The government acts, in terms of fundamentals, like a criminal here because it is initiating physical force (as a criminal does).

4. Ayn Rand, *The Virtue of Selfishness* (New York: Signet, 1964), p. 110.

5. Ibid.

6. For examples of the consistency of the view of rights presented here with that of John Locke, see John Locke, *The Second Treatise on Civil Government* (Amherst, NY: Prometheus Books, 1986 [1689]), pp. 9, 15–18, 20, 33–34, 36–37, 95, and 100.

7. Rand, *Virtue of Selfishness*, p. 50.

8. For more on the nature of the morality of self-sacrifice versus the morality of rational self-interest, see Simpson, *Markets Don't Fail!*, pp. 13–21.

9. Rand, *Virtue of Selfishness*, p. 13.

10. Ibid., p. 22.

11. This statement is not invalidated by the fact that pre-conceptual babies do not possess reason but still possess some rights, such as the right to life. We recognize that they are human beings and will eventually possess reason once they have developed enough physically. Hence, they possess the rights that are appropriate for the level of development they have reached.

12. For a thorough discussion of this topic, see Peikoff, *Objectivism*, pp. 39–52.

13. For one of these reports, see James Gwartney, Robert Lawson, Joshua Hall, and Ryan Murphy, *Economic Freedom of the World: 2019 Annual Report* (Vancouver, BC, Canada: Fraser Institute, 2019), pp. vi and 17–22.

14. Due to space limitations, I will not discuss here the evidence of the rejection of reason that is occurring today. I have done that elsewhere. See Simpson, *Markets*

Don't Fail!, pp. 158–61. For a thorough discussion of the subject, see Leonard Peikoff, *The Ominous Parallels* (New York: Stein and Day, 1982).

15. Ayn Rand, *Atlas Shrugged*, 35th anniversary edition (New York: Signet, 1992 [1957]), pp. 1015–16.

16. For a thorough critique of social contract theory, see Tara Smith, *Viable Values: A Study of Life as the Root and Reward of Morality* (Lanham, MD: Rowman & Littlefield Publishers, Inc., 2000), pp. 28–38.

17. On free will, see Rand, *Atlas Shrugged*, pp. 1012–13; Rand, *Virtue of Selfishness*, pp. 18–27; and Ayn Rand, *For the New Intellectual* (New York: Signet, 1961), pp. 14–15. On the volitional nature of objectivity and the fact that the concept "objective" is inapplicable to the information provided by the senses, see Peikoff, *Objectivism*, pp. 112 and 116–18.

18. Ayn Rand, *Philosophy: Who Needs It* (New York: Signet, 1982), pp. 62–63.

19. For a detailed discussion of arbitrary assertions and why they can be dismissed without consideration, see Peikoff, *Objectivism*, pp. 163–71.

20. Rand, *Atlas Shrugged*, p. 1016.

21. Rand, *Philosophy*, pp. 66 and 70.

22. Simpson, *Markets Don't Fail!*, pp. 5–23.

23. Ludwig von Mises, *Socialism* (Indianapolis, IN: Liberty*Classics* [sic], 1981 [1951]), pp. 95–194. While the edition of this book that I reference was published in 1981 and is a reprint of the second English edition that was published in 1951, the book was originally published in German in 1922, only a short time after the Russian Revolution and the establishment of a socialist state in Russia.

24. On the Nazi's rejection of reason, see Peikoff, *Ominous Parallels*, pp. 39–63 and 260–77. On the communist's abandonment of the mind, see Rand, *Philosophy*, p. 70 and *Atlas Shrugged*, pp. 1027, 1044–46, and 1054–56.

Chapter 2

Revising the Declaration of Independence

INTRODUCTION

There are a few procedural matters I must make clear before I begin revising the Declaration. First, I will not correct grammar and punctuation or make spelling in the Declaration consistent with modern conventions. Second, the text of the Declaration is presented in block quotation format. Third, my writing is bracketed by my initials (BPS). These latter two will help to distinguish my writing from the text of the Declaration.

In addition, I do not change the masculine nouns used in the Declaration, such as men and mankind. In fact, I use masculine nouns and pronouns in many instances throughout this book. I use the masculine terms because it helps to avoid awkward sentence structure and incorrect grammar. Using gender-neutral nouns and pronouns often leads to incorrect grammar and awkward sentence structure. As a personal preference, it also makes it easier for me to write, since I do not need to be concerned about which gender-specific term I should use in a particular case or how to construct more complex, gender-neutral sentences. It allows me to focus more effort on making sure that what I say is correct and clear. In any case, the use of masculine terms should not be taken to mean that the ideas discussed do not apply to women. The ideas apply to all human beings, whether they are ideas in the Declaration or in my own writing.

I now proceed to revise the Declaration to make it fully consistent with the protection of individual rights and freedom. This mainly involves reorienting the Declaration's philosophical focus from that of mysticism to secularism. As I discuss in chapter 1, mysticism, whether religious or otherwise, is filled with logical contradictions and does not agree with the facts of reality. It, therefore, cannot provide a valid philosophical foundation for defending individual rights. That foundation can only come from a reality-based philosophical viewpoint.

REVISING THE DECLARATION

In Congress, July 4, 1776.[1]
  The unanimous Declaration of the thirteen united States of America,
  When in the Course of human events, it becomes necessary for one people to dissolve the political bands which have connected them with another, and to assume among the powers of the earth, the separate and equal station to which the Laws of Nature and of Nature's God entitle them, a decent respect to the opinions of mankind requires that they should declare the causes which impel them to the separation.

BPS—I eliminate all references to God in the Declaration. While as a general rule not all references to God need to be eliminated, it is important to change those that attribute causal significance to God to have a proper philosophical orientation in the Declaration. Unfortunately, this is the case with all the references made to God in the Declaration. The reference in this particular case, at least in part, attributes the political standing of people to God. I will grant that the view of God expressed in this sentence is qualified by Jefferson's deist viewpoint. Nonetheless, it is still a mystical reference that attributes causal significance to God and is invalid metaphysically. Hence, it must be eliminated. So, the sentence should read: When in the Course of human events, it becomes necessary for one people to dissolve the political bands which have connected them with another, and to assume among the powers of the earth, the separate and equal station to which the Laws of Nature entitle them, a decent respect to the opinions of mankind requires that they should declare the causes which impel them to the separation.—BPS

  We hold these truths to be self-evident, that all men are created equal, that they are endowed by their Creator with certain unalienable Rights, that among these are Life, Liberty and the pursuit of Happiness.—

BPS—This sentence states that three things are self-evident: all men are created equal, they are endowed by their creator with certain inalienable rights, and among these rights are life, liberty, and the pursuit of happiness.[2]
  The first change that needs to be made in this sentence is that the term "self-evident" must be changed to "undeniable." This change is necessary, in part, because it is not self-evident that men are endowed with inalienable rights. According to the *Oxford English Dictionary*, "self-evident" means

evident of itself without proof; axiomatic. The definition was the same at the time of the American Revolution.[3] Perhaps the Founding Fathers meant that man's possession of these rights was clearly understood by them *based on their knowledge*. I am sure this was true, but self-evident does not refer to something being clearly understood based on knowledge one already possesses. It means something is clear *without proof*. Without proof implies that no other knowledge is necessary. In other words, a fact is directly observable, such as the fact that I am sitting on a chair as I write these words. Man's possession of rights is not self-evident because it takes a great deal of abstract knowledge—knowledge about ethics, political philosophy, and the nature of human beings—to understand the concept "rights."[4] "Undeniable" is a better term to use because the fact that humans possess these rights cannot legitimately be denied. Furthermore, "undeniable" is a better term because in what Jefferson referred to as his "original Rough draught" of the Declaration, he used the terms "sacred & undeniable" instead of "self-evident."[5] Hence, in using "undeniable" I am not only using an epistemologically more accurate term, I am merely reverting back to a term that is closer to what Jefferson originally used.

A change later in the sentence also necessitates changing the term "self-evident." I change "they are endowed by their Creator with certain unalienable Rights" to "they possess based on their nature as rational beings certain unalienable Rights." Referring to this latter fact as self-evident makes even less sense than referring to what it replaces as self-evident. If it is not self-evident that man possesses rights, it is certainly not self-evident that he possesses rights because he is a rational being.

Why is the change mentioned in the above paragraph needed? Obviously, the reference to man being endowed with rights by his creator needs to be changed because there is no creator. While many of the Founding Fathers believed that we are endowed with rights by a creator, that does not change the invalid nature of such a claim. As I have mentioned, the founders were also products of the Enlightenment and thus had great respect for reason. This provided a valid basis for their support of the protection of rights, despite their invalid belief regarding the source of rights. See chapter 1 for the nature and secular source of rights. There I show that the source of rights is the possession of reason by human beings. In recognition of this fact, I substitute "possess based on their nature as rational beings" for "are endowed by their Creator with."

Additionally, "all men are created equal" must be changed to "all men are born equally free." This change is needed, in part, because people are not created, like a painting is created by an artist. They are born. Being created implies there is a creator, and I have demonstrated that there is no creator. Hence, "born" will be substituted for "created."

Moreover, the change is needed to make it clear in what sense men are equal. Men, of course, are not equal in every respect. For example, they are not born with the same physical and mental endowments. However, all men are born equally free (or, at least, should be equally free). This was identified by George Mason in the Virginia Declaration of Rights. I adopt Mason's terminology here (with a slight modification) because it is more precise than what is stated in the Declaration of Independence.

The term "equally" also serves the important function of emphasizing that freedom applies to all people in the same way. It is not the case that some people possess freedoms that other people do not possess. People are equal under the law. Furthermore, I use "equally" to minimize the number of modifications to the terminology in the Declaration, while at the same time making sure the meaning is clear.

I could have used the phrase "all men are born equal" instead of "all men are born equally free." To the founders, the former phrase would have been clearly understood to mean that men are equally free. We can look to John Locke for evidence of this. The founders were quite familiar with Locke's work, and Jefferson drew heavily from Locke in drafting the Declaration. Equality to Locke referred to a situation in the original state of nature where there is no government and where all men are born equally free and independent, each with the same authority to protect his own rights. Further, according to Locke, no man (rightfully) has power, authority, or jurisdiction over other men. Locke states, "the equality I there spoke of as proper to the business in hand, being that equal right that every man hath to his natural freedom, without being subjected to the will or authority of any other man."[6] This is what equality refers to in this phrase of the Declaration. Nonetheless, making the argument clearer and more precise, as my changes have done, strengthens the argument, makes it comprehensible to a wider audience, and thus provides a more powerful case for a government limited to protecting freedom.

I considered using the statement "all men are equal under the law" instead of "all men are born equally free." To keep the focus of the Declaration on the fundamental nature of human beings, I did not include the former statement. The statement is true and provides an important understanding of the nature of a proper legal system. The statement is also consistent with the phrase I chose to use because saying that men are born equally free implies that they all have equal protection of rights under the law, as I mention above. However, the statement would have shifted the focus from the fundamental nature of human beings to the less fundamental issue of how people are to be treated by a proper legal system. This would have made the argument less powerful.

Next, I add property rights to the list of inalienable rights. While not including property rights does not make the Declaration inconsistent with the protection of freedom and rights, the lack of reference to property rights is a significant omission. Including property rights in this portion of the Declaration strengthens the protection of rights provided by the Declaration. I discuss the importance of the rights to life, liberty, property, and the pursuit of happiness in chapter 1. There I show that the right to property is necessary so that a man can exercise his right to life. If a man cannot keep what he produces—such as food, clothing, and shelter—he is, in essence, enslaved to those to whom he is forced to give his property. A slave does not have a right to his own life.

The right to property is also necessary for one to exercise his right to liberty and the right to pursue his own happiness. For example, a man must gain knowledge using his rational faculty and then apply that knowledge to pursue values, including the production of wealth. This is the right to liberty. This is intimately related to the right to property, since what people think about and act on directly or indirectly involves some type of property. Even in what seem like instances that involve no property, such as thinking about abstract issues in philosophy, property is involved. A man might think of such issues in the quiet and solitude of his own home or refer to a book on Aristotle to clarify his thinking on the subject. A home and a book are both property, and, of course, many more types of property can be involved as well. Moreover, since property rights are inextricably linked to the rights to life and liberty, they are likewise linked to the right to pursue happiness, since this right focuses on the results of the successful actions taken to further one's life and well-being.

Notice the careful choice of words by the Founding Fathers with regard to the pursuit of happiness. A person has a right to *pursue* happiness, not a right to happiness. Happiness is not guaranteed. It depends on many factors, including the mental state of the person doing the pursuing. A "right" to happiness could be used to force others to provide a man with things he claims he needs to achieve happiness (a job, home, car, etc.). However, what happens to the rights of the people forced to provide these things? This is why the right pertaining to happiness focuses on the pursuit of happiness, not the "right" to happiness.[7]

One might think that it is inappropriate to include property rights among the list of inalienable rights, since specific pieces of property are alienable. While it is true that the ownership right in a specific piece of property, such as a car, can be sold or given away, property rights qua property rights are inalienable. They cannot be transferred to another person; they cannot be legitimately abolished or restricted. They are fundamental rights because man's ability to survive and flourish fundamentally depends on the protection of property rights. Therefore, they must be protected and should be included in this part of the Declaration.

So, this sentence of the Declaration should read: We hold these truths to be undeniable, that all men are born equally free, that they possess based on their nature as rational beings certain unalienable Rights, that among these are Life, Liberty, Property, and the pursuit of Happiness—BPS

That to secure these rights, Governments are instituted among Men, deriving their just powers from the consent of the governed,—That whenever any Form of Government becomes destructive of these ends, it is the Right of the People to alter or to abolish it, and to institute new Government, laying its foundation on such principles and organizing its powers in such form, as to them shall seem most likely to effect their Safety and Happiness. Prudence, indeed, will dictate that Governments long established should not be changed for light and transient causes; and accordingly all experience hath shewn, that mankind are more disposed to suffer, while evils are sufferable, than to right themselves by abolishing the forms to which they are accustomed. But when a long train of abuses and usurpations, pursuing invariably the same Object evinces a design to reduce them under absolute Despotism, it is their right, it is their duty, to throw off such Government, and to provide new Guards for their future security.—Such has been the patient sufferance of these Colonies; and such is now the necessity which constrains them to alter their former Systems of Government. The history of the present King of Great Britain is a history of repeated injuries and usurpations, all having in direct object the establishment of an absolute Tyranny over these States. To prove this, let Facts be submitted to a candid world.

He has refused his Assent to Laws, the most wholesome and necessary for the public good.

He has forbidden his Governors to pass Laws of immediate and pressing importance, unless suspended in their operation till his Assent should be obtained; and when so suspended, he has utterly neglected to attend to them.

He has refused to pass other Laws for the accommodation of large districts of people, unless those people would relinquish the right of Representation in the Legislature, a right inestimable to them and formidable to tyrants only.

He has called together legislative bodies at places unusual, uncomfortable, and distant from the depository of their public Records, for the sole purpose of fatiguing them into compliance with his measures.

He has dissolved Representative Houses repeatedly, for opposing with manly firmness his invasions on the rights of the people.

He has refused for a long time, after such dissolutions, to cause others to be elected; whereby the Legislative powers, incapable of Annihilation, have returned to the People at large for their exercise; the State remaining in the mean time exposed to all the dangers of invasion from without, and convulsions within.

He has endeavoured to prevent the population of these States; for that purpose obstructing the Laws for Naturalization of Foreigners; refusing to pass others to encourage their migrations hither, and raising the conditions of new Appropriations of Lands.

He has obstructed the Administration of Justice, by refusing his Assent to Laws for establishing Judiciary powers.

He has made Judges dependent on his Will alone, for the tenure of their offices, and the amount and payment of their salaries.

He has erected a multitude of New Offices, and sent hither swarms of Officers to harrass our people, and eat out their substance.

He has kept among us, in times of peace, Standing Armies without the Consent of our legislatures.

He has affected to render the Military independent of and superior to the Civil power.

He has combined with others to subject us to a jurisdiction foreign to our constitution, and unacknowledged by our laws; giving his Assent to their Acts of pretended Legislation:

For Quartering large bodies of armed troops among us:

For protecting them, by a mock Trial, from punishment for any Murders which they should commit on the Inhabitants of these States:

For cutting off our Trade with all parts of the world:

For imposing Taxes on us without our Consent:

For depriving us in many cases, of the benefits of Trial by Jury:

For transporting us beyond Seas to be tried for pretended offences:

For abolishing the free System of English Laws in a neighbouring Province, establishing therein an Arbitrary government, and enlarging its Boundaries so as to render it at once an example and fit instrument for introducing the same absolute rule into these Colonies:

For taking away our Charters, abolishing our most valuable Laws, and altering fundamentally the Forms of our Governments:

For suspending our own Legislatures, and declaring themselves invested with power to legislate for us in all cases whatsoever.

He has abdicated Government here, by declaring us out of his Protection and waging War against us.

He has plundered our seas, ravaged our Coasts, burnt our towns, and destroyed the lives of our people.

He is at this time transporting large Armies of foreign Mercenaries to compleat the works of death, desolation and tyranny, already begun with circumstances of Cruelty & perfidy scarcely paralleled in the most barbarous ages, and totally unworthy the Head of a civilized nation.

He has constrained our fellow Citizens taken Captive on the high Seas to bear Arms against their Country, to become the executioners of their friends and Brethren, or to fall themselves by their Hands.

He has excited domestic insurrections amongst us, and has endeavoured to bring on the inhabitants of our frontiers, the merciless Indian Savages, whose known rule of warfare, is an undistinguished destruction of all ages, sexes and conditions.

In every stage of these Oppressions We have Petitioned for Redress in the most humble terms: Our repeated Petitions have been answered only by repeated injury. A Prince whose character is thus marked by every act which may define a Tyrant, is unfit to be the ruler of a free people.

Nor have We been wanting in attentions to our Brittish brethren. We have warned them from time to time of attempts by their legislature to extend an unwarrantable jurisdiction over us. We have reminded them of the circumstances of our emigration and settlement here. We have appealed to their native justice and magnanimity, and we have conjured them by the ties of our common kindred to disavow these usurpations, which, would inevitably interrupt our connections and correspondence. They too have been deaf to the voice of justice and of consanguinity. We must, therefore, acquiesce in the necessity, which denounces our Separation, and hold them, as we hold the rest of mankind, Enemies in War, in Peace Friends.

We, therefore, the Representatives of the united States of America, in General Congress, Assembled, appealing to the Supreme Judge of the world for the rectitude of our intentions, do, in the Name, and by Authority of the good People of these Colonies, solemnly publish and declare, That these United Colonies are, and of Right ought to be Free and Independent States; that they are Absolved from all Allegiance to the British Crown, and that all political connection between them and the State of Great Britain, is and ought to be totally dissolved; and that as Free and Independent States, they have full Power to levy War, conclude Peace, contract Alliances, establish Commerce, and to do all other Acts and Things which Independent States may of right do.

BPS—The phrase "Supreme Judge of the world" needs to be eliminated because it is a mystical reference (to God). I replace it with "ultimate arbiters of truth—reason and reality" because the only means to ascertain the truth is to use reason to understand the facts of reality. So the beginning portion of this sentence of the Declaration should read: We, therefore, the Representatives of the united States of America, in General Congress, Assembled, appealing to the ultimate arbiters of truth—Reason and Reality—for the rectitude of our intentions, ...—BPS

And for the support of this Declaration, with a firm reliance on the protection of divine Providence, we mutually pledge to each other our Lives, our Fortunes and our sacred Honor.

BPS—Divine Providence is a reference to God and must be eliminated. If one is going to pledge one's life, fortune, and sacred honor to fight for a cause, one better have confidence that the cause is morally right. Mysticism undermines confidence because it represents an abandonment of the tool humans possess that makes it possible to gain knowledge about the world and act successfully in it: reason. Hence, "protection of divine Providence" is replaced with "righteousness of our cause." The mind does not need the protection of a mystical being. It needs protection from those who would attempt to forcibly prevent individuals from acting on their rational judgement. That is, it needs freedom. So the last line of the Declaration should read: And for the support of this Declaration, with a firm reliance on the righteousness of our cause, we mutually pledge to each other our Lives, our Fortunes, and our sacred Honor.—BPS

CONCLUDING REMARKS

As one can see, there are not many changes to make to the Declaration to make it consistent with the protection of individual rights and freedom. That is a testament to the soundness of the document. The most significant changes focus on including property rights as one of the inalienable rights and eliminating the mystical references made in the document. The changes strip the inconsistencies from and provide a sound philosophical foundation for the document that established the first explicitly created free society in the world.

The complete revised Declaration is presented in Appendix A, at the end of the book. It provides a much more solid base upon which to build a free society. That is extremely important in creating and maintaining such a society. I encourage countries around the globe to adopt their own declarations for freedom based on the revised Declaration. Of course, I also encourage governments at all levels in the United States to reaffirm their commitment to protecting freedom and individual rights by making declarations of their own based on the revised Declaration. Such declarations will help immensely to advance peace and prosperity throughout the world.

In chapter 3, I begin revising the U.S. Constitution. We will see that far more revisions are necessary to make that document fully consistent with the protection of individual rights and freedom.

NOTES

1. The Declaration was obtained from the National Archives and Records Administration website, http://www.archives.gov/exhibits/charters/declaration_

transcript.html (accessed June 14, 2015). I do not include the signature block at the end of the Declaration.

2. I use the preferred spelling today of "inalienable" instead of "unalienable," which was the preferred spelling at the time the Declaration was written.

3. Jack N. Rakove, *The Annotated U.S. Constitution and Declaration of Independence* (Cambridge, MA: The Belknap Press, 2009), p. 78.

4. For further discussion of this issue, see Peikoff, *Objectivism*, pp. 354–55.

5. See "Jefferson's 'original Rough Draught' of the Declaration of Independence" in Julian P. Boyd, editor, *The Papers of Thomas Jefferson: Vol. 1, 1760–1776* (Princeton, NJ: Princeton University Press, 1950). See p. 423.

6. For the quotation, see Locke, *The Second Treatise*, p. 32. For more on this topic from Locke, see pp. 8–10 and 48–49.

7. On the relationship between the rights to life, liberty, property, and the pursuit of happiness, see Peikoff, *Objectivism*, pp. 352–53 and 355–56.

Chapter 3

Revising the U.S. Constitution

The Preamble through Article I, Section 7

INTRODUCTION

In this and the following two chapters, I revise the original Constitution. There are a few procedural matters I must make clear before I begin revising the Constitution. First, as with the Declaration, in the Constitution I will not correct grammar and punctuation or make spelling consistent with modern conventions. Also, as with the Declaration, the text of the Constitution is presented in block quotation format and my writing is bracketed by my initials.

Furthermore, to the extent that they do not violate individual rights or are legitimate options to choose from to protect rights, I am not considering changing clauses in the Constitution that focus on procedural issues (such as whether a judge has lifetime tenure, the pardon power of the president, and so forth) or the structure of the government (such as the division of the government into three branches or the creation of a bicameral legislature). This does not mean that in some cases I do not disagree with these kinds of provisions. However, to the extent they do not violate rights or are legitimate options to choose from, I am not concerned with such matters here. In setting up a government, sometimes various optional procedures and methods can be used that are all consistent with the protection of individual rights. So I will not change these types of provisions.

In addition, I will not consider making changes to portions of the Constitution that have been superseded by amendments, as long as those amendments are consistent with the protection of individual rights. I only consider whether to change portions of the Constitution that are still in force. This will help to properly delimit the task at hand, keep the book a reasonable length, and provide only the most relevant guidance to those seeking to amend the Constitution. Portions of the current Constitution that have been

45

amended or superseded will be set off in square brackets. This applies to the amendments as well. The amendments are addressed in chapters 6 and 7.

In some cases, amendments may need to be repealed because they violate rights. In those cases, the portions of the Constitution that they amended or superseded will now be in force and may need to be modified. Cases of this type will be identified.

To change the Constitution, I will amend it. I will identify the portion of the Constitution that each amendment I propose modifies or replaces in my discussion of the section that it modifies or replaces. I follow the same procedure in chapters 6 and 7. In chapters 8 and 9, I provide additional amendments to the Constitution that are necessary to further strengthen the protection of rights and freedom. In Appendix B, at the end of the book, I provide the revised Constitution without any intervening discussion. This will include the new amendments, starting with Amendment XXVIII. The Constitution presented in Appendix B will therefore include three sets of amendments: amendments to the original Constitution (the Preamble through Article VII), amendments to the current twenty-seven amendments to the Constitution, and any additional amendments to the Constitution that are necessary to protect rights consistently.

Also, I do not include expiration clauses in the amendments I propose. I focus on the provisions needed to protect rights. Expiration clauses can easily be added to the amendments if they are proposed for inclusion in the Constitution. Finally, I do not include provisions that state that Congress can enforce articles with appropriate legislation. Such provisions could be added to each proposed amendment as well.

Let us now begin to see how the original portion of the Constitution needs to be revised so that it consistently protects individual rights and freedom by discussing the Preamble through Article I, Section 7 in this chapter. Chapter 4 will cover Article I, Sections 8 through 10 and chapter 5 will cover Articles II through VII.

REVISING THE CONSTITUTION
THROUGH ARTICLE I, SECTION 7

Preamble

We the People of the United States, in Order to form a more perfect Union, establish Justice, insure domestic Tranquility, provide for the common defence, promote the general Welfare, and secure the Blessings of Liberty to ourselves and our Posterity, do ordain and establish this Constitution for the United States of America.[1]

BPS—The most important change to the Preamble is that a clause must be added to highlight the only proper function of government: protecting individual rights and freedom. This is the most important purpose of the Constitution and will establish the proper context for the Constitution. Everything else in the Constitution focuses on this purpose.

As discussed in the introduction to the book, I focus on both "freedom" and "individual rights" to emphasize the connection between them. It is important to focus on the connection so that people understand that to protect freedom, one must protect individual rights. Focusing on both in the new Constitution will better ensure the protection of rights and freedom.

In the new Preamble, I also establish the link between initiating physical force and violating rights and freedom. The only way to violate rights is by initiating physical force. This link is established in chapter 1. It is crucial to incorporate this link into the Constitution so that people understand clearly what is meant by freedom and individual rights. It will better secure the protection of freedom and rights by preventing statists from claiming the existence of false rights that we allegedly need to protect. For example, statists might claim that people have a right to a minimum amount of food to meet their nutritional needs and therefore that the government should provide food to the poor. However, by stating in the Constitution that the only way to violate freedom and rights is by initiating physical force, one can see that the government would be initiating physical against some people to provide food to the poor and thus violating rights and freedom, not protecting them.

It is important to understand that while rights are protected by banning the initiation of physical force, there are some exceptional cases in which the initiation of physical force does not violate rights and thus is permissible. These cases pertain mainly to children. Children do not possess all the rights of adults because their conceptual faculty is not fully developed. Hence, it is sometimes appropriate for parents to initiate force to protect the child or enforce certain rules. For example, if a child gets dangerously close to the edge of a cliff it might be necessary to grab him by the arm and hold him back. A parent might also have to physically prevent a child from eating candy before dinner if the child cannot be persuaded not to do so. These constitute initiations of force against the child but do not represent violations of rights. The only way to violate rights is by initiating physical force but initiating force in all cases does not violate rights. The rights of children will be discussed in this chapter in more detail in connection with Article I, Section 2 on the appropriate minimum age for U.S. representatives.

Another important change to the Preamble is that the General Welfare Clause must be eliminated. It is not a proper function of the government to promote the general welfare. As I have stated, the only proper function of the government is to protect individual rights.

If the government attempts to promote the welfare of any group or person, it cannot promote the general welfare. It will end up promoting the welfare of some groups or individuals at the expense of others. For example, the government can take money from taxpayers around the country to, say, build a bridge in Minneapolis, thus helping citizens of Minneapolis at the expense of all U.S. taxpayers outside of Minneapolis. The same would be true at the state and local level as well. For example, if a local government wants to spend money to build a school, it must be financed with taxpayer money, including from those taxpayers who do not have children and thus have no use for the school. This means the children who use the school and their parents benefit at the expense of taxpayers who have no children or whose children have grown and no longer need a school. The same is true of state-funded schools, highways, bridges, and so on.

The only way the government can, in fact, promote the *general* welfare, that is, the welfare of *everyone*, is by protecting rights so that people are free to promote their own welfare. This is the only way it will not end up helping some people at the expense of others. This is the case because a government uses force to achieve its ends; it compels people to obey laws. Hence, if it gives to some it must, by its nature, take from others. Therefore, the only way to promote the general welfare is for the government to refrain from taking anything from anyone, unless they have violated someone's rights. This means, as discussed in chapter 1, that it must use force only in a retaliatory manner.

Protecting rights provides both the incentive and the means for people to produce wealth and grow richer by making it possible for them to keep what they produce and benefit from it. I have more incentive to produce wealth if I can keep what I produce and benefit from it, and I will have a greater ability to produce if I can employ what I have previously produced to enhance my productive capability, such as by reinvesting wealth I have produced in a business I own and thus expanding the business. What this means is that violating rights harms the welfare of people. Taking from some people to give to others forces some people to be enslaved to the needs and desires of others and leads to less being produced and thus a lower standard of living being achieved for the average person. Why should I produce (or produce as much) only to watch the product of my effort (or some significant portion of the product of my effort)—of my thought, action, and hard work—be swallowed down the mouths of other people? I won't. And neither will anyone else.

Some of the founders appear to have recognized that the government cannot promote the general welfare by taking money from taxpayers across the country and spending it to provide goods and services in particular parts of the country. For example, Alexander Hamilton stated in his *Report on the Subject of Manufactures* that appropriations of money by Congress to build such things as roads and canals to assist manufacturers were required, by the General Welfare Clause, to be for general, not local, purposes.[2] In addition, during his presidency, James Monroe vetoed the Cumberland Road Bill because the bill would have been of benefit only to a specific region of the country. He vetoed it, in part, based on the General Welfare Clause.[3] Even though in these cases the government should not be building roads, canals, or engaging in similar activities because these activities are not a part of protecting individual rights (at least insofar as such activities are not directly related to the defense of the nation), it nonetheless appears from these examples that at least some of the founders understood that the government could not promote the general welfare by taking from some to give to others.

Another important reason to eliminate the reference to the general welfare is so that statists cannot use it to attempt to justify providing welfare—the redistribution of wealth and income—based on the Constitution. Even though the founders did not intend the clause to be used for this purpose, it is still possible for statists to use it to do this, and starting with the New Deal, the clause has been used to do just that, such as in the Supreme Court cases *Steward Machine Co. v. Collector of Internal Revenue* (1937) and *Helvering v. Davis* (1937), both of which justified certain provisions of the Social Security Act, in part, by reference to the General Welfare Clause.[4] The General Welfare Clause and the Commerce Clause have been the source of much of the expanded power of the government.[5]

While James Madison, in *The Federalist* No. 41, argued that the General Welfare Clause does not give the federal government broad powers, there were a number of Founding Fathers who believed that it did. Those are the people toward whom Madison was directing his argument. Madison even admitted in the same essay that the power in this clause could be misapplied and abused.[6] History has proven that those who Madison was directing his argument toward were correct.

If some people want to help others, they are free to do so through voluntary charity. This means private individuals choosing to help people with their own time and money. However, they have no right to use the government to force others to help people. I discuss the harmful nature of welfare in chapters 4, 6, and 8.

I contemplated eliminating the phrase "insure domestic Tranquility" from the Preamble because this could be interpreted in a way to justify violating individual rights. This would be the case if, for example, workers rioted to force employers to pay them higher wages, thus violating the rights of employers, and the government, in the name of achieving tranquility, passed legislation to impose higher wages on employers to get the workers to stop rioting. The government might "insure domestic tranquility," at least temporarily, but it would violate the rights of employers by helping workers, in essence, extort higher wages from employers.

Since achieving tranquility means, in essence, achieving peace, it is a legitimate function of government. However, the government is not to attempt to achieve it by violating individual rights. The revised Constitution will make it clear that the government cannot violate rights for the sake of "achieving peace" or for any other reason. The proper way for the government to achieve peace in the example of the workers rioting for higher wages is to quell the riots and administer justice against the rioters. This is how one protects individual rights under such a scenario.

One must also consider in this example that appeasing rioters does not actually achieve peace. It merely rewards and encourages rioting and other violations of rights. Just as Neville Chamberlain did not achieve "peace for our time" by appeasing Hitler and giving in to his demands in the Munich Agreement, in general one cannot achieve peace by conceding to dictators, thugs, and bullies. The only way to achieve lasting peace is to protect rights and freedom.

Given these changes, the following amendment is necessary: Amendment XXVIII–The Preamble to the Constitution of the United States shall be repealed and replaced with the following: Given that the only proper purpose of government is to protect Freedom and Individual Rights, and that the only way to violate Freedom and Individual Rights is by initiating physical force, we the People of the United States, in Order to form a more perfect Union, establish Justice, insure domestic Tranquility, provide for the common defence, and secure the Blessings of Liberty to ourselves and our Posterity, do ordain and establish this Constitution for the United States of America.

Some might think that it is not necessary to change the Preamble to ensure that it is consistent with the protection of individual rights because it has no legal significance. I am not going to discuss in this book whether the Preamble has any legal significance. I will only say that, regardless of whether it has legal significance, the Preamble is extremely important because it defines the purpose of the Constitution. That is why it is so crucial to make sure the proper purpose of government is established in the Preamble. The new Preamble, by stating that purpose and making the connection between rights, freedom, and force, provides important guidance in the interpretation of the rest of the document.—BPS

Article I

Section 1

All legislative Powers herein granted shall be vested in a Congress of the United States, which shall consist of a Senate and House of Representatives.

Section 2

The House of Representatives shall be composed of Members chosen every second Year by the People of the several States, and the Electors in each State shall have the Qualifications requisite for Electors of the most numerous Branch of the State Legislature.

No Person shall be a Representative who shall not have attained to the Age of twenty five Years, and been seven Years a Citizen of the United States, and who shall not, when elected, be an Inhabitant of that State in which he shall be chosen.

BPS—While I agree it is preferable that people gain a certain amount of knowledge and experience before becoming a representative and, therefore, from that perspective it is beneficial to have a minimum age requirement for representatives, such a requirement does not achieve equality before the law. Achieving equality before the law is an important part of consistently protecting individual rights and freedom.

Equality before the law is important because it means the law treats everyone the same. For example, everyone's rights are equally protected. In this instance, once individuals have reached the age of adulthood, the law should treat them in the same manner and therefore all individuals should be able to run for office. While there is no right to run for office, recognizing the ability of all adult citizens to run for the office of representative (who meet the inhabitant requirement) is similar to recognizing rights consistently in that all rights that apply to adults should apply to everyone that has reached the age of majority.

This raises the following question: What is the appropriate age for determining when individuals have reached adulthood and thus are eligible to run for the office of U.S. representative? The answer: the current age requirement for when one is eligible to vote is an acceptable age. Based on Amendment XXVI, that means the minimum age requirement should be eighteen years.

It is appropriate to set age requirements for voting, engaging in contractual relationships, and other activities that require an adult who has a fully developed conceptual faculty (from a physiological standpoint). As discussed in connection with the Preamble, children do not have all the rights that adults have (and should not be able to engage in all the activities in which adults are able to engage, such as voting and running for office) because they are not fully developed conceptual beings. One must keep the entire conceptual context in mind when recognizing the existence of rights and the eligibility for engaging in certain activities with regard to children. For instance, children are human beings and thus have the right to life. However, because their conceptual faculty is not fully developed, they do not have the right to, for example, engage in certain contractual relationships, and therefore, among other things, do not have the right to borrow money from a bank (which would require signing a loan contract).

For the same reason, children should not be eligible to vote. Once a child has reached physical maturity and thus has a conceptual (or rational) faculty that is fully developed, the child has the basic tool necessary to understand contractual relationships and issues related to voting (such as the differences in the positions of two candidates) and at that point should be able to engage in these activities. But until children reach the point of maturity, they do not possess a fully developed conceptual faculty and thus do not possess all rights and cannot engage in all activities in which adults can engage.

Of course, different people reach physiological maturity at different ages. However, to protect the rights of a large number of people in an efficient manner, the law must recognize the age that children generally reach adulthood. Exceptions can be made for geniuses and the mentally retarded. For example, a mentally retarded person may never be capable of functioning mentally beyond the capacity of a normally functioning eight-year-old child. Hence, such a person would never possess the right to engage in contractual relationships or be eligible to vote.

It is also true that some people might not behave in a mature manner even after they have reached physiological maturity. In addition, it is true that people do not necessarily reach full intellectual maturity at the time their conceptual faculty has reached physiological maturity. People can continue to gain knowledge about the world long after they have reached physiological maturity. However, since rights derive from our possession of a conceptual faculty, once one has a fully functioning conceptual faculty, all rights must be recognized. Rights are not dependent on how much knowledge a fully functioning adult might gain throughout his lifetime or whether he might behave like a child well into adulthood.

One could also argue that anyone who is old enough to take a job and pay taxes is old enough to run for office. Since people are legally able to work at the age of sixteen (and in some cases at an even younger age), one might argue that the minimum age at which one is eligible to run for representative should be placed at this lower level. However, children are typically still developing physiologically when they have reached the age at which they are legally able to work. Children often still go through a growth phase after this age. Hence, they may be able to perform some jobs but do not generally have the ability to perform more intellectually challenging jobs, such as that of representative.

Moreover, one must take into account the fact that in a capitalist society there would be no minimum age set by law at which children could work. There would be a minimum age at which individuals could enter into contracts, and this would prevent children below this age from working without their parents' consent (since the children would generally have to sign an employment contract). But as long as children do not represent a threat to the rights of others or themselves when performing certain jobs, they would be able to gain employment by having a parent or guardian sign the employment contract. Whether a child works or not is a matter to be decided by the parents (or guardians), the child, and the employer and is not a matter in which the government should generally be involved.

A detailed discussion of the issue of child labor is outside the scope of this book. I will only state that parents have the right to have their children work if they believe it is necessary to support the family (and for other reasons). By increasing the productivity of labor and average standard of living in the economy, capitalism has made it possible for more and more parents to be able to support their families, thus reducing the need for children to work.[7] Nonetheless, parents who are not able to earn enough to support their family may need their children to work. Therefore, it could be harmful to the children and their family if they are not able to work. If people do not want children to have to work, they are free to give to charities that support families who otherwise may need their children to work. However, they have no right to initiate force and violate the rights of parents who determine their family needs their children to work. Seen from this perspective, laws prohibiting child labor are against the interest of children who need to work to support themselves and the families to which they belong. Such laws are also immoral, since they violate the rights of the parents and prevent both the parents and the children from doing what is in their family's self-interest.

As one can see, the debate regarding what is the appropriate age for individuals to be eligible to run for the position of U.S. representative is really a debate about the age at which children generally reach the age of majority and thus when the rights and eligibilities of adulthood are recognized, including the eligibility to vote, the right to enter contractual relationships, and the eligibility to run for office. It may be reasonable in certain contexts—such as in a more rational culture where children develop intellectually in a much quicker fashion—to lower the age for voting and running for office. However, given that there is bound to be some disagreement on this issue and that the currently recognized voting age of eighteen years is a reasonable candidate for when children generally reach adulthood from a physiological standpoint, that is a good age to use.

One must understand that there are many options, with regard to some issues, about how to protect individual rights and determine voting and candidacy eligibility. This is one of those issues. For instance, with regard to protecting rights, optional methods exist in the possible punishments for crimes (i.e., whether those convicted will face fines and/or jail time) and how severe the punishment will be (i.e., the magnitude of fines, length of jail terms, and whether some of those convicted will face the death penalty for their crimes).

The method of determining whether individuals are violating rights can also be optional in many cases. For example, in an area in which driving under the influence is widespread, police roadblocks may be appropriate to apprehend offenders of this crime. However, in areas where such offenses are rare, judgment of individual police officers regarding whether to pull over a potential offender may be the only method relied upon. Note that driving under the influence is a violation of individual rights because it threatens the lives of pedestrians and other drivers. In addition, in a free society, since roads would be privately owned, private road owners would, more than likely, have rules against driving under the influence on their roads and thus it would violate the rules one agrees to follow when driving on someone else's road.

Furthermore, one must understand that the debate about whether to change the age at which people can run for office by a few years is not that significant of an issue. Even if the age was maintained at twenty-five years, it would not be that significant of an injustice. Not that many people below the age of twenty-five years would probably run for office and, of those who did, probably not that many people would vote for them. The issue becomes even less significant, of course, when considering the difference between the age of eighteen and, perhaps, sixteen years, especially given that one can argue that sixteen is not an appropriate age for eligibility based on the age at which physical maturity occurs.

In addition to changing the minimum age requirement in this portion of Article I, Section 2, the citizenship requirement must also be changed. Given that this is the Constitution of the *United States*, it is appropriate to require that representatives be American citizens. It is also appropriate that they be inhabitants of the state they represent. However, to achieve equality before the law for all citizens who meet the inhabitant requirement, there should be no length of time that one must be a citizen before one can run for office. Hence, as soon as one becomes a U.S. citizen, one should be eligible to run for office.

Since one will be representing U.S. citizens and taking an oath to support and defend the U.S. Constitution, it is important for one to become familiar with life in America and show some level of dedication to living for a significant period of time (if not permanently) in the United States before being eligible to run for office. Most importantly, living for a significant period of time in America could help protect individual rights by increasing the likelihood that the person who becomes a representative will have integrated himself into a culture that respects individual rights and thus will have become more familiar with how to protect rights himself. Familiarity with life in the United States and long-term residency can be achieved by requiring foreigners to live in America for a significant period of time before they are eligible to become citizens. Any rights-respecting, self-supporting foreigner has the right to come to the United States to seek employment and live here. However, that does not automatically make him eligible to become a citizen. It would be appropriate to require foreigners to live in the United States for a significant period of time before being eligible to become a citizen. This will help achieve the desired integration with American culture prior to being eligible to run for office. Such citizenship eligibility requirements can be achieved through appropriate legislation, which Congress is authorized to pass based on the Naturalization Clause in Article I, Section 8. These requirements should not be addressed in the Constitution.

Based on the preceding discussion, the Constitution should be amended as follows: Amendment XXIX—In Article I, Section 2 of the Constitution of the United States, the minimum age requirement for representatives shall be changed from twenty-five years to eighteen years and the citizenship requirement for representatives shall be changed from a minimum of seven years to only requiring individuals to be United States citizens before being eligible to become a representative.—BPS

[Representatives and direct Taxes shall be apportioned among the several States which may be included within this Union, according to their respective Numbers, which shall be determined by adding to the whole Number of free Persons, including those bound to Service for a Term of Years, and excluding Indians not taxed, three fifths of all other Persons.][8] The actual Enumeration shall be made within three Years after the first Meeting of the Congress of the United States, and within every subsequent Term of ten Years, in such Manner as they shall by Law direct. The Number of Representatives shall not exceed one for every thirty Thousand, but each State shall have at Least one Representative; and until such enumeration shall be made, the State of New Hampshire shall be entitled to chuse three, Massachusetts eight, Rhode-Island and Providence Plantations one, Connecticut five, New-York six, New Jersey four, Pennsylvania eight, Delaware one, Maryland six, Virginia ten, North Carolina five, South Carolina five, and Georgia three.

When vacancies happen in the Representation from any State, the Executive Authority thereof shall issue Writs of Election to fill such Vacancies.

The House of Representatives shall chuse their Speaker and other Officers; and shall have the sole Power of Impeachment.

Section 3

The Senate of the United States shall be composed of two Senators from each State, [chosen by the Legislature][9] thereof, for six Years; and each Senator shall have one Vote.

Immediately after they shall be assembled in Consequence of the first Election, they shall be divided as equally as may be into three Classes. The Seats of the Senators of the first Class shall be vacated at the Expiration of the second Year, of the second Class at the Expiration of the fourth Year, and of the third Class at the Expiration of the sixth Year, so that one third may be chosen every second Year; [and if Vacancies happen by Resignation, or otherwise, during the Recess of the Legislature of any State, the Executive thereof may make temporary Appointments until the next Meeting of the Legislature, which shall then fill such Vacancies.][10]

No Person shall be a Senator who shall not have attained to the Age of thirty Years, and been nine Years a Citizen of the United States, and who shall not, when elected, be an Inhabitant of that State for which he shall be chosen.

BPS—The age requirement for senators must be reduced to eighteen for the reasons discussed in Article I, Section 2 in connection with the age requirement for representatives. While I agree with the intention of the Framers in imposing a higher minimum age requirement on senators than on representatives—to have more experienced individuals become senators—it nonetheless is not consistent with achieving equality before the law, which is crucial in creating a government that consistently protects rights.

The citizenship requirement must also be changed in the same way and for the same reason that it was changed for representatives. Again, laws requiring foreigners to live in the United States for a specified number of years before they can become a U.S. citizen can be imposed that will require foreigners to become familiar with life in the United States and show a desire to live in the United States permanently before being eligible to become a senator.

Based on this, the Constitution should be amended as follows: Amendment XXX—In Article I, Section 3 of the Constitution of the United States, the minimum age requirement for senators shall be changed from thirty years to eighteen years and the citizenship requirement for senators shall be changed from a minimum of nine years to only requiring individuals to be United States citizens before being eligible to become a senator.—BPS

The Vice President of the United States shall be President of the Senate, but shall have no Vote, unless they be equally divided.

The Senate shall chuse their other Officers, and also a President pro tempore, in the Absence of the Vice President, or when he shall exercise the Office of President of the United States.

The Senate shall have the sole Power to try all Impeachments. When sitting for that Purpose, they shall be on Oath or Affirmation. When the President of the United States is tried, the Chief Justice shall preside: And no Person shall be convicted without the Concurrence of two thirds of the Members present.

BPS—I considered adding an amendment stating that the chief justice should preside over the impeachment trial of the vice president because this portion of the Constitution does not state that the vice president cannot preside over his own impeachment trial. I decided against this amendment because the vice president presiding over his own impeachment trial contradicts many provisions in the Constitution against self-dealing (e.g., the clause in Article I, Section 3 preventing the vice president from presiding over the president's impeachment trial and Amendment XXVII, which prevents senators and representatives from increasing their own pay without an intervening election). It also contradicts statements made by James Madison and Alexander Hamilton in *The Federalist* Nos. 10 and 80, respectively, rejecting the idea that a man should be a judge in his own cause.[11] Other writers have also rejected the idea that the vice president would be allowed to preside over his own impeachment trial based on similar considerations.[12]—BPS

> Judgment in Cases of Impeachment shall not extend further than to removal from Office, and disqualification to hold and enjoy any Office of honor, Trust or Profit under the United States: but the Party convicted shall nevertheless be liable and subject to Indictment, Trial, Judgment and Punishment, according to Law.

Section 4

> The Times, Places and Manner of holding Elections for Senators and Representatives, shall be prescribed in each State by the Legislature thereof; but the Congress may at any time by Law make or alter such Regulations, except as to the Places of chusing Senators.
>
> The Congress shall assemble at least once in every Year, and such Meeting shall [be on the first Monday in December,][13] unless they shall by Law appoint a different Day.

Section 5

> Each House shall be the Judge of the Elections, Returns and Qualifications of its own Members, and a Majority of each shall constitute a Quorum to do Business; but a smaller Number may adjourn from day to day, and may be authorized to compel the Attendance of absent Members, in such Manner, and under such Penalties as each House may provide.
>
> Each House may determine the Rules of its Proceedings, punish its Members for disorderly Behaviour, and, with the Concurrence of two thirds, expel a Member.
>
> Each House shall keep a Journal of its Proceedings, and from time to time publish the same, excepting such Parts as may in their Judgment require

Secrecy; and the Yeas and Nays of the Members of either House on any question shall, at the Desire of one fifth of those Present, be entered on the Journal.

Neither House, during the Session of Congress, shall, without the Consent of the other, adjourn for more than three days, nor to any other Place than that in which the two Houses shall be sitting.

Section 6

The Senators and Representatives shall receive a Compensation for their Services, to be ascertained by Law, and paid out of the Treasury of the United States. They shall in all Cases, except Treason, Felony and Breach of the Peace, be privileged from Arrest during their Attendance at the Session of their respective Houses, and in going to and returning from the same; and for any Speech or Debate in either House, they shall not be questioned in any other Place.

BPS—No changes to this clause are needed. However, some discussion on topics that this clause touches upon is required to understand how it protects rights consistently. First, let me discuss the privilege from arrest. This privilege was instituted to prohibit the arrest of representatives that would prevent them from representing their constituents in Congress. It has its origin in protecting representatives from the practice in England, where the crown would attempt to intimidate and prosecute members of Parliament when the monarch did not agree with their views. The privilege from arrest gives Congressmen immunity from civil arrest. Civil arrest was something common at the time the Constitution was created. It occurs when a person is detained by a lawful authority to answer a civil demand against him. Such arrests rarely, if ever, occur today. Based on the Framers' intent and Supreme Court rulings, the privilege does not provide immunity from arrest and prosecution for criminal acts. In addition, it does not provide immunity from civil process and other legal processes.[14] This is appropriate. The privilege should only protect Congressmen from attempts to prevent them from representing their constituents. It should not protect Congressmen from appropriate legal proceedings.

In addition, Congressmen also have immunity from being questioned about what they say on the floor of Congress. This was instituted to facilitate open debate and discussion during the legislative process. While I am uncomfortable with Congressmen having immunity from slander, it is important to prevent people from using legal methods to intimidate Congressmen with whom they disagree and prevent them from speaking freely on the House or Senate floor, especially given that such methods were used in England when this immunity did not exist. It is also important to note that while the clause may protect Congressmen from legal liability from which they should not be protected, they are still subject to disciplinary action by Congress should they engage in "disorderly behavior."[15] Hence, they could still be punished for inappropriate statements on the floor of Congress. Moreover, the clause only protects Congressmen from legal action against statements made on the floor of Congress. If Congressmen make statements or republish statements outside this venue, the slandered party is free to take legal action.[16]

The immunity this clause provides is needed to protect individual rights in the best manner possible. The clause not only protects the rights of Congressmen by preventing people from intimidating them, but by fostering open and honest debate, it can help Congress protect rights in a better fashion. Hence, it is necessary to maintain this immunity.

While this portion of the Constitution is necessary to protect individual rights, discussion on the use of the term "privilege" is necessary to understand its relation to rights. To the Founding Fathers, the word "privileges" referred to rights. However, the word was not originally used in this way, and it was not consistently used to refer to rights during the time the Constitution was written. Privileges originally referred to exemptions from laws enforced by the British Crown.[17] In some cases, these exemptions did protect rights, but they did not consistently do so and that was not their purpose.[18] For example, one privilege granted was monopoly trading privileges. These violate rights by forcibly keeping some people from entering an industry and engaging in voluntary trade. Another privilege granted land tenure only to British subjects (not to aliens). This protected the rights of British subjects by effectively establishing private property rights. Prior to this, all land was titled to the British Crown. However, this did not consistently protect rights, since land tenure was not extended to aliens. Another privilege that actually helped to protect rights was trial by jury.

Because of its origin and inconsistent usage, as well as because the word "privileges" is not generally used today to refer to rights and because there are many privileges today that some people want the government to provide that would, in fact, violate individual rights (such as the "privilege" of all young adults receiving a one-time payment from the government when starting out in life),[19] one must understand that the term "privilege" is used in a very narrow sense in the context of this clause of the Constitution. It refers to the protection of a very specific right that applies to Congressmen. Everyone, in effect, possesses this right. Everyone has the right to be free from being arrested at his place of employment and while traveling to and from his place of employment (unless, of course, the arrest relates to some violation of individual rights). However, because Congressmen face special circumstances relating to the activities of the government and are in a more vulnerable position, it is appropriate to identify this right in the Constitution to ensure the protection of their rights.

Finally, I could have changed this clause by referring to the privilege from arrest as a right instead of a privilege. However, as I state at the beginning of this chapter, my intention is to make only those changes that are necessary to ensure the consistent protection of individual rights. In the very narrow context that the term "privilege" is used in this clause, all that is necessary is a brief discussion to clarify what the term "privilege" refers to.—BPS

No Senator or Representative shall, during the Time for which he was elected, be appointed to any civil Office under the Authority of the United States, which shall have been created, or the Emoluments whereof shall have been encreased during such time; and no Person holding any Office under the United States, shall be a Member of either House during his Continuance in Office.

Section 7

All Bills for raising Revenue shall originate in the House of Representatives; but the Senate may propose or concur with Amendments as on other Bills.

Every Bill which shall have passed the House of Representatives and the Senate, shall, before it become a Law, be presented to the President of the United States; If he approve he shall sign it, but if not he shall return it, with his Objections to that House in which it shall have originated, who shall enter the Objections at large on their Journal, and proceed to reconsider it. If after such Reconsideration two thirds of that House shall agree to pass the Bill, it shall be sent, together with the Objections, to the other House, by which it shall likewise be reconsidered, and if approved by two thirds of that House, it shall become a Law. But in all such Cases the Votes of both Houses shall be determined by yeas and Nays, and the Names of the Persons voting for and against the Bill shall be entered on the Journal of each House respectively. If any Bill shall not be returned by the President within ten Days (Sundays excepted) after it shall have been presented to him, the Same shall be a Law, in like Manner as if he had signed it, unless the Congress by their Adjournment prevent its Return, in which Case it shall not be a Law.

Every Order, Resolution, or Vote to which the Concurrence of the Senate and House of Representatives may be necessary (except on a question of Adjournment) shall be presented to the President of the United States; and before the Same shall take Effect, shall be approved by him, or being disapproved by him, shall be repassed by two thirds of the Senate and House of Representatives, according to the Rules and Limitations prescribed in the Case of a Bill.

CONCLUDING REMARKS ON THE REVISION OF THE CONSTITUTION THROUGH ARTICLE I, SECTION 7

Only a few changes are needed through Article I, Section 7 of the Constitution to make this portion fully consistent with the protection of individual rights. The most important of these changes is to the Preamble. That change establishes the proper purpose of government and states what it means to violate rights at the very beginning of the Constitution. This change will significantly help to protect rights by clearly showing what, in very broad terms, the government must do and what it is impermissible for the government to do. It must, of course, protect individual rights and it cannot initiate physical force.

More changes are needed in the next three sections of Article I. Those sections are the focus of the next chapter.

NOTES

1. The Constitution was obtained from the National Archives and Records Administration website, http://www.archives.gov/exhibits/charters/constitution_trans cript.html (accessed June 14, 2015). I do not include the signature block at the end of the Constitution, which would be included in chapter 5.

2. Alexander Hamilton, *Report on Manufactures*, December 5, 1791, http://www .constitution.org/ah/rpt_manufactures.pdf (accessed November 10, 2017). See p. 17 of the document. While Hamilton refers to the General Welfare Clause in Article I, Section 8, his statement is equally applicable to the General Welfare Clause in the Preamble.

3. James Monroe, "Veto Message," May 4, 1822, published online by Gerhard Peters and John T. Woolley, *The American Presidency Project*, https://www.presiden cy.ucsb.edu/documents/veto-message; and James Monroe, "Special Message to the House of Representatives Containing the Views of the President of the United States on the Subject of Internal Improvements," May 4, 1822, published online by Gerhard Peters and John T. Woolley, *The American Presidency Project*, https://www.presiden cy.ucsb.edu/documents/special-message-the-house-representatives-containing-the-v iews-the-president-the-united. Both were accessed June 27, 2020. While Monroe refers to the General Welfare Clause in Article I, Section 8, his statements are equally applicable to the General Welfare Clause in the Preamble.

4. *Steward Machine Co. v. Collector of Internal Revenue*, 301 U.S. 548, pp. 586–88 (1937) and *Helvering v. Davis*, 301 U.S. 619, pp. 640–44 (1937). Again, while these cases focus on the General Welfare Clause in Article I, Section 8, they are equally applicable to the General Welfare Clause in the Preamble.

5. On this point, see John R. Vile, *Re-Framers: 170 Eccentric, Visionary, and Patriotic Proposals to Rewrite the U.S. Constitution* (Santa Barbara, CA: ABC-CLIO, LLC, 2014), p. 318. The Commerce Clause will be discussed in chapter 4. Vile

is probably referring to the General Welfare Clause of Article I, Section 8, but both instances of the clause need to be eliminated to ensure the clause is not used to justify government violations of rights.

6. See James Madison, Alexander Hamilton, and John Jay, *The Federalist Papers*, edited by Isaac Kramnick (London: Penguin Books, 1987), pp. 266 and 272–73. Again, while Madison was referring to the General Welfare Clause of Article I, Section 8, his statements are equally applicable to the clause in the Preamble.

7. For a detailed discussion of the issues pertaining to child labor, see George Reisman, *Capitalism: A Treatise on Economics* (Ottawa, IL: Jameson Books, 1996), pp. 642–46 and 661–62.

8. Modified by Amendment XIV, Section 2. This portion of the Constitution has also been modified by the revised Constitution, specifically Amendments XXXI, XXXVI, and L. These amendments prevent all confiscatory means of financing the government.

9. Changed by Amendment XVII.

10. Changed by Amendment XVII.

11. See Madison, Hamilton, and Jay, *The Federalist Papers*, pp. 124 and 448.

12. See Brian C. Kalt, "Pardon Me?: The Constitutional Case against Presidential Self-Pardons," *The Yale Law Journal* vol. 106, no. 3 (December 1996), pp. 779–809. See pp. 793–96, 798, and 803–4. Also, see Akhil Reed Amar, *America's Unwritten Constitution: The Precedents and Principles We Live By* (New York: Basic Books, 2012), pp. 6–14.

13. Changed by Amendment XX, Section 2.

14. David F. Forte and Matthew Spalding, editors, *The Heritage Guide to the Constitution*, 2nd edition (Washington, DC: Regnery Publishing, 2014), pp. 99–100.

15. Ibid., p. 102.

16. Ibid., p. 100.

17. On the early uses of not only the term "privileges" but "immunities" as well, see Robert G. Natelson, "The Original Meaning of the Privileges and Immunities Clause," *Georgia Law Review* vol. 43 (Summer 2009), pp. 1117–93. See, in particular, pp. 1130–36. Also, see Thomas H. Burrell, "A Story of Privileges and Immunities: From Medieval Concept to the Colonies and United States Constitution," *Campbell Law Review* vol. 34, no. 1 (Fall 2011), pp. 7–120. See, in particular, pp. 10–89.

18. For examples of cases of privileges and immunities not protecting rights or not consistently protecting rights, see David R. Upham, "*Corfield v. Coryell* and the Privileges and Immunities of American Citizenship," *Texas Law Review* vol. 83, no. 5 (April 2005), pp. 1483–534. See, specifically, p. 1496. Also, see Natelson, "The Original Meaning," pp. 1149, 1153–54, and 1166–67; and Burrell, "A Story of Privileges and Immunities," pp. 15, 28–30, and 35.

19. For examples of "privileges and immunities" from a contemporary writer on the Constitution that would violate rights, see Bruce Ackerman, "Post by Bruce Ackerman," *The Constitution in 2020*, March 11, 2005, http://constitutionin2020.blog spot.com/2005/03/post-by-bruce-ackerman.html (accessed April 17, 2016).

Chapter 4

Revising the U.S. Constitution

Article I, Sections 8 through 10

INTRODUCTION

The main changes in this chapter include eliminating the Commerce Clause and eliminating the ability of the government to engage in confiscatory taxation. The Coinage Clause is modified as well to limit the government's power, with regard to money, to codifying the use of money established in the marketplace. In addition, the government's power to create post offices and post roads is eliminated. Just why these changes are necessary to establish a free society will be discussed. Other modifications and topics are also discussed. I follow the same procedures in this chapter for making changes to the Constitution that I follow in chapter 3.

REVISING ARTICLE I, SECTIONS 8–10 OF THE CONSTITUTION

Article I

Section 8

> The Congress shall have Power To lay and collect Taxes, Duties, Imposts and Excises, to pay the Debts and provide for the common Defence and general Welfare of the United States; but all Duties, Imposts and Excises shall be uniform throughout the United States;

BPS—This portion of the Constitution requires significant changes. The first change that is needed, as discussed in connection with the Preamble, is that the phrase "general welfare" must be eliminated. It should be replaced with "protection of individual rights of citizens." So this portion will read: to pay the Debts and provide for the common Defence and protection of Individual Rights of citizens of the United States. . . .

Next, the clause pertaining to laying and collecting taxes must be changed. It must be changed to ensure that the government is financed through voluntary, not confiscatory, methods. This change needs to be made because confiscatory taxation is inappropriate.

Why is confiscatory taxation inappropriate? It is inappropriate because it violates individual rights; it requires the initiation of physical force to implement. It is money that is forcibly expropriated from individuals. To the extent a person earns his money through honest, voluntary trade, he does not use force against anyone to obtain the money. When the government uses force to collect money through taxes, it is the first user of force. It initiates physical force and thus violates the rights of the person who earned the money.

If you do not think confiscatory taxes are taken through the threat and use of force, try not paying your taxes and see what happens. Note here that when I use the term "confiscatory," I am not referring to the taking of what is considered to be an excessive amount of money through the use of force. I am referring to the taking of *any* amount of money through the use of force. It does not matter whether the government takes one cent or $1 million from a person through the initiation of force. Either way, it is confiscatory.

When speaking to people, if I mention that the government of a capitalist society must be financed through voluntary means, people sometimes roll their eyes or snicker. They think such an idea is ludicrous and would never work. Based on the systems of government they are familiar with—mixed economies with heavy doses of statism, like the United States—they are right to react this way. Voluntary taxation would never work in the context of a society with massive government interference. I would never pay taxes voluntarily in such a society. This is because the government uses my tax dollars to engage in a whole host of inappropriate activities. For instance, the government uses my tax dollars to subsidize, among other groups, farmers, bankrupt corporations, pet projects (such as golf courses and businesses that produce "environmentally friendly" products), the poor, the unemployed, the old, and entire nations (even some that are hostile to the United States). It is not in my self-interest for the government to give my money to these groups.

However, it *is* in my self-interest to pay for the police, military, and courts. This is what is needed for the government to protect individual rights, including my own rights. The police protect us from having our rights violated by domestic criminals, the military protects us from foreign aggressors, and the courts provide an objective means of determining guilt and innocence in criminal trials and resolving disputes in a peaceful manner in civil matters. Financing these appropriate activities of government is extremely inexpensive when compared to the vast sums of money governments spend today on inappropriate activities—activities that have nothing to do with protecting individual rights and, in fact, in many cases violate rights.

Consider that the federal government's expenditures for 2019 amounted to about $4.9 trillion and the state and local governments' 2019 expenditures amounted to about $3 trillion.[1] The far greater portion of these expenditures focuses on activities that either have nothing to do with protecting individual rights or actually violate rights, including regulating the economy, redistributing wealth and income, and providing educational services. I estimate that only about 20 or 25 percent of all government spending is for expenditures that are related to the protection of rights, including spending for courts, the military, law enforcement, legislatures, and government executive offices (i.e., mayors, governors, and the president).[2] This means the expenditures to protect rights are only about $1.6 to $2 trillion at the federal, state, and local levels combined. This is a much more manageable expenditure. It reduces the average tax payment per member of the U.S. labor force that would be necessary to finance all government spending from about $47,800 annually to between $9,600 and $11,900.[3]

It is not in my self-interest or anyone else's self-interest to pay for welfare for the poor, bail out bankrupt corporations, subsidize nations hostile to the United States (or any nations at all, for that matter), finance people's retirement (through Social Security), and so forth. No one will voluntarily pay for all that. However, it is in people's self-interest to spend a much smaller amount of money to protect individual rights. People would be willing to voluntarily pay for that. There are a number of methods that can be used to finance these expenditures.

First, lotteries could be used. They are already used today to some extent for education. While lotteries to finance government spending in a free society would face more competition than they do today, since privately sponsored lotteries would not be illegal, the net proceeds from government lotteries could still be used to help finance some portion of spending on the police, military, and courts. Second, even voluntary donations could be used. In 2019, a GoFundMe campaign raised over $20 million in about a month for the border wall that President Trump wanted to build.[4] If this much can be raised in such a short period of time for a border wall (even with the massive taxation we have in the United States), much larger amounts could easily be raised for the police, military, and courts.

Next, parties to contracts who wish to purchase the right to have any disputes that arise from those contracts redressed in a court of law could pay a fee for this right. They would pay this fee upfront, before any disputes arise. These fees could help cover not just potential court costs but the cost of other activities of the government that protect individual rights. People could still

enter into contracts without paying the fee. They just would not be able to
have any disputes that arise that are related to the contracts resolved through
the court system. This would include not being able to have resolutions to
disputes legally enforced by the government.[5]

Also, businesses have a strong incentive to pay taxes and require their
workers to do the same. This is particularly true for large businesses. To the
extent a business has millions—or even billions—of dollars of assets that
can be exposed to theft, vandalism, and embezzlement, businesses will want
to make sure their rights are protected. Many businesses will probably even
require, as a condition of employment, that employees pay a small portion
of their wages to the government to protect rights. This would be voluntary
because the payments would be paid based on both parties voluntarily agreeing to the employment contract. If the workers do not want to pay the taxes,
they do not have to work for an employer that requires them to do so.

In addition, the government could sell off some of the organizations and
land that it owns—which it should not own—to temporarily help fund the
government. These assets include Amtrak and state and national parks. This
would help to make the transition to a system of voluntary taxation smoother.
Property the government owns that it should not own is discussed in detail in
chapter 8 in connection with Amendments LVII and LVIII.

Import duties could also be charged by the government to cover the cost
of inspecting goods coming into the country to ensure that such goods do not
threaten people's rights in any way. Similar fees could be charged to persons attempting to immigrate to the country. These might cover the cost of
background checks to prevent dangerous individuals who would threaten the
rights of citizens (such as terrorists and criminals) from entering the country.
The duties and fees might also cover other functions of the government that
protect rights. They should vary depending on the nature of the threats the
country faces. If little or no threat exists and less substantial inspections are
required, then lower duties and fees should be charged. If a great threat exists,
more serious inspections and higher duties and fees would be justified.

One must understand that the purpose of the duties and fees is not to discourage imports or immigration. The purpose is to help finance the proper
functions of the government. Rights-respecting, self-supporting foreigners
have a right to come to this country to seek a better life if they want to. No one
has the right to stop them. Americans also have the right to hire foreigners to
work for them if they want to. In addition, rights-respecting foreigners (and
U.S. citizens) have the right to bring goods produced in foreign lands into the
country. Again, no one has the right to stop them. If some Americans would
rather purchase foreign-made goods instead of American-made goods, they
have the right to do this as well. Of course, such freedoms are an economic
benefit to U.S. citizens due to the talent and productive effort foreign workers

will bring to the country and the less expensive and wider variety of goods U.S. citizens will be able to obtain if goods can be imported from abroad.[6] I discuss international trade and immigration in more detail in chapter 8.

It is important to note that while workers and companies have a right to choose not to pay taxes, people also have the right to boycott such companies and workers by choosing not to buy their goods or hire them. In fact, it is well within the rights of people to denounce such companies and workers for not contributing to the protection of individual rights. So, while taxes are voluntary, there will be repercussions for not paying taxes.

Some might be worried that the government will not be able to collect enough funds through voluntary financing to protect individual rights due to the so-called free-rider problem. That is, some people may want to benefit from the protection of rights by the government but not be willing to pay as long as they can "free ride" off of other people's willingness to pay. This will not be a major obstacle to raising the necessary funds for a few reasons. First, as I mention above, the amount of government spending necessary to finance will be greatly reduced and thus much more easily met with payments by fewer individuals (or much smaller payments). Second, as I also mention above, those who want or require certain services from the government (such as inspection services and the right to resolve disputes on contracts through the court system and have those resolutions legally enforced) will be charged fees for such services. Individuals will be required to pay these fees if they want to purchase the services. Third, as is also mentioned above, individuals have the right to castigate and boycott those who do not pay. This will encourage payment. Fourth, Americans gave $428 billion to charity in 2018 and, beyond a tax deduction, they do not materially benefit from that at all.[7] I do not see a problem achieving payments less than four or five times that amount for something from which all Americans will materially benefit. As I discuss in my book *Markets Don't Fail!*, the "free-rider problem" does not present an insurmountable obstacle to overcome.[8]

A brief word needs to be said about why it is not in the self-interest of individuals to be forced to provide welfare to the poor, bailout companies, and so forth. People might claim that, for instance, if the poor do not receive welfare, they will commit more crime to obtain what they need to survive. Hence, according to this argument, welfare actually helps to protect individual rights. Likewise, if large companies on the brink of bankruptcy are not bailed out (such as financial firms deemed "too big to fail"), it could create a domino effect and cause firms to fail throughout the entire economy, thus causing a large financial crisis and depression.

These concerns are, at best, misplaced. Being poor does not justify committing crimes. If people are poor, they need the freedom to gain skills and find jobs to lift themselves out of poverty. If they are incapable of working (such as the retarded or severely crippled), they need others to be free to do these things so that a standard of living can be achieved such that people can afford through charitable means to take care of those who cannot take care of themselves. This means they need the protection of individual rights. Since the rise of capitalism in the late eighteenth century and the protection of individual rights it makes possible, the poor have become richer than kings and queens of past eras in many ways. For example, poverty today comes with color television, cable television, cellular phones, air conditioning, automobiles, refrigerators, and many more products.[9] The poor today have access to products that kings and queens from past eras could not have imagined. The fact that the poor can afford these products is not due to the existence of welfare. All the welfare in the world will not bring these products into existence. What has made the production of these products possible is the freedom of scientists, inventors, engineers, entrepreneurs, and businessmen to discover the scientific principles that make these products possible and then design and develop these products, obtain the necessary financing, and create the businesses to bring them to the market. They then had to continuously improve upon these products and the methods of production necessary to produce them so that the cost of producing them was radically reduced and thus a mass market could be achieved such that the products were brought within reach of the poor. This is how freedom—how capitalism—has continuously raised the standard of living of the rich and poor alike.[10]

Moreover, as discussed in chapter 1, a rational code of morality—the morality of rational self-interest—tells us that one does not have a duty to help the poor. The morality of rational self-interest also tells us that if poor people commit crimes, they should be tried and convicted in a proper legal proceeding. They should not be allowed to, in essence, threaten to commit crimes against people if someone does not give them a handout. That's extortion! The purpose of the government is to stop crimes like extortion, not participate in their perpetration.

Further, as I intimate in chapter 1, if one wants to help the poor, one has the right to do so. However, no one has the right to force other individuals to help the poor by enacting welfare legislation. Such legislation violates individual rights and is immoral.

Lastly on this topic, by establishing a society in which individual rights are respected and that teaches everyone—including the poor—that no one owes them a living, we will reduce crime and raise the standard of living. With knowledge of the importance of protecting rights widely disseminated, fewer people will turn to crime because more people will have a fundamental understanding of why it is morally wrong. In addition, with more people working (including the poor), the productive capability and average standard of living will be increased, especially that of the poor.

On the issue of bailing out large companies, large companies do not need to be bailed out to prevent the financial collapse of the economic system. This is a subject too complex to discuss in detail in a book on how to change the Constitution and Declaration to protect rights consistently, so I will refer the reader to my work on this subject in my two-volume book *Money, Banking, and the Business Cycle.*[11] I will only say here, briefly, that most monetary and financial instability that our economic system experiences comes from government interference in the form of regulations that create perverse incentives for banks and other companies to take on exorbitant risk. These regulations include, for example, federal deposit insurance and bailouts of large firms that get into financial trouble. Such regulations lead to, among other things, banks operating with too much debt and too little reserves because the banks and depositors know they can count on government assistance if they get into financial trouble. This puts the banks in a financially precarious position. The existence of the Federal Reserve and its manipulation of the supply of money and credit is a primary factor that contributes to the instability as well. It leads to wild swings in the business cycle, continuously rising prices, and the corresponding decrease in the value of the dollar. To achieve stability, we need to establish a complete free market in money and banking. This means abolishing the Federal Reserve and federal deposit insurance and constitutionally preventing the government from bailing out bankrupt companies. It also means constitutionally preventing the government from issuing money. This and a number of other protections of individual rights that I discuss in my two-volume book will create a free market in money and banking and will lead to a gold standard, as well as banks keeping far higher reserves and using much less debt to finance their business activities.

One might think that the above describes what existed in the monetary and banking system in the United States during the nineteenth century. However, one would be mistaken if one thought this. Even though the Federal Reserve did not exist in the United States during the nineteenth century, and the United States was on a gold standard, many forms of regulation existed that created significant instability in the economy. These include, but are not limited to, the creation of fiat money (greenbacks) during the Civil War, state government deposit insurance schemes, state government chartering systems for banks that restricted competition, and federal regulation through the National Bank Act of 1863. To understand the types of interference and how they led to instability, see my book *Money, Banking, and the Business Cycle, Volume 2.*[12]

It will be instructive to briefly consider what an appropriate response would be to financial crises and recessions in the context of the government interference that exists today in the economy. The appropriate response is for the government to reduce its spending, cut taxes, pay down government debt (if it is able to achieve budget surpluses), and deregulate the economy as much as possible. This type of response leads to the quickest recovery because it reduces costs of production, helps to restore spending in the economy and the profitability of businesses, and in general gets the government out of the way so that individuals can adjust quickly and in the best way to mitigate the negative effects of the crisis on their own lives. It also frees up funds in the loan market through reduced government borrowing and thus makes more funds available to businesses and individuals. Unfortunately, the last time the government responded in this manner was during the depression of the early 1920s. As a result, the economy recovered rapidly from that depression.[13]

Given that the government has control of the money supply today, it should also ensure that the money supply does not shrink by providing adequate reserves to banks through the Federal Reserve. This is not an ideal response, but it is the best that can be hoped for with the government interference in money and banking that exists today. This will help to prevent spending in the economy from decreasing, which is important to maintain the solvency of companies and individuals.[14]

One thing the government should not do, as I have previously mentioned, is bailout individuals, companies, and financial institutions. Bailouts and the inflation of the money supply used to finance them sow the seeds for future crises and can lead to longer recovery periods. The government should also engage in quick adjudication of bankruptcies to ensure that markets can function as smoothly as possible.

Essentially the same response applies to the economic crisis caused by the government shutting down the economy in response to the COVID-19 pandemic. However, there are some differences. For instance, given the large number of firms that have been forced to shut down, businesses, individuals, borrowers, creditors, landlords, and tenants should be encouraged to work out adjustments to loans, leases, and other agreements to avoid bankruptcies, evictions, and other economic dislocations as much as possible. This should include requiring parties in any relevant legal proceedings, such as bankruptcy and eviction proceedings, to first try to work out adjustments to their contractual agreements.

It is important to understand, in connection with this issue, that freedom does not include the "freedom" to spread an infectious disease through interactions with others. This violates the rights of those infected. This is not only true if one knows one has the disease but, during a pandemic, it is true if one unknowingly spreads the disease as well. Hence, shutting down localized areas of the economy—perhaps small sections of cities at most—may be appropriate in an emergency to protect individual rights by detecting and isolating those who are infected, although shutdowns must be based on evidence that a disease is spreading in specific areas and is a threat to individuals. Shutdowns should also occur for only a very limited period of time (only the time needed to detect and isolate the infected).

Once the emergency abates, as a part of protecting rights, the ability to produce, trade, and interact with others in general must be restored as quickly as possible (with appropriate precautions). As indicated above, it would be appropriate for the government to require individuals who have the disease to be quarantined. This means, as is also indicated above, that the government should be testing people for the disease. In addition, it should trace the contact people have had with those who test positive to limit the spread of the disease as much as possible. But protecting individual rights during a pandemic means focusing on both protecting people from being exposed to the virus and respecting the right of individuals to engage in production and voluntary trade (again, this latter while following appropriate precautions). Focusing on only one or the other does not protect rights consistently. Those who do not want to be exposed to the risk of interacting with others can choose to isolate themselves from others. However, people must be free to choose what level of risk is acceptable to them and, therefore, those who are willing to take on added risk have the right to interact with others once the emergency subsides.

Furthermore, as with economic crises more generally, one thing governments should *not* provide during a pandemic is bailouts, loans, "stimulus packages," or "relief checks" whether to individuals, companies, and other governments, including bailouts and loans to state and local governments by the federal government. This violates the rights of taxpayers and, among other things, keeps inefficient and poorly run businesses in business, provides incentives for people to not work who could, and bails out financially irresponsible governments. People must save for unexpected unemployment and downturns in business (or mandatory shutdowns due to pandemics). It is a well-known principle that everyone should have a "rainy day fund" for such events. This includes private organizations and governments.

It is not a valid argument to claim that one could not have possibly saved for the pandemic because the pandemic and the shutdown in response to it are unprecedented. Recessions, depressions, and financial crises are common, and people should be saving for the possibility of these types of crises. If they have not saved (or cannot afford to save), they must rely on voluntary charity, help from family and friends, or mutual aid societies. The extensive handouts and bailouts the government has provided during the last several decades have created strong incentives for businesses and individuals to consume too much, take on too much debt (and too much risk more generally), not work and save enough, make poor investment decisions, and behave in a more financially irresponsible manner. Stability in the economy is achieved, in part, by requiring individuals and businesses to be responsible for their own choices and actions. Taxpayers should not be forced to protect people from the consequences of their poor choices.

So, it is not in one's self-interest to have taxpayer-financed subsidies, welfare, bailouts, and so on. It is in one's self-interest to establish a capitalist society. Capitalism protects the freedom and individual rights on which economic prosperity and human life depend. This point cannot be emphasized too strongly. Eliminating confiscatory taxation and radically reducing the size and scope of government will lead to an explosion in the production of wealth. This will be caused by large increases in innovation, business formation, and capital formation, which will result from eliminating the government interference (i.e., government violations of individual rights) that makes all of these harder, if not impossible in some cases, to achieve. This will lead to a massive increase in the productive capability, rate of economic progress, and standard of living. This is what the modifications I am making to the Constitution will help to accomplish. I will provide many more examples throughout this book of the benevolence of capitalism and the economic prosperity it creates, as well as the malevolence and economically destructive nature of government interference in the economy.

One thing that it is important to understand when discussing the topic of financing the government of a capitalist society is that establishing the methods of financing such a government is the last step to take in implementing a capitalist society. First, the government must be pared back to its appropriate functions. This means, as indicated above, a radical reduction in the activities in which the government engages. Once the size of the government is reduced to an appropriate level, implementing the appropriate methods of financing the government and obtaining the necessary funds through voluntary means should be a relatively easy task.

The opening clause of Section 8 needs to be changed to reflect the changes discussed above. Here is the amendment: Amendment XXXI—The following portion of Article I, Section 8 of the Constitution of the United States shall be repealed: The Congress shall have Power To lay and collect Taxes, Duties, Imposts and Excises, to pay the Debts and provide for the common Defence and general Welfare of the United States; but all Duties, Imposts, and Excises shall be uniform throughout the United States. It shall be replaced with the following: The Congress shall have Power To lay and collect Duties on imports, to collect voluntary Taxes and Fees and use other voluntary methods to raise revenue, to pay the Debts and provide for the common Defence and protection of Individual rights of citizens of the United States; but all Duties, Fees, and other methods of raising revenue, besides Taxes, shall be uniform throughout the United States.

The reason why I explicitly refer to imports in connection with duties is because duties can be placed on exports as well (see Article I, Sections 9 and 10 of the Constitution). Duties are sometimes also used to refer to taxes more generally. So the term "imports" needs to be included here to ensure that the meaning is clear.

Additionally, the reason I do not include taxes in the Uniformity Clause is because the imposition of taxes will be out of the control of Congress. Taxes will be voluntary contributions from citizens. Hence, the federal government will not have the power to make them uniform or non-uniform, although it can certainly make recommendations for uniform taxes. The Uniformity Clause is worth keeping because it requires the government to make the methods of financing the government that are under its control as consistent as possible throughout the United States.—BPS

> To borrow Money on the credit of the United States;
>
> To regulate Commerce with foreign Nations, and among the several States, and with the Indian Tribes;

BPS—This clause must be eliminated. While the original intent of the Commerce Clause was to prevent the states from erecting barriers to trade, that is not how the clause has been interpreted and it is not what "to regulate" refers to today. Moreover, one of the earliest and most influential Supreme Court Chief Justices, John Marshall, stated in *Gibbons v. Ogden* (1824) that the power of Congress to regulate interstate commerce "is complete in itself, may be exercised to its utmost extent, and acknowledges no limitations other than are prescribed in the Constitution." He went on to say in the ruling that "The wisdom and the discretion of Congress . . . and the influence that their constituents possess at elections are . . . the sole restraints on which they have relied, to secure them from its abuse."[15] In essence, he stated that Congress can regulate interstate commerce however it sees fit, subject only to the will of the voters and the limits of the Constitution. This provides very little limitation on the power of Congress to regulate interstate commerce, as history demonstrates. In fact, if the voters want more regulations, it provides a positive political force to expand the regulatory power of Congress. This has been the general trend throughout much of the history of the United States, especially since the latter nineteenth century. Since that time, the power of Congress to regulate in general (not just interstate commerce) has been expanded based on the Commerce Clause.

While the historical influence of this clause is interesting, to have a proper understanding of why this clause must be eliminated, one must understand what it means for the government to regulate. Regulation in this context refers to the government interfering in the market by initiating physical force to change some outcome that government officials do not like.[16] Regulation is not the same as protecting individual rights. When the government protects rights, it bans the initiation of physical force, such as when it protects people from fraud. When the government regulates, it violates individual rights *because* it initiates physical force. The government regulates for many reasons, including to forcibly change the wages workers can earn in the market (through minimum wage laws), to impose laws based on environmental ideology (through the Environmental Protection Agency), and to impose drug safety and efficacy rules on drug manufacturers (through the Food and Drug Administration [FDA]).

I mention fraud above because sometimes it is believed that to protect people from fraud, the government must regulate businesses. This is not true. Fraud is an indirect case of someone initiating physical force, since the person committing the fraud takes something of value from an individual against his will by intentionally providing false information. For example, if someone convinces me to buy a watch by telling me it is a genuine Rolex, when it is really a cheap imitation, they have taken my money from me against my will because I would not have purchased the watch had I known it was not a Rolex. The situation is, in terms of essentials, no different than if an armed robber took the same money from me at gunpoint. In both cases, the money is taken from me against my will.

To protect people from fraud, the government must punish those who intentionally deceive people when attempting to sell them products and services. It must not impose requirements on the marketplace that force all businesses to provide certain types of information about their products, such as information about food ingredients, nutritional characteristics, and the pricing of automobiles. The vast majority of businesses provide accurate and adequate information to buyers—without regulation—so that the buyers can make properly informed decisions. It is in their self-interest to do this so that they have satisfied customers and can thus obtain good word-of-mouth advertising and repeat business. The government does not know what information customers of firms care about obtaining and are willing to pay for (in the form of higher priced products) because it does not act on the profit motive.

Moreover, believing the government must force businesses to provide certain types of information assumes people are guilty until proven innocent. That is, even those businesses that have not engaged in fraud are presumed guilty. It heads a nation down the slippery slope of violating individual rights. The interpretation becomes, in essence, that since the government must allegedly violate rights to prevent fraud, it is acceptable for the government to violate rights to achieve other goals. The result of this precedent, when taken to its logical and consistent end, is a police state.

Regulation is not necessary to prevent fraud, increase wages, improve working conditions, improve the safety and quality of products and services, protect us from financial crises and depressions, improve the environment, and so forth. In fact, regulation makes it harder to make improvements in all of these areas. As just one example, I refer the reader back to chapter 1 where I discuss how regulation of the safety and efficacy of drugs by the FDA raises costs and causes more harm than it prevents. Pharmaceutical companies have strong incentives to provide safe and effective drugs without regulation. First, their reputation, and thus their profitability and survival, depend on it. If they produce drugs that harm their customers, they will not have very many customers. The resulting lawsuits would create an added incentive to provide safe and effective drugs. Doctors that prescribe drugs also have a strong incentive to ensure that the drugs they prescribe to their patients are safe and effective. Their reputations and careers depend on it. Independent evaluation organizations may also arise to provide third-party review of drugs, such as Underwriters Laboratories and Consumer Reports do with regard to con-sumer products.

I discuss many of the topics mentioned in the previous paragraph in chap-ters 5 and 6 of *Markets Don't Fail!*[17] As mentioned previously, in *Money, Banking, and the Business Cycle* I discuss how government regulation of the monetary and banking system causes financial crises, recessions, depressions, and the business cycle more generally. I show how a free market in money and banking is necessary to solve these problems.

Since the government has no business regulating the economy—whether with regard to trade among the states, with foreign nations, or with the Indian tribes—this clause should not merely be modified. The entire clause must be struck from the Constitution. Hence, the next amendment is as follows: Amendment XXXII–The following clause in Article I, Section 8 of the Constitution of the United States shall be repealed: To regulate Commerce with foreign Nations, and among the several States, and with the Indian Tribes.

Some might fear that without the Commerce Clause state governments may interfere with trade between the states. As I stated, the original purpose of the Commerce Clause was to prevent the states from interfering with interstate trade. This will not be an issue with the new Constitution. Adequate provisions will be provided to prevent all governments—at the federal, state, and local levels—from interfering with all trade.—BPS

> To establish an uniform Rule of Naturalization, and uniform Laws on the sub-ject of Bankruptcies throughout the United States;
> To coin Money, regulate the Value thereof, and of foreign Coin, and fix the Standard of Weights and Measures;

BPS—Significant changes need to be made to this clause. The government should not have the ability to coin money or regulate the value thereof, whether foreign or domestic coin. This has nothing to do with protecting individual rights and, in fact, leads to violations of rights to the extent the government uses this power to prevent individuals and businesses from creating and using their own money. It also undermines stability in the economy and the rate of economic progress to the extent the government uses this power to create fiat money and inflates the fiat money at rapid rates, which governments have done throughout the history of fiat money.

In a free market, individuals in the marketplace will choose what money they use in the same manner and for the same reason that they choose which goods to buy and sell: it is a part of individuals furthering their own well-being and exercising their right to liberty. However, this does not mean the government cannot decide through court cases and codify through statute what must be used as money in cases where there are disputes over what is to be used or over amounts of money owed by one party to another party. The government should possess the ability to recognize legal tender, but such ability should be limited to money already widely accepted in the marketplace. Moreover, market participants should be free to agree on means of payment other than what has been legally recognized by the government and have those agreements legally enforced.

Of course, in a free market, the government must also use some type of money. Since it cannot create money, it must use whatever is chosen by individuals in the marketplace as money, whether gold, silver, private banknotes, or something else. The only restriction on the government's use of money is that it must hold only standard money or banknotes and checking deposits backed 100 percent by standard money. This restriction should exist because the government should not engage in any lending whatsoever, whether to college students, small businesses, farmers, large businesses, banks, homeowners, foreign nations, and so on, and accepting money not 100 percent backed by standard money puts the government, at least implicitly, in the position of a lender. Lending money is not a part of the government's proper function of protecting individual rights, and to ensure that the government does not go beyond its appropriate function, it should be legally prevented from lending money.

I impose restrictions on the government in these and related areas in Amendments LVII and LXI of the revised Constitution, which are discussed in chapters 8 and 9. However, I am not going to discuss in detail in this book why accepting money not 100 percent backed by standard money turns the government into a lender. I am also not going to discuss in detail the nature of standard money. I will only say about the latter that standard money is money that has ultimate debt-paying power and is not a claim to any further item. Today, the government's fiat money is standard money. On a gold standard, gold is standard money.

About the former, I will only say that bank money—checking deposits and banknotes—that is not 100 percent backed by standard money is a claim to the standard money *and* the loans that back it. As a result, those who hold the money are, at least implicitly, financing the lending operations of the bank. Hence, they are creditors lending money not depositors depositing money for safekeeping.[18] For a detailed discussion of the topics mentioned in this and the previous paragraphs, see volumes 1 and 2 of my book *Money, Banking, and the Business Cycle.*[19]

Standards of weights and measures should also be established in the marketplace. However, to help in resolving disputes, again, the government may recognize such standards through court cases and codify through statute what has been established in the marketplace or what has been decided in the court cases. Of course, market participants should be free to use the legally recognized standards or other standards.

Based on this discussion, the next amendment is as follows: Amendment XXXIII–The following portion of Article I, Section 8 of the Constitution of the United States shall be repealed: To coin Money, regulate the Value thereof, and of foreign Coin, and fix the Standard of Weights and Measures. It shall be replaced with the following: To make Money that has been widely accepted in the marketplace a Tender in Payment of Debts and fix the Standard of Weights and Measures based on what has been widely accepted in the marketplace, but individuals may use alternative Money or Standards of Weights and Measures if agreed upon.

One might ask here: How is one to determine what is a "widely accepted" form of money or standard? I do not think one set of criteria can be used to determine what it means for something to be "widely accepted." But such details should not be placed in a constitution. A constitution should focus on defining the basic structure of government and the crucial laws necessary to protect individual rights. The details of what it means for money or standards of weights and measures to be "widely accepted" are left to be determined through court cases and legislation. However, to provide some guidance, one example would be that Congress should not recognize as legal tender money that is accepted only in one state or territory or even only in a few states within the country. It should recognize as legal tender money that is accepted throughout the country (or, at least, it should recognize the money that is most widely accepted across the country). Of course, whatever it recognizes should apply throughout the nation.

One might also ask here: How do we make the transition from the government's established standards of weights and measures and the fiat money it has established as legal tender to what market participants decide to use? With regard to money, this involves moving to a free market in money. This means establishing a gold standard. I discuss how to do this (and why gold is free-market money) in volume 2 of my book *Money, Banking, and the Business Cycle.*[20]

Regarding standards of weights and measures, since the government's standards have already been established, these could continue to be used. However, market participants should be free to use other standards. This might require some changes to statutes pertaining to these issues. But since the standards established by the government are already widely used and are sensible, I do not anticipate any changes in the marketplace occurring in connection with standards of weights and measures. It should be noted also that when it comes to protecting individual rights, this is not a significant issue.

But things are different with money. Money is a significant issue with regard to protecting rights. Moreover, the stability of the economy and the rate of economic progress depend on individuals in the marketplace being able to choose what types of money they will use.

One last point I will make here pertains to a statement I make in volume 2 of *Money, Banking, and the Business Cycle.* I state there that the government should not be able to pass legal tender laws.[21] However, here I state that the government will make money that has been widely accepted in the marketplace a legal tender in the payment of debts. What I am proposing that the government do here does not contradict what I say the government should not be able to do in *Money, Banking, and the Business Cycle.* The government must recognize some method for debts to be paid off in legal disputes. That is what the clause mentioned above enables it to do. In the earlier book, I am saying the government cannot require that its own money or any specific money be accepted in trade *to the exclusion of all other types of money.* In other words, the government cannot create a monopoly in its money (or any specific type of money). What I am proposing in this book is consistent with the earlier book, since here I am also stating that individuals are free to accept any form of money that is mutually agreed upon.—BPS

To provide for the Punishment of counterfeiting the Securities and current Coin of the United States;

BPS—The government should punish people for counterfeiting U.S. government securities. However, since the government will not be creating money, it will not need to punish people for counterfeiting coins of the U.S. government, although it should punish people for counterfeiting money used in the United States. The latter duty of the government should be included in the Constitution because it is an important part of protecting rights. So, the next amendment is as follows: Amendment XXXIV—The following clause in

Article I, Section 8 of the Constitution of the United States shall be repealed: To provide for the Punishment of counterfeiting the Securities and current Coin of the United States. It shall be replaced with the following: To provide for the Punishment of counterfeiting the Securities of, and Money used in, the United States.—BPS

To establish Post Offices and post Roads;

BPS—This clause needs to be eliminated. Delivering mail is a commercial activity and is not a part of protecting individual rights. In fact, forcing tax-payers to subsidize the Post Office violates their rights. Hence, the government should neither establish post offices nor roads, whether post roads or any kind of road except those that are needed for military purposes. Private companies should provide these goods and services if they are demanded. Of course, private companies will be able to provide such services with far greater efficiency than the government. The fact that the Post Office is noto-riously inefficient is an indication of this. The monopoly in the delivery of first-class mail that the Post Office possesses is one of the main reasons for its inefficiency.[22]

Note also that the government should not provide postal services so that it can subsidize the delivery of mail in rural areas and thus provide it more cheaply to those who live in such areas. This is an altruist justification of government-provided mail service, where those who live in the city are sac-rificed to those who live in rural areas. As discussed in chapter 1, the altruist code of morality is antithetical to human life. It, therefore, does not provide a proper moral justification for mail-delivery service or anything else. In addi-tion, forcing city dwellers to subsidize mail delivery in rural areas violates the rights of city dwellers and is immoral from this standpoint as well. So, the next amendment is as follows: Amendment XXXV—The following clause in Article I, Section 8 of the Constitution of the United States shall be repealed: To establish Post Offices and post Roads.—BPS

To promote the Progress of Science and useful Arts, by securing for limited Times to Authors and Inventors the exclusive Right to their respective Writings and Discoveries;

BPS—Protecting patents and copyrights is an important part of protecting individual rights. It protects intellectual property rights. Protecting intellec-tual property rights is extremely important economically. It helps to increase the productive capability and standard of living by increasing the incentive and ability to develop new inventions and copyrightable material.[23]

While the essential protection of rights that this clause provides must be maintained, the justification for this protection is not correct. The proper justification for protecting patents and copyrights is because each person has a right to his own life and thus the right to the products of his own mind, including the intellectual property he creates. As a consequence, such protection will "promote the progress of science and useful arts." But this is an effect of protecting these rights, not the reason they should be protected. Nonetheless, this clause can remain as is since it still serves its crucial function.—BPS

To constitute Tribunals inferior to the supreme Court;

To define and punish Piracies and Felonies committed on the high Seas, and Offences against the Law of Nations;

To declare War, grant Letters of Marque and Reprisal, and make Rules concerning Captures on Land and Water;

To raise and support Armies, but no Appropriation of Money to that Use shall be for a longer Term than two Years;

To provide and maintain a Navy;

To make Rules for the Government and Regulation of the land and naval Forces;

BPS—Government regulation *of the economy* violates individual rights, as was shown in the discussion of the Commerce Clause. Regulation of the armed forces by the government is appropriate, since it is an arm of the government that directly uses force against others. The use of force by the military must be rigidly controlled to ensure that it is not used inappropriately—that is, to violate rights. This is what the regulation of the armed forces will do.—BPS

To provide for calling forth the Militia to execute the Laws of the Union, suppress Insurrections and repel Invasions;

To provide for organizing, arming, and disciplining, the Militia, and for governing such Part of them as may be employed in the Service of the United States, reserving to the States respectively, the Appointment of the Officers, and the Authority of training the Militia according to the discipline prescribed by Congress;

To exercise exclusive Legislation in all Cases whatsoever, over such District (not exceeding ten Miles square) as may, by Cession of particular States, and the Acceptance of Congress, become the Seat of the Government of the United States, and to exercise like Authority over all Places purchased by the Consent of the Legislature of the State in which the Same shall be, for the Erection of Forts, Magazines, Arsenals, dock-Yards, and other needful Buildings;—And

> To make all Laws which shall be necessary and proper for carrying into Execution the foregoing Powers, and all other Powers vested by this Constitution in the Government of the United States, or in any Department or Officer thereof.

BPS—During the ratification debates, the Anti-Federalists referred to this clause as "the sweeping clause." They thought it would give Congress unlimited power to legislate. It has not provided Congress that kind of power. The Commerce Clause has been far worse. The ability of Congress to legislate to exercise the powers given to it in the Constitution is indispensable to having an effective constitution and government. This clause should remain in the Constitution for that reason. The key to limiting the power of Congress—and the power of the government in general—is to ensure that the "Powers vested by this Constitution in the Government of the United States" are appropriately restricted. If the Constitution limits the powers of the government, then the laws "necessary and proper" to execute those powers will be correspondingly limited. The problem is the portions of the Constitution that give the government powers it should not have, such as the power to regulate commerce through the Commerce Clause. By repealing these portions of the Constitution, and further limiting the power of the government through a number of other important changes to the Constitution, one can limit the power of the government *and* its ability to make laws so that both are used only for the purpose of protecting individual rights.—BPS

Section 9

> The Migration or Importation of such Persons as any of the States now existing shall think proper to admit, shall not be prohibited by the Congress prior to the Year one thousand eight hundred and eight, but a Tax or duty may be imposed on such Importation, not exceeding ten dollars for each Person.

BPS—This refers to the importation of slaves. Slavery, of course, is a gross violation of individual rights and is immoral. Not outlawing slavery was a major flaw in the original Constitution. Fortunately, that flaw was corrected by Amendment XIII, with related corrections in Amendments XIV, XV, and XXIV.—BPS

> The Privilege of the Writ of Habeas Corpus shall not be suspended, unless when in Cases of Rebellion or Invasion the public Safety may require it.

BPS—While no change to this clause is necessary, discussion is required to better understand the nature of this clause, its relation to the protection of individual rights, and its relation to other clauses that use similar terminology. The privilege of the writ of habeas corpus is the right of a prisoner, or someone acting on the prisoner's behalf, to petition a court to determine if the prisoner's detainment is legally justifiable. This is an important right, and its protection is a necessary part of a free society. My comments will focus on the use of the term "privilege" versus the term "right."

The term "privilege," as it is used in the context of this clause, refers to a right.[24] It is similar to the term's use in Article I, Section 6 in the Privilege from Arrest Clause that applies to Congressmen. One of the problems with the use of the term "privilege," as highlighted in my discussion pertaining to Section 6, is that sometimes it refers to rights but sometimes it does not. The term, in a general sense, refers to special advantages or benefits given to some people but not to others. The privileges bestowed upon high rollers at casinos, such as being given free luxury suites to use during their stay and being provided with free drinks, are examples of privileges in this general sense. They are benefits the casinos choose to give to these gamblers because of the large sums of money with which they gamble. Such privileges can be taken away at any time by the casinos if the gambler does not continue to gamble with large enough sums of money or the casino decides it is not in its self-interest to offer such privileges. The privileges given to prison inmates for good behavior (such as, perhaps, having access to better jobs within the prison or being able to spend more time out of their cells) are also examples of privileges in this general sense. Again, they are benefits given to some inmates but not to others and can be taken away from the inmates.

A clear distinction must be made between privileges in the general sense and the privilege of the writ of habeas corpus, as well as the privilege from arrest of senators and representatives when attending their sessions in Congress or traveling to or from those sessions. The latter are rights the government must protect. The former are merely special benefits given to some people but not to others.

There is a fundamental difference between the privileges of the prison inmate or high roller and the privilege of the writ of habeas corpus or the privilege from arrest of senators and representatives. All the privileges involve benefits bestowed upon these individuals given the rules that apply to them in their situations. However, the similarity stops there.

The fundamental difference lies in the fact that the latter privileges protect freedom. Habeas corpus protects the freedom of individuals who are wrongly incarcerated. The privilege from arrest of senators and representatives protects their freedom to travel and perform their duties as Congressmen and, ultimately, the ability of the government of a free society to function properly and pass laws that maintain such a society. Providing benefits to high rollers and inmates does not protect freedom. We see here that the term "privilege" can be used in two fundamentally different ways conceptually. To ensure that rights are consistently protected, one must understand that in the Constitution "privilege" is used to identify rights. It is not used to identify mere benefits bestowed on some people.

Moreover, it is not the proper purpose of the government to provide benefits or special advantages to some people and not to others or at the expense of others. The proper purpose of the government is to protect the rights of individuals. To do this, as discussed in chapter 1, it must protect freedom; that is, it must protect people from the initiation of physical force. This point will also be important to remember when the Privileges and Immunities Clause of Article IV, Section 2 and the Privileges or Immunities Clause of Amendment XIV of the Constitution are discussed.

Finally, the second portion of this clause refers to the conditions under which the privilege of the writ of habeas corpus can be suspended. The writ can only be suspended in emergency circumstances, when it is not possible to enforce such writs or it could threaten the ability of the government to otherwise protect the rights of citizens if it attempted to enforce such writs. The privilege cannot be suspended arbitrarily. Notice also that this is only a *temporary* suspension. The suspension is lifted once order is restored and the government is able to issue and act on such writs or acting on them no longer poses a threat to the rights of citizens.—BPS

No Bill of Attainder or ex post facto Law shall be passed.

BPS—This clause must be left as is. Bills of attainder are not a part of an objectively valid legal system; they generally violate individual rights. Ex post facto laws should not be a part of a valid legal system as well, although there are some exceptions. They often violate individual rights. Bills of attainder are laws passed by the legislature that single out particular individuals for punishment. They have been used to seek retribution against political rivals. Obviously, these laws do not achieve equality before the law and violate the rights of the individuals who are targeted by them. Ex post facto laws are laws that are applied retroactively. For instance, they can make an act illegal even though the act was legal when committed. It is unjust to convict someone of a crime if the action that is now a crime was legal at the time the person engaged in the action and thus the person thought he was engaging in a lawful act.

Even though this clause does not need to be changed, some discussion of ex post facto laws is needed because of the controversy surrounding such laws (such as when the Ex Post Facto Clause is considered to be applicable). In general, ex post facto or retroactive laws are seen as unjust because they, in essence, change the rules of the game after the game has been played. Rules in professional sports are often changed from one season to the next. Imagine if the rules were changed retroactively. For instance, rules in American football have been significantly changed to reduce the likelihood of injury. Imagine if all games in the past were reviewed in an attempt to determine if the outcome should have been changed based on rule changes that were made after the games took place. This would be immensely unjust (not to mention impossible to do). It would be unjust because justice means giving people what they have earned, and if the athletes could not have known that certain actions violated the rules, one is not giving them a proper chance to obey the rules and win the game. Outcomes may be arbitrarily determined based on whether players happen to violate (or not violate) rules they did not know about.

Retroactive laws can be either criminal or civil. The least controversial retroactive laws are criminal laws. These include, as previously mentioned, criminal laws that make actions illegal after the acts have been committed. They also include laws that increase the severity of punishment of a criminal act after the act has been committed. In addition, they include laws that change the rules of evidence, after a crime has been committed, so that less evidence is required to convict the accused. The types of laws that are generally considered to be in violation of the Ex Post Facto Clause were outlined by Supreme Court Justice Samuel Chase in the Court's decision in *Calder v. Bull* (1798).[25]

Not all retroactive criminal laws have been viewed as violating the Ex Post Facto Clause. These include primarily laws pertaining to procedures followed at trial. For example, *Thompson v. Missouri* (1898) dealt with a case in which a Mr. Thompson was convicted of first-degree murder. At trial, handwriting samples in the form of handwritten letters written by Thompson were admitted into evidence to compare to a forged strychnine prescription. As the murder was carried out through strychnine poisoning, this was an important piece of evidence. Thompson challenged the admission of the writing samples because at the time the murder was committed such samples were inadmissible. However, the Missouri legislature had subsequently passed legislation that allowed such samples to be submitted as evidence. The Supreme Court rejected the claim and upheld the conviction. The Court stated, quoting from its decision in *Thompson v. Utah* (1898), "that the accused is not entitled of right to be tried in the exact mode, in all respects, that may be prescribed for the trial of criminal cases at the time of the commission of the offense."[26] It also stated, quoting from Thomas M. Cooley's treatise *Constitutional Limitations*:

> But, so far as mere modes of procedure are concerned . . . it would create endless confusion in legal proceedings if every case was to be conducted only in accordance with the rules of practice, and heard only by the courts in existence, when its facts arose. The legislature may abolish courts and create new ones,

and it may prescribe altogether different modes of procedure in its discretion, though it cannot lawfully, we think, in so doing, dispense with any of those substantial protections with which the existing law surrounds the person accused of [a] crime.[27]

A similar ruling was made by the Court in *Dobbert v. Florida* (1977). In this case, the defendant killed two of his children when a Florida law required that in a case in which the prosecution was seeking the death penalty, the defendant would receive death unless a majority of the jury recommended life without parole. However, after the murders, this law was invalidated and the state legislature passed a new law that stated a trial court could overrule a jury, and impose the death penalty, if the jury recommended life. The defendant was sentenced to death under the new law after a majority of the jury recommended life in prison and the trial court overruled the recommendation. The Court ruled this did not violate the Ex Post Facto Clause.

It must be noted that the cases mentioned above were appeals to the Supreme Court of verdicts reached in state courts. This means the State Ex Post Facto Clause in Article I, Section 10 applies to these cases. Article I, Section 10 prohibits states from passing ex post facto laws. Nonetheless, the discussion of these cases applies to ex post facto laws in general and thus is still applicable to the Ex Post Facto Clause in Article I, Section 9, which prohibits the federal government from passing ex post facto laws.

The Ex Post Facto Clause is generally believed to not be applicable to civil law. One reason is that it would prevent virtually all civil laws from being enacted, since almost all civil laws have some form of retroactive aspect to them.[28] Furthermore, some ex post facto civil laws actually help to protect individual rights and, for that reason, should not be prohibited. For example, imagine that the government was to pass a law recognizing the proper procedure to follow to claim ownership of unused land in unsettled portions of the country and a part of this procedure involves filing a claim with the government within a fixed period of time after one settles on the land. However, imagine also that the government does not provide the means to implement the procedure for a period of time, after the legislation is passed, that is substantially greater than the fixed period within which one is supposed to file a claim with the government after settling on the land. Perhaps the government does not make the law widely known or does not allow for the funding of the department to process such claims. In this case, the government might pass a retroactive law recognizing that those who have settled upon the effected land, during the time period when the law could not be implemented, are the rightful owners of the land even though they were not able to file a claim within the stipulated time period.[29] This type of ex post facto law is known as a curative law, and there is no objection to such laws because they help protect rights. In this case, they help protect the rights of individual landowners who have acquired ownership of land through legitimate means (i.e., there was no violation of rights in the acquisition of the land).

A couple of examples of different types of retroactive laws that violate individual rights will help one gain a better understanding of the nature of ex post facto laws. The first example is a type of law that is known as a weakly retroactive law. Imagine that a usury law is passed that says the interest rate on all loans that are either still outstanding or made by banks on or after the date the law is passed cannot be above a maximum rate, which is less than the current interest rate and the interest rate on previous loans made. Interest paid starting on the date of the law's enactment would be lower on all loans. A weakly retroactive law applies the law starting on the date the law was enacted but alters preexisting obligations, such as preexisting loans.

To understand strongly retroactive law, we can take the example above and modify it as follows: imagine that the usury law applies to all loans made starting two years prior to the date the law was passed. Banks would have to refund any excess interest paid by borrowers who took on new loans in the two years prior to the law's enactment. A strongly retroactive law applies the law starting on a date before the enactment of the law.[30]

As stated by one lawyer, "it is hard to conceive of many legitimate justifications for either strongly or weakly retroactive legislation."[31] Moreover, the laws in these examples would be unconstitutional—based on a constitution that consistently protects individual rights—given that they violate the rights of banks and their customers to agree on a mutually acceptable interest rate. In other words, the government violates the rights of banks and their customers by forcibly preventing them from agreeing to a rate above the legal maximum.

Even though some laws that are retroactive in nature would be allowed because they are consistent with the protection of individual rights, the retention of the Ex Post Facto Clause is necessitated by the fact that there are certain types of retroactive laws that would be unjust if passed. Furthermore, the clause needs to be retained in the general form in which it exists. Some might think more specification in the Constitution of the types of laws to be prohibited would be helpful in enforcing the clause. However, a constitution is by necessity a very general statement of the law. The supreme law of the land cannot anticipate how to protect individual rights under all possible scenarios. There are just too many variables and unknowns to consider. The details must be worked about by the legislature and judiciary. Of course, laws and rulings made based on the Ex Post Facto Clause should always be fundamentally guided—as all laws and rulings should be—by the government's only proper function: to protect individual rights.

Finally, there are other clauses of the Constitution that are related to the Ex Post Facto Clause, such as the Obligation of Contracts Clause in Article I, Section 10 and the Takings Clause of Amendment V. These also prevent ex post facto laws and will be dealt with below.—BPS

No Capitation, or other direct, Tax shall be laid, [unless in Proportion to the Census or enumeration herein before directed to be taken.][32]

BPS—In the opening lines of Article I, Section 8, the revised Constitution states that only voluntary methods can be used by the federal government to raise revenues. That is the positive statement of what the federal government can do. Here, the negative statement about what it cannot do must be made. Specifically, the government must be banned from using confiscatory taxation. Note also that the portion of the Constitution above that is changed by Amendment XVI must be repealed as well, since that amendment will be repealed. Accordingly, this clause should be amended as follows: Amendment XXXVI—The following clause in Article I, Section 9 of the Constitution of the United States shall be repealed: No Capitation, or other direct, Tax shall be laid, unless in Proportion to the Census or enumeration herein before directed to be taken. It shall be replaced with the following: No confiscatory Tax shall be laid.—BPS

No Tax or Duty shall be laid on Articles exported from any State.
No Preference shall be given by any Regulation of Commerce or Revenue to the Ports of one State over those of another: nor shall Vessels bound to, or from, one State, be obliged to enter, clear, or pay Duties in another.

BPS—Since Congress will not regulate commerce, there is no need to mention it here. Congress may show a preference for one port over others under certain, very limited, circumstances. For example, it may show a preference when deciding where to build a naval base or where to locate a port of entry. However, the purpose under these circumstances is not to give an arbitrary preference but to protect freedom in the most efficient and effective manner possible. Hence, the next amendment is as follows: Amendment XXXVII—The following clause in Article I, Section 9 of the Constitution of the United States shall be repealed: No Preference shall be given by any Regulation of Commerce or Revenue to the Ports of one State over those of another. It shall be replaced with the following: No Preference shall be given to the Ports of one State over those of another, except for the purpose of protecting the rights of United States citizens in the best manner possible.

Ships bound to or from one state should not be required to enter, clear, or pay duties in another state. Hence, the second clause in this portion of the Constitution remains unchanged.—BPS

No Money shall be drawn from the Treasury, but in Consequence of Appropriations made by Law; and a regular Statement and Account of the Receipts and Expenditures of all public Money shall be published from time to time.

No Title of Nobility shall be granted by the United States: And no Person holding any Office of Profit or Trust under them, shall, without the Consent of the Congress, accept of any present, Emolument, Office, or Title, of any kind whatever, from any King, Prince, or foreign State.

Section 10

No State shall enter into any Treaty, Alliance, or Confederation; grant Letters of Marque and Reprisal; coin Money; emit Bills of Credit; make any Thing but gold and silver Coin a Tender in Payment of Debts; pass any Bill of Attainder, ex post facto Law, or Law impairing the Obligation of Contracts, or grant any Title of Nobility.

BPS—As discussed in connection with the Coinage Clause in Article I, Section 8, the government should not determine what is used as money. This includes the state governments. However, it is appropriate for governments, including state governments, to legally recognize money that has been widely accepted in the marketplace. Through statutes, state governments can codify what the market and the courts (through civil disputes) have established as money within a state. They cannot attempt, by fiat, to make any particular item money. Of course, individuals may choose to use money not recognized by the government in their transactions. This portion of the Constitution needs to be changed to reflect these facts.

I will also eliminate from this portion of the Constitution the clauses referring to the states not being able to coin money, emit bills of credit, and impair the obligation of contracts. These restrictions will be imposed on all levels of government, along with a number of other related restrictions, in Amendment LXI in chapter 9.

Hence, the next amendment shall read: Amendment XXXVIII—The following clauses in Article I, Section 10 of the Constitution of the United States shall be repealed: No State shall . . . coin Money; emit Bills of Credit; make any Thing but gold and silver Coin a Tender in Payment of Debts; pass any . . . Law impairing the Obligation of Contracts, ... They shall be replaced with the following: No State shall . . . make any Thing but Money widely accepted in the marketplace a Tender in Payment of Debts, but individuals may use alternative Money if agreed upon; . . . .

When joined with the clauses in this portion of the Constitution that remain in force, this portion of the revised Constitution reads as follows: No State shall enter into any Treaty, Alliance, or Confederation; grant Letters of Marque and Reprisal; make any Thing but Money widely accepted in the marketplace a Tender in Payment of Debts, but individuals may use alternative Money if agreed upon; pass any Bill of Attainder or ex post facto Law, or grant any Title of Nobility.

Note that even though the federal government is given the power to recognize legal tender in Article I, Section 8, the state governments are given this power as well because it could be that some forms of money are used only within a state or region of the country, as occurred prior to the Civil War with banknotes that were issued by state-chartered banks. It therefore makes sense for states to have the power to recognize these as legal tender. It could help the states protect rights in contractual disputes. It is also important to note that just because the government might recognize a particular type of money as legal tender to deal with cases where no explicit agreement was made regarding the means of payment or where it is unclear what the means of payment was to be between parties engaged in a transaction, that does not mean that the use of money not recognized as legal tender cannot be legally enforced through the courts when individuals have agreed to use such money. This, of course, applies at both the federal and the state level.

At this point, one might ask: How will we determine what is money? This, of course, applies to this clause as well as the relevant clause in Article I, Section 8. The Constitution already assumes knowledge of money, since it references money in several locations. The revised Constitution retains many of these references. To determine what is money, we must do what is currently done: look to the definition of money. Money is an asset readily acceptable in exchange in a given geographic location and is sought for the purpose of being re-exchanged.[33] That, of course, has included gold and silver in the past. Today it includes government fiat money. It could also include notes issued by private banks. It could include anything commonly accepted by market participants in payment for debts and goods.—BPS

No State shall, without the Consent of the Congress, lay any Imposts or Duties on Imports or Exports, except what may be absolutely necessary for executing it's inspection Laws: and the net Produce of all Duties and Imposts, laid by any State on Imports or Exports, shall be for the Use of the Treasury of the United States; and all such Laws shall be subject to the Revision and Controul of the Congress.

BPS—As in Article I, Section 8, the duties the state governments can impose must be limited. They must be limited to duties on imports for the purpose of protecting individual rights. Duties on imports may be appropriate for the state governments to impose, whether the imports are coming from outside the country or from other states. However, the state and federal governments should not be duplicating their efforts. Generally, to ensure uniform inspection laws at the national level, the federal government should be responsible for inspecting goods coming from outside the country, while states should be responsible for inspecting goods coming across their borders from other states. However, such inspections could be performed by either level of government, if necessary.

Inspection of goods being imported from other states may be necessary in some cases. For example, animals and plants being imported from another state could threaten the rights of property owners in a state (such as farmers) if such goods threaten crops or livestock in the destination state with disease or infestation. Duties on and inspections of imports are only permitted to the extent there are objective threats to individual rights.

It is appropriate to give Congress ultimate control over the state power to inspect and impose duties on imports. This will ensure such duties and inspections are not redundant and that they are necessary to protect rights. It will also help ensure that the inspections and duties are uniform throughout the United States, to the extent that such uniformity is necessary.

Based on the above, the next amendment is as follows: Amendment XXXIX—The following portion of Article I, Section 10 of the Constitution of the United States shall be repealed: No State shall, without the Consent of the Congress, lay any Imposts or Duties on Imports or Exports, except what may be absolutely necessary for executing it's inspection Laws: and the net Produce of all Duties and Imposts, laid by any State on Imports or Exports, shall be for the Use of the Treasury of the United States; and all such Laws shall be subject to the Revision and Controul of the Congress. It shall be replaced with the following: No State shall lay any Duties on Exports; and No State shall lay any Duties on Imports, except what may be necessary for the protection of individual rights; and all such Duties on Imports shall require the Consent of Congress and be subject to the Revision and Control of Congress.

Note that I have eliminated the requirement that net amounts from duties imposed on imports by the state governments be paid to the U.S. Treasury. This requirement was imposed, as one lawyer from late-eighteenth/early-nineteenth century America stated, "to prevent evasion under colour of securing only the right of inspection."[34] State governments will need to finance their inspections and charging duties on imports, so long as those duties are to finance the protection of individual rights, is a legitimate way to do so. Moreover, since the revised Constitution will have far greater protections of individual rights, one does not have to be as concerned about the state governments charging duties for inappropriate reasons. Nonetheless, all duties require the consent of the Congress and are subject to revision and control by Congress.

Note also that state governments shall not be permitted to impose any taxes on exports, since these are not consistent with the protection of individual rights. The only allowable option here is for states to impose duties on imports.

Finally, I considered adding a clause in this amendment stating that state governments can only use voluntary methods of financing their activities. However, I decided not to because this section of the Constitution focuses mainly on what the states cannot do. In my amendment to Amendment XIV (Amendment XLIX of the new Constitution), I prevent the states from violating the rights of their citizens. This effectively incorporates all relevant parts of the Constitution and thus applies them to the states, which, of course, includes only being able to use voluntary methods of financing.—BPS

> No State shall, without the Consent of Congress, lay any Duty of Tonnage, keep Troops, or Ships of War in time of Peace, enter into any Agreement or Compact with another State, or with a foreign Power, or engage in War, unless actually invaded, or in such imminent Danger as will not admit of delay.

BPS—Since ports and waterways will be privately owned (except for those created or developed for military purposes), the government—whether federal, state, or local—has no business imposing duties based on the weight of ships that pass through waters within the United States. Private owners may charge fees for the use of their ports and waterways. However, that is not an issue to be addressed in the Constitution, since it does not pertain to restricting the government to its appropriate function of protecting individual rights. Private providers of ports and waterways will, like private providers of roads, railroads, and airports, do a far better job of providing them than the government because they will be responding to the demand for such goods and services based on the profit motive. This gives them a much stronger incentive and ability to provide what people want and to do so in the most efficient manner that is possible.

Based on the above discussion, the next amendment shall read as follows: Amendment XL—The following portion of Article I, Section 10 of the Constitution of the United States shall be repealed: No State shall, without the Consent of Congress, lay any Duty of Tonnage, ... It shall be replaced with the following: No State shall lay any Duty of Tonnage and, without the Consent of Congress, ...

This portion of Article I, Section 10 shall now read, in its entirety: No State shall lay any Duty of Tonnage and, without the Consent of Congress, keep Troops, or Ships of War in time of Peace, enter into any Agreement or Compact with another State, or with a foreign Power, or engage in War, unless actually invaded, or in such imminent Danger as will not admit of delay.

One might ask, why explicitly prohibit states from laying duties on the weight of ships' cargo when duties on imports are already prohibited in the previous portion of Section 10 in the revised Constitution, except when necessary to protect rights? Doesn't the previous modification cover duties on tonnage? The answer is: it does to some extent. Duties on tonnage could be imposed for reasons not associated with the importation of goods (such as duties imposed for merely traveling on waterways within a state). Given that the original Constitution allowed states to impose duties on tonnage with the consent of Congress, it is important to make it explicit that this is not allowed in the revised Constitution, even with the consent of Congress. There is some redundancy between this and the previous portion of Section 10 of the revised Constitution, but redundancy in the protection of individual rights in a constitution is good. It will help to better ensure that rights are protected.

It must be emphasized that redundancy in the Constitution to protect individual rights is a virtue despite the traditional rule of legal interpretation that says that a law should not be read in a way that renders any of its parts redundant. This is a weak objection to redundancy because Constitutional protections often overlap. Even the Bill of Rights is a redundancy. As stated by Timothy Sandefur, leading authors of the Constitution argued that a Bill of Rights was unnecessary because the Constitution gave the federal government only specific, limited powers, and therefore the people's rights were protected by the Constitution without the Bill of Rights.[35]

Redundancy can provide individuals multiple provisions with which to protect their rights. It may be the case that in different contexts one provision might be more suitable for protecting the rights of an individual than another provision. Multiple constitutional provisions protecting similar rights can also be used as a cudgel with which to deliver multiple blows against the government when it attempts to violate rights. This will better secure people's rights. In addition, multiple provisions protecting similar rights can help people better understand what rights are protected. If they do not understand what right is protected based on one provision, they may be able to understand what right is protected based on another provision (or both provisions together).—BPS

CONCLUDING REMARKS ON THE REVISION OF ARTICLE I, SECTIONS 8–10 OF THE CONSTITUTION

A number of important changes have been made to Sections 8, 9, and 10 of Article I of the Constitution. The most significant change is the one that establishes a system of voluntary taxation. This will help protect the right of people to keep money that rightfully belongs to them and help restrict the government to its appropriate function of protecting individual rights by limiting the funds it has available to it and requiring the government to provide beneficial services to *all* citizens in order to get them to fund the government. Another significant change is the elimination of the Commerce Clause. This will help prevent the federal government from regulating trade. Eliminating regulation will lead to a dramatic increase in innovation and a rapidly rising standard of living.

Some might think that the changes I am making to the Constitution make the Constitution look more like the Articles of Confederation. For example, Congress did not have the power to tax in the Articles and it will not have the power to engage in confiscatory taxation in the revised Constitution. Also, Congress did not have the power to regulate trade and commerce in the Articles and it will not have that power in the revised Constitution (see Amendment XXXII in this chapter and Amendment LV in chapter 8). In general, the revised Constitution creates a less powerful central government, and this was one complaint which led to the abandonment of the Articles and the creation of the Constitution. This raises the question: If the changes I propose make the Constitution more like the Articles and the Articles were considered inadequate and led to the creation of the Constitution, why do I think the modified Constitution I propose will be successful?

The answer to this question is that while there are some similarities between the revised Constitution and the Articles, there are also many differences. That is why the new Constitution will succeed. For example, take the case of Congress not being able to regulate trade and commerce in the new Constitution. One of the problems with the Articles was that it gave Congress no power to prevent states from imposing trade restrictions when some of them began to do so. The original purpose of the Commerce Clause was to enable Congress to prevent the states from restricting trade. Unfortunately, the Commerce Clause is no longer used for that purpose by Congress but is used to regulate trade. The changes I propose in the new Constitution will not only prevent Congress from regulating trade but will prevent the states from imposing trade barriers and regulating trade as well. This is completely different than the Articles. See Amendments XXXVIII, XXXIX, XL, LV, LVI, LIX, LXI, and LXIII.

In addition, Congress will not have the power to engage in confiscatory taxation in the new Constitution, but the states will not have this power either (see Amendment XLIX in chapter 7, which, as mentioned in this chapter in the discussion of Amendment XXXIX, incorporates all relevant sections of the Constitution to the states, including only being able to use voluntary methods of financing the government). This latter provision is radically different than the Articles, where the states still retained the power to engage in confiscatory taxation. While neither will have the power to engage in confiscatory taxation in the revised Constitution, they will both be able to charge fees on contracts if those engaging in the contracts want to retain the right to have disputes that arise from those contracts resolved in a court of law. Both can still impose duties on imports as well. The federal government can also charge fees for immigration to the United States. These, along with the voluntary methods of taxation I mention in this chapter, should more than cover the costs of protecting rights. Of course, confiscatory means of taxation will not be taken away until the government has been reduced to its appropriate functions and the voluntary mechanisms for financing the government are put into place.

There are other differences between the revised Constitution and Articles as well. For example, there were no federal courts under the Articles, but there are under the revised Constitution. There was no executive office in the federal government to enforce the law under the Articles. There is under the revised Constitution. The one area in which the revised Constitution most certainly weakens the federal government (and state and local governments as well) is in the area of violating rights. The revised Constitution eliminates this ability completely. The one area with respect to which the revised Constitution increases the power of all levels of government is in protecting rights. This is the fundamental distinction between the revised Constitution and both the Articles and current Constitution. It is what makes the revised Constitution immensely superior to the Articles and current Constitution.

NOTES

1. Federal government 2019 expenditures obtained from U.S. Bureau of Economic Analysis, "Federal Government Total Expenditures," retrieved from FRED, Federal Reserve Bank of St. Louis, https://fred.stlouisfed.org/series/W019R C1A027NBEA. State and local government 2019 expenditures obtained from U.S. Bureau of Economic Analysis, "State and Local Government Current Expenditures," retrieved from FRED, Federal Reserve Bank of St. Louis, https://fred.stlouisfed.org/ series/ASLEXPND. Both accessed September 6, 2020.

2. These estimates are based on defense spending being about 15 percent of federal government spending, with the other functions of the federal government to protect rights estimated to be about 10 percent of federal government spending. Police and corrections are about 7 percent of state and local government spending, with the other functions of state and local governments to protect rights estimated to be around 10 percent of state and local government spending. For defense spending relative to total federal government spending, see *Economic Report of the President* (February 2020), p. 420, https://www.whitehouse.gov/wp-content/uploads/2020/02 /2020-Economic-Report-of-the-President-WHCEA.pdf. For spending on police and

corrections relative to total state and local government spending, see Urban Institute, "Police and Corrections Expenditures," https://www.urban.org/policy-centers/cross-center-initiatives/state-and-local-finance-initiative/state-and-local-backgrounders/police-and-corrections-expenditures. Both accessed September 6, 2020. The 10 percent estimates are based on values that were obtained from various sources.

3. Civilian labor force for 2019 obtained from *Economic Report of the President*, p. 393. In addition, values assume that all government spending is financed with taxes. Government borrowing could decrease the tax burden relative to spending during the years the government runs a deficit. Of course, during the years the government runs a surplus, the tax burden would be greater than government spending.

4. See the GoFundMe webpage at https://www.gofundme.com/thetrumpwall (accessed January 17, 2019).

5. On lotteries and fees on contracts to finance government spending, see Rand, *Virtue of Selfishness*, pp. 135–40.

6. On the economic benefits of free immigration and free international trade, see Reisman, *Capitalism*, pp. 350–56 and 362–67.

7. On the charitable giving of Americans, see Una Osili and Sasha Zarins, "American Giving Lost Some Ground in 2018 Amid Tax Changes and Stock Market Losses," *The Conversation*, June 18, 2019, https://theconversation.com/american-giving-lost-some-ground-in-2018-amid-tax-changes-and-stock-market-losses-118892 (accessed September 6, 2020).

8. Simpson, *Markets Don't Fail!*, pp. 181–88.

9. Robert Rector and Rachel Sheffield, "Understanding Poverty in the United States: Surprising Facts About America's Poor," *Backgrounder* no. 2607, September 13, 2011, http://thf_media.s3.amazonaws.com/2011/pdf/bg2607.pdf (accessed November 17, 2017).

10. Simpson, *Markets Don't Fail!*, pp. 5–13.

11. Brian P. Simpson, *Money, Banking, and the Business Cycle, Vol. 1: Integrating Theory and Practice* (New York: Palgrave Macmillan, 2014), pp. 57–85 and 133–37; and Brian P. Simpson, *Money, Banking, and the Business Cycle, Vol. 2: Remedies and Alternative Theories* (New York: Palgrave Macmillan, 2014), pp. 113–85 and 219–42.

12. Simpson, *Money, Banking, and the Business Cycle, Vol. 2*, pp. 195–99.

13. For more on the appropriate response, see Simpson, *Money, Banking, and the Business Cycle, Vol. 1*, pp. 133–37, 215, and 226.

14. I previously stated the government should reduce its own spending during a crisis. Some readers might think this will reduce spending in the economy. However, this, by itself, will not reduce spending in the economy. As long as taxes or government borrowing from the public is reduced to the same extent as government spending, reductions in government spending will not decrease spending in the economy. Only reducing government spending that is financed through inflation (i.e., the creation of new money) will reduce spending in the economy. But reducing spending financed through inflation will benefit the economy overall. The proper way to restore spending in the economy is as I have already stated in the main text. For more on the effects that government spending has on spending in the economy, see ibid., pp. 36–39. On the effects of inflation, see Simpson, *Money, Banking, and the Business Cycle, Vol. 2*, pp. 225–31.

15. *Gibbons v. Ogden*, 22 U.S. 1, pp. 196–97 (1824).

16. Simpson, *Markets Don't Fail!*, p. 101.

17. Ibid., pp. 101–65. In addition, on the harm caused by the FDA and alternatives to it, see Mary J. Ruwart, *Death by Regulation: How We Were Robbed of a Golden Age of Health and How We Can Reclaim It* (Kalamazoo, MI and San Francisco, CA: SunStar Press and Liberty International, 2018), pp. 2–3, 9, 25, 29, 35, 48–53, 75–77, 80–85, 95, 97–98, 103–4, 110–12, 121–23, 163–65, 209–11, and 215–28.

18. For depositors at traditional banks, they are lending money both to the bank and, at least implicitly, to those to whom the bank lends money. For depositors (i.e., shareholders) in money market mutual funds, they are lending, at least implicitly, to those to whom the mutual fund lends money.

19. Simpson, *Money, Banking, and the Business Cycle, Vol. 1*, pp. 9–22 and *Vol. 2*, pp. 151–75.

20. Simpson, *Money, Banking, and the Business Cycle, Vol. 2*, pp. 159–60 and 243–59.

21. Ibid., p. 153.

22. For more on this topic, see Simpson, *Markets Don't Fail!*, pp. 11–12, 31–33, and 46–47.

23. For more on this topic, see ibid., pp. 31–33 and 43–46. On the justification of intellectual property rights, see Fred D. Miller, Jr. and Adam Mossoff, "Political Theory: A Radical for Capitalism," in *A Companion to Ayn Rand*, edited by Allan Gotthelf and Gregory Salmieri (Malden, MA: Wiley Blackwell, 2016), pp. 187–202. See, in particular, pp. 199–201. Also, see Rand, *Capitalism*, pp. 130–134; and Adam Mossoff, "What Is Property? Putting the Pieces Back Together," *Arizona Law Review* vol. 45 (Summer 2003), pp. 371–443. In the latter, see in particular pp. 413–27.

24. For another author who refers to the privilege of the writ of habeas corpus as a right, see Upham, "*Corfield v. Coryell* and the Privileges," p. 1528.

25. *Calder v. Bull*, 3 U.S. 386, pp. 390–91 (1798).

26. *Thompson v. Missouri*, 171 U.S. 380, p. 386 (1898).

27. Ibid.

28. Daniel E. Troy, "Toward a Definition and Critique of Retroactivity," *Alabama Law Review* vol. 51, no. 3 (2000), pp. 1329–53. See p. 1330.

29. The ownership-of-unused-land example is derived from an example provided in Robert G. Natelson, "Statutory Retroactivity: The Founders' View," *Idaho Law Review* vol. 39 (2003), pp. 489–529. See pp. 494–95.

30. The interest rate examples are based on examples provided in ibid., pp. 497–98.

31. Troy, "Toward a Definition and Critique of Retroactivity," p. 1337.

32. Changed by Amendment XVI.

33. Simpson, *Money, Banking, and the Business Cycle, Vol. 1*, p. 9.

34. William Rawle, *A View of the Constitution of the United States of America*, 2nd edition (Colorado Springs, CO: Portage Publications, 2011 [1829]), p. 63.

35. Sandefur, *The Conscience of the Constitution*, p. 112. Sandefur makes this statement as a part of an argument against the objection to redundancy. He makes other arguments against the objection to redundancy as well.

Chapter 5

Revising the U.S. Constitution
Articles II through VII

INTRODUCTION

This chapter completes the revision of the original Constitution. It changes the requirements for being eligible to become president and modifies the Privileges and Immunities Clause to ensure that it is consistent with the protection of rights. It also limits the laws the government can make in U.S. territories. Finally, it shows how sovereign immunity must be limited to ensure that the government and government agents are held responsible for acts they engage in that violate the rights of others. Other topics are discussed as well. As in chapter 4, I follow the same procedures for making changes in this chapter that I follow in chapter 3.

REVISING ARTICLES II THROUGH
VII OF THE CONSTITUTION

Article II

Section 1

The executive Power shall be vested in a President of the United States of America. He shall hold his Office during the Term of four Years, and, together with the Vice President, chosen for the same Term, be elected, as follows

Each State shall appoint, in such Manner as the Legislature thereof may direct, a Number of Electors, equal to the whole Number of Senators and Representatives to which the State may be entitled in the Congress: but no Senator or Representative, or Person holding an Office of Trust or Profit under the United States, shall be appointed an Elector.

[The Electors shall meet in their respective States, and vote by Ballot for two Persons, of whom one at least shall not be an Inhabitant of the same State with themselves. And they shall make a List of all the Persons voted for, and of the Number of Votes for each; which List they shall sign and certify, and transmit sealed to the Seat of the Government of the United States, directed to the President of the Senate. The President of the Senate shall, in the Presence of the Senate and House of Representatives, open all the Certificates, and the Votes shall then be counted. The Person having the greatest Number of Votes shall be the President, if such Number be a Majority of the whole Number of Electors appointed; and if there be more than one who have such Majority, and have an equal Number of Votes, then the House of Representatives shall immediately chuse by Ballot one of them for President; and if no Person have a Majority, then from the five highest on the List the said House shall in like Manner chuse the President. But in chusing the President, the Votes shall be taken by States, the Representation from each State having one Vote; A quorum for this Purpose shall consist of a Member or Members from two thirds of the States, and a Majority of all the States shall be necessary to a Choice. In every Case, after the Choice of the President, the Person having the greatest Number of Votes of the Electors shall be the Vice President. But if there should remain two or more who have equal Votes, the Senate shall chuse from them by Ballot the Vice President.][1]

The Congress may determine the Time of chusing the Electors, and the Day on which they shall give their Votes; which Day shall be the same throughout the United States.

No Person except a natural born Citizen, or a Citizen of the United States, at the time of the Adoption of this Constitution, shall be eligible to the Office of President; neither shall any Person be eligible to that Office who shall not have attained to the Age of thirty five Years, and been fourteen Years a Resident within the United States.

BPS—The minimum age requirement for the president must be reduced to eighteen years for the reasons stated in chapter 3 in the discussion on Article I, Section 2 in connection with the age requirement for representatives. While I agree with the intention of the Framers in imposing a higher minimum age requirement on the president than on senators and representatives—to have more experienced individuals become president—to achieve equality before the law, the minimum age must be lowered.

The citizenship requirement must be changed as well. To achieve equality before the law, both citizens born in the United States and foreign-born individuals who become U.S. citizens must be eligible for the Office of the President. As discussed previously, Congress can pass laws to provide appropriate time requirements for living in the United States before foreigners can become U.S. citizens. This will limit the ability of foreigners to become president. They will be required to have spent sufficient time in the United States, and presumably learn about American culture and become better acquainted with the importance of rights and how to protect them, before being eligible to become president.

The residency requirement must also be changed. It is appropriate to require residency, but as long as one is a citizen and a resident, one should be eligible to become president. This is also a part of achieving equality before the law. If individuals do not want a person to be president who has not achieved a certain length of residency in the United States, they should support someone for president who has the desired length of residency.

In addition, this clause requires being a resident instead of an inhabitant. The latter pertains to being eligible to be a representative or senator. While there are differences in the meanings of "inhabitant" and "resident," the differences do not rise to a high enough level of significance to warrant discussion in this book.[2] They represent optional methods that can be applied as rules pertaining to the government and are both consistent with the protection of individual rights.

Based on this discussion, the next amendment should read as follows: Amendment XLI—The citizenship requirement for the Office of the President shall be changed from being a natural born citizen of the United States to only requiring individuals to be a citizen of the United States. The minimum age requirement for the Office of the President shall be changed from thirty-five years to eighteen years. The residency requirement for the Office of the President shall be changed from a minimum of fourteen years to only requiring individuals to be a resident of the United States.—BPS

[In Case of the Removal of the President from Office, or of his Death, Resignation, or Inability to discharge the Powers and Duties of the said Office, the Same shall devolve on the Vice President, and the Congress may by Law provide for the Case of Removal, Death, Resignation or Inability, both of the President and Vice President, declaring what Officer shall then act as President, and such Officer shall act accordingly, until the Disability be removed, or a President shall be elected.][3]

The President shall, at stated Times, receive for his Services, a Compensation, which shall neither be increased nor diminished during the Period for which he shall have been elected, and he shall not receive within that Period any other Emolument from the United States, or any of them.

Before he enter on the Execution of his Office, he shall take the following Oath or Affirmation:—"I do solemnly swear (or affirm) that I will faithfully execute the Office of President of the United States, and will to the best of my Ability, preserve, protect and defend the Constitution of the United States."

Section 2

> The President shall be Commander in Chief of the Army and Navy of the United
> States, and of the Militia of the several States, when called into the actual Service
> of the United States; he may require the Opinion, in writing, of the principal
> Officer in each of the executive Departments, upon any Subject relating to the
> Duties of their respective Offices, and he shall have Power to grant Reprieves and
> Pardons for Offences against the United States, except in Cases of Impeachment.

BPS—There may be cases in which the power to grant reprieves and pardons
is consistent with protecting individual rights. For example, if new evidence
is brought forward that shows a person has been wrongfully convicted, it
could be appropriate for the president to grant a pardon.[4] Pardons could also
be used to make deals with those accused of crimes in order to prosecute
accomplices.[5] In addition, reprieves could provide for the lessening of sentences that are determined to be too harsh. Nonetheless, pardons and reprieves
can also be used inappropriately, such as to benefit political supporters, family members, friends, or allow those who violated rights to go free too soon.

One could argue that it would be better to place the pardon power in the
judicial branch because it would be more conducive to following objective
standards when pardoning individuals.[6] While this might be true, judges
may also be more hesitant to overturn judgments emanating from their own
branch of government. Giving the power to the executive branch strengthens
the checks and balances between the branches of government. Moreover, it
would be difficult for the judicial branch to act in a quick fashion in cases
where quick action is needed.[7]

One could also argue that this power should be placed in the legislative
branch. This would make it less likely that the power would be used arbitrarily, since it would not be placed in the hands of one person, but it would
also prevent quick use of the power when needed. In addition, it would
maintain the checks and balances between the branches of government.
There are good arguments for placing the power in any of the three branches
of government. This is a case of there being optional methods to protecting
individual rights.

There is also a good case for placing a check on the pardon power of the
president so that it is more difficult to use inappropriately. In fact, an amendment was proposed in the 93rd Congress by Senator Walter Mondale to place
such a check on the pardon power. That proposed amendment stated that no
pardon granted to an individual shall be effective if two-thirds of each House
of the Congress disapproved of the pardon within 180 days of granting the
pardon.[8]

Placing a check on the president's pardon power or placing the power in one
of the other two branches would also address the issue of the president being

able to pardon himself, which, based on the current text of the Constitution, the president is able to do. As with the vice president's ability to preside over his own impeachment trial, the president pardoning himself is inconsistent with the Constitution's provisions against self-dealing and the rule of law that the Constitution upholds, and it would most likely not stand up to a legal challenge. Nonetheless, placing a check on the president's pardon power would make it much more difficult for the president to pardon himself and placing the power in the judicial or legislative branch would eliminate the power of self-pardon.[9]

Despite these benefits, I do not make any changes to the pardon power of the president because no matter where the power resides there is the potential for it to be used in a manner that is not consistent with the protection of rights. For example, even if Congress has the power to nullify a presidential pardon, the power could still be used in a manner inconsistent with the protection of rights. Congress could reject a legitimate pardon or not overturn an inappropriate pardon. In fact, even with the congressional check, there is no guarantee that the president could not pardon himself with a particularly corrupt Congress that is friendly to the president. Moreover, to minimize the changes to the Constitution and because all the options available are consistent with the protection of rights (even though some of the options might be better than others), here I choose to leave the power with the executive branch and provide no check on the power by Congress.—BPS

> He shall have Power, by and with the Advice and Consent of the Senate, to make Treaties, provided two thirds of the Senators present concur; and he shall nominate, and by and with the Advice and Consent of the Senate, shall appoint Ambassadors, other public Ministers and Consuls, Judges of the supreme Court, and all other Officers of the United States, whose Appointments are not herein otherwise provided for, and which shall be established by Law: but the Congress may by Law vest the Appointment of such inferior Officers, as they think proper, in the President alone, in the Courts of Law, or in the Heads of Departments.
>
> The President shall have Power to fill up all Vacancies that may happen during the Recess of the Senate, by granting Commissions which shall expire at the End of their next Session.

Section 3

> He shall from time to time give to the Congress Information of the State of the Union, and recommend to their Consideration such Measures as he shall judge necessary and expedient; he may, on extraordinary Occasions, convene both Houses, or either of them, and in Case of Disagreement between them, with Respect to the Time of Adjournment, he may adjourn them to such Time as he

shall think proper; he shall receive Ambassadors and other public Ministers; he shall take Care that the Laws be faithfully executed, and shall Commission all the Officers of the United States.

Section 4

The President, Vice President and all civil Officers of the United States, shall be removed from Office on Impeachment for, and Conviction of, Treason, Bribery, or other high Crimes and Misdemeanors.

Article III

Section 1

The judicial Power of the United States, shall be vested in one supreme Court, and in such inferior Courts as the Congress may from time to time ordain and establish. The Judges, both of the supreme and inferior Courts, shall hold their Offices during good Behaviour, and shall, at stated Times, receive for their Services, a Compensation, which shall not be diminished during their Continuance in Office.

Section 2

The judicial Power shall extend to all Cases, in Law and Equity, arising under this Constitution, the Laws of the United States, and Treaties made, or which shall be made, under their Authority;—to all Cases affecting Ambassadors, other public Ministers and Consuls;—to all Cases of admiralty and maritime Jurisdiction;—to Controversies to which the United States shall be a Party;—to Controversies between two or more States;— [between a State and Citizens of another State,][10]—between Citizens of different States,—between Citizens of the same State claiming Lands under Grants of different States, [and between a State, or the Citizens thereof, and foreign States, Citizens or Subjects.][11]

BPS—No changes to this section are needed, but this is a good place to discuss sovereign immunity. Sovereign immunity is relevant to the portions of Article III, Section 2 that were superseded or modified by Amendment XI. The superseded portion states that the Supreme Court's judicial power extends to cases between a state and citizens of another state. Amendment XI made it so the Court's judicial power does not extend to these cases. Amendment XI also made it so that the Court's judicial power does not extend to suits brought against the states by foreign citizens and subjects. While Amendment XI is consistent with the protection of individual rights, it is important to make sure that sovereign immunity is properly understood so that it can be properly applied. This is the purpose of the following discussion.

Sovereign immunity refers to the idea that since a government creates the law and therefore does not have to look to a higher authority from which it derives its power, it cannot be sued or held accountable to others for exercising that power, even if it is exercised in an unlawful manner. Sovereign immunity stems from the adage that "the king can do no wrong." It has a long tradition in Anglo-American jurisprudence, dating back to the twelfth century, and while sovereign immunity included the idea that the government cannot be sued, in practice monarchs were often sued through various means.[12]

The legitimate aspect of sovereign immunity refers to the idea that if nations, and their governments, are, indeed, to be sovereign, they must be immune from suits brought forth in the courts of other governments. Short of war, how would such suits be enforced? For example, how would legal action taken against the United States in the courts of Canada be enforced? The fact that the two countries are sovereign over their respective territories implies that wrongs cannot be redressed in courts external to the countries. Of course, a country can agree to a suit in a court external to it (such as in an international court); however, that does not mean the country is not sovereign. The country's sovereignty does not preclude it from giving up its immunity in certain cases. But the decision belongs to the sovereign entity itself. To be able to make such choices is one characteristic of a sovereign nation.

What is not legitimate about sovereign immunity is the idea that a government cannot be sued in its own courts or held accountable in its own courts for wrongs it commits. This characteristic of sovereign immunity stands in contradiction to justice and the rule of law.[13] If justice, the rule of law, and the protection of individual rights are to prevail, governments and government officials cannot be immune to suits in their own courts. A government must obey its own laws. This means an appropriate government not only protects individual rights but also provides appropriate compensation to victims if it violates rights or causes certain types of harm to individuals in the process of protecting rights.

Of course, the government is in a special situation. It is the entity responsible for creating and enforcing the laws that protect rights. This gives rise to many special circumstances in which it might be appropriate for the government or government officials to be protected by immunity. For example, take the case of a police officer who acts reasonably and in good faith to protect the rights of citizens by apprehending a suspect and yet harms an innocent bystander in the process. Assume also that the suspect has, in fact, violated someone's rights and is a danger to the public. In this case, the officer and the government in general must be immune from suits by the injured party. The government and the officer cannot be held accountable for harm caused in the legitimate exercise of their power. One cannot expect rights to go unprotected because innocent people might get hurt. In this type of case, it is, in fact, the violator of rights (the apprehended suspect) that is responsible for the harm done to the innocent person. This is true even if the violator did not directly cause the harm, but the apprehending officer did. The violator of rights is responsible because without his actions there would have been no need for the officer to take the action he took to apprehend the suspect. Hence, in this case, the person harmed has a legitimate case against the rights violator, not the government or the government's agent.[14]

A different example is the case of the prosecution of an individual for a crime who is eventually found not guilty (and is, in fact, innocent). Even if the case is prosecuted in good faith, it may damage the reputation of the individual to such an extent that it makes it hard for him to earn a living and, in general, live his life in the same manner that he did prior to the prosecution. Here, the government is responsible for causing the harm, so the government has a responsibility to compensate the individual for the damage caused. Note that the prosecutor and judge involved should have personal immunity as long as they acted in good faith, but the government should be required to pay to the extent there is significant harm done to the defendant.[15]

Because of the differences between the case of prosecuting an innocent man, in the one instance, and a police officer apprehending a suspect on the street and harming an innocent bystander in the process, in the other instance, they require different levels of culpability on the part of the government. Even though both involve reasonable actions, because the police officer had to act quickly to protect the rights of citizens, one cannot hold him or the government to the same level of responsibility in that situation. The actions of the suspect require an immediate response to defend rights. Furthermore, it is, in fact, the violator of rights that is ultimately responsible for the harm done to the innocent bystander.

In the case of the prosecution of an innocent man, however, the prosecutor has ample time to make an appropriate decision. Therefore, the level of culpability on the part of the government is greater. In addition, there is no one besides the government that is, in fact, responsible for the harm done in the case of the prosecution of an innocent man (assuming no inappropriate actions by other parties, such as dishonest testimony by witnesses). In the case of the police officer, there may also be the fact that no other method was possible for the police officer to use to apprehend the suspect. However, if a prosecutor is prosecuting the wrong man, he has made a mistake, even if it is an innocent one. Nonetheless, even if it is determined that the police officer could have responded in a different way to apprehend the suspect and not have harmed an innocent bystander in the process, if he acted reasonably, he and the government should not be held responsible because of the exigent circumstances created by the suspect.

Another example is the case of military action that harms innocent people. When the United States carpet-bombed German cities during World War II or dropped the atomic bombs on Japan, innocent people were killed. When I use the term "innocent" here, I do not use it synonymously with "civilian." Many German and Japanese civilians were guilty of supporting their rights-violating governments by, among other means, working in factories that produced weapons used in the war by these countries and by providing moral support for their countries as well. Nonetheless, I am sure there were innocent individuals in these countries during the war, and by innocent I mean individuals who actively attempted to overthrow their governments or who supported them in no way (or only under duress). If U.S. bombs killed these people, the U.S. military or government should not be held responsible, either morally or legally. The moral and legal responsibility is on the shoulders of the aggressor. One cannot expect a person or a country to collapse in the face of aggression merely because innocent people might get hurt if one attempts to defend oneself. If someone violates my rights by shooting at me with a gun on a crowded street and I defend myself by shooting back (and this is a reasonable response to protect myself), if I hurt or kill innocent bystanders the moral and legal responsibility falls on the shoulders of the aggressor. The innocent people harmed (or their families) have a legitimate case against the rights violator (or his family), not me.

The same is true with regard to military action. The innocent victims have a legitimate case against the rights violator. This is true even in the case of, say, a hospital or orphanage that is bombed in a military conflict because of terrorists who decide to hide behind the occupants while continuing to attack others and violate their rights. If the military determines the best option available—that is, the one that minimizes the casualties of the rights-defending army or other people that the terrorists may be attacking—is to bomb the hospital or orphanage, the innocent victims or their families do not have a legitimate case against the rights-defending army. Again, the moral and legal responsibility is on the shoulders of the aggressors, which in this case are the terrorists.

In this scenario, the rights-defending army should try to limit the casualties of the innocent. However, it has no moral obligation to do so. It should not sacrifice its soldiers and others the terrorists may be attacking to the people the terrorists have forced to act as a human shield.

The last example I will discuss involves the case of a government defaulting on loan payments. Immunity should not apply in this case. Just as a private individual must be held responsible for his actions, including being responsible for paying off debt he takes on, the government must be held responsible as well. Requiring individuals and organizations—including governments—to make good on their contractual obligations is a part of protecting individual rights and upholding the rule of law. Allowing individuals and organizations—including governments—to renege on their contractual obligations would be an injustice. It would be a case of giving something to someone (or some entity) that he (or it) has not earned. As a result, governments should not be immune from lawsuits due to contract violations, whether in connection with unpaid debts or any other contractual obligation.

The possible cases are too numerous to identify all the scenarios that could arise. My goal here is to provide an indication of how these cases should be dealt with on principle. In addition, I will say that the government must pass laws to determine when the government should and should not be immune in cases where general rules can be identified. The courts must be relied upon in those cases that do not fall under a general rule.[16] Of course, in certain cases it may better protect rights if the legislature codifies rulings from court cases in statute, especially if there are repeated cases of certain types. The key is that the government follows its own laws and be held responsible in situations where it is negligent, acts unreasonably, or is the ultimate cause of the harm done to innocent individuals. One cannot have a government that is consistent with the protection of individual rights and the rule of law if the government is above the law.

Moreover, it is not legitimate for the government to pass laws that completely absolve itself of responsibility. That is also inconsistent with protecting individual rights and with laws that determine when individuals (or organizations) are liable for harmful outcomes. A law that completely absolves the government of responsibility for harmful action that it caused would mean that laws used to determine the responsibility of parties would not be consistently applied to individuals and the government. To achieve equality before the law, such laws must be applied consistently.

Given that governments are not completely immune from responsibility for their own actions, does sovereign immunity apply to the state governments at all? The answer is: yes. States should be immune from legal action brought against them in other countries, just as any sovereign nation would be. However, states should also be immune from legal action brought against them in other states. The reason for this is essentially the same as why sovereign nations have immunity against legal action brought against them in other nations. Compared to other states, an individual state is like a sovereign nation. In fact, after the Declaration of Independence but before the U.S. Constitution was adopted, the states were essentially sovereign nations that had agreed to band together for purposes of defense and trade. Some aspects of this relationship were retained after the adoption of the Constitution, such as the need to extradite prisoners from one state at the request of another state.

In addition, while it would probably be better to make it possible for states to be sued by individuals in federal courts because it would provide more objective oversight of the states and help lead to impartial decisions,[17] it can be consistent with the protection of individual rights to require, as Amendment XI does, that suits by out-of-state citizens against states be brought in the states' respective courts, as long as the states pass legislation that requires them to respect their own laws and be held responsible for certain harms they cause. There are optional methods that can be used to ensure the protection of individual rights in this situation.

If the state courts are not impartial, Amendment XI can always be abolished so that citizens can bring suits against other states in federal court. This will provide objective, third-party oversight of the states. However, what if the federal courts are not impartial in cases involving the federal government? Even worse, what happens if the federal government does not agree to be sued? On the latter question, I refer back to my discussion of the proper purpose of government. The proper purpose of government is to protect rights. Rights cannot be protected consistently if any person or organization, including the government, is above the law. Hence, an inherent part of a government that consistently protects rights is that it agrees to be sued in its own courts. The legislature can aid in this process by passing laws that determine how people can seek redress from the government.

Of course, even if the federal government passes appropriate legislation establishing how to seek redress from it, there is still the question of what happens if the federal courts are not impartial and thus do not protect rights. This is a potential that exists because humans have free will and can decide for myriad reasons to violate individual rights. The first solution is to ensure that the judiciary is as independent as possible from the legislative and executive branches. The solution also involves the same advice offered by Thomas Jefferson as the ultimate guarantor of freedom: eternal vigilance by the people. It might be that stricter laws must be passed to prevent bias for the federal government in the federal courts. It might be that further suits must be brought forward to demonstrate the injustice of such rulings. People should take all legal and legislative action that is possible against these and all violations of rights.

One might think that the solution is to allow appeals of rulings in federal courts in the state courts. However, this would not foster the protection of individual rights. One court must be supreme. It would lead to judicial chaos (or judicial stalemates) if individuals who did not like the ruling made in one court could file endless appeals in other courts. If one court was not supreme and different courts made different rulings, how would the conflicting rulings be enforced? How would the judicial stalemate be resolved? It would lead to countless, unresolved legal conflicts. It would lead to, as Alexander Hamilton stated in *The Federalist* No. 80, "a hydra in government from which nothing but contradiction and confusion can proceed."[18] The only resolution is to have the rulings of one court be supreme. Again, if the highest court in the land rules in a way that does not protect individual rights, people must take action in the legislature to right the wrong or take legal action against individuals involved in the ruling if there is evidence of malice or corruption.

One question that might arise is: What will happen if states and the federal government are held responsible for their actions and are required to obey their own laws, and this prevents them from protecting individual rights properly due to the burden of lawsuits? This is unlikely. The legal system already essentially requires federal and state governments to do this. I do not believe any additional burden placed on federal and state governments to meet this standard will be overly taxing.

Another question that might arise is why there should not be a provision in the Constitution stating that the government (whether local, state, or federal) should be held responsible for wrongful actions it commits. This is an important question. It is answered in chapter 10.—BPS

> In all Cases affecting Ambassadors, other public Ministers and Consuls, and those in which a State shall be Party, the supreme Court shall have original Jurisdiction. In all the other Cases before mentioned, the supreme Court shall have appellate Jurisdiction, both as to Law and Fact, with such Exceptions, and under such Regulations as the Congress shall make.

BPS—This section is fine as is. However, there is much controversy surrounding the meaning of the statement "with such Exceptions, and under such Regulations as the Congress shall make." Some have claimed this portion of the Constitution gives Congress the power to limit the cases the Supreme Court can hear on appeal. In fact, some claim that Congress has plenary power to limit the cases the Supreme Court can hear on appeal.[19] It is legitimate for Congress to have the power to impose regulations and exceptions on the Supreme Court's appellate jurisdiction. However, having plenary power to do so is not legitimate.

The power to regulate that is given to Congress in this portion of the Constitution is legitimate because it is the power to regulate some aspect of another branch of government. There is no initiation of physical force if that power is used appropriately, unlike the regulation of private action by the government. The power to regulate in this case can be used to create a more efficient judiciary and to protect rights more consistently.

The power to regulate and make exceptions to the appellate jurisdiction of the Supreme Court does not imply the power to eliminate the appellate jurisdiction of the Court. "Exceptions" refer to an instance or a limited number of instances that do not conform to some general rule or norm. The general rule here is that the Supreme Court shall have appellate jurisdiction in the other cases mentioned in the relevant clause. In order to have exceptions from that general rule, the rule must be maintained. Making exceptions does not provide for the ability to create a completely different rule.

"Regulation" in a general sense refers to making rules pertaining to some activity to control the activity. Regulating here means creating rules relevant to the Supreme Court's appellate jurisdiction to control or limit its jurisdiction. Creating rules pertinent to its appellate jurisdiction presupposes the existence of that jurisdiction.[20]

What about the question regarding when a large number of exceptions lead to a different rule being created? Does Congress have the power to make many small exceptions that lead, cumulatively, to a substantial change in the appellate jurisdiction of the Supreme Court? The answer is: no. If the changes are to be exceptions from the general rule, then many exceptions made over a period of time cannot create a new rule. The basic rule as laid out in the Constitution must remain intact. Constitutionally, Congress must stop making exceptions (or be prevented from doing so) before the old rule is transformed and becomes a new rule.[21]

When this point would be reached is a different question, and different individuals may provide different answers that are equally valid. There is no bright-line test to determine when Congress has gone beyond the point of making exceptions to a rule to creating a different rule. However, just because there is no agreement on the exact point when the exceptions become the rule does not deny that there is a difference between exceptions being made to a specific rule and the specific rule being morphed into another rule by a large number of small exceptions. The former is constitutionally acceptable. The latter is not.

That the Exceptions and Regulations Clause does not give plenary power to Congress to strip the Supreme Court of its appellate jurisdiction is seen in the debates surrounding the creation and adoption of the Constitution. Probably the strongest evidence is the fact that a motion at the Constitutional Convention to give Congress plenary power over the Court's appellate jurisdiction was defeated. The rejected language stated, "In all the other cases before mentioned the judicial power shall be exercised in such manner as the legislature shall direct."[22] This would have replaced the appellate jurisdiction granted to the Court being subject to the exceptions and regulations Congress shall make. What was approved provides much less power to Congress.

The fact that the Framers of the Constitution wanted to create a government with three separate branches that would provide a system of checks and balances and thus prevent any one branch from becoming too powerful belies the notion that the intention of the Exceptions and Regulations

Clause was to give Congress plenary power over the appellate jurisdiction of the Supreme Court. The Framers wanted the three branches to remain as independent as possible. Moreover, the Framers' intention with the judicial branch was to keep the other two branches in check by determining whether the laws created are consistent with the Constitution. This is intimated in *The Federalist* No. 81, in which Alexander Hamilton states, "still less could it be expected that men who had infringed the Constitution in the character of legislators would be disposed to repair the breach in the character of judges."[23] Hamilton makes this statement as a part of his argument that the judiciary should be a separate branch of government from the legislature. The repairing of the breach that Hamilton refers to highlights the fact that the purpose of the judicial branch is to determine the constitutionality of the laws passed. This responsibility was made explicit in *Marbury v. Madison* (1803).

The inconsistency of Congress having plenary power over the appellate jurisdiction of the Supreme Court with the intentions of the Framers is clearly seen in the fact that the Framers were especially concerned about the vulnerability of the judiciary to encroachments of power by the other branches of government and the violations of freedom that would occur as a result.[24] Hamilton, in *The Federalist* No. 78, states:

> The judiciary is beyond comparison the weakest of the three departments of power; that it can never attack with success either of the other two; and that all possible care is requisite to enable it to defend itself against their attacks. . . . [T]hough individual oppression may now and then proceed from the courts of justice, the general liberty of the people can never be endangered from that quarter; I mean so long as the judiciary remains truly distinct from both the legislature and the Executive. . . . [L]iberty can have nothing to fear from the judiciary alone, but would have everything to fear from its union with either of the other departments.[25] [footnote omitted]

There is also evidence in *The Federalist* No. 81 that the Exceptions and Regulations Clause was included in the Constitution for a specific purpose that provided only very limited ability to Congress to make exceptions to the Supreme Court's appellate jurisdiction and was not intended to provide plenary power to Congress over that jurisdiction. In that essay, Hamilton discusses how the clause can be used to prevent findings of fact in jury trials from being re-examined on appeal to the Supreme Court. It was a concern of many of the delegates at the Constitutional Convention that jury verdicts in state courts might be overturned through appeal to the Supreme Court. The Exceptions and Regulations Clause was added to assuage these concerns.[26] As stated by Hamilton:

It is therefore necessary that the appellate jurisdiction should, in certain cases, extend in the broadest sense to matters of fact. It will not answer to make an express exception of cases which shall have been originally tried by a jury because in the courts of some of the States *all causes* are tried in this mode; and such an exception would preclude the revision of matters of fact, as well where it might be proper as where it might be improper. To avoid all inconveniencies, it will be safest to declare generally that the Supreme Court shall possess appellate jurisdiction both as to law and *fact*, and that this jurisdiction shall be subject to such *exceptions* and regulations as the national legislature may prescribe. This will enable the government to modify it in such a manner as will best answer the ends of public justice and security.

This view of the matter, at any rate, puts it out of all doubt that the supposed *abolition* of the trial by jury, by the operation of this provision, is fallacious and untrue.[27] [emphases in original; footnote omitted]

There have been a number of Supreme Court cases related to the Exceptions and Regulations Clause, and there have been a wide range of interpretations of the rulings in these cases.[28] It has even been stated that the rulings can be used to support all competing views of the clause, including the view that it gives Congress plenary power over the Supreme Court's appellate jurisdiction, the view that it gives Congress only very limited power to modify the appellate jurisdiction of the Court, and everything in between.[29] It has also been stated that the Court has attempted to avoid ruling on the plenary power of Congress to change the appellate jurisdiction of the Court.[30]

The literature on the interpretations of the Supreme Court rulings is very interesting. My own view is that the rulings only justify a very limited ability of Congress to modify the Court's appellate jurisdiction.[31] However, I am not going to present an analysis of the rulings and interpretations. Such a presentation is not necessary to show what is needed to create a constitution that is consistent with the protection of individual rights. All one must understand is that plenary power of Congress over the Supreme Court, whether over the original or appellate jurisdiction (or both), is not consistent with protecting rights. This would undermine the contribution to the system of checks and balances that the Supreme Court provides.

Although the Exceptions and Regulations Clause should not be used to create a plenary power of Congress over the Supreme Court's appellate jurisdiction, the clause should be retained because it can be used in a way that is consistent with the protection of individual rights. Unfortunately, however, the clause can also be used to violate rights. Examples of attempts to do the latter include instances in which Congress has used the clause to prevent the Supreme Court from reviewing a number of controversial cases. These include attempting to pass laws to prevent the Court from reviewing cases involving abortion, school desegregation, obscenity laws, and more.[32]

Regarding using the Exceptions and Regulations Clause in a manner that is consistent with the protection of individual rights, at the Virginia ratifying convention for the Constitution, John Marshall, the fourth Chief Justice of the Supreme Court, correctly identified the important underlying issue about how the clause should be used when he stated, "Congress is empowered to make exceptions to the appellate jurisdiction, as to law and fact, of the Supreme Court. These exceptions certainly go as far as the legislature may think proper for the interest and liberty of the people."[33] The key point to understand in that quotation is that valid use of the clause entails protecting individual liberty.

Within this context, Congress has passed laws to establish the type of inferior courts that shall exist, determine the rules and procedures the Supreme Court and inferior courts shall follow, and determine the number of districts, justices, and other characteristics pertaining to these courts. The most prominent law of this type is the Judiciary Act of 1789. It has had many amendments as well. The Act of 1789 established, among other things, regulations pertaining to the number of federal court districts within the United States and the number of justices on the Supreme Court. It also established the minimum value in certain cases that must be under dispute in order for cases to be eligible for reexamination on appeal to the Supreme Court. Cases that do not meet the minimum standard are exceptions to the cases that can be appealed to the Court.

Amendments IV through VIII to the Constitution represent further exceptions and regulations, initiated by Congress, that are consistent with the protection of individual rights. Among other things, these amendments dictate various procedures the courts must follow, including that warrants can be issued only upon probable cause, criminal defendants cannot be required to testify against themselves, accusations of certain crimes require an indictment of a grand jury to proceed to trial, and particular rules must be followed in order for findings of fact in certain jury trials to be reexamined on appeal. They also dictate how trials must be conducted, such as recognizing the right to a speedy and public trial and the right of the accused to confront witnesses against him.

In addition, the Exceptions and Regulations Clause could be used to achieve efficiency in the legal system.[34] For example, using the clause to reduce the caseload of the Supreme Court while at the same time ensuring that rights are protected could be a legitimate goal. This may involve allowing cases in specialized areas that have little or no national application to be appealed to Article III courts other than the Supreme Court. This could, among other things, help protect the Court from being inundated with cases.[35]

However the clause is employed, the important consideration is that it be used in a manner that is consistent with the protection of individual rights and freedom.—BPS

> The Trial of all Crimes, except in Cases of Impeachment, shall be by Jury; and such Trial shall be held in the State where the said Crimes shall have been committed; but when not committed within any State, the Trial shall be at such Place or Places as the Congress may by Law have directed.

Section 3

> Treason against the United States, shall consist only in levying War against them, or in adhering to their Enemies, giving them Aid and Comfort. No Person shall be convicted of Treason unless on the Testimony of two Witnesses to the same overt Act, or on Confession in open Court.
>
> The Congress shall have Power to declare the Punishment of Treason, but no Attainder of Treason shall work Corruption of Blood, or Forfeiture except during the Life of the Person attainted.

Article IV

Section 1

> Full Faith and Credit shall be given in each State to the public Acts, Records, and judicial Proceedings of every other State. And the Congress may by general Laws prescribe the Manner in which such Acts, Records and Proceedings shall be proved, and the Effect thereof.

Section 2

> The Citizens of each State shall be entitled to all Privileges and Immunities of Citizens in the several States.

BPS—This clause needs to be modified to ensure that only privileges and immunities that are consistent with the protection of individual rights are safeguarded by the Constitution. Previous clauses that referred to privileges—the Privilege from Arrest Clause in Article I, Section 6 (discussed in chapter 3) and the Suspension (of Habeas Corpus) Clause in Article I, Section 9 (discussed in chapter 4)—did not require modification because they referred to the protection of very specific rights. However, the Privileges and Immunities Clause uses "privileges and immunities" in an open-ended fashion. Because of the issues related to the use of these terms that were discussed in connection with the previous clauses mentioned, the open-ended use of the terms in this section must be qualified to ensure the Privileges and Immunities Clause is not used to justify violations of individual rights.

To be completely accurate, I must state that in connection with the previous clauses mentioned I mainly discussed the term "privilege." However, "privilege" and "immunity" refer essentially to the same thing. As one scholar states, "'privilege' and 'immunity' were reciprocal ways of saying the same thing [during the eighteenth century]."[36] The terms were used to refer to various rights but were not used to refer to so-called natural rights. For example, "privileges" might have been used to refer to the right to a free press but not the right to life, the latter of which was considered a natural right—a right that exists in the "state of nature" and that is an allegedly inherent right of human beings.[37] Nonetheless, because the terms had essentially the same meaning, I use them synonymously for my purposes here.

As stated in the discussion of the term "privileges" in connection with the clauses of the Constitution mentioned above, the term was not originally used to refer to rights but to exemptions from laws enforced by the British Crown.[38] Some of the privileges granted did protect rights, but some of them violated rights.[39] More and more, however, privileges and immunities began to be associated with rights and were used to a greater extent to protect rights. Americans in the eighteenth century associated them with rights, although the terms were not used consistently in this manner in America during that period. Today the terms are not generally used to refer to rights. In fact, there are many privileges and immunities today that some want the government to provide that would violate rights. These include one proposal that would provide each citizen $80,000 when starting out in life as a young adult.[40]

In the discussion of the privilege of habeas corpus in Article I, Section 9, we saw that the general use of the term "privilege" today does not focus on the protection of rights. The general use of the term "immunity" today also does not focus on the protection of rights. Focusing on its legal meaning, it generally refers to exemption from liability of some type, including criminal or civil liability. For example, as discussed in connection with Article III, Section 2, sovereign immunity refers to the government's, or government officials', immunity from being sued for enforcing the law. We also saw in that discussion that sovereign immunity *can be* consistent with the protection of individual rights.

Because the term "privileges and immunities" is not synonymous with rights, its use in this clause must be qualified to ensure the consistent protection of rights. So, the next amendment is as follows: Amendment XLII—The following clause of Article IV, Section 2 of the Constitution of the United States shall be modified: The Citizens of each State shall be entitled to all Privileges and Immunities of Citizens in the several States. The modified clause is as follows: The Citizens of each State shall be entitled to all Privileges and Immunities of Citizens in the several States, but all Privileges and Immunities shall be consistent with the protection of Individual Rights.

The revised wording recognizes that the purpose of the government is to protect individual rights and that state governments cannot pass laws that violate rights.

To some readers, it might seem that I am being redundant in my use of the qualifying statement at the end of this clause. This might appear to be the case because privileges and immunities were essentially used synonymously with rights by the Founding Fathers. This makes it seem that, in its modified form, the clause says, essentially, that all rights shall be consistent with the protection of individual rights. Nevertheless, this does not, in fact, represent a redundancy because, as previously stated, the term "privileges and immunities" was not originally used to refer to individual rights, has never been used consistently to refer to rights, and is used by many today to advocate violations of rights. The qualifying statement is not a redundancy but a necessity given the history and inconsistent use of the term "privileges and immunities."

In addition, the qualifying statement allows me to modify the Constitution with as few changes as possible. This is one of the requirements I set for myself at the outset of this endeavor. This requirement includes not eliminating key terms, if possible, that are used in a number of locations. "Privileges" is used in four locations (Article I, Sections 6 and 9; Article IV, Section 2; and Amendment XIV) and "immunities" in two locations (Article IV, Section 2 and Amendment XIV).

It is also important to understand that the Privileges and Immunities Clause refers to the rights of out-of-state citizens and that retaining the use of the term "privileges and immunities" is helpful because not all rights apply to out-of-state citizens. For example, out-of-state citizens have the right to travel within a state; establish residence; acquire, hold and sell real and personal property; among other rights.[41] However, out-of-state citizens should not be able to vote, run for political office, or serve as a juror.[42] It is perfectly legitimate, within the context of protecting rights, to prevent out-of-state citizens from engaging in these latter activities, although states would need to identify the process by which out-of-state citizens could become citizens and thus acquire the ability to engage in these activities.

By using the term "privileges and immunities," it is easier to distinguish between the rights possessed by out-of-state citizens and what out-of-state citizens are not able to do. If the term "rights" was used instead of "privileges and immunities," one would then have to identify what out-of-state citizens are not able to do. However, it is already well understood that certain activities are excluded from the privileges and immunities. It is just a matter of making sure that the standard of protecting individual freedom is used when determining what to exclude.—BPS

> A Person charged in any State with Treason, Felony, or other Crime, who shall flee from Justice, and be found in another State, shall on Demand of the executive Authority of the State from which he fled, be delivered up, to be removed to the State having Jurisdiction of the Crime.
>
> [No Person held to Service or Labour in one State, under the Laws thereof, escaping into another, shall, in Consequence of any Law or Regulation therein, be discharged from such Service or Labour, but shall be delivered up on Claim of the Party to whom such Service or Labour may be due.][43]

BPS—This is known as the Fugitive Slave Clause and was superseded by Amendment XIII. Hence, no change to this portion of the constitution is required.—BPS

Section 3

> New States may be admitted by the Congress into this Union; but no new State shall be formed or erected within the Jurisdiction of any other State; nor any State be formed by the Junction of two or more States, or Parts of States, without the Consent of the Legislatures of the States concerned as well as of the Congress.
>
> The Congress shall have Power to dispose of and make all needful Rules and Regulations respecting the Territory or other Property belonging to the United States; and nothing in this Constitution shall be so construed as to Prejudice any Claims of the United States, or of any particular State.

BPS—This clause is fine except for the word "Regulations." As stated in chapter 4 in my discussion of the Commerce Clause in Article I, Section 8, government regulation of the economy violates individual rights because it initiates physical force to achieve certain outcomes in the marketplace. Hence, the government has no business imposing regulations on the states, federal property within the states, or federal territories. So, the reference to regulations must be eliminated here.

Given the above, the next amendment shall be as follows: Amendment XLIII—The reference to "Regulations" in Article IV, Section 3 of the Constitution of the United States shall be eliminated. Henceforth, the clause in this section of the Constitution that previously referred to regulations shall state: The Congress shall have Power to dispose of and make all needful Rules respecting the Territory or other Property belonging to the United States.

Nothing else in this portion of the Constitution needs to be changed. However, further discussion is necessary to ensure a clear understanding of the types of rules that can be made by the federal government.

Before discussing the rules, one must distinguish in this portion of the Constitution between the terms "territory" and "property." Territory refers to lands that have not been incorporated into the United States as one of the states of the union but over which the U.S. government exercises some control. These may include such places as Puerto Rico, the Samoa Islands, and territories in what is now the contiguous United States before these areas became states (such as the Northwest Territory, which was governed by the Northwest Ordinance of 1787). Property refers to land owned or controlled by the federal government within the U.S. states, such as military bases, national parks, conservation areas, federal buildings, and so on. In a free society, the government—whether federal, state or local—would not own parks or conservation areas. It would not own any land except that needed for protecting individual rights. This means the government would own land used for military bases, courts, police stations, legislative buildings, and so forth. Any rules pertaining to this property would fall under the authority of the Constitution and thus would have to be consistent with the protection of individual rights.

In territories outside the states within the union but over which the U.S. government exerts some control, rights may not be consistently protected. These are territories that have not joined the union of states and thus the U.S. Constitution may not be the supreme law of the land in them. Nonetheless, in order for the federal government to comply with the proper purpose of government—to protect individual rights—any rules established by it in these territories must be consistent with the protection of individual rights.

Although the only proper purpose of government is to protect individual rights, not all governments will do so. The United States will certainly come into contact with such governments and may form relations with such governments and embrace some of these lands as U.S. territories. As long as these governments do not threaten the rights of American citizens, it is not the duty of the U.S. government to enforce the consistent protection of individual rights in these territories. Nonetheless, to the extent the United States can move these countries or areas in the direction of protecting rights consistently without sacrificing its own interests, it should do so. If these countries or areas want to remain U.S. territories, they should at least embrace the principle of respecting individual rights, even if they do not implement the principle consistently. If they want to become a state, they, of course, would have to establish laws consistent with the U.S. Constitution. If they do not show at least a minimum level of respect for protecting individual rights and freedom, they show no significant movement in this direction, or it is not in the interest of the United States to move them in this direction, they should lose their status as U.S. territories. The United States may maintain peaceful and perhaps even friendly relations with these countries or areas, but it is not appropriate for a rights-respecting country to maintain these areas as territories. Such a relationship stands in opposition to the appropriate function of government.—BPS

Section 4

> The United States shall guarantee to every State in this Union a Republican Form of Government, and shall protect each of them against Invasion; and on Application of the Legislature, or of the Executive (when the Legislature cannot be convened), against domestic Violence.

BPS—No changes to this section are needed; however, some comments are necessary on a republican form of government. Such a form of government entails the power of voters to elect political officials to represent them. These representatives must adhere to the rule of law. This form of government is not the only form that is consistent with the protection of individual rights. A limited monarchy is another form of government that could be consistent with this. The point of this section of the Constitution is to state that this is the specific form of government guaranteed in each state by the U.S. government rather than a monarchy or dictatorship, the latter of which is not consistent with the protection of individual rights.—BPS

Article V

> The Congress, whenever two thirds of both Houses shall deem it necessary, shall propose Amendments to this Constitution, or, on the Application of the Legislatures of two thirds of the several States, shall call a Convention for proposing Amendments, which, in either Case, shall be valid to all Intents and Purposes, as Part of this Constitution, when ratified by the Legislatures of three fourths of the several States, or by Conventions in three fourths thereof, as the one or the other Mode of Ratification may be proposed by the Congress; Provided that no Amendment which may be made prior to the Year One thousand eight hundred and eight shall in any Manner affect the first and fourth Clauses in the Ninth Section of the first Article; and that no State, without its Consent, shall be deprived of its equal Suffrage in the Senate.

BPS—The portion referring to the first and fourth clauses of Article I, Section 9 is related to slavery and thus does not need to be addressed, since slavery has been abolished.—BPS

Article VI

> All Debts contracted and Engagements entered into, before the Adoption of this Constitution, shall be as valid against the United States under this Constitution, as under the Confederation.

This Constitution, and the Laws of the United States which shall be made in Pursuance thereof; and all Treaties made, or which shall be made, under the Authority of the United States, shall be the supreme Law of the Land; and the Judges in every State shall be bound thereby, any Thing in the Constitution or Laws of any State to the Contrary notwithstanding.

The Senators and Representatives before mentioned, and the Members of the several State Legislatures, and all executive and judicial Officers, both of the United States and of the several States, shall be bound by Oath or Affirmation, to support this Constitution; but no religious Test shall ever be required as a Qualification to any Office or public Trust under the United States.

Article VII

The Ratification of the Conventions of nine States, shall be sufficient for the Establishment of this Constitution between the States so ratifying the Same.

The Word, "the," being interlined between the seventh and eighth Lines of the first Page, The Word "Thirty" being partly written on an Erazure in the fifteenth Line of the first Page, The Words "is tried" being interlined between the thirty second and thirty third Lines of the first Page and the Word "the" being interlined between the forty third and forty fourth Lines of the second Page.

Attest William Jackson Secretary

done in Convention by the Unanimous Consent of the States present the Seventeenth Day of September in the Year of our Lord one thousand seven hundred and Eighty seven and of the Independance of the United States of America the Twelfth In witness whereof We have hereunto subscribed our Names.

CONCLUDING REMARKS ON THE REVISION OF THE ORIGINAL CONSTITUTION

As one can see, there are many changes necessary to make the original Constitution completely consistent with the protection of individual rights and freedom. It is a great document but can be made greater still by eliminating the portions that allow violations of rights to take hold and persist. Note that while many changes are necessary to make the Constitution fully consistent with the protection of individual rights, the fundamental structure of the document has not changed. Fundamentally, the Constitution is sound and, in a more philosophically sound (i.e., rational) culture, could be used as is to protect individual rights. However, a document that is fully consistent with the protection of rights will help protect them even when the culture is closer to the irrational end of the philosophical spectrum. This topic will be discussed more in the epilogue.

NOTES

1. Superseded by Amendment XII.

2. For a brief discussion of the differences, see Forte and Spalding, *The Heritage Guide*, p. 247.

3. Changed by Amendment XXV.

4. Alexander Hamilton makes a point consistent with this statement in *The Federalist* No. 74. See Madison, Hamilton, and Jay, *The Federalist Papers*, p. 422.

5. James Wilson made the same point at the Constitutional Convention. See Max Farrand, editor, *The Records of the Federal Convention of 1787*, Vol. II (New Haven, CT: Yale University Press, 1911), p. 426.

6. On this view, hear Stephen Plafker, "Structure of the American Constitution," audio recording (Irvine, CA: The Ayn Rand Institute, 2006). Hear Lecture 1.

7. Hamilton makes this point in *The Federalist* No. 74. See Madison, Hamilton, and Jay, *The Federalist Papers*, p. 423.

8. Senate Joint Resolution 241, 93rd Congress (1974), https://www.congress .gov/bill/93rd-congress/senate-joint-resolution/241 (accessed December 27, 2017).

9. For a discussion of the president's pardon power, including the power to self-pardon, see Kalt, "Pardon Me?," pp. 779–809. Also, see William F. Duker, "The President's Power to Pardon: A Constitutional History," *William & Mary Law Review* vol. 18, no. 3 (Spring 1977), pp. 475–538. See, in particular, pp. 535–38 in the latter article.

10. Superseded by Amendment XI.

11. Modified by Amendment XI.

12. Melvyn R. Durchslag, *State Sovereign Immunity: A Reference Guide to the United States Constitution* (Westport, CT: Praeger, 2002), pp. 3–4.

13. On the contradiction with justice, see Christopher Shortell, *Rights, Remedies, and the Impact of State Sovereign Immunity* (Albany, NY: State University of New York Press, 2008), p. 16.

14. On immunity when government agents act reasonably and in good faith, see Louis L. Jaffe, "Suits against Governments and Officers: Damage Actions," *Harvard Law Review* vol. 77, no. 2 (December 1963), pp. 209–39. See p. 216.

15. Ibid., pp. 219–21 and 224 on the immunity of judges and other government officials.

16. Ibid., pp. 229 and 239.

17. This was identified by Alexander Hamilton in *The Federalist* No. 80. See Madison, Hamilton, and Jay, *The Federalist Papers*, pp. 445 and 447.

18. Ibid., p. 446. Also, see Mark Strasser, "Taking Exception to Traditional Exceptions Clause Jurisprudence: On Congress's Power to Limit the Court's Jurisdiction," *Utah Law Review* vol. 1 (2001), pp. 125–87. See p. 183. In addition, see Ira Mickenberg, "Abusing the Exceptions and Regulations Clause: Legislative Attempts to Divest the Supreme Court of Appellate Jurisdiction," *The American University Law Review* vol. 32, no. 2 (1983), pp. 497–542. See pp. 536–38.

19. Mickenberg, "Abusing the Exceptions and Regulations Clause," p. 501.

20. Ibid., pp. 508–11. Also, see Scott Douglas Gerber, *To Secure These Rights: The Declaration of Independence and Constitutional Interpretation* (New York: New York University Press, 1995), pp. 134–39.

21. For additional discussion on these kinds of questions, see Strasser, "Taking Exception," pp. 143–46.

22. Farrand, *The Records of the Federal Convention*, pp. 425 and 431. For a discussion of the rejection of this proposed amendment, see Leonard G. Ratner, "Majoritarian Constraints on Judicial Review: Congressional Control of Supreme Court Jurisdiction," *Villanova Law Review* vol. 27, no. 5 (1982), pp. 929–58. See pp. 944–46.

23. Madison, Hamilton, and Jay, *The Federalist Papers*, p. 452.

24. On these points, see Strasser, "Taking Exception," pp. 146–47.

25. Madison, Hamilton, and Jay, *The Federalist Papers*, pp. 437–38.

26. For an extensive discussion of this topic, see Mickenberg, "Abusing the Exceptions and Regulations Clause," pp. 513–15.

27. Madison, Hamilton, and Jay, *The Federalist Papers*, p. 457.

28. For a discussion of many of the cases and different interpretations of them, see Mickenberg, "Abusing the Exceptions and Regulations Clause," pp. 516–30; and Strasser, "Taking Exception," pp. 149–55. Also, see Gordon G. Young, "Congressional Regulation of Federal Courts' Jurisdiction and Processes: *United States v. Klein* Revisited," *Wisconsin Law Review* (1981), pp. 1189–262. See, in particular, p. 1218. In addition, see William W. Van Alstyne, "A Critical Guide to *Ex Parte McCardle*," *Arizona Law Review* vol. 15 (1973), pp. 229–69. See, in particular, pp. 232–33 and 260.

29. Strasser, "Taking Exception," p. 160.

30. Martin J. Katz, "Guantanamo, *Boumediene*, and Jurisdiction-Stripping: The Imperial President Meets the Imperial Court," *Constitutional Commentary* vol. 25 (2009), pp. 377–423. See pp. 388–89.

31. Mickenberg, "Abusing the Exceptions and Regulations Clause," pp. 516–30 provides the most comprehensive and logically rigorous analysis of the rulings.

32. On attempts to pass laws pertaining to these and other issues, see ibid., pp. 497 and 500–7.

33. As quoted in Neil H. Coghan, editor, *The Complete Bill of Rights: The Drafts, Debates, Sources, & Origins*, 2nd edition (New York: Oxford University Press, 2015), p. 840.

34. Katz, "Guantanamo, *Boumediene*, and Jurisdiction-Stripping," pp. 403–6.

35. Strasser, "Taking Exception," pp. 146–47 and 173–74.

36. Natelson, "The Original Meaning," p. 1134. Also, see the surrounding discussion on pp. 1130–39.

37. Ibid., p. 1141, note 127 and pp. 1166–67 and 1174 for discussion related to this issue.

38. See Burrell, "A Story of Privileges and Immunities," p. 118. Also, see David S. Bogen, "The Individual Liberties within the Body of the Constitution: A Symposium: The Privileges and Immunities Clause of Article IV," *Case Western Reserve Law Review* vol. 37 (1987), pp. 794–861. See, in particular, pp. 801–3.

39. See Burrell, "A Story of Privileges and Immunities," p. 119 for examples of rights protected as privileges (such as the right to travel) and pp. 70 and 90 for violations of rights (such as the granting of monopolies).

40. See Ackerman, "Post by Bruce Ackerman."

41. See Upham, "*Corfield v. Coryell* and the Privileges," p. 1528. Upham identifies a number of legitimate rights—rights that are consistent with individual freedom—associated with the Privileges and Immunities Clause. However, he also discusses "rights" that are not, in fact, rights. For instance, he discusses the right of citizens of an entire state to hold property in common, such as, perhaps, a state park or the right to fish in coastal waters. But property rights are not properly held in common by all the citizens of a state (unless all the citizens have acted as a group in some manner to acquire property, such as forming a corporation, but then it is not as citizens of the state that they hold the property but as owners of the corporation). States would not generally own property in a free society, including parks or fishing rights in coastal waters. Individuals who own the park or first regularly fish in the waters would possess the property rights. State governments would only own property that is necessary for the protection of individual rights, such as police stations, court houses, legislative buildings, and so forth. These, however, would not be held in common by citizens of the state but would be owned by the state government itself.

42. Ibid., pp. 1500 and 1505.

43. Superseded by Amendment XIII.

Chapter 6

Revising the Amendments to the U.S. Constitution

The Bill of Rights

INTRODUCTION

In this chapter, I focus on revising the Bill of Rights. I follow the same procedural rules that I follow for the original portion of the Constitution. See the introduction to chapter 3 for these rules.

REVISING THE BILL OF RIGHTS

The first ten amendments to the Constitution, known as the Bill of Rights, were proposed by Congress on September 25, 1789 and ratified on December 15, 1791.[1] Here is my discussion on the revision of these amendments.

Amendment I

Congress shall make no law respecting an establishment of religion, or prohibiting the free exercise thereof; or abridging the freedom of speech, or of the press; or the right of the people peaceably to assemble, and to petition the Government for a redress of grievances.

BPS—The next amendment is as follows: Amendment XLIV—The first article of amendment to the Constitution of the United States is hereby repealed and shall be replaced with the following: Congress shall make no law respecting an establishment of religion, or prohibiting the free exercise or rejection thereof, or approving or disapproving of religion or religious sayings, ceremonies, or symbols; or abridging the freedom of thought, of association, of speech, or of the press; or the freedom to not associate with others; or the right of the people peaceably to assemble, and to petition the government for a redress of grievances.

The protection against the unification of politics and religion must be strengthened. As I discuss in chapter 1, religion is based on faith—the abandonment of reason—and leads to disaster when united with politics. One has seen evidence of this in the Crusades and the Inquisition, and one sees it in the unification of Islam and politics in the Middle East today. This occurs because faith and force are corollaries.[2] When one abandons his mind—his only means of understanding and dealing successfully with the world—he must ultimately resort to force to get others to "accept" his views (i.e., forcibly impose his views on others). When one abandons observation and reasoning—that is, rational argument—force is all one has left to "convince" others of the "validity" of his views.

Hence, to protect individual rights it is important to ensure there is no unification of politics and religion. In the words of the Supreme Court in *Everson v. Board of Education of Ewing Township* (1947) when referring to Jefferson's "wall of separation between church and state": "that wall must be kept high and impregnable."[3] That means not only protecting the freedom *of* religion but, more importantly, protecting the freedom *from* religion. The latter right is more important because of the irrational nature of religion. The irrational nature of religion was demonstrated in chapter 1 and is due to its embracement of faith and mysticism and thus its abandonment of reason (our *rational* faculty). People have a right to believe in religion and engage in peaceful religious practices. However, people also have the right to embrace rational ideas and thus the right to not believe in or practice religion and be free of religious individuals attempting to forcibly impose religious ideas on them. This is why the portion stating that Congress shall make no law prohibiting the rejection of religion must be added.

I want to make it clear that I am not condoning the government's ability to prevent people from believing in or practicing religion. Just as it would be a violation of individual rights for the government to require individuals to accept religion, it would also be a violation of rights for the government to forcibly prevent people from embracing religion. The freedom to believe in and practice religion, of course, is already protected in the Constitution with the clause that states Congress shall make no law prohibiting the free exercise of religion.

To make the wall between religion and politics impregnable, even more is needed. Congress should not only be prevented from passing laws establishing a religion and preventing the free exercise or rejection of religion, it should also be prevented from merely approving of religion or religious sayings, ceremonies, or symbols. This would include preventing such approvals as having a monument of the Ten Commandments on government property, adopting "In God We Trust" as the official motto of the United States, or requiring government officials to refer to God or place their hand on a Bible when taking an oath of office. No support of religion should occur, whether that support is implicit through the approval of religious sayings, ceremonies, or symbols or whether that support is explicit.

Approving of or praising religion or religious sayings, ceremonies, or symbols is different than establishing a religion. Even if the government is prevented by law from establishing a religion, it may be accepted that the government is allowed to approve of religion, whether explicitly or implicitly. The government approving of a religion may not be seen as a threat, since it may involve as little as politicians in their official capacity as agents of the government expressing approval of religion. What harm could come from that? No harm may immediately come from that. However, since the protection of rights is so crucially important to human life and the union of religion and politics is an objective threat to the protection of rights, to ensure that the government does not move even one step toward using religion to violate rights, laws are needed to prevent the government from merely approving of religion or religious sayings, ceremonies, or symbols. This will make the separation of religion and government undeniably clear.

One issue that arises in connection with this topic is the issue of religious symbols, such as crosses, on graves in government-owned military cemeteries. It would be appropriate for the government to allow family members of the deceased to choose to place crosses or other religious symbols on the graves of their loved ones. It would even be appropriate for the government to pay for the headstones. This would not be an endorsement of religion, or any aspect of religion, by the government, since the government is not choosing the symbol. Even if the government pays for the headstone, it is not a case of the government endorsing religion as long as the government does not favor the symbol of one religion over another or religious symbols over nonreligious symbols. However, the government should not place religious symbols or sayings of its own choosing on gravestones. This would be an implicit endorsement of religion.

Of course, the government should not pass laws condemning religion or religious sayings, ceremonies, or symbols either. The government should be consistently areligious. It should not reward or punish people for accepting or rejecting religion and it should neither endorse nor denounce religion, again, either implicitly or explicitly.

It may be appropriate under certain circumstances to ban gatherings of religious individuals. If individuals who adhere to a particular religion are using such gatherings to plan acts of violence against others, it may be appropriate for the government to ban such gatherings not in the name of condemning a religion or its practices but in the name of preventing the planning of violating the rights of others. If, for example, in the current war against Islamic totalitarianism it is determined that Muslims are routinely planning terrorist acts at mass prayers, it would be appropriate to ban such prayers. This would not be a violation of the free exercise of religion. In this case, it is a religious activity that is being used to plan massive violations of individual rights. It is the planning of the violations of rights that is being banned. If a religious activity is a part of that, it is not the religious activity as such that is being banned. Nonetheless, it may be necessary to ban the religious activity, in this type of special circumstance, to protect individual rights.

Some might claim that if Congress acts to prevent the existence of religious sayings, ceremonies, and symbols on government property that it is disapproving of them. However, this is not a case of disapproving of religious sayings, ceremonies, and symbols but a case of preventing the government from sanctioning these things. The absence of a positive is not a negative. For example, preventing the government from taking action to approve of religion by displaying religious symbols on its property is not the same as the government taking action to condemn religion or religious sayings, ceremonies, and symbols. Preventing the government from putting a sign on its property saying all men should follow Jesus is not the same as the government putting a sign on its property saying Christianity is evil. Silence on this matter is neither approval nor condemnation.

Another important point to understand regarding the religious aspects of this amendment is that even though the government may not endorse religion, politicians and other government officials most certainly have the right to personally believe in religion and even use religious ideas to guide them in their decision making (of course, as long as they respect rights). This is irrational, but it is within their rights. It is the government as an institution and politicians and other government officials acting in their official capacity as agents of the government that cannot sanction religion or religious sayings, ceremonies, or symbols. This will help to prevent any incursion of religion into government and thus help to prevent violations of rights on religious grounds.

One additional point pertaining to religion is the issue of whether religious people should be exempt from certain laws, such as laws requiring individuals to take oaths as a condition to serve in a government office or laws requiring jury duty in cases involving capital punishment even though people might object to capital punishment on religious grounds. There is no problem in allowing individuals who object to oaths to make affirmations instead, as long as they in some way promise to uphold the law of the land and perform their other required duties while in office. This could easily be accomplished by passing appropriate legislation or including the appropriate options in the Constitution (which is already done, such as in Article II, Section 1). Slight changes in wording to accommodate different beliefs, whether religious or otherwise, are not a problem as long as the meaning of the promise is fundamentally the same. It is merely a procedural matter and does not inhibit the ability of the government to protect individual rights. Moreover, there would be no favoring of any religion or ideological belief since the government could accommodate all beliefs in this manner.

The same is essentially true of jurors being able to opt out of cases that focus on issues that are an affront to their beliefs, again, whether religious or otherwise. The jury selection procedures can easily accommodate such scenarios. Here one must also consider that in a free society, one would not be required to serve on a jury. Jury duty involves initiating force against individuals and thus violates rights to make them serve on juries. Jury duty would be voluntary in a free society. The methods used to obtain sufficient numbers of jurors might involve paying jurors enough to obtain an adequate number of people to voluntarily serve on juries. Regardless of how adequate numbers of jurors are obtained, the point here regarding jury duty in a free society is that one would not have to be concerned about providing exemptions from jury duty to individuals based on ideological grounds because it would be voluntary. I discuss jury duty in more detail in chapter 9 in my discussion of Amendment LXII, which prohibits compulsory jury service. Nevertheless, even when a government violates rights by requiring jury duty, it is not inconsistent with the protection of individual rights to allow exemptions from such duty based on ideological grounds (and, of course, it does not make sense to allow individuals to serve on juries if they are ideologically opposed to a specific law that is related to a particular case).

It is important to note here that there should be no religious exemptions to laws that protect individual rights. Protecting and respecting rights is a fundamental requirement of human life, and, as should be abundantly clear by now, the proper function of government and its sole purpose in a capitalist society is to protect rights. No one is justified in violating rights, whether based on religious or any other grounds.[4]

One final point, pertaining to religion, that is related to this discussion is that *the freedom of religion, properly interpreted, protects only the freedom to peacefully practice religion.* Some religions (or, at least, specific religious statements) call for violence against nonbelievers. For example, the Koran states "kill the polytheists wherever you find them. And capture them, and besiege them, and lie in wait for them at every ambush."[5] Islam is not the only religion to call for violence against nonbelievers. Judaism and Christianity do as well. For example, the Old Testament of the Bible states:

> If your brother, the son of your mother, or your son, or your daughter . . . or your friend . . . entices you secretly, saying, "Let us go and serve other gods," . . . you shall not yield to him or listen to him . . . but you shall kill him.[6]

Acting on such statements would, of course, violate rights and thus is strictly forbidden.[7]

The next addition to the First Amendment that I will discuss is the protection of the freedom of thought. This needs to be added because the freedom of thought is broader than the freedom of religion. The freedom of thought applies to both religious and nonreligious beliefs. It also underlies the freedom of speech and freedom of the press and fits in well in that clause.

While it is difficult to control what people think and punish them for their thoughts, it could be possible to punish a person for thinking that an idea is true and expressing this belief. The most famous example of this is, of course, Galileo. People have also been killed for expressing what they think in writing and refusing to recant their beliefs, such as the Italian mathematician Giordano Bruno. Punishing people for what they say will, of course, make them fear continuing to believe in ideas they think are correct and thus violates the freedom of thought. Given that the freedom of thought is the fundamental freedom that underlies the freedom of religion, speech, and the press, it is important to name it explicitly to make sure it is protected.[8]

One might wonder why I include the freedom of thought in the Constitution and not the freedom of conscience. I include the freedom of thought because throughout the history of rights, the freedom of conscience has been closely related to the freedom of thought. The two have often been used interchangeably. However, the freedom of thought is the more fundamental right and subsumes the freedom of conscience. Conscience, as defined by *Merriam Webster's Collegiate Dictionary* (tenth edition), is the sense or consciousness of the moral goodness or blameworthiness of one's own conduct, intentions, or character together with a feeling of obligation to do right or be good. To understand whether one's character or conduct is moral requires observing facts and considering logical arguments. It also requires introspection. These are all aspects of thinking. Hence, if the freedom of thought is protected, freedom of conscience is necessarily protected as one of its most important components.

One might also believe that including the freedom of thought is unnecessary because it is implicitly protected through the freedom of religion, speech, and press. In fact, the freedom of thought is even implicitly protected by the right to peaceably assemble and petition the government, since underlying the peaceful assemblies and petitions are ideas and thoughts. Moreover, leading authors of the Constitution thought that the Bill of Rights was unnecessary because the rights protected in the Bill of Rights were already protected by the original Constitution, since the original Constitution gave the federal government only specific, very limited powers.[9] Why include redundant protections of rights?

As I argue in chapter 4, redundancy in defense of rights is a virtue. For one thing, the freedom of thought needs to be included to make it clear that both religious and nonreligious thought is protected. In addition, it will provide explicit protection for intellectual freedom and thus provide stronger overall protection for the rights and freedoms on which the First Amendment focuses.

The last freedom I add is the freedom of association, as well as the freedom to not associate with others. The right of association is closely related to the right to assemble. The two rights are often used interchangeably. The Supreme Court has referred to these rights almost synonymously, as in *National Association for the Advancement of Colored People (NAACP) v. Alabama* (1958).[10] Nonetheless, the right to association is a broader right that encompasses the right to assemble. Association refers to the right to join groups or organizations while assembly refers to the right of groups to gather together, whether in public or private spaces. One aspect of associating with others is the ability to meet with them, whether publicly or privately.

Because of its close relation with the right to assemble, it is often stated that the right of association is implicitly protected in the First Amendment. However, to ensure that the right of association is fully protected, language explicitly protecting the right to associate needs to be added. This will protect the right to associate in a stronger fashion.

More importantly, the right to not associate with others must be protected. Individuals and private organizations, including corporations, have a right to not associate with others if they do not want to—even for irrational reasons, such as racism. For example, Ku Klux Klan members have the right to not allow black people to join their group. I must emphasize here that I am a staunch opponent of racism *because* it is irrational—it is an abandonment of the mind. I will discuss in detail why it is irrational and destructive in chapter 8. Nonetheless, being a racist is within the scope of people's rights, so long as they do not initiate physical force against others.

While the right to not associate with others is implicitly protected in the right to associate, unfortunately, the right to not associate with others is often violated today. For example, antidiscrimination laws that exist today violate the right to not associate with others. One may not like individuals and private organizations discriminating for irrational reasons, but to protect rights consistently one must protect the right of people to engage in irrational activities (again, so long as the irrational activities do not initiate physical force against others).

The landmark case of *Heart of Atlanta Motel, Inc. v. United States* (1964) upheld the ability of Congress to pass antidiscrimination laws. Using the Commerce Clause, the Supreme Court upheld Title II of the Civil Rights Act of 1964, which outlaws discrimination based on race, religion, and other criteria in motels, restaurants, and other places of "public accommodation" engaged in interstate commerce.[11] While the new Constitution will abolish the Commerce Clause and thus prevent Congress from regulating commerce based on this clause, it is still necessary to explicitly protect the right to not associate with others because the Court has also held that preventing discrimination does not violate the freedom of association.

The Supreme Court case *Runyon v. McCrary* (1976) is relevant to this issue. In this case, the Court decided that private schools could support segregation but could not refuse admission to applicants based on race, which clearly violates the right to not associate with others. It was also claimed that this decision does not violate the freedom of association.[12] The type of interaction between individuals referred to in *Runyon* (as well as in *Heart of Atlanta Motel, Inc.*) will also be covered by Amendment LV on the freedom to trade and not trade with others, which is discussed in chapter 8. Nonetheless, since the Court referred to the right to association in this case, the case provides a strong reason why the right to not associate with others needs to be explicitly protected in the Constitution. Importantly, in chapter 8 one will also learn about the practical benefits of protecting the right to not associate with others, including the right to engage in irrational discrimination.

The case of *Roberts v. United States Jaycees* (1984) provides another reason why this right needs to be explicitly protected. In that case, the Court decided that compelling the U.S. Jaycees to accept women as full members did not violate the Jaycees right to association.[13] One might not agree with a group such as the Jaycees refusing full membership to women—I certainly do not agree with it—however, again, they have the right to refuse membership to anyone for any reason. No one has the right to, in essence, reach for a gun (i.e., use government coercion) to force groups to accept people for membership that the groups do not want to accept.

As I mention, in chapter 8, I add an amendment on the right to trade and not trade with others. The right of association can include the right to trade. *Runyon* provides an example of this, where parents engaged in trade with a private school to educate their children. When one engages in a contract with others to provide work or produce a product (such as an employment contract or a contract to build a home), one is associating with the person or company one is working for or for whom one is producing the product. However, in cases where one joins a group to advocate for certain ideas or a particular cause (such as the NAACP), one is not typically engaging in trade. Trade might be involved in some cases pertaining to this type of scenario. For instance, those who are paid as employees by an organization to provide specific services to further its cause do engage in trade with the organization. Nonetheless, since the two rights can focus on different activities, both need to be separately protected. This is particularly true of the right to trade, since that right has been routinely violated. Protecting both rights will create some redundancy in the Constitution but, as I have stated, redundancy in the protection of rights is a virtue. It can only serve to better protect rights.

It is important to understand that the freedoms protected by the First Amendment also apply to corporations. After all, corporations, whether created for commercial, charitable, or other purposes, consist of individuals who have associated with each other to create, own, oversee, and/or run the corporation. Hence, these individuals have the right to exercise their freedom of thought, speech, press, assembly, and so on through the corporation.

In addition, the protections of the First Amendment apply to commercial speech and advertising in the same way that they apply to noncommercial speech, such as political and religious speech. This, unfortunately, has not been the case in the past but needs to be the case in the future. Commercial enterprises have just as much of a right to speak and write about their opinions as do noncommercial enterprises. The protection of commercial speech is also economically beneficial because it leads to a more informed public and greater competition.[14]

Of course, the protections the First Amendment provides do not apply to fraudulent and misleading statements. Fraud, as I discuss in chapter 4, represents an indirect initiation of physical force and thus violates individual rights. Hence, commercial speech that is fraudulent or misleading is not protected, whether it comes from corporations or individuals.

Finally, the freedom of speech does not impose a duty on individuals, companies, corporations, and other organizations (including private universities) to allow people to make speeches on their property or post content on their websites. Private property owners have the right to determine who can speak on their property or post on their websites. This is not a violation of free speech but an exercise of private property rights. It would initiate physical force and thus violate private property owners' rights to force them to allow someone to speak on their property or post on their websites against their wishes.

Moreover, when private organizations limit speech on their property, it is not censorship. Private property owners should not be forced to provide a forum for speakers with whom they disagree. For example, a socialist should not be forced to allow an advocate of laissez-faire capitalism to speak on his property. When property owners choose who can and cannot speak on their property, it is the opposite of censorship. It is an exercise of free speech. They have the right to promote ideas they consider valid and denounce ideas they consider false and vicious. Censorship applies only to government action, and to protect rights it must be strictly prohibited. The First Amendment protects us from the government violating the freedom of speech, not from private property owners restricting speech on their own property.[15]—BPS

Amendment II

A well regulated Militia, being necessary to the security of a free State, the right of the people to keep and bear Arms, shall not be infringed.

BPS—The right to keep and bear arms is constantly under attack today by advocates of gun control. Therefore, we must strengthen the Second Amendment to provide greater protection of this right. The changes will acknowledge that the use of force to protect rights has been delegated to the government but will also make it clear that individuals have the right to keep and bear arms for self-defense, hunting, and other purposes that are consistent with the protection of individual rights. This will remove all doubt that the right to keep and bear arms applies to individuals, while at the same time acknowledging that the government has the primary responsibility for protecting rights. It is important to acknowledge that the government has the primary responsibility to use force to protect rights so that it does not appear that the amendment endorses anarchy or "competing governments." The topic of anarchy will be briefly examined in chapter 10.

Based on the above discussion, the next amendment should read as follows: Amendment XLV—The second article of amendment to the Constitution of the United States is hereby repealed and shall be replaced with the following: While it is acknowledged that the use of force to protect rights has been delegated by the people to the government, the right of individuals to keep and bear arms for self-defense, hunting, and other purposes that respect individual rights shall not be infringed.

One of the major debates regarding the Second Amendment, as currently written, is whether it applies to individuals or states. That is, does it protect the right of individuals to own and use firearms or does it only protect the right of states to maintain organized military units? Based on the text of the Constitution itself and the historical evidence, including court cases, U.S. law, and what the term "militia" referred to at the time of the ratification of the Second Amendment, it is clear that the amendment protects the right of individuals to keep and bear arms. Nonetheless, to remove any doubt that the right of individuals is protected, the amendment needs to be changed.

Even though the revised Constitution will make it clear that the right of individuals to keep and bear arms is protected, it will be instructive to consider the evidence demonstrating that the Second Amendment, as originally written, protects that same right. The most important evidence to consider is the text of the amendment itself. It specifically states that *the right of the people* to keep and bear arms shall not be infringed. It does not say the right of the states to raise armies shall not be infringed or the right of the states to keep and bear arms shall not be infringed. If the Framers of the amendment had intended it to apply solely to the states' right to raise armies or keep and bear arms, why did they not explicitly say this?[16]

Consider also that the phrase "the people" is used in four other places in the Bill of Rights, and it always refers to individuals, not governments. For example, the First Amendment refers to the right of the people peaceably to assemble and to petition the government for a redress of grievances. The Fourth Amendment states that the right of the people to be secure in their persons, houses, papers, and effects, against unreasonable searches and seizures, shall not be violated. Clearly these refer to rights of individuals. The Ninth and Tenth Amendments use the phrase "the people" to refer to individuals as well. Based on the usage of the phrase "the people" throughout the Bill of Rights, the use of the phrase "the right of the people" in the Second Amendment refers to individuals. While it is true that the Second Amendment protects the right of states to raise and maintain organized military units, it also protects the right of individuals to keep and bear arms.[17]

Next, one must consider the primary meaning of the term "militia" as used in the late eighteenth century. It referred to all able-bodied male citizens who were subject to being called upon for military service.[18] Prior to the founding of the United States, colonists were not merely allowed to keep their own arms, they were required to do so to protect themselves from criminals and attacks by Indians and colonial rivals. One must keep in mind here that police forces were not available at the time for protection, and the army of the mother country was not close by to defend colonists. Hence, individuals were expected to protect themselves.

In addition, in the 1939 case *United States v. Miller* the Supreme Court recognized that the militia constitutes all able-bodied male citizens and that these citizens are expected to supply their own arms.[19] U.S. law also recognizes the militia as constituting all able-bodied males. Title 10, Section 311 of the United States Code states, "The militia of the United States consists of all able-bodied males at least 17 years of age and . . . under 45 years of age." In the debates surrounding the ratification of the Second Amendment and in state and colonial law, as well as in other sources, there is additional evidence that the Second Amendment refers to an individual's right to keep and bear arms.[20] Based on the evidence, it is clear that the amendment refers to the right of individuals to keep and bear arms.

Moreover, this is what the Supreme Court decided in *District of Columbia v. Heller* (2008). The decision in that case unequivocally recognized the individual's right to keep and bear arms unrelated to service in a militia. The

Court provides a substantial amount of textual, legal, and historical evidence to support this decision.[21]

The fact that the debate over the meaning of the Second Amendment persists, even though the evidence clearly shows that it protects the right of individuals, provides a strong reason to change the amendment to ensure that individual rights are consistently protected. It will help to eliminate any confusion about whether the right of individuals or the right of the states is protected.

Ultimately, we do not need to be concerned about whether the rights of individuals or the states are protected by the amendment as it was originally written because, as I show in chapter 1, all rights belong to individuals and the proper purpose of government is to protect individual rights. Thus, it is individuals that possess the right to keep and bear arms, and, of course, it is the purpose of the revised Constitution to ensure the protection of individual rights, including the rights pertaining to arms.

Why do individuals have a right to keep and bear arms? To answer this question, one must simply recall the purpose of rights. Rights protect individual freedom. Freedom refers to the absence of the initiation of physical force. Individuals have a right to engage in any activity so long as it does not initiate physical force against others or threaten others with force. Owning and using arms as such does not initiate physical force against others. Firearms can be used in a rights-respecting manner. In fact, firearms can be used to protect one's rights if they are used for the purpose of self-defense. However, even if not used for self-defense they can be used in ways that do not violate the rights of others. This is the case if, for example, firearms are used for hunting, for target practice at a shooting range, or as museum pieces.

The practical benefits of the right to keep and bear arms for the purpose of self-defense must be stressed. Evidence shows that when more guns are owned by rights-respecting individuals, crime rates decrease. When gun control laws are imposed, murder rates and other crime rates tend to increase. Evidence for the link between high rates of gun ownership and low crime rates is widespread throughout the United States. However, there is also international evidence for the link between low (or reduced) crime rates and high rates of gun ownership. In addition, evidence for the link between gun control laws and higher crime rates is seen in cities such as Chicago and Washington, D.C., which have high crime rates and some of the strictest gun control laws in the United States. There is also a significant amount of international evidence on this issue.

Here is just a small sampling of the evidence. In states that have adopted right-to-carry laws, large drops in overall violent crime, murder, rape, and aggravated assault have been seen, and the crime rates in these categories consistently remained much lower than they were before the laws. In addition, Washington, D.C. experienced higher murder rates in the years after a handgun ban was imposed in 1977 and Chicago also experienced higher murder rates in the years after a ban on virtually all new handguns in 1983. Internationally, England and Wales experienced a 340-percent increase in deaths and injuries from gun crime in the eight years after Great Britain banned handguns in 1997. Finally, Switzerland is one of the most heavily armed countries in the world on a per capita basis and is also one of the safer countries in the world.[22] For a comprehensive presentation of the evidence, see the excellent book titled *More Guns, Less Crime* by John Lott, Jr.[23] Gun control laws keep guns out of the hands of law-abiding citizens and make them easy prey for criminals, who are obviously not concerned with obeying the law (including gun control laws). Protecting the right to own guns makes people safer, not less safe.

Thinking of the issue in terms of fundamentals, low crime rates are not caused by low rates of gun ownership and high crime rates are not caused by high rates of gun ownership (or vice versa). Fundamentally, crime is caused by a lack of rational moral values, including a lack of respect for the rights of others. The revised Constitution will help create greater respect for rights— and, indeed, requires greater respect for rights in order to be implemented— and thus will help to reduce crime.

While a firearm can be used to violate rights, one must understand that it is the actions of the individual who uses it to violate rights that is the rights violator. It is not the firearm itself that violates rights. Many devices can be used as weapons to violate rights. For instance, an automobile can be used as a weapon to violate rights. However, again, it is not the automobile itself that violates rights but the person who uses it as a weapon that violates rights. It is the rights violators that must be punished. Individuals who use firearms and automobiles in ways that respect rights should not be punished for the violations of rights by other individuals.

It is important to understand that the right to keep and bear arms that individuals possess does not imply a right to keep and bear any type of weapon. One must assess whether the possession of a weapon is an objective threat to others and thus a violation of individual rights. Remember, protecting rights involves banning the initiation of physical force *and the threat of force*. A nuclear bomb in a neighbor's backyard is an objective threat. Tanks, howitzers, and nerve gas being used in a neighbor's yard constitute an objective threat as well. However, automatic rifles safely stowed in someone's attic or used at a shooting range following appropriate safety precautions do not represent a threat. The same is true of handguns. This is generally the case even if the handgun is carried in a concealed manner in an urban area.

If it can be shown that weapons are routinely used to violate rights or that by their nature they threaten the rights of others, it may be appropriate to ban such weapons for use in the ways or areas in which they represent a threat. For example, it may be appropriate to ban long guns for self-defense in urban areas because of their greater ability to penetrate walls and people and thus become a threat to innocent bystanders. A storeowner might be an accurate shot and hit the armed robber with which he is confronted; however, if the rifle he uses is capable of delivering a bullet that pierces its target, penetrates the walls of adjacent buildings or the front of the store, and still has enough velocity left to harm innocent bystanders (a likely possibility with many long guns), it may be appropriate to prohibit the use of such guns for self-defense in urban areas, where they represent a threat to the rights of others. The same might be true of shotguns, whose spray might not only hit the armed robber but innocent bystanders. Nonetheless, this does not mean such guns cannot be safely stored in urban areas and used for other purposes in a safe manner, such as at a shooting range.[24] In such areas, individuals would still possess the right to use them for purposes that do not threaten the rights of others. In urban areas, it may be that the right to keep and bear arms for the purpose of self-defense applies only to handguns, which do not have the penetrating power of long guns.

Whatever weapons are banned, in order to protect rights, one must be able to provide evidence to show that the possession or use of such weapons is an objective threat to others. With extreme weapons (such as nuclear weapons), it is easy to show that they are objective threats and thus one does not need a demonstration based on the use of the weapons in practice to justify banning them. However, in borderline cases, one would need to see evidence of the weapon's threat, based on its use, to demonstrate that it is an objective threat to individual rights. This is why it is difficult to make a general statement about which weapons should be banned. In many cases, one will probably have to assess the weapons on a case-by-case basis to determine if they are a threat to individual rights.

In the same way that the right to keep and bear arms is consistent with banning the possession of some weapons, it is also consistent with preventing some individuals from possessing firearms. For example, to protect individual rights it would be appropriate for the government to prohibit ex-convicts with violent records and individuals with severe mental disorders from possessing firearms. The key with regard to determining who can own guns—as with anything the government does—is that the guiding principle should always be the protection of individual rights.—BPS

Amendment III

No Soldier shall, in time of peace be quartered in any house, without the consent of the Owner, nor in time of war, but in a manner to be prescribed by law.

BPS—The Third Amendment needs to be changed to protect rights consistently. The next amendment is as follows: Amendment XLVI—The third article of amendment to the Constitution of the United States shall be repealed and replaced with the following: No Soldier shall, at any time, be quartered in any house, without the consent of the Owner.

It requires the initiation of physical force and is a violation of the property rights of homeowners to require them to quarter soldiers they do not want to quarter. People must be able to object to a war—even a just war—as long as they do not "aid and comfort" the enemy. It is possible for rational people to disagree about whether a war is just.

Some might think that not quartering soldiers during a time of war is a form of aiding the enemy in the sense that it makes it harder for the troops to fight the enemy, since they may have to live outside. However, the absence of aid to your own army is not the same as giving aid to the enemy, even though it might have the same effect in the sense of making it easier for your enemy to fight your army. The absence of action to help someone whose rights are being violated is not the same as taking action to aid the rights violator and thus actually violating rights oneself. This is a crucial distinction to make. The person who does not act is not initiating physical force and thus is not violating rights. Hence, the government has no business forcing a person to act in this situation to provide lodging.

This issue can be related to the draft, which will be discussed in detail in chapter 9. Some might claim that the government should be able to force people to join the army to fight a war because if people refuse to fight this could be seen as a form of aiding the enemy, since there will be fewer soldiers to fight the enemy. Leaving aside the well-known fact that volunteer armies are generally superior to armies that consist of draftees, and therefore it does not necessarily aid the enemy to not have a draft, one who refuses to fight is not initiating physical force and thus is not violating rights, as one would be doing if one aided the enemy by, for instance, joining its army. The draft is a gross violation of individual rights because the government initiates force against a man when he is just starting out in life to make him fight and possibly die in a war he might consider unjust and in which he might not want to fight.

In the same way, not helping someone escape from or defend himself against a murderer is not the same as helping the murderer commit his crime and thus violating rights oneself along with the murderer one is aiding. Again, not taking action to protect rights might have the same effect as taking positive action to aid the rights violator, in the sense that the result in both cases is that it is easier for the rights violator to violate rights, but the means by which these effects are brought about are fundamentally different from each other.—BPS

Amendment IV

> The right of the people to be secure in their persons, houses, papers, and effects, against unreasonable searches and seizures, shall not be violated, and no Warrants shall issue, but upon probable cause, supported by Oath or affirmation, and particularly describing the place to be searched, and the persons or things to be seized.

BPS—While no modifications to this amendment are necessary, a discussion of the right to privacy and its relation to this amendment is necessary. I considered adding a provision on the right to privacy to this amendment, since the limits placed on searches and seizures help to protect the right to privacy. However, I was convinced by the article on the right to privacy titled "Beyond Reductionism: Reconsidering the Right to Privacy" by Amy Peikoff that the right to privacy derives from and is protected by the rights to property, liberty, and contract and therefore there should be no legal right to privacy.[25] For instance, a woman's right to obtain an abortion was protected in *Roe v. Wade* (1973) based on the right to privacy.[26] However, the rights that protect a woman's right to obtain an abortion are the rights to her own life and liberty. It is the freedom of a woman to do with her life and body what she wants (and the right to engage in a contractual relationship with a doctor) that is being exercised when a woman obtains an abortion. The right to abortion is discussed in more detail in chapter 8.

Likewise, what protects a person's right to make phone calls without someone listening to them or having the activities he engages in while in his home monitored is his right to property. For example, in the case of phone calls, it is the right to his property in the form of the phone and the right to engage in contractual relationships with the phone service provider (which is based on the right to property as well) that protects the privacy of a person when making phone calls.[27] Furthermore, if one takes the appropriate precautions to ensure people cannot hear or see what he is doing in his home (such as closing his doors, windows, and blinds), it is his right to property in the form of his home that protects his privacy in this instance.[28]

Peikoff also argues that recognizing a legal right to privacy reduces the security of the rights to property, liberty, and other rights. For example, federal legislation and case law consistent with a legal right to privacy have limited the ability of employers to listen to telephone conversations of employees while in the workplace during work hours and using employer owned telephones. This violates the property rights of employers. In addition, she argues that recognizing a legal right to privacy, as ironic as it might seem, weakens the protection of privacy. This is because the protection of privacy has been reduced to whether a judge or jury believes that a person has a reasonable expectation to privacy. It is no longer based on the property one owns and the contracts in which one enters. She provides extensive discussion on these topics.[29] For these reasons, the right to privacy should not be explicitly recognized in the Constitution.—BPS

Amendment V

No person shall be held to answer for a capital, or otherwise infamous crime, unless on a presentment or indictment of a Grand Jury, except in cases arising in the land or naval forces, or in the Militia, when in actual service in time of War or public danger; nor shall any person be subject for the same offence to be twice put in jeopardy of life or limb; nor shall be compelled in any criminal case to be a witness against himself, nor be deprived of life, liberty, or property, without due process of law; nor shall private property be taken for public use, without just compensation.

BPS—The only change that is needed here pertains to the Takings Clause. The government should not be able to take private property for public use, even if it compensates the property owner. It is a violation of property rights to force an individual to sell property if he does not want to. The Takings Clause should state the following: nor shall private property be taken for public or private use or purpose.

The first change to highlight here is that the phrase "without just compensation" must be eliminated. In addition, the government should not be able to take private property to transfer it to another *private* party. Hence, the addition of the government not being able to take private property for private use (in addition to public use). It should also not be able to take private property for public or private *purposes*. Hence, the addition of the government not being able to take property for public or private purposes (in addition to public or private uses).

The Framers of the Constitution did not intend for the government to be able to take private property so that other private individuals or organizations could use it, but the Takings Clause has been interpreted in that manner, as in *Kelo v. City of New London* (2005). In that case, taking property from private landowners so that it could be redeveloped by private businesses and increase tax revenues for the city was considered a permissible "public use."[30] One could debate about whether this is a public use, since the property was taken so that it could be used by other private individuals. Nonetheless, to ensure that the government does not take property for use by private individuals, the reference to banning the taking of property for private use is necessary.

Further modification to the clause is needed because an even looser standard than taking property for public use has emerged in the last several decades. The Supreme Court has ruled in favor of taking property for public purposes as well. This represents a more serious threat to private property rights because it is easier to justify taking property for this reason. Interpreted literally, taking property for public use requires that the public be able to use the property in some way, such as for a road or park. Taking property for a public purpose justifies a broader range of takings. For example, a public purpose could include the government taking property from lower middle-class homeowners and giving it to private businesses to, at least in part, build more expensive homes for wealthier individuals and thus increase tax revenues for a local government. This was the justification for taking the property in *Kelo*. In this case, the property taken would not have been used by the public but by the private businesses and wealthier homeowners. I say the property taken "would not have been used" as opposed to "is not used" by the public because after the property was taken the redevelopment projects were abandoned. The land taken by the government became a vacant lot.

The public purpose justification could also be used to take property from large landowners to give the land to lessees who built and resided in homes on the land, as occurred in *Hawaii Housing Authority v. Midkiff* (1984). The property taken was used by the former lessees, not the public. Eliminating concentrated property ownership was viewed as a legitimate public purpose in this case. Including the ban in the Constitution on taking property for public purposes is necessary to prevent these types of violations of property rights.

One topic related to this issue that is important to understand is that private property can properly be taken by the government as punishment for a crime or in a settlement in a civil suit (and given to the plaintiff, if appropriate), as long as the government follows appropriate due process. If an individual violates rights, it may be proper to take property from him as punishment, as a settlement, or to prevent future violations of rights. This is consistent with the protection of individual rights. Moreover, this issue is addressed by the Due Process Clause of Amendment V. Hence, the revised (or current) Takings Clause does not apply in these cases. That is, it does not prevent the government from taking property in these cases.

The Takings Clause also does not prevent the government from occupying, using, or destroying property to repel an invader. If the government needs to occupy land to fight the invader, it has every right to do so without providing compensation to the landowner. This is true even if the landowner objects to the war. Given the imminent threat if an enemy has, in fact, invaded the country, there will be no debate about the fact that the rights of Americans are being threatened. Perhaps one might argue that we can debate over which lands the government needs to occupy to repel the invader, but if an army has invaded, the threat is of the nature that the government cannot wait for it to be decided in the courts or determined elsewhere what land it is appropriate to occupy to repel the invader. The government must act immediately to protect rights.

If the landowner wants to seek compensation for the occupation and any damage to his land or property by the government in repelling an invader, his only legitimate case is against the rights violator—that is, the invader. When the enemy is repelled and defeated, as a part of its surrender, such compensation might be obtained, to the degree that it can be. But the government repelling the invader has no duty to compensate landowners.

One might think there is an inconsistency between my statement above on repelling an invader and my change to Amendment III. I say in the discussion of Amendment III that the government cannot quarter troops on property without the owner's consent, even in wartime. Why is consent needed to quarter troops in wartime but not to occupy land to repel an invader? Consent is needed to quarter troops in wartime because such an action is not necessary to defend against an imminent threat of the rights of citizens. The army has other options available to quarter its troops. Moreover, quartering troops in time of war could occur even if there is no invasion (i.e., the country is fighting a war on foreign soil). And even if there is an invasion, quartering soldiers could occur far from the fighting. However, if an enemy has invaded and troops must fight to repel the invader, swift and unrestricted action must be taken to protect rights in the areas where the fighting is taking place.

In addition, some might think that a statement is needed in the amended Constitution to prevent regulatory takings. It is true that regulation of property that restricts the use or disposal of the property can reduce the value of the property and thus, in effect, represent a type of taking. There is some controversy over whether such regulation constitutes a taking covered by the current Takings Clause, since there is no physical taking of the property by the government, and therefore whether reductions in the value of the property that result should be compensated based on the Takings Clause.[31] Nonetheless, this form of taking does not need to be addressed in the amended Constitution. Other parts of the amended Constitution will prevent the government from engaging in regulation—that is, in initiating physical force in the marketplace to achieve outcomes preferred by government officials. The revised Takings Clause along with the other portions of the amended Constitution that will prevent government regulation of any type will be sufficient to prevent any form of taking, whether through physical confiscation or through regulation.

The last issue that needs to be addressed is the economic implications of abolishing eminent domain. Some might claim that if we abolish the government's ability to take property through the process of eminent domain, it will be impossible, or very costly, to build roads, pipelines, and so on.

It may be true that in a few exceptional cases, a road or pipeline may end up with an extra turn or bend due to some property owner refusing to sell. However, in the great majority of cases, property owners will be glad to sell their property at a price higher than what they could otherwise obtain for it. In most cases, this will not represent a prohibitive cost to the road or pipeline builder but will be in line with the greater value of the land to the builder, in accordance with the more valuable economic activity for which the land will be used. A result of the requirement that land be purchased through voluntary trade is that it will be used for its most important economic purpose. Only those newly discovered economic employments for land that are sufficiently profitable will provide the means for individuals to be able to offer enough to the current landowners to get them to sell voluntarily.

Such an outcome is similar to what currently happens when, for example, a developer buys land from a farmer to build residential housing on the land or an oil company pays a landowner to drill for oil on his land. In some instances, acquisition of land from many property owners even occurs through voluntary means in cities to redevelop property. In addition, private railroads in the past often purchased land to obtain rights-of-way to build their railroads. It is relatively easy for landowners and those who wish to purchase their land to find a price that is beneficial to both. Landowners are happy to sell (or rent) their land in these cases because of the relatively high prices they can obtain for their land. Things are quite different when landowners are forced to sell to the government at "fair market value"—a price at which landowners may not want to sell. The sale of land in the former case takes place within the context of a spirit of goodwill and mutual respect for the rights of others. The sale of land to the government through eminent domain creates animosity and discontent and leads to the land being used for purposes that are not the most economically important (i.e., it leads to the production of products and services that are not the most highly demanded by the public).[32]

In addition, developers, oil companies, and so forth will have to plan well in advance to ensure the appropriate rights-of-way are obtained. It would be well understood in a free market that the rights-of-way would need to be obtained long before an area could be developed. As a part of this planning, developers could make provisions for rights-of-way in the deeds of the property they sell to buyers of parcels of land.[33]

Moreover, as I discuss in chapter 1, the protection of individual rights—including private property rights—is the precondition for economic progress. Hence, while there may be the occasional hindrance to development, the overall effect will be positive because without the protection of individual rights no economic progress will take place. In fact, economic decline will occur and a much lower standard of living will exist.[34]

Based on the above discussion, the following amendment must be made to the Constitution: Amendment XLVII—In the fifth article of amendment to the Constitution of the United States, the following clause shall be repealed: nor shall private property be taken for public use, without just compensation. It shall be replaced with the following: nor shall private property be taken for public or private use or purpose.—BPS

Amendment VI

In all criminal prosecutions, the accused shall enjoy the right to a speedy and public trial, by an impartial jury of the State and district wherein the crime shall have been committed, which district shall have been previously ascertained by law, and to be informed of the nature and cause of the accusation; to be confronted with the witnesses against him; to have compulsory process for obtaining witnesses in his favor, and to have the Assistance of Counsel for his defence.

BPS—The Sixth Amendment needs to be modified to protect rights by preventing the right to counsel from turning into a form of welfare. The modification shall include the following addition: In all criminal prosecutions, the accused shall enjoy the right . . . to have the assistance of counsel for his defense *but any counsel provided by the government shall be limited to no more than the minimum necessary to achieve justice and counsel shall not be provided by the government in civil trials.*

This is a tough area to determine how to protect rights. Welfare should not be provided to the poor. However, it seems assured that if criminal defendants who cannot afford an attorney are not provided with one, innocent people will be sent to jail and guilty people will remain free. This would violate rights. The solution is to allow for the provision of a minimum level of representation to defendants in criminal trials so that rights can be protected.

The Constitution, as currently written, does not require counsel to be provided by the government, but the Supreme Court has ruled that counsel should be provided by the government. This occurred for trials in state courts in the seminal case *Gideon v. Wainwright* (1963), in which the Court ruled that states are required under the Sixth Amendment to provide counsel in criminal cases to defendants who are unable to pay for their own. To protect rights in the criminal justice system in the United States, an attorney advocating for the defendant is generally necessary to ensure his rights are properly defended. A prosecutor, who presents the case to prove the guilt of the person accused of a crime, and an impartial judge provide the other two components necessary to ensure that a trial is fair and that rights are protected. The legal system is too complicated for most people to represent themselves in criminal cases. Hence, the rights of accused individuals would not be properly defended without some minimum representation by a lawyer who understands the law and the appropriate procedures to follow throughout the entire process of determining the guilt or innocence of an individual.

What constitutes the minimum representation necessary to achieve justice should be determined through the courts and, if necessary, codified in statute. The minimum should not be established in a constitution, since a constitution does not focus on such details. Also, I will not (and cannot) provide an analysis to establish the minimum here because there are too many factors to consider. I will only mention some of the factors that should be considered. These factors include the type of cases in which counsel should be provided. For example, should counsel be provided in all criminal cases or just a subset of cases, such as capital cases and cases involving imprisonment? The modified amendment does not require counsel to be provided by the government and it may be determined that rights can be properly protected in certain cases even if the defendant has no attorney. Other factors to consider in determining the minimum level of representation might include the budgets allocated to the provision of public defenders and the amount of trial experience and the number of years practicing law required of public defenders, as well as the amount of training they should receive.

Besides *Gideon*, a number of Supreme Court cases have already established some of these minimum standards. For example, in *Argersinger v. Hamlin* (1972) the Supreme Court extended the right to counsel to misdemeanor cases in which the defendant faces imprisonment. In *Alabama v. Shelton* (2002), the Court extended the right to counsel to misdemeanor cases in which a suspended sentence is imposed. The level of representation provided by the government today seems adequate to protect rights. The key is to ensure that the provision of counsel is not extended too far. That is why a statement in the amendment is needed that limits the provision of counsel.

If people want defendants who cannot afford an attorney to have better representation than that provided by the government, they can take action through private means to provide better representation. They can form or donate to charities that provide representation. They can also become an attorney themselves and work for such a charity or provide their services pro bono to poor defendants.

The limits on the provision of counsel include the government not providing counsel in civil cases. The right to counsel is currently being extended to civil cases through both court rulings and legislation.[35] However, rights can be protected in civil trials through judges ensuring trials are fair and the provision of attorneys, if necessary, through voluntary means. It is more important to have attorneys for defendants in criminal cases because the consequences are more severe, since the liberty and lives of those convicted can be at stake. Moreover, criminals who have violated rights can be a threat to the rights of the public in general. For example, if a person has murdered or raped someone, he could be a threat to others. To protect rights, it is crucial that the correct individual is convicted in criminal trials. In civil cases, the disputes are generally between two or only a small number of individuals or private entities and the defendants generally do not represent a threat to the rights of anyone else. So the provision of counsel by the government is not justified in civil cases.

The limits on the provision of counsel by the government are included to ensure as best as possible that the provision of legal services does not go beyond the government's appropriate function of protecting rights and become a type of welfare for poor defendants. It is not appropriate for the government to provide welfare. The purpose of providing counsel should be to protect rights, not to provide poor people lawyers because they need lawyers. We need to make sure we protect the rights of individuals through the criminal justice system, but we also need to protect the rights of taxpayers. Taxpayers should not be sacrificed to poor defendants.

The altruist code of morality, discussed in chapter 1, provides the moral justification for welfare. As I show in that chapter, altruism is a vicious code of morality and is not an appropriate justification for action under any circumstances. In particular, it is not an appropriate justification for government action. Politically, altruism justifies collectivism, statism, and the sacrifice of some people for the sake of others. Altruism is destructive because it stands in opposition to the requirements of human life. It enslaves some people to the needs and desires of others. But human life requires the pursuit and attainment of values, not giving up or sacrificing values. That is, as I also discuss in chapter 1, human life requires rational egoism. Based on this latter code of morality, individuals have a right to their own lives and a right to live as they see fit, based on their own rational judgment. According to this morality, they have no duty to help others obtain what they want or need.

To those who believe we do have a duty to help others, I ask "Why?" Why should we sacrifice ourselves to others? There is no rational answer to that question because sacrifice is destructive to human life. Even worse, why do some people (government officials) think they have a right to force other people (taxpayers) to sacrifice themselves? They do not. This is immoral on two counts. First, it is based on an immoral code of morality and, second, it requires violations of individual rights to implement.

Some might claim that, in a fully free society, since taxes are voluntary, once such a society is achieved, then force will not be used against taxpayers when the government pays for poor defendants' attorneys and thus it would be acceptable to have the government pay for more than the minimum level of legal representation. However, this argument could be applied to *any* government expenditure in a free society. For example, one could argue that it is acceptable for the government to provide food stamps and Social Security in a free society because no one will be forced to pay taxes in a free society and thus people can choose if they want to pay taxes to finance government spending on these types of welfare. But the government should not provide any type of welfare, even if taxes are voluntary. Government has a legal monopoly on the use of force and to ensure that force is used only to protect rights and not to violate them, we must rigidly limit what the government can do. As mentioned, if one wants to provide more than the minimum level of legal representation to the poor, one can do so through private means.

One last topic that is related to this amendment must be discussed. No changes need to be made in connection with this topic. However, it must be made clear why this portion of the Sixth Amendment is consistent with the protection of individual rights. The portion I am referring to states, "The accused shall enjoy the right . . . to have compulsory process for obtaining witnesses in his favor." Subpoenas are consistent with the protection of individual rights, whether are used in favor of the defense or prosecution. Focusing first on the prosecution, if a witness whose testimony would lead to the conviction of a criminal refuses to testify, that person is an accessory after the fact, hindering prosecution, and/or obstructing justice and it would be legitimate for these types of crimes to be prosecuted. Instead of bringing cases against such witnesses, it makes more sense for the government to possess subpoena power.

The justification is essentially the same for the defense to have the power to subpoena witnesses.[36] If a witness could exonerate an innocent defendant but the witness refuses to testify and the defendant is convicted in the case as a result, the witness is a causal factor in the wrongful conviction of the defendant. Since it is the refusal of the witness to testify that is responsible for the wrongful conviction, it is the witness who, ultimately, is responsible for this injustice against the defendant.

In such a situation, the defendant should be able to seek redress through the courts by suing the witness for this injustice. This would force the witness to answer the claim against him and achieve essentially the same outcome as the subpoena. However, this would be a drawn-out process that would take place after the conviction of the defendant and thus cause an innocent person to spend time in jail. Hence, it is a more efficient and effective way of achieving justice to provide subpoena power to defendants.[37]

Some might wonder how a person who has been convicted of a crime would successfully be able to sue a witness who refused to testify in his favor at his trial (if subpoena power for defendants did not exist). In the eyes of the law, the defendant is guilty. How could he show that the witness is responsible for his conviction? Here, one must remember that in civil trials, the burden of proof is based on a preponderance of the evidence. This is a much lower burden of proof than in criminal trials, where the standard is beyond a reasonable doubt. Proving something to be true based on a preponderance of the evidence involves proving that something has a greater probability of being true than not being true (i.e., the claim has greater than a 50 percent chance of being true). If a convicted person can show that it is more likely than not that if the witness testified he would have been acquitted, he can win the case. This is not impossible. Just as it was not impossible for O.J. Simpson to be held responsible for the deaths of Nicole Brown-Simpson and Ronald Goldman in a civil trial even though he was acquitted of their murders in the criminal trial.

Some might also wonder how a person can be held responsible for the acquittal of a guilty defendant for merely refusing to testify. The person did not take any positive action to cause the acquittal. He simply did not act. Some might think this is similar to someone being held at least partially responsible for a crime that takes place because the person witnessed the crime and could have stopped it if he acted. Like the witness who refused to testify, he is held responsible for the occurrence of an event because he refused to act. How can the person who refuses to act in either scenario be held responsible?

These two scenarios are fundamentally different from each other and, therefore, in the case of the witness not testifying, he should be held responsible. In the case of the crime that is committed, the witness should not be held responsible. For example, if person A murders person B and person C witnesses the murder but refuses to act to stop the murder, C is not a causal factor in the murder of B, even if C could have stopped the murder by taking action. Person C did nothing to cause B's murder. That responsibility falls completely on A. However, whether C likes it or not he is now a part of the wider event of the criminal case against A because of his involvement as a witness. This means he is a part of the wider activity of protecting rights in this case. In the context of the wider event, if he refuses to testify to help convict the murderer and the murderer is acquitted because of his refusal to testify, he is responsible for the acquittal of the murderer. He should be held responsible for preventing the administration of justice and helping the murderer to go free in this case. But as I mention, it makes more sense for the government to have subpoena power instead.

Finally, to ensure that the rights of witnesses are protected, qualifications on the use of subpoena power should be imposed. These qualifications include, but are not limited to, when the power can be used (For example, what types of trials can it be used in and what types of evidence must witnesses possess to justify using subpoena power against them?), how the power can be used (For instance, should witnesses be compensated for any inconvenience to them?), who can issue subpoenas (Should attorneys be able to issue them or only the courts?), and what precautions need to be taken to ensure the safety of witnesses (such as in cases where witnesses against a defendant are being threatened). These qualifications do not deny that subpoena power is consistent with the protection of individual rights. They merely represent a debate, within the context of the use of subpoena power, regarding how to protect the rights of all parties involved, including defendants, victims of crimes, the public, *and* potential witnesses. The details of how to implement the power of subpoena are not something to be addressed in a constitution. They should be worked out in the courts and through legislation.

So, based on the discussion on the Sixth Amendment, the following amendment must be made to the Constitution: Amendment XLVIII—The phrase "but any counsel provided by the government shall be limited to no more than the minimum necessary to achieve justice and counsel shall not be provided by the government in civil trials" shall be added after "defence" in the sixth article of amendment to the Constitution of the United States. Henceforth, the last clause shall read as follows: and to have the Assistance of Counsel for his defence but any counsel provided by the government shall be limited to no more than the minimum necessary to achieve justice and counsel shall not be provided by the government in civil trials.—BPS

Amendment VII

In Suits at common law, where the value in controversy shall exceed twenty dollars, the right of trial by jury shall be preserved, and no fact tried by a jury, shall be otherwise re-examined in any Court of the United States, than according to the rules of the common law.

Amendment VIII

Excessive bail shall not be required, nor excessive fines imposed, nor cruel and unusual punishments inflicted.

Amendment IX

The enumeration in the Constitution, of certain rights, shall not be construed to deny or disparage others retained by the people.

Amendment X

The powers not delegated to the United States by the Constitution, nor prohibited by it to the States, are reserved to the States respectively, or to the people.

CONCLUDING REMARKS ON THE
REVISION OF THE BILL OF RIGHTS

The important changes to the Bill of Rights include protecting the freedom *from* religion and strengthening the freedom of thought and association. They also include strengthening the right to keep and bear arms. In addition, they strengthen private property rights by preventing the government from taking private property. Finally, they place a limit on the provision of counsel by the government. These changes help to better secure the protection of individual rights. The next chapter addresses the rest of the existing amendments to the Constitution.

NOTES

1. The Bill of Rights were obtained from the National Archives and Records Administration website, http://www.archives.gov/exhibits/charters/bill_of_rights.htm l (accessed May 18, 2016).

2. Rand, *Philosophy*, pp. 66 and 70.

3. The quotation from Jefferson is from a letter he wrote to the Danbury Baptist Association, 1802. See Adrienne Koch and William Peden, editors, *The Life and Selected Writings of Thomas Jefferson* (New York: The Modern Library, 1998), p. 307. On the quotation from the Supreme Court, see *Everson v. Board of Education of Ewing Township*, 330 U.S. 1, p. 18 (1947).

4. For more on this topic, see Tara Smith, *Judicial Review in an Objective Legal System* (New York: Cambridge University Press, 2015), pp. 255–57.

5. Talal Itani, translator, *Quran in English*, https://www.clearquran.com/dow nloads/quran-in-english-clearquran.pdf (accessed April 24, 2019). See chapter 9, verse 5 on p. 139 of the document.

6. *Holy Bible*, Revised standard version (Nashville, TN: Thomas Nelson, Inc., 1972), Deuteronomy, chapter 13, verses 6–9, pp. 168–69.

7. For more on the nature of religious freedom, see Craig Biddle, "Weighing Gary Johnson for President," August 29, 2016, https://www.theobjectivestandard.co m/2016/08/weighing-gary-johnson-for-president/ (accessed March 3, 2018). See the comment section as well.

8. Of course, speaking and writing help further thought as well. For example, discussing one's ideas with others can help an individual identify correct ideas and thus help improve one's thinking. Therefore, the freedom of speech is crucial to the freedom of thought. For more on this relationship, see Craig Biddle, "Freedom of Speech is Freedom to Think," September 19, 2017, https://www.theobjectivestanda rd.com/2017/09/freedom-of-speech-is-freedom-to-think/ (accessed March 4, 2018).

9. On the belief that the Bill of Rights was unnecessary, see Sandefur, *The Conscience of the Constitution*, p. 112.

10. *NAACP v. Alabama*, 357 U.S. 449, pp. 461–62 (1958).

11. *Heart of Atlanta Motel, Inc. v. United States*, 379 U.S. 241, pp. 241–42, 250–51, and 253–58 (1964).

12. *Runyon v. McCrary*, 427 U.S. 160, pp. 160–61 and 175–76 (1976).

13. *Roberts v. United States Jaycees*, 468 U.S. 609, pp. 609–10, 621–24, and 628–29 (1984).

14. On the topics discussed in this paragraph, see Adam Thierer, "Advertising, Commercial Speech, and First Amendment Parity," *Charleston Law Review* vol. 5, no. 3 (2011), pp. 503–19.

15. Public universities should not be able to restrict speech on their campuses, since the government must treat everyone equally under the law. However, public universities would, of course, be able to set rules that speakers must follow to be approved to deliver their speeches (as long as those rules do not arbitrarily exclude some speakers or topics). Whether the government should own or operate universities is a separate and important question. See the discussion on education in chapter 8 for the answer.

16. Sanford Levinson asks essentially the same question in his article "The Embarrassing Second Amendment," *The Yale Law Journal* vol. 99, no. 3 (December 1989), pp. 637–59. See pp. 644–45.

17. On this interpretation of the second amendment, see Nelson Lund, "The Second Amendment, Political Liberty, and the Right to Self-Preservation," *Alabama Law Review* vol. 39 (1987), pp. 103–30. See pp. 105, 107–8, 111, and 122–23.

18. On this subject, see Don B. Kates, Jr., "Handgun Prohibition and the Original Meaning of the Second Amendment," *Michigan Law Review* vol. 82, no. 2 (November 1983), pp. 204–73. See pp. 214–18.

19. *United States v. Miller*, 307 U.S. 174, pp. 178–82 (1939).

20. See Kates, "Handgun Prohibition," pp. 214–51 for a thorough discussion of the evidence.

21. *District of Columbia v. Heller*, 554 U.S. 570, pp. 570–633 (2008).

22. For the examples mentioned, see John R. Lott, Jr., *More Guns, Less Crime: Understanding Crime and Gun-Control Laws*, 3rd edition (Chicago, IL: The University of Chicago Press, 2010), pp. 259–61, 306, and 315–17; and Richard Poe, *The Seven Myths of Gun Control: Reclaiming the Truth About Guns, Crime, and the Second Amendment* (Roseville, CA: FORUM, 2001), p. 64.

23. In particular, see Lott, *More Guns, Less Crime*, pp. vii, 20–21, 48–51, 164, 235, 259–64, 294–95, and 306–21. Also, see Poe, *The Seven Myths of Gun Control*, pp. 62–64, 94–97, and 100–1.

24. See Kates, "Handgun Prohibition," pp. 257–67 for a discussion of laws prohibiting the use of firearms that, in some cases, are consistent with the protection of individual rights.

25. Amy L. Peikoff, "Beyond Reductionism: Reconsidering the Right to Privacy," *New York University Journal of Law & Liberty* vol. 3, no. 1 (2008), pp. 1–47. See pp. 3, 5, and 43–44.

26. *Roe v. Wade*, 410 U.S. 113, pp. 114, 120, 129, 152–55, and 159 (1973).

27. Peikoff, "Beyond Reductionism," p. 35.

28. Ibid., pp. 15–16.

29. Ibid., pp. 24–46. The most relevant pages on these topics are pp. 38–40 and 43–46.

30. *Kelo v. City of New London*, 545 U.S. 469, pp. 469, 476, 494, and 500–1 (2005).

31. See Richard A. Epstein, *Supreme Neglect: How to Revive Constitutional Protection for Private Property* (Oxford: Oxford University Press, 2008), pp. 97–99.

32. On eminent domain, see Institute for Justice, "Myths and Realities of Eminent Domain Abuse" (June 2006), https://ij.org/wp-content/uploads/2015/03/CC_Myths _Reality-Final.pdf (accessed July 25, 2020).

33. For more on eminent domain, see Reisman, *Capitalism*, pp. 421–23.

34. On the connection between rights and economic progress, see Simpson, *Markets Don't Fail!*, pp. 5–26.

35. Laura K. Abel, "A Right to Counsel in Civil Cases: Lessons from *Gideon v. Wainright*," *Temple Political & Civil Rights Law Review* vol. 15 (2006), pp. 527–55. See pp. 527–29, 542, and 544.

36. For additional discussion of this and another justification for subpoena power, see The Association of Objective Law, "Highlights of TAFOL Panel Presentation at The Jefferson School: Subpoena Power," *Bulletin #3* (Spring 1989), pp. 2–3, http://www.tafol.org/bulletinsindex.html (accessed November 19, 2016).

37. For more discussion related to this topic, see Smith, *Judicial Review*, pp. 109–10.

Chapter 7

Revising Amendments XI through XXVII to the U.S. Constitution

INTRODUCTION

In this chapter, I focus on revising the last seventeen amendments to the Constitution. I address them in the order they were ratified. I follow the same procedural rules that I follow for the original portion of the Constitution. See the introduction to chapter 3 for these rules.

REVISING AMENDMENTS XI THROUGH XXVII

These amendments were ratified between 1795 and 1992. Interestingly, Amendment XXVII was proposed by Congress in 1789 as a part of the Bill of Rights. It was not ratified by the states until 1992. Here is my discussion of how to modify these amendments to make them fully consistent with the protection of individual rights.

Amendment XI[1]

The Judicial power of the United States shall not be construed to extend to any suit in law or equity, commenced or prosecuted against one of the United States by Citizens of another State, or by Citizens or Subjects of any Foreign State.

Amendment XII[2]

The Electors shall meet in their respective states and vote by ballot for President and Vice-President, one of whom, at least, shall not be an inhabitant of the same state with themselves; they shall name in their ballots the person voted for as

President, and in distinct ballots the person voted for as Vice-President, and they shall make distinct lists of all persons voted for as President, and of all persons voted for as Vice-President, and of the number of votes for each, which lists they shall sign and certify, and transmit sealed to the seat of the government of the United States, directed to the President of the Senate; – The President of the Senate shall, in the presence of the Senate and House of Representatives, open all the certificates and the votes shall then be counted; – The person having the greatest number of votes for President, shall be the President, if such number be a majority of the whole number of Electors appointed; and if no person have such majority, then from the persons having the highest numbers not exceeding three on the list of those voted for as President, the House of Representatives shall choose immediately, by ballot, the President. But in choosing the President, the votes shall be taken by states, the representation from each state having one vote; a quorum for this purpose shall consist of a member or members from two-thirds of the states, and a majority of all the states shall be necessary to a choice. [And if the House of Representatives shall not choose a President whenever the right of choice shall devolve upon them, before the fourth day of March next following, then the Vice-President shall act as President, as in case of the death or other constitutional disability of the President. —][3] The person having the greatest number of votes as Vice-President, shall be the Vice-President, if such number be a majority of the whole number of Electors appointed, and if no person have a majority, then from the two highest numbers on the list, the Senate shall choose the Vice-President; a quorum for the purpose shall consist of two-thirds of the whole number of Senators, and a majority of the whole number shall be necessary to a choice. But no person constitutionally ineligible to the office of President shall be eligible to that of Vice-President of the United States.

Amendment XIII[4]

Section 1

Neither slavery nor involuntary servitude, except as a punishment for crime whereof the party shall have been duly convicted, shall exist within the United States, or any place subject to their jurisdiction.

Section 2

Congress shall have power to enforce this article by appropriate legislation.

Amendment XIV[5]

Section 1

All persons born or naturalized in the United States, and subject to the jurisdiction thereof, are citizens of the United States and of the State wherein they reside. No State shall make or enforce any law which shall abridge the privileges or immunities of citizens of the United States; nor shall any State deprive any person of life, liberty, or property, without due process of law; nor deny to any person within its jurisdiction the equal protection of the laws.

BPS—The Privileges or Immunities Clause must be changed. It needs to be changed to ensure it is understood that what the state laws cannot abridge are rights. As discussed in connection with the Privileges and Immunities Clause of Article IV, Section 2, privileges and immunities did not start out in history being used to refer to rights. Further, once they began to refer to rights, they were not consistently used in this manner. Moreover, they are often used today to justify benefits to citizens that would violate individual rights. Hence, the need for the change.

In Article IV, I opted to place a qualifier on the Privileges and Immunities Clause to ensure the clause refers only to privileges and immunities that are consistent with the protection of rights. In Amendment XIV, "privileges or immunities" needs to be replaced with "rights." This replacement is necessary for a few reasons. First, the replacement is necessary so that the Constitution is made fully consistent with the protection of individual rights with as few changes as possible.

Furthermore, the Privileges and Immunities Clause in Article IV refers to the equal protection in each state of the rights of citizens from other states. As I mention in connection with my discussion in Article IV, citizens from one state, when traveling, doing business, temporarily residing, and so on in another state do not have all the same rights as citizens of that state. The use of "privileges and immunities" in Article IV makes it easier to distinguish between rights possessed by citizens of one state when visiting another state and rights possessed by citizens when in the state of which they are a citizen.

However, the Privileges or Immunities Clause of Amendment XIV refers to the equal protection by a state of the rights of its own citizens. It is not referring to a subset of rights (such as the privileges and immunities that out-of-state citizens possess) or a specific right (such as the privilege of the writ of habeas corpus). It is referring to the protection of individual rights in general. Therefore, it is more important here to use the term "rights."

Moreover, because the term "privileges or immunities" is used in an open-ended fashion to refer to all rights, it is more likely that the term could be misused in an attempt to provide privileges or immunities that violate rights, such as the "privilege" of having enough money to start out with in life as a young adult (a "privilege" mentioned in the discussion of Article IV, Section 2). The use of the term "rights" will help prevent misuse of the clause.

In addition to swapping out "privileges or immunities" for "rights," there is another modification of the Privileges or Immunities Clause that needs to be made. In the Supreme Court's decision in *The Slaughter-House Cases* (1873), rights were divided into the rights of citizens of the individual states and the rights of citizens of the United States. It was also concluded in the decision that the Privileges or Immunities Clause prevents the states from abridging the latter but not the former.[6] This interpretation significantly restricted the protection of rights the Privileges or Immunities Clause provided because the rights of citizens of the United States that were listed are a very narrow set of rights. They include the right to come to the seat of government and engage in business with it, to have access to the seaports, to protection of life, liberty, and property when on the high seas, among other rights.[7] However, state laws should be prevented from abridging all rights. It does not matter whether those rights are recognized through individuals' U.S. or state citizenship. Hence, the clause needs to be changed to ensure that no rights of either type of citizen are abridged by state law (which will essentially restore the meaning of the clause to what had existed based on how the clause was interpreted prior to *The Slaughter-House Cases* decision). To do this, the phrase "or its own citizens" must be added at the end of the Privileges or Immunities Clause. So the modified clause will read: No State shall make or enforce any law which shall abridge the rights of citizens of the United States or its own citizens.

The problem with the Fourteenth Amendment, as written, is that it says that states cannot abridge the privileges or immunities of U.S. citizens. Therefore, the Privileges or Immunities Clause focuses only on U.S. citizenship. The clause does not mention state citizenship. Hence, this amendment can be interpreted as providing no protection from states abridging the privileges or immunities that individuals possess based on their state citizenship. This is why it is necessary to make it explicit that both the rights individuals possess as U.S. and state citizens cannot be abridged by state law.

One last change that is necessary to Section 1 is that local governments, including both city and county governments, must be prevented from violating the rights of individuals, depriving individuals of due process of the law, and denying individuals equal protection of the law. While local governments are subsidiaries of state governments and thus the requirements for states to protect rights, provide due process, and provide equal protection of the law apply to local governments, local governments sometimes do not do these things (even with regard to already existing state laws).[8] Hence, it is important to explicitly state that these requirements apply to local governments to better ensure that they protect rights consistently.

Based on the discussion above, the next amendment to the Constitution shall read as follows: Amendment XLIX—The clause in Section 1 of the fourteenth article of amendment to the Constitution of the United States that says "No State shall make or enforce any law which shall abridge the privileges or immunities of citizens of the United States" shall be repealed and replaced with the following: No State shall make or enforce any law which shall abridge the rights of citizens of the United States or its own citizens. In addition, the following clause shall be added to the end of Section 1 of the fourteenth article of amendment to the Constitution of the United States: nor shall any local government make or enforce any law which shall abridge the rights of citizens of the United States or the several states, deprive any person of life, liberty, or property without due process of law, or deny to any person the equal protection of the law. Henceforth, the last sentence of Section 1 of the fourteenth article of amendment shall read: No State shall make or enforce any law which shall abridge the rights of citizens of the United States or its own citizens; nor shall any State deprive any person of life, liberty, or property, without due process of law; nor deny to any person within its jurisdiction the equal protection of the laws; nor shall any local government make or enforce any law which shall abridge the rights of citizens of the United States or the several states, deprive any person of life, liberty, or property without due process of law, or deny to any person the equal protection of the law.

Preventing the states from violating the rights of both U.S. citizens and their own citizens finishes the job of incorporating relevant rights in the Constitution so that they are all applicable to the states. The Supreme Court had been applying the Bill of Rights to the states through Amendment XIV using a selective process, where only certain rights within the Bill of Rights were deemed applicable to the states. Since the states can violate no rights now, no additional "incorporation" is necessary. With the changes made pertaining to local governments, the same applies to local governments as well.—BPS

Section 2

Representatives shall be apportioned among the several States according to their respective numbers, counting the whole number of persons in each State, excluding Indians not taxed. But when the right to vote at any election for the choice of electors for President and Vice-President of the United States, Representatives in Congress, the Executive and Judicial officers of a State, or the members of the Legislature thereof, is denied to any of the male inhabitants of such State, [being twenty-one years of age,][9] and citizens of the United States, or in any way abridged, except for participation in rebellion, or other crime, the basis of representation therein shall be reduced in the proportion which the number of such male citizens shall bear to the whole number of male citizens twenty-one years of age in such State.

Section 3

No person shall be a Senator or Representative in Congress, or elector of President and Vice-President, or hold any office, civil or military, under the United States, or under any State, who, having previously taken an oath, as a member of Congress, or as an officer of the United States, or as a member of any State legislature, or as an executive or judicial officer of any State, to support the Constitution of the United States, shall have engaged in insurrection or rebellion against the same, or given aid or comfort to the enemies thereof. But Congress may by a vote of two-thirds of each House, remove such disability.

Section 4

The validity of the public debt of the United States, authorized by law, including debts incurred for payment of pensions and bounties for services in suppressing insurrection or rebellion, shall not be questioned. But neither the United States nor any State shall assume or pay any debt or obligation incurred in aid of insurrection or rebellion against the United States, or any claim for the loss or emancipation of any slave; but all such debts, obligations and claims shall be held illegal and void.

Section 5

The Congress shall have the power to enforce, by appropriate legislation, the provisions of this article.

Amendment XV[10]

Section 1

The right of citizens of the United States to vote shall not be denied or abridged by the United States or by any State on account of race, color, or previous condition of servitude—

Section 2

The Congress shall have the power to enforce this article by appropriate legislation.

Amendment XVI[11]

The Congress shall have power to lay and collect taxes on incomes, from whatever source derived, without apportionment among the several States, and without regard to any census or enumeration.

BPS—This amendment needs to be abolished. As I state in the discussion of Article I, Section 8, only voluntary taxation is consistent with the protection of individual rights. The government may not use confiscatory means to obtain tax revenue. This includes taxing income. See Article I, Section 8 for the methods of financing the government that are acceptable. Based on this, the next amendment to the Constitution shall read as follows: Amendment L—The sixteenth article of amendment to the Constitution of the United States is hereby repealed.—BPS

Amendment XVII[12]

The Senate of the United States shall be composed of two Senators from each State, elected by the people thereof, for six years; and each Senator shall have one vote. The electors in each State shall have the qualifications requisite for electors of the most numerous branch of the State legislatures.

When vacancies happen in the representation of any State in the Senate, the executive authority of such State shall issue writs of election to fill such vacancies: *Provided,* That the legislature of any State may empower the executive thereof to make temporary appointments until the people fill the vacancies by election as the legislature may direct.

This amendment shall not be so construed as to affect the election or term of any Senator chosen before it becomes valid as part of the Constitution.

Amendment XVIII[13]

Section 1

After one year from the ratification of this article the manufacture, sale, or transportation of intoxicating liquors within, the importation thereof into, or the exportation thereof from the United States and all territory subject to the jurisdiction thereof for beverage purposes is hereby prohibited.

Section 2

The Congress and the several States shall have concurrent power to enforce this article by appropriate legislation.

Section 3

This article shall be inoperative unless it shall have been ratified as an amendment to the Constitution by the legislatures of the several States, as provided in the Constitution, within seven years from the date of the submission hereof to the States by the Congress.

Amendment XIX[14]

The right of citizens of the United States to vote shall not be denied or abridged by the United States or by any State on account of sex.

Congress shall have power to enforce this article by appropriate legislation.

Amendment XX[15]

Section 1

The terms of the President and the Vice President shall end at noon on the 20th day of January, and the terms of Senators and Representatives at noon on the 3d day of January, of the years in which such terms would have ended if this article had not been ratified; and the terms of their successors shall then begin.

Section 2

The Congress shall assemble at least once in every year, and such meeting shall begin at noon on the 3d day of January, unless they shall by law appoint a different day.

Section 3

If, at the time fixed for the beginning of the term of the President, the President elect shall have died, the Vice President elect shall become President. If a President shall not have been chosen before the time fixed for the beginning of his term, or if the President elect shall have failed to qualify, then the Vice President elect shall act as President until a President shall have qualified; and the Congress may by law provide for the case wherein neither a President elect nor a Vice President elect shall have qualified, declaring who shall then act as President, or the manner in which one who is to act shall be selected, and such person shall act accordingly until a President or Vice President shall have qualified.

Section 4

The Congress may by law provide for the case of the death of any of the persons from whom the House of Representatives may choose a President whenever the right of choice shall have devolved upon them, and for the case of the death of any of the persons from whom the Senate may choose a Vice President whenever the right of choice shall have devolved upon them.

Section 5

Sections 1 and 2 shall take effect on the 15th day of October following the ratification of this article.

Section 6

This article shall be inoperative unless it shall have been ratified as an amendment to the Constitution by the legislatures of three-fourths of the several States within seven years from the date of its submission.

Amendment XXI[16]

Section 1

The eighteenth article of amendment to the Constitution of the United States is hereby repealed.

Section 2

The transportation or importation into any State, Territory, or possession of the United States for delivery or use therein of intoxicating liquors, in violation of the laws thereof, is hereby prohibited.

BPS—Section 2 of Amendment XXI needs to be repealed. It has made possible the regulation of alcoholic beverages by the states (and local governments), including restricting sales from out-of-state suppliers and creating "dry" areas.[17] While Section 2 is interpreted by the Supreme Court today as granting a narrower set of powers to the states to regulate the production and consumption of alcoholic beverages than in the past, this could easily change.[18] The interpretations of the amendment by the courts have gone through wide swings.[19]

As I state in chapters 1 and 4, regulation of the economy violates rights through the government's initiation of physical force to achieve certain outcomes in the marketplace, such as limiting the prices goods can be purchased at and limiting the sale of alcoholic beverages. The manufacture, importation, transportation, sale, and consumption of alcoholic beverages, as such, do not violate individual rights. Rights-respecting individuals have the right to produce and consume alcoholic beverages. Hence, Section 2 of this amendment is a violation of freedom.

Repealing Section 2 will not prevent governments from passing laws to protect rights in connection with the consumption of alcoholic beverages. For example, if individuals drink and drive, they become a threat to others. Thus, it is proper for the government to pass laws banning this and similar activities. Likewise, if drunken individuals or drinking establishments disturb the peace or engage in disorderly conduct, it would be appropriate for the government to prosecute those who engage in such activities.

It may also be appropriate for the government to pass laws banning the sale and advertisement of alcoholic beverages to minors. Whether such laws are necessary depends on if minors are being routinely targeted by sellers of alcoholic beverages and whether minors engaging in the consumption of alcohol become a routine problem that endangers their lives and violates the rights of others. Establishing laws that prevent minors from drinking can be consistent with the protection of individual rights to the extent that minors are routinely harming themselves and violating the rights of others by consuming alcohol. As I state in chapter 3, children do not possess all the rights that adults possess because their conceptual faculty is not fully developed from a physiological standpoint. For example, they do not possess the right to engage in contractual relationships. Once they become adults and are fully developed physiologically, they have the tool—a fully developed human brain—to understand the implications of their decisions and make fully rational decisions. At that point, they acquire all the rights of fully functioning adults, including the right to determine what they will ingest.

As I allude to above, passing laws prohibiting minors from drinking and prohibiting the advertisement of alcoholic beverages to minors may not be necessary. Sellers may restrict the sale and advertisement of alcoholic beverages to minors to obtain good public relations, due to public pressure, or due to their own belief that minors should not consume the product (or be targeted by advertising). To keep the government limited to protecting rights, before it acts, it must be established that there is a proper basis for its actions. In this case, it must be established that rights are being violated or threatened or that individuals are acting outside the scope of their rights. If the issue can be dealt with through voluntary means, that is best. This is consistent with how it is often dealt with in Europe, since many European countries do not have a minimum legal age for consuming alcohol. However, if drinking by minors becomes a widespread threat to minors themselves and the rights of others, then the government is justified in taking action.

If Section 2 is repealed, it will help to prevent the states from regulating economic activity related to alcohol production and consumption. However, states regulated (and even banned in some cases) the use of alcohol long before Prohibition. Therefore, additional constitutional provisions are required to ensure the government does not violate individual rights in connection with alcohol. To ensure the freedom to engage in the production and consumption of alcoholic beverages, an amendment will be added to prevent the government from abridging the freedom of production and trade. This will apply to producing and trading in general, which, of course, includes producing and trading alcohol. An amendment will also be added to ensure individuals have control of their own bodies, including what they ingest. These amendments will be presented and discussed in chapter 8. The benefits of consistently protecting the right to produce and consume alcohol will also be discussed in chapter 8 in connection with a discussion of the war on drugs.

Based on the preceding discussion, the next amendment to the Constitution is as follows: Amendment LI—Section 2 of the twenty-first article of amendment to the Constitution of the United States is hereby repealed.—BPS

Section 3

This article shall be inoperative unless it shall have been ratified as an amendment to the Constitution by conventions in the several States, as provided in the Constitution, within seven years from the date of the submission hereof to the States by the Congress.

Amendment XXII[20]

Section 1

No person shall be elected to the office of the President more than twice, and no person who has held the office of President, or acted as President, for more than two years of a term to which some other person was elected President shall be elected to the office of the President more than once. But this Article shall not apply to any person holding the office of President when this Article was proposed by the Congress, and shall not prevent any person who may be holding the office of President, or acting as President, during the term within which this Article becomes operative from holding the office of President or acting as President during the remainder of such term.

Section 2

This article shall be inoperative unless it shall have been ratified as an amendment to the Constitution by the legislatures of three-fourths of the several States within seven years from the date of its submission to the States by the Congress.

BPS—Term limits are not consistent with the protection of individual rights. They are arbitrary restrictions placed on popular politicians. They are also not consistent with laws that treat people equally. They are essentially equivalent to bills of attainder. Laws should not single people out and punish them because they are popular. To have a system of laws in which people are equal before the law, once people reach the age of adulthood, they should be able to run for political offices regardless of how many times they have been re-elected.

It might be claimed that rights can be protected better by imposing term limits because politicians could gain too much power by remaining in office too long and exercise this power in a manner that violates rights. However, there is no inherent reason why a person in office for a long period of time would be more likely to violate rights (or not protect them adequately) relative to a person in office a short period of time. Whether a politician violates or protects rights depends on the type of ideas he embraces, not how many times he is re-elected. If a politician violates rights after holding office for a long period of time, the voters can vote him out of office (if they have retained any respect for protecting rights).

In fact, politicians who violate rights are voted into office by voters who want political leaders who violate rights. It is the fundamental ideas generally accepted in the culture—and thus generally accepted by voters and politicians—that lead both voters and politicians to want to violate (or respect) rights.[21] Term limits cannot change this. A change in the fundamental ideology that is prevalent in the culture is necessary to make such a change. If term limits are imposed in a society where rights are generally violated, one will merely end up with a series of politicians who want to violate rights being voted into office. You will not somehow magically end up with politicians in office who want to protect rights just because a new person must be elected periodically.

Finally, I considered briefly whether an amendment should be added to the Constitution to ban term limits. I rejected the idea. The issue of term limits is a minor issue; it is not a major inconsistency with the protection of rights. Hence, abolition of this amendment is adequate. Therefore, the next amendment to the Constitution shall read as follows: Amendment LII—The twenty-second article of amendment to the Constitution of the United States is hereby repealed.—BPS

Amendment XXIII[22]

Section 1

The District constituting the seat of Government of the United States shall appoint in such manner as the Congress may direct:

A number of electors of President and Vice President equal to the whole number of Senators and Representatives in Congress to which the District would be entitled if it were a State, but in no event more than the least populous State; they shall be in addition to those appointed by the States, but they shall be considered, for the purposes of the election of President and Vice President, to be electors appointed by a State; and they shall meet in the District and perform such duties as provided by the twelfth article of amendment.

Section 2

The Congress shall have power to enforce this article by appropriate legislation.

BPS—Amendment XXIII needs to be repealed and replaced with an amendment that fully recognizes the ability of citizens of the seat of the national government to vote and be represented. Fortunately, a proposal for such an amendment already exists. It was proposed in 1978. Unfortunately, the proposed amendment was not ratified by three-quarters of the state legislatures before it expired in 1985. The proposed amendment was House Joint Resolution 554 of the 95th Congress, submitted to the state legislatures on August 22, 1978. The article contained a provision requiring it to be ratified by three-quarters of the state legislatures within seven years of its submission to the states, or it would be inoperative.

The next amendment to the Constitution employs sections 1–3 of the 1978 article: Amendment LIII—Section 1: For purposes of representation in the Congress, election of the President and Vice President, and article V of this Constitution, the District constituting the seat of government of the United States shall be treated as though it were a State. Section 2: The exercise of the rights and powers conferred under this article shall be by the people of the District constituting the seat of government, and as shall be provided by the Congress. Section 3: The twenty-third article of amendment to the Constitution of the United States is hereby repealed.

The ability of all citizens of the United States to vote and be represented must be appropriately recognized. This is a part of achieving equality before the law, which is necessary to consistently protect rights.[23] Citizens of the District are subject to all provisions of the Constitution, all federal laws, and pay all federal taxes. However, they do not have voting representation in the House of Representatives and have no representation in the Senate. To achieve equality before the law, citizens of the District need the same voting representation in the House and Senate that any state with the same population would have. The District also needs to be able to participate in the process of amending the Constitution, as any state would be able to.

Other remedies for the lack of representation at the federal level for District citizens are not appropriate. One possibility is to grant statehood to the District. This means the federal government would not have exclusive legislative authority in the District constituting the seat of national government. It could lead to the very real problem, recognized by James Madison in *The Federalist* No. 43, of the national government not being able to protect its representatives. This occurred in 1783, when angry, unpaid Continental Army soldiers threatened the Confederation Congress meeting in Philadelphia in Independence Hall. Pennsylvania refused to provide assistance. Congress had to adjourn, and its members fled to New Jersey.[24] The proposed amendment would maintain legislative authority for Congress over the District.

Another possibility is for Congress to grant voting representation to the District through the legislative process. Under this approach, Congress could pass a law to enable residents in the District to vote for voting representatives in the House and Senate and to enable the District to participate in the

ratification process for amendments to the Constitution. This can be justified based on the Enclave Clause of the Constitution, since that clause gives
Congress the exclusive power to pass legislation affecting the District.[25]
However, the Constitution also states that the House of Representatives shall
be composed of members *chosen by the people of the several states*. Similar
language pertaining to Senators is used in Amendment XVII. In addition,
Article V refers to amendments to the Constitution being ratified by the
states. While there is nothing in the Constitution that says Congress cannot
pass legislation treating the District as if it were a state, since the Constitution
also contains provisions that are applicable specifically to the states, the constitutionality of Congress's authority to grant the ability to vote in federal
elections to the District and allow the District to participate in the ratification
process as if it were a state is unclear.

Ken Starr has argued that Congress has the authority to treat the District as
if it were a state.[26] He cites Supreme Court decisions that affirm the authority
of Congress to treat the District as a state in different contexts. According to
Starr, this sets the precedent for Congress to treat the District as a state for
voting purposes. However, also according to Starr, others have interpreted
the Constitution as not providing Congress the authority to treat the District
as a state for voting purposes.[27] Given that the controversy persists, the only
way to end it is to ratify a Constitutional amendment granting the ability to
vote in national elections and participate in the ratification of amendments to
residents of the District.

Another possibility is to cede the District back to Maryland (except for,
perhaps, the White House, Capitol, and Supreme Court) and have citizens of
the District vote in the national elections in that state and be represented by
that state in the process to ratify amendments. Another possibility is to treat
citizens of the District as if they are citizens of Maryland for the purpose of
voting in national elections. These proposals run into problems similar to the
proposals already discussed.

While citizens in the District should possess the ability to vote, Congress
should continue to have the exclusive power to enact legislation in the
District. The incident described above that occurred in Philadelphia in
1783 provides enough evidence to justify that provision of the Constitution.
However, Congress should certainly use its legislative power to enact laws
that protect the rights of citizens of the District and their ability to participate
in local self-governance. The revised Constitution, while not guaranteeing
any specific characteristics of the local government of the District, makes it
much easier for citizens of the District to protect their own rights.

Some might think that if the ability of citizens of the District to participate
in national elections and the ratification of amendments is protected that, to be
consistent, this ability should be protected for all U.S. territories, including,

for instance, Puerto Rico. However, protecting this ability in all U.S. territories cannot be extrapolated from its protection in the District. First, many U.S. territories do not pay all federal taxes, but the District does. Moreover, if they are unincorporated, the Constitution does not apply fully to them. The five permanently inhabited territories of the United States are currently unincorporated.[28] Since the District was formed from the cession of land from two states and it is the seat of the federal government, it is incorporated into the United States. Since the other territories being referred to here are unincorporated, they must gain the ability to vote in national elections and gain access to the amendment ratification process through the process of becoming a state.

Finally, the main concern with this new amendment pertains to how the District will be represented during the ratification of amendments. It would not be appropriate for Congress to be directly involved during the ratification process. The ratification process is reserved for the states. Fortunately, the amendment ensures that Congress will not become directly involved. Section 2 of the amendment states, "The exercise of the rights and powers conferred under this article shall be *by the people of the District constituting the seat of government*, and as shall be provided by the Congress" (emphasis added). It is clear that the rights and powers are to be exercised by the people of the District, not by Congress. The role of Congress is to pass appropriate legislation to enable the people of the District to exercise these rights and powers. So, while the specifics about *how* the rights and powers will be exercised are not provided in the amendment, the amendment makes clear *who* is to exercise the rights and powers. Congress will provide the specifics with regard to how.—BPS

Amendment XXIV[29]

Section 1

> The right of citizens of the United States to vote in any primary or other election for President or Vice President, for electors for President or Vice President, or for Senator or Representative in Congress, shall not be denied or abridged by the United States or any State by reason of failure to pay any poll tax or other tax.

Section 2

> The Congress shall have power to enforce this article by appropriate legislation.

BPS—This amendment needs to be modified to ensure that it applies not only to national elections but state and local elections as well. The amendment mentions only national elections, and while the Supreme Court held in

Harper v. Virginia State Board of Elections (1966) that poll taxes in state elections are unconstitutional because they violate the Equal Protection Clause of Amendment XIV, there were dissents in that case. The dissents were based on, among other reasons, the claim that the state poll tax is not irrational or unreasonable.[30] To prevent the Court from overruling itself in a later case, the amendment needs to be changed.

Why is a poll tax inappropriate? Here, we can, in essence, agree with Justice William Douglas, who wrote the opinion for the Court in *Harper*.[31] Wealth and income are not pertinent to whether one is capable or qualified to vote. Once a person has reached the legal age of adulthood, the ability to vote must be recognized for all citizens (except, perhaps, those individuals in prison). This is the point when they have reached full, physical maturity and possess all rights as human beings and citizens.

The dissenting opinions in *Harper* claimed in part that the government could rationally use the poll tax to raise revenue and ensure that voters were sufficiently interested in public affairs by requiring them to pay a tax. While it might be true that these are possible uses of the tax, one must remember that in a fully free society, taxation is voluntary. Hence, individuals cannot and should not be forced to pay a tax, whether as a requirement to vote or for any other purpose.

Some might argue that the voting process requires resources to provide and that all individuals should be required to help pay for these resources. A poll tax could certainly be used for this purpose. However, as stated in the discussion on Amendment XXIII, universal suffrage is the result of individuals being equal before the law. Poll taxes have been used to discriminate against poor people in the past, especially black people in the United States. There is no reason to believe this might not happen in the future. The way to prevent this from occurring is through an appropriate constitutional amendment.

In addition, while it is best that individuals be interested enough in government affairs to become sufficiently informed on the issues on which they are voting, each individual has the right to determine his own level of interest, sans the poll tax. Individuals should have the ability to participate in the process that determines the laws that will apply to them and that will elect the individuals who will create and enforce those laws. Individuals, whether rich or poor, will be subject to those laws and thus should have the ability to play a role in determining what those laws will be. Of course, this entire process must take place within the limits that the Constitution sets to ensure that the majority of voters do not violate the rights of the minority.

Based on this discussion, the next amendment shall read as follows: Amendment LIV—Section 1 of the twenty-fourth article of amendment to the Constitution of the United States shall be repealed and replaced with the following: The right of citizens of the United States to vote in any primary or other election for President or Vice President, for electors for President or Vice President, for Senator or Representative in Congress, or in any State or Local primary or election, shall not be denied or abridged by the United States or any State or Local Government by reason of failure to pay any poll tax or other tax.

The above amendment protects citizens from poll taxes being put into place by all levels of government. Notice that it does not say that everyone possesses the ability to vote. Voters must be able to understand the issues on which they are voting. They cannot do this if they do not have the mental competence to understand the issues. Hence, it is appropriate to prevent certain people from voting. This is true for children and those whose brains are defective or damaged and thus are incapable of thinking at the conceptual level of an adult, such as the mentally retarded. Provisions of the Constitution focusing on the ability to vote must sufficiently delimit the ability so that only those who can properly exercise it have the ability protected.

As mentioned previously, it may also be appropriate to limit or prevent voting by those adults who are in prison. That is because these people have broken the law and, as a part of the punishment, it might be appropriate to prevent them from participating in the voting process. This is especially true of those who have committed serious crimes. Why should such individuals be able to participate in the process pertaining to the establishment of the laws in a country if they have not obeyed the laws? Nonetheless, this is an optional issue. Either choice is consistent with the protection of individual rights.—BPS

Amendment XXV[32]

Section 1

In case of the removal of the President from office or of his death or resignation, the Vice President shall become President.

Section 2

Whenever there is a vacancy in the office of the Vice President, the President shall nominate a Vice President who shall take office upon confirmation by a majority vote of both Houses of Congress.

Section 3

Whenever the President transmits to the President pro tempore of the Senate and the Speaker of the House of Representatives his written declaration that he is unable to discharge the powers and duties of his office, and until he transmits to them a written declaration to the contrary, such powers and duties shall be discharged by the Vice President as Acting President.

Section 4

Whenever the Vice President and a majority of either the principal officers of the executive departments or of such other body as Congress may by law provide, transmit to the President pro tempore of the Senate and the Speaker of the House of Representatives their written declaration that the President is unable to discharge the powers and duties of his office, the Vice President shall immediately assume the powers and duties of the office as Acting President.

Thereafter, when the President transmits to the President pro tempore of the Senate and the Speaker of the House of Representatives his written declaration that no inability exists, he shall resume the powers and duties of his office unless the Vice President and a majority of either the principal officers of the executive department or of such other body as Congress may by law provide, transmit within four days to the President pro tempore of the Senate and the Speaker of the House of Representatives their written declaration that the President is unable to discharge the powers and duties of his office. Thereupon Congress shall decide the issue, assembling within forty-eight hours for that purpose if not in session. If the Congress, within twenty-one days after receipt of the latter written declaration, or, if Congress is not in session, within twenty-one days after Congress is required to assemble, determines by two-thirds vote of both Houses that the President is unable to discharge the powers and duties of his office, the Vice President shall continue to discharge the same as Acting President; otherwise, the President shall resume the powers and duties of his office.

Amendment XXVI[33]

Section 1

The right of citizens of the United States, who are eighteen years of age or older, to vote shall not be denied or abridged by the United States or by any State on account of age.

Section 2

The Congress shall have power to enforce this article by appropriate legislation.

Amendment XXVII[34]

No law, varying the compensation for the services of the Senators and Representatives, shall take effect, until an election of Representatives shall have intervened.

CONCLUDING REMARKS ON THE
REVISION OF AMENDMENTS XI–XXVII

As one can see, there are several changes that need to be made to the last seventeen amendments to the Constitution to make it consistent with the protection of individual rights and freedom. Six amendments in total are needed. These changes are presented along with the rest of the changes to the Constitution in Appendix B, without any intervening discussion. This way one can see the fully revised Constitution without interruption. First, however, in chapters 8 and 9, I present and discuss additional amendments that need to be made to strengthen the protection of individual rights and freedom that the Constitution provides.

NOTES

1. Passed by Congress March 4, 1794. Ratified February 7, 1795. Article III, Section 2 of the Constitution was modified by Amendment XI.

2. Passed by Congress December 9, 1803. Ratified June 15, 1804. A portion of Article II, Section 1 of the Constitution was superseded by Amendment XII.

3. Superseded by Section 3 of Amendment XX.

4. Passed by Congress January 31, 1865. Ratified December 6, 1865. A portion of Article IV, Section 2 of the Constitution was superseded by Amendment XIII.

5. Passed by Congress June 13, 1866. Ratified July 9, 1868. Article I, Section 2 of the Constitution was modified by Section 2 of Amendment XIV.

6. *The Slaughter-House Cases*, 83 U.S. 36, pp. 74–75 (1873).

7. Ibid., pp. 79–80.

8. For a recent example of local governments not enforcing a state law that protects rights more consistently, see Gary Robbins, "What You Need to Know about Buying Recreational Marijuana in San Diego," *The San Diego Union-Tribune*, November 10, 2017, https://www.sandiegouniontribune.com/news/science/sd-me -marijuana-qanda-20171108-story.html (accessed July 27, 2019).

9. Changed by Section 1 of Amendment XXVI. The copy of the Constitution I obtained from the National Archives and Records Administration website contained a note referring to the change in voting age from what is given in Amendment XIV. It did not contain a note referring to the change from only males being able to vote at the time Amendment XIV was ratified to both males and females being able to vote with the ratification of Amendment XIX. It also did not contain a note referring to the fact that Amendment XV supersedes the portion of Section 2 of Amendment XIV that states that representation will be reduced if the right to vote is denied to any male inhabitant (who is eligible to vote).

10. Passed by Congress February 26, 1869. Ratified February 3, 1870.

11. Passed by Congress July 2, 1909. Ratified February 3, 1913. Article I, Section 9 of the Constitution was modified by Amendment XVI.

12. Passed by Congress May 13, 1912. Ratified April 8, 1913. Article I, Section 3 of the Constitution was modified by Amendment XVII.

13. Passed by Congress December 18, 1917. Ratified January 16, 1919. Repealed by Amendment XXI.

14. Passed by Congress June 4, 1919. Ratified August 18, 1920.

15. Passed by Congress March 2, 1932. Ratified January 23, 1933. Article I, Section 4 of the Constitution was modified by Section 2 of this amendment. In addition, a portion of Amendment XII was superseded by Section 3.

16. Passed by Congress February 20, 1933. Ratified December 5, 1933.

17. For the ways in which Section 2 has made possible the regulation of alcoholic beverages, see John Foust, "State Power to Regulate Alcohol Under the Twenty-First Amendment: The Constitutional Implications of the Twenty-First Amendment Enforcement Act," *Boston College Law Review* vol. 41, no. 3 (2000), pp. 659–97. See pp. 660–61, 665, 686–88, 692–93, and 696–97. Also, see Jonathan M. Rotter and Joshua S. Stambaugh, "What's Left of the Twenty-First Amendment?," *Cardozo Public Law, Policy & Ethics Journal* vol. 6, no. 3 (Summer 2008), pp. 601–49. See pp. 609–10, and 644.

18. On the change in interpretation, see Foust, "State Power," pp. 679–86; and Rotter and Stambaugh, "What's Left," pp. 601–2 and 643–44.

19. For the wide variation in interpretations, see Rotter and Stambaugh, "What's Left," pp. 604 and 644.

20. Passed by Congress March 21, 1947. Ratified February 27, 1951.

21. For a discussion of the fundamental ideas that underlie (or undermine) the protection of rights, see chapter 1.

22. Passed by Congress June 16, 1960. Ratified March 29, 1961.

23. Ayn Rand, "Politics of a Free Society," Radio Interview of Ayn Rand (1965), https://campus.aynrand.org/works/1965/01/01/politics-of-a-free-society (accessed December 21, 2016).

24. On the incident in 1783, see Forte and Spalding, *The Heritage Guide*, p. 186.

25. See Article I, Section 8, Clause 17 of the Constitution, which states, "The Congress shall have Power . . . To exercise exclusive Legislation in all Cases whatsoever, over such District . . . as may . . . become the Seat of the Government of the United States . . . ."

26. See Kenneth W. Starr, "Testimony of the Hon. Kenneth W. Starr Before the House Government Reform Committee," *DC Vote*, June 23, 2004, http://www.dcvote.org/sites/default/files/kstarr062304_0.pdf (accessed December 17, 2016). See pp. 5–6.

27. Ibid., p. 5.

28. On the applicability of the Constitution and tax laws to U.S. Territories, see United States General Accounting Office, *Report to the Chairman, Committee on Resources, House of Representatives – U.S. Insular Areas: Application of the U.S. Constitution* (November 1997), https://www.gao.gov/archive/1998/og98005.pdf (accessed May 6, 2018). See, in particular, pp. 23–37.

29. Passed by Congress August 27, 1962. Ratified January 23, 1964.

30. *Harper v. Virginia State Board of Elections*, 383 U.S. 663, pp. 673–74, 677, and 684–85 (1966).

31. Ibid., p. 668.

32. Passed by Congress July 6, 1965. Ratified February 10, 1967. Article II, Section 1 of the Constitution was affected by Amendment XXV.

33. Passed by Congress March 23, 1971. Ratified July 1, 1971. Amendment XIV, Section 2 of the Constitution was modified by Section 1 of Amendment XXVI.

34. Originally proposed September 25, 1789. Ratified May 7, 1992.

Chapter 8

Additional Amendments to the Constitution, Part 1

INTRODUCTION

In this and the following chapter, I put forth amendments that do not repeal, replace, or revise specific parts of the Constitution or the amendments to the Constitution. There are a number of additional amendments to the Constitution that are required so that it consistently protects individual rights. They range from broad, sweeping amendments that protect very general rights (such as the right to produce and trade) to narrow amendments that protect very specific rights (such as free speech protection for contributions to political campaigns).

A constitution should be a very general document that is as brief as possible. This results from the nature of the document: it establishes the basic structure and function of the government. However, to ensure that rights are protected from those in a country who would most like to violate them, a sufficient number of important rights must be explicitly protected. This is particularly important for rights that have been routinely violated. A part of this protection includes making it as difficult as possible for judges to interpret the Constitution in a way that leads to violations of rights.

Enumerating specific rights might lead to some redundancy in the Constitution. For instance, explicitly stating that each person has the right to the control of his or her own body (Amendment LVI below) is a specific instance of a person's right to his or her life and liberty. However, as I have stated, redundancy is desirable (and necessary) in the protection of individual rights. One cannot merely state that the fundamental, abstract rights should be protected (such as the right to life and liberty) and expect them to be protected in all cases. If people want to violate rights, they will ignore and evade the meaning of the fundamental, abstract rights so that they can violate them.

Redundancy in the identification and protection of rights in the Constitution will do a better job protecting them. For example, it can provide multiple clauses in the Constitution that those who have had their rights violated can refer to as a means to protect their rights. They can make stronger arguments in their favor that will be harder to ignore. It will also educate people on the nature of rights and provide a guide to help people recognize and protect rights not named.

By not naming all rights, some might be concerned that some rights will go unprotected. This was a concern of the Framers in creating a Bill of Rights. That is why they included Amendment IX in the Bill of Rights. It would be impossible to list all rights in the Constitution (and inappropriate to do so even if you could). It would make the Constitution too long and move it away from its purpose. The rights listed in the Constitution must be limited to the fundamental rights and important rights that are routinely violated. If other rights end up being routinely violated, they could be added. Of course, such rights could also be protected by passing legislation to protect them.

Let us now begin the discussion on the additional amendments needed to make the Constitution fully consistent with the protection of individual rights. In this chapter, I do not present the proposed amendments in block quotation format and I do not bracket my discussion of the amendments with my initials, unlike in previous chapters where I present the text of the Constitution and my discussion of it using these methods. The proposed amendments, in this chapter, are differentiated from the discussion of them by italicizing the amendments.

ADDITIONAL AMENDMENTS TO
THE CONSTITUTION

Amendment LV

No law shall be made abridging the freedom of production and trade. No law shall also be made abridging the freedom to choose to not trade with others.

The first of the new amendments focuses on the right most in need of protection: the right to produce and trade. This is the right that is most routinely violated today, whether it is violated through minimum wage laws, pro-labor union legislation, licensing laws, environmental regulations, building codes and zoning laws, financial and banking regulations, and many more regulations imposed on individuals and businesses by a multitude of regulatory agencies. This is the one change to the Constitution identified in Ayn Rand's *Atlas Shrugged.*[1] By protecting this right, the productive capability and standard of living will rise dramatically for everyone in the United States. It will be easier to get a job, gain skills, open a business, expand one's business, develop products, innovate, build and buy residential housing, and so forth. It will be much easier to support oneself and the people one cares about.[2]

It is important to ensure that no government in the United States, whether federal, state, or local, can violate the right to produce and trade (and to not trade). As I discuss in chapter 7, the Bill of Rights has been applied to the states by the Supreme Court through Amendment XIV, but not all rights within the Bill of Rights have been applied to the states. Amendment XLIX, discussed in chapter 7, requires state and local governments to protect all rights. But Amendment XLIX is an abstract statement. Amendment LV provides a concrete example of one right that needs to be protected and will better ensure the protection of this important right, as well as the protection of rights in general. Moreover, even though local governments are essentially subordinate governments to state governments, and thus any relevant law applying to the states applies to local governments, to ensure rights are fully protected, it is important to make sure this law applies to local governments. As I mention in chapter 7, there have been cases of local governments ignoring state law. Stating that "no law shall be made" ensures that this amendment can be applied to any level of government, whether federal, state, or local, that violates the amendment.

It is also important to understand the full meaning of the right to produce and trade. It means, for instance, that people in the United States can trade with foreigners if they wish, including by hiring immigrants, producing goods abroad and selling them back in the United States, and importing goods produced by foreign companies. Voluntary trade with foreigners or immigrants, in and of itself, does not violate the rights of anyone, and thus the government has no business restricting it.

Free international trade and free immigration are enormous economic benefits to Americans. Let me briefly discuss the benefits of free international trade here. I will discuss the benefits of free immigration in this chapter in connection with Amendment LIX, which protects the right of foreigners to immigrate to the United States. Free international trade is a benefit because it raises the productive capability and standard of living by allowing people to gain access to goods that can be produced at a lower cost in other countries or that cannot be produced at all in the country that imports them (such as oil or minerals that do not exist in the country). This means a greater supply of goods will exist in the country that imports the goods and a higher standard of living will be achieved.

Free international trade does *not* cause unemployment. Jobs will be eliminated in sectors of the economy that cannot compete with foreign manufacturers. But jobs will be created in areas that export goods to other countries. In addition, jobs will be created in areas that experience greater demand because of the savings those in the United States will experience from the less expensive foreign goods. This savings can be used, in whole or in part, to purchase U.S. made goods. More significantly, jobs will be created as businesses in the United States that use less expensive foreign inputs expand or are formed (and would not have been able to expand or form otherwise). This latter is a significant job creator because more than 50 percent of all imports are used by businesses as inputs.[3] The net result is that free international trade is neutral to employment. It creates jobs in more efficient domestic industries and eliminates jobs in inefficient domestic industries. The key is that labor markets remain free so workers can leave industries in which jobs are eliminated and enter industries in which jobs are created.

In addition, we do *not* lose money from international trade, even if we have a trade deficit. With our fiat money, which for the most part is spent only in the United States, the money spent on imports comes back to the United States in the form of loans, other investments, or spending on goods and services in the United States. Imports do not constitute a loss because we obtain the goods. Consider this: I have a trade deficit every week with the grocery store—I buy goods from the grocer but he does not buy any goods from me—but that is not a loss to me because I obtain food to eat.[4] The same, in terms of essentials, is true with regard to international trade.

Trade with foreigners is a benefit for the same reason that trade with people in other states, counties, cities, or the people next door is a benefit. It takes better advantage of the division of labor, which increases efficiency and the production of wealth. If free international trade is harmful because it creates losses in terms of money or jobs, then logically we should stop all trade. If Californians import goods from Nevadans, this would allegedly cause Californians to lose jobs and money to Nevadans. Similarly, if residents of San Diego County import goods from the Imperial County, San Diego County allegedly loses jobs and money. Likewise for residents of cities, neighborhoods, and individual homes. According to the arguments of the anti-free traders, we should produce all goods on our own. This, of course, would be disastrous to our standard of living.

Trade is beneficial because it is a win-win relationship. *Both sides* gain from the trade. That's why people engage in trade. If they did not stand to gain, they would not trade. I gain when I trade with the person next door, in the next city, county, state, or in another country. It is restrictions on trade, such as tariffs, that are harmful. They make goods more expensive by forcing us to pay tariffs (i.e., taxes) on imported goods and by keeping inefficient domestic producers in business due to protection from the tariffs.

Furthermore, by engaging in free international trade, we do not import lower wages from poorer countries. Our higher wages exist because of the greater skills and abilities of the workforce and, more importantly, the greater supply of capital goods we possess (such as machines and devices) and the more advanced technology we use. All of these lead to a higher productivity of labor—a greater ability of individual workers to produce. As productivity goes, so goes real wages. Imports that we obtain at lower costs enhance real wages because they increase the supply of goods available to individuals.

While it is true that there might be short-run losses for some Americans who compete with the more efficient foreigner producers, the overwhelming majority of the population will not be competing with the foreigners and will stand to benefit *immediately* from the imported goods. Moreover, even those who lose in the short-run gain in the long-run. Their standard of living rises in the long-run due to the overall greater productive capability and rate of economic progress.

Nonetheless, those Americans who lose in the short-run do not have the right to, in essence, reach for a gun and force other Americans to pay tariffs to get them to buy domestic producers' inefficiently made products. This, of course, is a violation of rights. We have no duty to "buy American." We should buy the best products we can find at the lowest prices, regardless of who produces them. The only morally and economically sound trade policy for a country to follow is one of unilateral free trade. Through this policy, we benefit from free trade regardless of how other countries might harm their own economies with tariffs and quotas.[5]

One issue that has arisen in the last few years in connection with international trade is the infringement of intellectual property rights by the Chinese. This is a problem that must be addressed. The "solution" that is generally put forward is to restrict trade with the Chinese. However, it should be clear by now that we punish ourselves with trade restrictions because we make it harder to obtain goods that Americans prefer to purchase from the Chinese. The proper solution to the infringement of intellectual property rights is to punish, enjoin, and/or obtain compensation from the perpetrators through appropriate legal action (whether civil or criminal and whether through Chinese, American, and/or international courts). To the extent that intellectual property rights need to be protected in a better fashion in China, the Chinese should be pushed to reform their laws. But violating the rights of Americans who want to buy Chinese goods is not justified to attempt to stop the Chinese violations of intellectual property rights.

Another issue that has received attention recently is how we allegedly need restrictions on international trade to improve the stability of our supply chains. This issue has been raised in connection with the COVID-19 pandemic due to the difficulty of obtaining some products from foreign manufacturers (such as some medical equipment). However, one does not need trade restrictions to improve the stability of a company's or industry's supply chain. In fact, trade restrictions make supply chains less stable because they eliminate potential sources of goods and make goods more expensive. If a supply chain becomes unstable, companies must be left free to make adjustments on their own to improve its stability. But the stability of the supply chain is not the only factor that must be taken into consideration by companies when choosing from whom to purchase their inputs. They must also take into account, among other factors, cost and quality. It is in the self-interest of companies to take all necessary factors into account when making purchases because that is what helps them run profitable businesses. But trade restrictions, due to the higher costs and more limited options they impose on businesses, make it harder to run successful businesses. They therefore make it harder for people to get the goods they need not only to fight disease but also to live their lives in general.

Lastly in connection with international trade, some state that we should produce some products in the United States for national security reasons and that limiting imports of these products can help to achieve this goal. For example, based on this view, some claim we should produce more military hardware and, as stated by some during the COVID-19 pandemic, more medical equipment in the United States. But this does not require trade restrictions. The main purpose of the government is to protect rights. If the government determines that it is best to buy products needed to protect rights from manufacturers in the United States, it can easily do that. All it needs to do is pay prices that make it profitable for firms to produce the products here.[6] Nonetheless, it may be a more effective alternative to buy the less expensive foreign-made products and stockpile them to use during emergencies. Whatever the government does, it should not rationalize violating the rights of Americans based on the pretense that the violations are needed for national security.[7]

The right to produce and trade also means individuals have the right to produce and trade illicit goods, including illicit drugs. While I strongly object to the use of such drugs because their use is harmful to human life and thus irrational, people have the right to use them so long as their use is not involved with violating the rights of others. This means, for instance, that driving under the influence would still be illegal because it threatens the rights of others.

Also, children can properly be prevented from using drugs. As I discuss in chapter 3, because children are not fully developed physiologically and thus do not have a fully developed rational faculty, they do not possess all the rights of adults. Children do not have the mental tools to understand all the implications of their actions, including using illicit drugs. The rights they possess must recognize this conceptual context.

The right to trade also applies to prostitution. Let me make it clear that I am staunchly opposed to prostitution because it devalues sex. It devalues sex because it rejects the integration of mind and body that sex represents to a rational individual. One should select sexual partners based on both physical *and* rational mental attributes (intelligence, wit, kindness, sense of humor, etc.). One should not reduce sex to a mere physical act, like a dog does when it humps a person's leg.[8] However, as long as prostitution occurs between consenting adults, it violates no one's rights and should be legal. The government has no right to stop it. The same is true of pornography. Again, of course, these rights do not apply to children.

It is important to protect the right of adults to engage in depraved activities. These are areas that are the most vulnerable to rights being violated by the government because people should not be engaging in these activities. Hence, these areas are the easiest places for statists to start violating rights and thus begin the process of creating a statist government—one that generally violates rights.

Ultimately, the purpose of protecting the rights of individuals to engage in depraved activities is not to make it possible for irrational people to engage in such activities. The purpose of protecting the rights of the irrational is to recognize that rights must be protected on principle. Rights are not protected if the principle one acts on is: I'll protect the right of people to engage in activities I think are acceptable. Such a society operates not on the principle of protecting individual rights but on the principle that violating rights is acceptable (at least to some extent).

Allowing the violation of rights, by the government, of those who engage in depraved activities puts a society on the path to justifying greater violations of rights. For example, many people think earning large profits from, say, producing and selling prescription drugs is not acceptable. In fact, some people believe that earning *any* profits is unacceptable. If the government can prevent activities merely because they are considered "unacceptable," then no activity is safe from the government banning it, even rational, life-supporting activities. Hence, protecting the rights of the irrational, ultimately, is necessary to protect the rights of the rational. And as ironic as it might seem to some people, if we achieve a level of rationality in our culture such that we recognize and protect the right of individuals to engage in irrational activities, the frequency of occurrence of such activities will be greatly reduced. Of course, such an outcome is not, in fact, ironic. It is not ironic because such activities are *irrational* and will therefore not be engaged in by the rational individuals who exist in larger numbers in a more rational culture.

There will be a number of concrete beneficial effects to legalizing illicit activities. One benefit is that crime will decrease. For instance, evidence suggests that the murder rate in the United States is 25–75 percent higher due to drugs being illegal.[9] Violence and crime increase when drugs are prohibited because the prices of drugs increase dramatically and, as a result, criminal gangs who are willing to evade the law to provide the outlawed substances that are still demanded are enriched with the large profits they can make. Such gangs often engage in violence to protect their profits (i.e., they engage in turf wars to preserve their market share), and the large profits give them far more resources with which to engage in such battles. Increased crime, including murder rates, was clearly seen during Prohibition in the United States.[10] More recently, violence in Mexico has increased dramatically since that country has engaged in far tougher law enforcement against the illegal drug trade.[11]

In addition, more crime is often engaged in by the users of the banned substances to obtain the extra money that is needed to pay the higher prices for the drugs.[12] Estimates for cocaine show that its price is twenty times higher because it is illegal and that alcohol was three times more expensive during Prohibition than prior to that period.[13] This requires a significant amount of extra money to finance one's drug habit and can lead to significant increases in crime.

Some might think that large increases in the quantity of drugs consumed will occur when drugs are legalized because drug prices will be dramatically lower. While it is true that one would expect to see increases in the quantity demanded, the increases will probably be smaller than most people expect because drugs have what economists call inelastic demand. That is, the quantity demanded does not increase that much for a large decrease in price. This is probably why after Prohibition ended alcohol consumption in the United States did not rise dramatically. In fact, it remained approximately constant.[14]

One does not eliminate the demand for products that are made illegal. One just pushes the provision of the product to the black market. Along with this comes the attendant corruption of political officials and law enforcement when criminal gangs seek to pay off local politicians and police officers to "look the other way."[15] Of course, the criminal gangs have far more money to pay off officials due to the high profits that can be made from selling the illegal substances. Injury and death due to tainted products become more frequent as well, since people cannot seek remedy through the court system from harm caused by contaminated products in illegal industries. Lack of access to the court system leads to lower quality products because potential lawsuits from customers provide an incentive for firms to produce higher quality products to avoid the potential lawsuits.

Billions of dollars are spent by the government each year to enforce drug laws: almost $50 billion annually in the United States.[16] Budgets for the so-called war on drugs have been increased massively. From 1971 to 2015, the federal government's budget for the war on drugs increased from $100 million ($575 million in 2015 prices) to $26 billion—and we are no closer to eliminating drug use![17] With every drug seizure by law enforcement, prices are increased, which provides a stronger incentive for criminal gangs to produce and sell the banned substances. Furthermore, hundreds of thousands of people are incarcerated for drug law violations—offenses that do not violate the rights of anyone! The number incarcerated has increased by a factor of nine from 1980 to 2016: 50,000 to 450,000.[18]

The solution to reducing drug use is not a policy of forcibly trying to prevent people from producing and consuming drugs. That policy, by its very nature, must fail abysmally, so it is no accident that that is exactly what has happened. The solution involves teaching people a rational philosophy that will enable them to think long-range, embrace life-promoting values, and take responsibility for their actions. Such a philosophy teaches them that if they make bad decisions, they will suffer the consequences, including being punished for violating the rights of others, whether the violations of rights are drug related or not. More importantly, it teaches them that life requires rational thought and action, and they will reap the rewards of thinking and acting in a rational manner. Fortunately, such a philosophy has been developed. It is the philosophy of Objectivism, developed by Ayn Rand.

It is important to highlight that Amendment LV protects not only the right *to* trade but the right *not* to trade. It recognizes that individuals should not be forced to trade with anyone with whom they do not want to trade. Forcing people to trade when they do not want to initiates physical force against them and violates their rights. Given the existence of affirmative action laws and other "antidiscrimination" laws, as well as recent violations of rights that have occurred in the form of forcing bakers and florists to provide their services to gay and lesbian couples for their weddings, this is an important right to explicitly protect.

Before discussing this issue further, I must emphatically state that I am staunchly opposed to discrimination, such as that based on race, gender, and sexual preference. Such discrimination should be morally condemned because it represents an abandonment of the mind and thus stands in opposition to the requirements of human life, since our mind is our basic tool of survival. Someone who judges others based on irrelevant characteristics or characteristics they have no control over (such as race) does not use his mind to judge others based on the abilities people possess that are relevant to a job or their ability to pay for a product or service.

Even so, it is within a person's rights to refuse to do business with others for irrational reasons, so long as he does not violate the rights of others. If he burns a cross on someone's property or attacks an individual because of the individual's race or sexual preference, he should be punished for such a violation of rights. However, if he merely prefers not to do business with certain individuals and exercises this preference in a peaceful, rights-respecting manner, he is acting fully within his rights.

One must remember that protecting rights implies voluntary trade. Voluntary trade involves both sides agreeing to the trade. If I choose not to trade with others, I do not initiate physical force against them and thus I do not violate their rights. They are free to trade with someone else or produce the good on their own. However, if the government forces me to trade with people that I do not want to trade with, the government is the first user of force and thus violates my rights.

Even though discrimination based on racism, sexism, sexual preference, and so on would be legal in a free society, such a society would discourage discrimination. Moreover, such a society is the only society fundamentally inconsistent with discrimination. How could this be so? How could a society in which discrimination is legal be fundamentally incompatible with discrimination?

First, free trade punishes discrimination. For example, if an employer hires based on race, he will lose access to the pool of talent in all the racial groups he discriminates against. He will even lose access to the talent of those individuals in the racial groups he is willing to hire but who do not want to work for a bigot. This will put him at a competitive disadvantage relative to those employers who hire the best workers, regardless of their race. His competitors will have access to a larger pool of talent to the degree he discriminates.

In addition, if one is only willing to sell to specific racial groups, he will reduce his potential customer base by refusing to sell to individuals who are willing and able to purchase the product but who belong to the racial groups to which he refuses to sell. He also loses as potential customers those in the racial groups he is willing to sell to but who do not want to do business with a bigot. Again, this will put such a seller at a competitive disadvantage relative to those who are willing to sell to anyone—regardless of the person's race—as long as the person is willing and able to purchase the good.

In a free market, if one wants to do well in business, one judges others based on their ability and willingness to pay, whether they are qualified for a job, or other rational standards. Judging others by race or any other irrational standard will tend to lead to failure. As a result, those who discriminate will tend to become less influential in a free market. Hence, a free market tends to eliminate racism, and other forms of discrimination, due to the economic motivations involved.[19]

Even though economic incentives tend to eliminate racism, they cannot, by themselves, completely eliminate racism and other forms of discrimination. That requires eliminating the underlying racism, sexism, and other prejudices people embrace, which brings me to a more fundamental issue underlying discrimination: individualism versus collectivism.

A free society is based on individualism. Individualism says the individual is the fundamental unit of value. It says each individual is an end in himself, not a means to the ends of others. It says each individual has a right to his own life and the right to live it as he sees fit, based on the judgment of his own mind. Individualism also requires that one judge others based on their abilities, not based on their membership in some group or collective (such as their race or gender). As a result, a free society is antithetical to discrimination.

To see this even more clearly, one must understand that discrimination is based on collectivism. A person's value or character, according to collectivism, is determined by accidental or irrelevant characteristics, such as the person's genetic lineage, gender, or sexual preference. Accordingly, collectivism says that one should judge individuals not based on their own merits or lack thereof but on their membership in some group, such as their race or gender. Stated differently, with collectivism, one does not judge others based on rational considerations, such as the characteristics they possess that are relevant to a job (i.e., whether they have the ability to perform the tasks required of the job, whether they are responsible and hardworking, and so forth). According to collectivism, one judges others based on irrational considerations. This is an abandonment of one's mind; it is an abandonment of the basic human tool of survival: reason.

So, a free society is based on underlying ideas—such as individualism and the acceptance of reason as our basic means to knowledge—that lead to a rejection of discrimination and the collectivism on which it is based. This means that not only do the economic incentives in a free society discourage discrimination, but discrimination is inconsistent with the ethical and epistemological foundations of a free society. A free society is economically, politically, ethically, and epistemologically opposed to discrimination.

I must highlight here, as I did previously, that protecting the rights of the irrational is not an end in itself but a means to an end. It is the means of protecting the freedom of rational individuals. This is no less true with regard to discrimination than it is with regard to the use of depraved goods. The protection of freedom will enable the rational to prevail over the irrational.

In fact, a free society cannot be achieved without significant elements of rationality existing in a culture because rationality is needed to, among other things, identify that freedom is a fundamental requirement of human life. So, rationality and freedom are reinforcing. Rationality requires freedom and freedom requires rationality.

It is also important to recognize that force is no substitute for rationality. Force perpetuates irrationality because it rejects the requirements of the mind. The mind requires freedom so people can use their minds to weigh the evidence, draw logical conclusions, act based on those conclusions, and succeed at living their lives. Those who want to forcibly prevent discrimination have the abandonment of reason in common with those who engage in discrimination. The latter reject judging others based on rational considerations, primarily the ability of individuals to use their minds, while the former reject the conditions that rational thought and action require.

Moreover, antidiscrimination laws force people to discriminate based on criteria such as race and gender. For example, laws that require employers to hire based on race or gender, such as laws that require hiring certain quotas of workers of a particular race or gender, require employers to judge workers, at least in part, based on their skin color or gender to ensure that the employers do not violate the law. Hence, such laws are racist and sexist laws. They will not end racism and sexism. One does not solve the problem of racism and sexism with more racism and sexism. To end racism and sexism, one needs to abandon judging others based on race and gender regardless of the reason for judging others based on those criteria (i.e., regardless of whether one wants to hire or not hire—or reward or punish—people based on their race or gender).

As contradictory as it might seem, protecting the right of individuals to be racist, sexist, and so on is the means to eliminating racism, sexism, and other forms of irrationality. Attempting to forcibly prevent individuals from engaging in irrational behavior that does not violate rights merely perpetuates it. Of course, there is, in fact, no contradiction. There only appears to be a contradiction to those who do not understand the requirements of reason. Protecting rights places logic and facts above all other considerations. It reserves the highest place for the one tool that makes the elimination of racism and sexism—and any form of irrationality—possible: reason.

In a free society, those who choose not to go by reason can be ignored. They cannot legally violate rights, and their numbers will be small. They can be left to stagnate together, while the rest of society leaves them behind.[20]

Finally, it is important to note that the right to discriminate does not apply to the government. That is, the government is not free to discriminate. It must protect the rights of *all* individuals equally. Protecting rights requires equality before the law and equality before the law means the law is color-blind (as well as gender blind, sexual-preference blind, religion blind, etc.). It violates individual rights (or sanctions violations of rights) to apply the law in any other manner. Hence, the right to discriminate applies only to individuals and private entities (such as businesses, corporations, charities, religious organizations, schools, etc.).

Amendment LVI

The right of each individual to the control of his or her own body shall not be infringed, and the right to do as he or she chooses with his or her own person, including engaging in voluntary, consensual, or contractual relationships with others, shall not be infringed.

The wording of this amendment is taken from the constitution developed by Roderick T. Long. It employs some of the wording in Part Two, Sections 2.2.3 and 2.2.4.[21]

This amendment focuses on individuals being able to do what they choose with their own bodies. It is an exercise of a person's right to life and liberty. Even though these rights are already protected in the Constitution, this specific manifestation of these rights needs to be called out and protected since it has been routinely violated. These rights mean that individuals can put in their bodies what they want (including illicit drugs). It also means being able to put on—or not put on—their bodies what they want, including helmets and seatbelts, although private road owners could require the use of helmets and seatbelts as a condition for being able to use their roads. It means that individuals have the right to commit suicide and, along with the protection of the freedom to trade, to doctor-assisted suicide. Further, it means, along with the freedom to trade, that individuals have the right to sell their organs if they choose, whether while alive or after they die.

This amendment separately highlights the rights of men and women because in one important way it applies to men and women differently. I am referring here to a woman's right to terminate a pregnancy. Rights, properly understood, apply only to actual human beings. They do not apply to potential human beings, which means they do not apply to a fetus. A fetus is essentially a growth in a woman and is thus biologically dependent on the woman. It therefore has no rights. If we are to give rights to the fetus, then what about the rights of the pregnant woman? Why does the government get to force her to be an incubator for the fetus, as well as a mother to an unwanted child after the baby is born (assuming no one is willing to adopt the baby)?

It may be appropriate to limit how far into a pregnancy a woman can end her pregnancy. For example, it may be appropriate to limit the ability of women to obtain an abortion to the first trimester. I am not going to discuss that issue here. The point to emphasize here is that the right to an abortion is an exercise of a woman's right to her own life and liberty.

What limits should be placed on when a pregnancy can be terminated is a task for the legislature to decide. At some point, the woman must take responsibility for the fact that she has a potential human being growing inside her. Different limits on when an abortion can take place can be consistent with the protection of the rights of the woman. However, any limits must recognize that a woman's body is her own and she has the right to terminate a pregnancy as a result. Thus, the one limit that is not consistent with the protection of individual rights is altogether preventing women from terminating pregnancies. Women must be given sufficient time to learn that they are pregnant and make an informed decision regarding whether to terminate the pregnancy. Current laws in the United States that make it possible for women to do this through the first trimester give women adequate time. This is one of those areas in which different options can be employed to protect individual rights.[22]

The right to do what one wants with one's body and person includes the right to marry. This not only applies to traditional marriages but to same-sex marriages as well. Marriage is ultimately a contract between individuals to unite their lives. Hence, if two men or two women want to marry, it violates no one's rights and should be legal.

While the government must recognize the validity of same-sex marriages because they are ultimately contractual relationships between individuals and recognizing the legitimacy of such relationships is a part of treating everyone equally under the law, private organizations have no duty to recognize the validity of these relationships or sanction them in any way. Hence, if religious organizations do not want to perform such marriages or admit members into their ranks who have participated in such marriages, they have every right to refuse to perform such ceremonies, refuse to recognize the legitimacy of such relationships, and refuse to admit individuals involved in such marriages into their organizations. Relationships and agreements between individuals and private organizations are voluntary, thus all parties must agree to them. It would require the initiation of physical force to make individuals and organizations accept such marriages (and the people who participate in them) if they do not want to.

In addition, it may be that legally these relationships are recognized through different means. For instance, same-sex marriages may be recognized as civil unions or in other ways. However, the result must be the same: that the lives of the parties are united in the same way under the law.

The above rights generally do not apply to minors. For example, parents or guardians should generally decide whether minors should wear safety devices, such as seatbelts or helmets, or whether babies and small children should be placed in child-safety seats. However, if the lack of use of such devices routinely leads to children being physically harmed, it might be appropriate for the government to require the use of these devices.

Amendment LVII

No federal, state, or local government shall own, operate, or provide financial assistance or any other type of assistance to any commercial enterprise, educational enterprise, or private organization; nor shall it provide financial assistance or any other type of assistance to any individual or other government, unless such ownership, operation, or assistance is directly necessary for the protection of individual rights of citizens of the United States.

No federal, state, or local government shall provide assistance to individuals and organizations in the form of loans.

This amendment is based on Article III, Sections 3(a) and (b) and Article VI, Section 19 of Bernard Siegan's constitution presented in his book *Drafting a Constitution for a Nation or Republic Emerging into Freedom.*[23] Since the proper function of the government is to protect individual rights, it has no business owning, operating, or supporting in any way any organization, activity, or individual, including other governments, unless said ownership, operation, or support serves the function of protecting individual rights. One would think it would not have to be explicitly stated that the government must not be involved in these activities given that it is stated in the revised Constitution that the only proper function of the government is the protection of individual rights. However, given that people can ignore and evade the implications of the abstract statement of the government's proper functions, it must be explicitly stated to ensure as best as possible that rights are protected. It ends up creating redundancy in the constitution, but as I have stated before, redundancy in the protection of rights is not only good, it is necessary.

The list of organizations the government shall not own, operate, or support include post offices, universities and colleges, primary and secondary schools, vocational schools, fire departments, libraries, museums and galleries, and businesses. While not an exhaustive list, it does give an idea of the types of organizations with which the government should not be involved. These organizations do not protect individual rights. Likewise, the type of assistance the government shall not provide to individuals or organizations includes but is not limited to welfare (whether in the form of unemployment "insurance," Social Security, Temporary Assistance for Needy Families, food stamps, etc.), health care, bailouts, subsidies, and passing special laws that favor some individuals or businesses by violating the rights of others (such as laws restricting who can compete in a given trade, business, or geographic region).

This book would be too long if I tried to address the process by which government provision of all the things mentioned in the paragraph above should be eliminated or how private provision of these things would be beneficial economically and lead to improved quality of any services provided (to the extent the services should be provided at all), as well as an overall higher standard of living being achieved in the economy (even for welfare recipients). Fortunately, these issues are discussed in detail elsewhere by others (and me), although I do address the topics of Social Security and education below.[24]

Loans are called out specifically in the amendment because this is a widespread type of assistance the government provides, such as through mortgage loans and college loans (or the guaranteeing of such loans), that is not consistent with the government's appropriate function. The government should not be lending money (or guaranteeing loans) under any circumstances.

The exception, of course, to the government providing assistance (except for loans) involves cases in which the government might have to be involved to protect rights. The last clause of the main portion of the amendment has been added to make this as clear as possible. As an example, it is appropriate for the government to own and run military schools and academies. This involves training military leaders so they are prepared in the best possible way to protect rights. It might also be the case that the government determines that the best way to protect rights is to own an organization that produces various types of military hardware. In addition, the government might determine that owning and operating research organizations for the purpose of developing new technology for use by the military is the best way to develop technology needed for the purpose of defending rights. Furthermore, if the United States becomes involved in a war or conflict and the government determines that the best way to defend the rights of U.S. citizens is to fund governments, private organizations, or citizens in foreign lands to fight armies that threaten the rights of Americans, the government must have such options available to it. The litmus test is whether the government is engaging in the activity to protect rights.

Of course, intellectually dishonest people can rationalize many activities being performed by the government by claiming they are necessary to protect rights. For example, they could claim that general education (i.e., primary, secondary, and university education) must be provided by the government to protect rights. If people are not educated, it could be claimed, the country will not be ensured of having an educated populous who can advance science and technology that could be used to develop the necessary weapons to defend the country from potentially hostile nations. Government provision of primary and secondary education might also be rationalized based on the claim that the country could potentially not have enough properly educated young adults prepared to enter the military academies and thus, eventually, a shortage of capable people to run the military. This is why I add "directly" in front of "necessary." Educating military officers in the art of warfare so they can properly run the military is directly necessary to protect rights. Building weapons and developing technology to be used by the military is directly necessary to protect rights. However, having a generally educated population is not directly necessary. It is indirectly necessary. Educating the general population is one step removed from the military academies and organizations that develop weapons and technology used by the military. By restricting the government so that it can only be involved with activities that are directly necessary for the protection of rights, this clause will help the revised Constitution better restrict the activities of the government to its appropriate functions. We do not need to be concerned about having enough well-educated people in the country in a free market because the profit motive, freedom in the field of education (discussed below), and a greater ability to benefit from one's own talent and ability will provide a much greater incentive and ability than our present system does for people to become educated.

Given the numerous organizations the government owns today that are not involved with the protection of rights, what is the government to do with these organizations? A system should be devised for selling off or closing down these organizations, whether they include schools, post offices, transportation organizations (such as Amtrak), and so on. A provision can be incorporated into the amendment to allow for enough time to do this, if necessary.

As previously mentioned, one issue I address here is Social Security (SS). SS is a system of retirement and disability benefits paid for by the government and financed by a tax on workers' incomes. It is a coercive system of redistribution from employers and current workers to, mainly, retirees.[25] It diverts taxpayers' money from savings to consumption by the government. It undermines saving, capital accumulation, and the rate of economic progress by discouraging workers from saving for their retirement to the extent they think they can count on SS when they retire. It also makes it harder for workers to save for their retirement to the extent they are forced to pay into the system. This is money the workers could have saved instead. This lowers the standard of living that the average retiree could achieve. The standard of living for the average retiree would be greater without SS due to the greater productive capability that would be made possible by the greater incentive and ability to save, invest, and thus produce wealth.

It gets worse. SS is multi-trillion-dollar fraud because of the deceptive way in which it is implemented. It is put forward as a system of insurance. SS is the commonly used term for the Old-Age, Survivors, and Disability *Insurance* program. But it is not a system of insurance at all. Taxes paid into SS are either used to fund payments to current retirees or government consumption. If taxes are not used to make payments to current retirees, surplus funds are loaned to the government and spent on other government programs. If a private insurance company spent money it received in this fashion, its executives would be thrown in jail (as they should be). After covering the cost of running its business and compensating investors, an insurance company saves and invests the rest of the premium payments it receives to help pay for future claims made by those it insures. In contrast, the government lends the money to itself (i.e., one agency of the government, the Social Security Administration [SSA], lends the money to another agency of the government, the Treasury, and receives nonmarketable Treasury bonds in exchange). The government then spends the money and the money is gone. It does not save and invest the funds. It needs to collect additional taxes to be able to use the bonds, which are held in what is called the Social Security Trust Fund (SSTF), as a means to pay future SS recipients. This is true even if the government reduces spending elsewhere or prints money to pay off the bonds.

It is important to note that the SSTF is not, in fact, a trust fund. This is a part of the deceptive nature of the system. The bonds in the SSTF are not a net asset to the government because they are both an asset and an equally offsetting liability to the government. The asset is the loan made by the SSA, and the liability is the money borrowed by the Treasury. Hence, on net they have no value to the government.

SS is not insurance; it's a Ponzi scheme. It depends on current contributors (i.e., taxpayers) paying into the system to make payments to current retirees. It needs enough funds being paid into the system from workers and employers to cover the payments received by current retirees. In 1950, SS had almost seventeen workers paying into the system for every retiree. Due to demographic changes, it now has about 2.5 workers per retiree. By 2030, it is projected to have about two workers per retiree. Surplus funds from taxes being paid into the system turned to deficits in 2010. Eventually, payments to retirees will have to be significantly reduced or taxes will have to be significantly increased to maintain the system.[26]

One might wonder how this Ponzi scheme has been able to last so long relative to other Ponzi schemes. The answer: other schemes collapse in a quicker fashion because those who run the schemes need to get patsies to voluntarily contribute to the schemes. In contrast, taxpayers are forced to pay into SS; they cannot choose to not participate. Take away the coerced participation and SS would collapse very quickly.[27]

So how can the system be abolished? The age at which retirees can receive payments could gradually be raised. Over twenty or twenty-five years, the age could be raised to the point where not many people would be old enough to receive payments.[28] Once this point is reached, the system could be easily abolished. The remaining recipients could be paid a one-time present value equivalent of what they expect to receive from the system.[29]

This method of abolishing SS will force younger workers to pay into the system without receiving benefits when they retire. However, this is the lesser of two evils. The worse evil would be to abolish the system immediately. This would eliminate payments to current retirees who have been forced to pay into the system and may no longer be able to work. If the system is abolished after, say, twenty years, younger workers would at least have significant time to save for their retirement. Moreover, the system would be a declining burden on them, as fewer people would receive payments from the system due to the rising age necessary to receive payments. SS-related taxes could then be reduced along with the payments.

Abolishing SS is both practical and moral. From a practical, economic standpoint, it will encourage people to save and invest for their future, encourage greater productive spending (spending on business activities—activities that produce wealth), and reduce consumption by the government.

This will increase the overall productive capability of the economy and raise the standard of living, including the standard of living of retirees.[30]

More fundamentally, SS is immoral because it sacrifices workers and employers to retirees. Abolishing SS will end the sacrifice and respect the rights of taxpayers. That is why abolishing it is the moral thing to do. No one has the right to, in essence, reach for a gun and force individuals to pay for other people's retirement. Individuals have a right to keep the income they earn.

In addition, people must save for their own retirement. If they cannot afford to do so, they will need to work later in life or rely on voluntary charity and mutual aid societies. Of course, capitalism makes it possible for more and more individuals to be able to afford to retire earlier. This is one of the many benevolent features of capitalism.

I now focus on education. There is no right to an education, and the government should not provide it. Taxpayers have no duty to fund other people's education. As with Social Security, it is immoral, based on an objectively valid code of morality—the morality of rational self-interest—and a violation of the rights of taxpayers to force them to provide for others' education. Moreover, I argue in chapters 1 and 4 that private firms in a free market can do the best job developing and producing goods and services for individuals to purchase. The free market leads to the highest quality and greatest abundance of goods and services that are possible. This applies to education as well. The government monopoly in education has contributed significantly to creating hordes of ignorant children in America. Increasingly they cannot read, write, think critically, think long range, and think based on rational principles.[31] A system of private education in which individuals can provide education for profit would create a strong incentive to provide innovative and better ways of educating children (and adults). Of course, private, not-for-profit education enterprises could provide education as well. All private enterprises would have a strong incentive to keep costs low and improve quality. Otherwise, they would lose business.[32]

One problem with government-provided education is that it prevents competition in the education industry because the service is provided to the student at no cost or at a very minimal cost. This makes it virtually impossible for private providers to compete. How can private businesses compete against government providers in the provision of a service in which the government providers have a 100-percent subsidy of their costs by taxpayers and therefore the government educators do not have to charge any fee to the consumers of the service? The answer: not very easily. With a price charged of zero, the government educators can provide an extremely low-quality education and still get most parents to send their children to such schools. Most parents would probably consider an education that costs 100 percent less a better option even if the education provided was 50 percent or even 75 percent lower in quality. The only market in which private educators can compete is in the market for the education of the children of wealthy parents, who can afford to pay for the improved services the private educators provide.

Government regulation also makes it much costlier for private educators to provide education services due to the imposition of, for example, zoning laws and building code regulations, which add to the cost of building schools. In addition, requiring classes on specific subjects (such as physical education) and imposing maximum student to teacher ratios and minimum education, certification, and licensing requirements for teachers adds to the cost of providing an education to children. All of this makes it harder for private educators to compete and thus prevents the education industry from reaping the benefits of competition.

Government provided education also violates the freedom of conscience of taxpayers who are forced to pay for the teaching of ideas with which they disagree. For example, religious taxpayers who believe in intelligent design are forced to pay for the teaching of Darwin's theory of evolution. Only privately provided education avoids this. If parents do not like the curriculum of a school, they do not have to send their children to that school.[33]

Note that a voucher system is not consistent with a free market. Voucher systems involve taxes being handed over to parents to be spent for their children's education at government approved schools, which could include government run schools. Voucher systems entail significant government interference in the education system. A free society means a complete separation of the state from education. This is the only way to protect the rights of taxpayers, parents, and children.[34]

One might ask, how will poor people's children be educated in a free society if no one pays for it? If one wants to help educate the children of the poor, one has every right to do that. However, no one has the right to force some people to pay for the education of other people, whether those others are the children of the poor or anyone else.

Donating to charities that help educate the poor is one way for people who want to do so to engage in these activities. Charity for education, as for other things, would be forthcoming in great amounts in a free society. Because a free society leads to a much wealthier society, it leads to a much greater ability to give to charity. In addition, as discussed above, education would be much less expensive and educators much more innovative because there will be much greater freedom to try new ways of providing education services. So, the poor will have more opportunities to become better educated in a free society than they would have in a society of government provided education.

One must also keep in mind that the worst government run schools exist in the poorest areas, such as inner cities. They are probably worse than the students having no formal education at all. Such schools produce large numbers of uncivilized individuals who learn about ideas that are antithetical to human life and well-being, such as ideas based on mysticism, altruism, collectivism, and statism. Even the lowest quality private schools will be able to do a much better job than that.[35]

Parents *do* have a duty to provide their children with a minimal education. Having a child is a chosen responsibility that comes with certain obligations. These include providing the child with the appropriate physical conditions to grow into a rational, self-supporting adult. It would obviously be a violation of the child's rights to physically abuse the child. However, it would also be a violation of the child's rights if the parents did not provide a minimal education. The basic tool of survival for human beings is the mind. If parents do not help the child develop his mind, at least minimally, so he can become a fully functional adult, the parents are violating the child's right to his life. Parents must understand that when they have a child, they have brought a helpless, rights-possessing being into existence that requires sustenance, nurturing, protection, and an education to develop both physiologically and cognitively to be able to live as a rational adult. Hence, they have a duty to provide for the child so that he can reach the state of a fully functioning adult.

Of course, providing an education for a child does not mean parents have to send their child to the best schools or any school at all. Vocational training, home schooling, or even apprenticeship on a family farm (and many more examples) are all legitimate options for providing a child training so that he will be able to support himself as an adult. The point is that the parents must provide some minimal education. If the parents abuse the child physically or mentally or fail to provide him with a minimally acceptable education, it would be proper for the state to intervene and, if necessary, take the child from the parents and provide him with alternative care (such as through foster care, an orphanage, relatives, etc.). If the child is taken from the parents, however, the parents should still be required to pay for the upbringing of the child. What constitutes a minimally acceptable education would be determined through court cases and codified in the legislature.[36]

Finally, while parents have a duty to provide their own children a minimal education, no child (or adult) has a right to an education. No one, other than his parents, owes a child an education. It is not the duty of taxpayers, siblings, extended relatives, friends of the parents, neighbors, and so on to provide a child with an education. The parents chose to have the child. They are the ones that brought a rights-possessing, helpless being into existence. Taxpayers, neighbors, extended relatives, and so on did not. Hence, it is the parents—and only the parents—that have taken on this *chosen* responsibility. The child has the right to be taken care of and nurtured to some minimum extent *by his parents* so that he can become a fully functioning, self-supporting adult.

However, it would be a violation of the rights of individuals to force them to provide an education to a child they did not choose to bring into existence.

Amendment LVIII

No federal, state, or local government shall purchase or own any property, except that which is directly necessary to protect individual rights.

This amendment is based in part on Article III, Section 3(a) of Bernard Siegan's constitution.[37] It is necessary to prevent the government from owning any property other than court houses, police stations, the homes of heads of state, legislative buildings, military bases and hardware, and any other property that is necessary to protect rights and freedom. This means the government cannot purchase or own educational buildings, national, state, county or city parks, bridges, roads, and so forth. If there is a road or bridge that must be built to protect rights (such as in time of war), the government is fully authorized to build and own such a road or bridge. However, in times of peace, roads and bridges would not normally be built or owned by the government.

Purchasing and owning roads, bridges, and the like is not generally necessary to protect rights. The government building roads and bridges is also not necessary to ensure that these goods are provided in sufficient quantities. The provision of these goods by private individuals based on the profit motive will ensure that they are provided in sufficient quantities. In fact, the private road and bridge owners will do a much better job than the government at providing the roads that individuals demand. They will also provide them in a much more efficient manner. Governments are notorious for doing things in an extremely inefficient manner because they do not (and should not) act on the profit motive, so they have much less incentive than private road owners would have to keep costs low. In addition, the government generally does a poor job at providing such goods as roads because it has less incentive than private road owners would to provide what the market demands, again, because it does not act on the profit motive. Government officials often have other priorities based on what their most influential constituents want, such as preventing the use of land for building roads based on the influence of the environmentalist movement.

It is important to note that even though some people consider roads, bridges, and so forth to be "public goods," it still does not justify the government providing them. I have written at length on the nature of so-called public goods. I demonstrate that so-called public goods that are appropriate for the market to provide can be provided in a much more efficient and effective manner by private individuals.[38]

Note also that the government does not own unused land, such as forests, the frozen tundra in Alaska, or the open prairies. The government should not own *any* unused land. To protect rights, land remains ownerless until an individual uses the land in some way to create a value, such as by building a home, a road, or a factory on the land. The role of the government in the case of unused land is to determine the appropriate process through which individuals can acquire ownership of the land. Individuals do not buy the land from the government but merely follow the process established to appropriate the land from nature. The Homestead Act of 1862 provides a good example of the type of legislation that is required.

Given the large amounts of property the government owns that it should not own—including vast tracks of land in the west and Alaska in the form of parks and conservation areas—a system should be devised for selling off the property or allowing the property to revert to becoming unused property that no one owns. This could be a part of the same system that was mentioned in connection with Amendment LVII that would allow the government to sell off organizations it should not own.

Amendment LIX

Foreign nationals shall have the right to immigrate to and become citizens of the United States and the several states. Foreign nationals in the United States who are not citizens shall be entitled to all the privileges and immunities of citizens of the United States and the several states, but all privileges and immunities shall be consistent with the protection of individual rights.

This amendment is needed because of the desire of many to violate the rights of foreigners—and U.S. citizens who want to hire the foreigners or sell to them—by keeping the foreigners out of the country, whether through travel bans on foreigners or restrictions on immigration. The amendment is based in part on Article VI, Section 18 of Bernard Siegan's constitution.[39] Siegan focuses on guaranteeing all the rights and freedoms in the constitution he created to foreign nationals. However, foreign nationals do not (and should not) possess all the rights of the citizens of the country or a particular state. For example, foreign nationals have the right to travel, work, own property, and open a business. However, they should not have the ability to vote or run for office. This is why I use the term "privileges and immunities" in the second clause of this amendment. Privileges and immunities include many rights that citizens possess but not all the rights.[40] The rights that foreign nationals possess are similar to the rights that U.S. citizens possess when traveling in a state other than the state of which they are a citizen. This is why the same terminology is used in this amendment as in Article IV, Section 2 of the Constitution.

As long as the foreign nationals are not violating or threatening the rights of others, they have the right to engage in any peaceful activity within the United States. This means that known terrorists, criminals, people with infectious diseases, or people who represent a threat to the rights of U.S. citizens in any other way do *not* have the right to come to the United States. However, everyone else does.

In a sense, the right of foreign nationals to come to a nation is a recognition of the rights of the citizens of the nation. For example, the citizens have the right to hire foreign workers and sell their goods to foreign nationals. In fact, some citizens of a nation might actually want foreigners to immigrate to the nation so the citizens can sell their goods to the foreigners and hire them.

The government or citizens of a nation have no right to keep foreigners out of a nation based on the collectivist premise that they "own" the country. The government has jurisdiction over the country, which means it has a monopoly on the enforcement of laws within the country. Individuals and associations of individuals (such as corporations) own certain portions of land and other property within the nation. Governments own *some* property as well, such as court houses. But neither own the country.

U.S. citizens should welcome foreigners because we stand to benefit from them economically. To the extent that talented, ambitious, and productive individuals come to the United States, they will help increase the productive capability and standard of living. A free society is particularly attractive to talented and productive individuals. To the extent they live in countries that violate their rights, they cannot benefit from their own talent and productiveness, at least not to the extent they can benefit from them in a free society. Talent comes to freedom and those who live in a free society benefit from the goods produced, services provided, and capital employed by the immigrants. Think of the enormous benefits we have derived from immigrants such as Elon Musk, Andrew Carnegie, Albert Einstein, Ayn Rand, Bob Hope, Knute Rockne, Nikola Tesla, and many, many more.

Even poor, unskilled immigrants are a benefit to citizens of the country to which they immigrate. They are often willing to perform unpleasant jobs that citizens do not want to perform, and they do so at lower wages. These wages usually represent a significant increase in the wages the immigrants could earn in their home country (that is why they leave their home country). The lower wages also allow the businesses that employ such workers to lower their costs and thus prices to customers. This helps raise the overall standard of living by lowering the cost of living. As long as immigrants are self-supporting, rights-respecting individuals, they are an economic benefit to the country to which they immigrate, regardless of whether they are rich or poor, skilled or unskilled. Moreover, as poor, unskilled immigrants (and their offspring) save, open businesses, employ capital, and gain an education, they become that much more of an economic benefit to the rest of the country by increasing the productive capability even more.

It is true that there might be short-run losses for Americans who compete with the foreigners, in the form of lost jobs and lower wages. However, the overwhelming majority of the population will not be competing with the foreigners and thus will stand to *immediately* benefit from the foreigners. Moreover, even those who lose in the short-run generally gain in the long-run. Once they find new positions in the economy, their standard of living will most likely be raised due to the overall greater productive capability and rate of economic progress.[41]

It is important to understand that when foreigners come to work in a country, they do not, on net, reduce the number of jobs available to citizens of the country. There is a potentially limitless amount of work to do in an economy and thus the potential for a limitless number of jobs. The key to ensuring that everyone who wants a job can obtain one is that freedom in the labor markets exist so that employers can offer, and workers can accept, wages that are in their self-interest. Thus, wages need to be free to fluctuate in response to supply and demand. Moreover, workers need to have the freedom of migration protected so they can move to where the jobs are. Foreign workers will create as many jobs as they take from citizens based on their demand for goods and the businesses they open. Immigration is neutral to the unemployment rate. However, it has a clearly positive effect on the productive capability and standard of living.[42]

Foreign nationals not only have the right to come to a country and travel, work, or open a business, but they have the right to become citizens. It is up to Congress to determine the process for foreigners to become citizens based on the Naturalization Clause of Article I, Section 8. As I state in chapter 3 in my discussion of citizenship requirements for becoming a representative, it would be appropriate to require foreigners to live in the United States for a significant period of time before being eligible to become a U.S. citizen so that they can be sufficiently integrated into American culture and to ensure that they plan on living here permanently.

A number of other arguments against free immigration are not legitimate either. For example, immigrants do not commit crimes at greater rates than native-born U.S. citizens. In fact, their crime rates are lower.[43]

Immigrants also do not abuse the welfare system. Poor immigrants use welfare at much lower rates than poor Americans.[44] The welfare system is immoral because it is based on the morality of altruism—the belief that taxpayers should be sacrificed to the poor. We should not oppose immigration to prevent immigrants from receiving welfare. We should abolish welfare programs to prevent anyone from receiving welfare, including native-born Americans. This will solve the entire problem.

Immigrants do not bring more statist ideas to America either. They tend to admire American institutions. That is one of the reasons why they leave their familiar homelands and come to a strange, foreign land to make a new life for themselves.

Likewise, a nation does not undermine its cultural values, such as giving up the main language spoken in a nation, by having large numbers of immigrants. Even today, immigrants to America—including Mexicans, America's most numerous immigrant group—assimilate into the culture as well as or better than immigrants from 100 years ago. Again, immigrants have chosen to come to a nation, so they have a strong motivation to learn about and embrace that nation's culture.

With the move to a free society and free immigration, the question naturally arises of what we should do with the immigrants that came here illegally based on current immigration law. The answer: we should give them amnesty. This would at least implicitly recognize that the current immigration laws are immoral and violate the rights of both immigrants and citizens of the United States who want to do business with them. Immigration laws based on the revised Constitution should apply in the same manner to immigrants who came here illegally under the current laws as they would to those immigrants who come here after a system of free immigration is established.

There are many other arguments against free immigration which are not legitimate. See the online essay "The 14 Most Common Arguments Against Immigration and Why They Are Wrong" by Alex Nowrasteh that I cited in the discussion on immigration. The essay does a good job of dispelling the myths of immigration, including the myths I have discussed here. It provides many good references on the subject as well.

CONCLUSION

The amendments in this chapter focus to a great extent on the protection of rights that are already protected by the Constitution. However, the protection as it exists now is provided by abstract rights. The rights protected in the amendments presented here are concrete manifestations of these abstract rights. For example, Amendment LVI, which secures the right of a person to do with his or her body what he or she wants, is protected by the right to liberty. The freedom of production and trade, protected in Amendment LV, is also protected by the right to liberty. But the right to liberty, because it is very abstract, can be misapplied (or not applied at all) when it is necessary to protect specific rights that fall under it. Hence, to ensure that the protection of rights is as strong as possible, it helps to explicitly protect specific, concrete rights that fall under the right to liberty or other abstract rights. Moreover, as I have said, redundancy in a constitution can better ensure that rights will be protected.

The redundancy even occurs between the amendments to the Constitution discussed in this chapter. For example, Amendments LVII and LVIII are to some extent redundant, in that they both focus on preventing the government from owning certain types of property. However, their focus is different enough to warrant separate amendments. One focuses on certain types of enterprises, while the other focuses on physical property. They are both necessary because, in different ways, they help to prevent the government from going beyond its appropriate function of protecting rights. For example, Amendment LVII prevents the government from owning such enterprises as the Post Office and Amtrak, while Amendment LVIII prevents the government from owning parks and "conservation areas." Given the widespread ownership of property and enterprises by the government that it should not own, these amendments are desperately needed.

Still more amendments are needed to fully protect individual rights in the revised Constitution. In the next chapter, I complete the task of providing the necessary amendments.

NOTES

1. Rand, *Atlas Shrugged*, p. 1168.
2. On these topics, see Reisman, *Capitalism*; and Simpson, *Markets Don't Fail!*.
3. Benjamin Powell, "The Trump Policy that Will 'Shrink the Economy and Make the U.S. Poorer,'" November 18, 2016, http://www.independent.org/news/article.asp?id=8929 (accessed May 10, 2019).
4. This point was made in John Cochrane, "Trump's Tariffs Will Hurt Trade, and Trade Is a Good Thing – Really," March 5, 2018, https://www.foxnews.com/opinion/trumps-tariffs-will-hurt-trade-and-trade-is-a-good-thing-really (accessed May 10, 2019).
5. For a comprehensive analysis of the economic benefits of free international trade, see George Reisman, "Globalization: The Long-Run Big Picture," November 17, 2006, http://capitalism.net/articles/Globalization.htm (accessed May 11, 2019). Also, see Reisman, *Capitalism*, pp. 350–56.
6. It should also abolish regulations that raise costs of production because such regulations can push manufacturing outside the United States. Of course, the new Constitution will make it unconstitutional to regulate the economy.
7. It can be appropriate for the government to prevent Americans from doing business in foreign countries if the activity represents a threat to the rights of Americans. For example, the government should prevent Americans from doing

business in countries that are at war with the United States. In addition, selling military hardware to countries that could use it to threaten the rights of Americans should be prevented. In these situations, the government is not violating the rights of Americans but protecting their rights.

8. For more on why prostitution devalues sex, see Rand, *For the New Intellectual*, pp. 98–101. Also, see Ayn Rand, "Of Living Death," in *The Voice of Reason: Essays in Objectivist Thought*, edited by Leonard Peikoff (New York: Meridian, 1989), pp. 46–63. See, in particular, p. 47. Finally, see Harry Binswanger, editor, *The Ayn Rand Lexicon: Objectivism from A to Z* (New York: Penguin Books, 1986), p. 459.

9. Jeffrey A. Miron, "Violence and U.S Prohibitions of Drugs and Alcohol," NBER Working Paper 6950 (February 1999), https://www.nber.org/papers/w6950.pdf (accessed May 12, 2019). See p. 1 of the document.

10. Ibid., p. 13. Also, see Jeffrey A. Miron and Jeffrey Zwiebel, "The Economic Case Against Drug Prohibition," *Journal of Economic Perspectives* vol. 9, no. 4 (Fall 1995), pp. 175–92. See p. 178.

11. Transform Drug Policy Foundation, "The War on Drugs: Creating Crime, Enriching Criminals," http://www.countthecosts.org/sites/default/files/Crime-brief ing.pdf (accessed May 12, 2019). See p. 9 of the document.

12. Miron and Zwiebel, "The Economic Case," p. 180.

13. Ibid., p. 177.

14. Ibid., pp. 185–86.

15. Transform Drug Policy Foundation, "The War on Drugs," p. 7. Also, see Miron and Zwiebel, "The Economic Case," p. 179.

16. Drug Policy Alliance, "Drug War Statistics," http://www.drugpolicy.org/issu es/drug-war-statistics (accessed September 10, 2020).

17. Transform Drug Policy Foundation, "The War on Drugs," p. 10; and Drug Policy Alliance, "The Federal Drug Control Budget: New Rhetoric, Same Failed Drug War" (February 2015), https://www.drugpolicy.org/sites/default/files/DPA _Fact_sheet_Drug_War_Budget_Feb2015.pdf (accessed May 12, 2019). See p. 1 of the latter document.

18. Drug Policy Alliance, "Making Economic Sense," http://www.drugpolicy.org /issues/making-economic-sense (accessed September 10, 2020); and Drug Policy Alliance, "Drug War Statistics."

19. Noah Smith, "Companies That Discriminate Fail (Eventually)," September 23, 2016, https://www.bloomberg.com/opinion/articles/2016-09-23/companies-that -discriminate-fail-eventually (accessed December 26, 2019).

20. For more on these topics, including why a free society is fundamentally incompatible with racism and how statism perpetuates racism, see Robert Tracinski, "America's 'Field of Blackbirds': How the Campaign for Reparations for Slavery Perpetuates Racism," *The Intellectual Activist: An Objectivist Review* vol. 15, no. 6 (June 2001), pp. 21–31. Also, see Andrew Bernstein, "The Welfare State Versus the Mind," *The Intellectual Activist: An Objectivist Review* vol. 15, no. 10 (October 2001), pp. 11–24. In addition, see Reisman, *Capitalism*, pp. 194–99. Finally, see Rand, *Virtue of Selfishness*, pp. 147–57; and Ayn Rand, *The New Left: The Anti-Industrial Revolution*, Revised edition (New York: Signet, 1975), pp. 167–69.

21. See Roderick T. Long, "Imagineering Freedom: A Constitution of Liberty, Part IV: The Rights of the People," *Formulations* vol. 2, no. 4 (Summer 1995), http://www.freenation.org/a/f24l2.html (accessed February 26, 2017).

22. For a thorough discussion of the issues pertaining to a woman's right to obtain an abortion, see Andrew Bernstein, *Capitalist Solutions: A Philosophy of American Moral Dilemmas* (New Brunswick, NJ: Transaction Publishers, 2012), pp. 123–36. Also, see Binswanger, *The Ayn Rand Lexicon*, pp. 1–2 for a compilation of excerpts by Ayn Rand on why a woman possesses the right to obtain an abortion.

23. Bernard H. Siegan, *Drafting a Constitution for a Nation or Republic Emerging into Freedom*, 2nd edition (Fairfax, VA: George Mason University Press, 1994), pp. 84 and 91.

24. On welfare, see Tom G. Palmer, editor, *After the Welfare State* (Ottawa, IL: Jameson Books, 2012), sections I–III. On the provision of private fire protection services, see John R. Guardiano, David Haarmeyer, and Robert W. Poole, Jr., "Fire Protection Privatization: A Cost-Effective Approach to Public Safety" (October 1992), https://reason.org/wp-content/uploads/files/c2bbfe415eccfdff424a2bf7c8 a20585.pdf. On health care, see George Reisman, "The Real Right to Medical Care Versus Socialized Medicine" (1994), http://capitalism.net/articles/SOC_MED_files/ The%20Real%20Right%20to%20Medical%20Care%20Versus%20Socialized%20 Medicine.html. On government interference with businesses, see Simpson, *Markets Don't Fail!*, chapters 2 and 3. On leisure and recreational services, including the provision of parks, museums, and galleries, see Robert W. Poole, Jr., "Leisure and Recreational Services," in *The Theory of Market Failure: A Critical Examination*, edited by Tyler Cowen (Fairfax, VA: George Mason University Press, 1988), pp. 327–39. Online content accessed August 16, 2019.

25. While payments are also made through SS to workers who become disabled and cannot work and to surviving spouses and children, here I focus only on payments to retirees.

26. See James D. Gwartney, Richard L. Stroup, Russell S. Sobel, and David A. Macpherson, *Macroeconomics: Private and Public Choice*, 15th edition (Stamford, CT: Cengage Learning, 2015), pp. 414–17 on some of the points made in this and the previous two paragraphs.

27. The other schemes also collapse in a quicker fashion because they are illegal and are shut down once they are discovered. Whereas, SS is, of course, legal. Nonetheless, SS would still collapse very quickly if participation was voluntary.

28. A provision could be placed in the amendment to allow sufficient time to eliminate SS.

29. See Reisman, *Capitalism*, pp. 976–78 for more details on this method of abolishing SS.

30. See ibid., pp. 441–56 on the difference between economically productive and consumptive activity, the importance of economically productive activity to the standard of living, and why the government is a consumer.

31. On the low quality of education in America, see Leonard Peikoff, "The American School: Why Johnny Can't Think," in *The Voice of Reason*, pp. 209–29. Also, see Reisman, *Capitalism*, pp. 107–12. On the decline in learning of American

students, see Richard K. Vedder, *Restoring the Promise: Higher Education in America* (Oakland, CA: Independent Institute, 2019), pp. 47–50, 56–57, and 63–68.

32. On the superiority of privately provided education relative to government-provided education, see Andrew J. Coulson, "On the Way to School: Why and How to Make a Market in Education," in *Freedom and School Choice in American Education*, edited by Greg Forster and C. Bradley Thompson (New York: Palgrave Macmillan, 2011), pp. 17–42. See, in particular, pp. 17–29. Privatizing the education industry is not the main change that is needed to improve that industry. The main change that is needed is the embracement of a pro-reason philosophy in the culture. Nonetheless, privatizing education will certainly help make improvements in that industry.

33. See Reisman, *Capitalism*, pp. 386–87 and 986 for more on the subjects discussed in the last few paragraphs.

34. On how a voucher system involves government interference, see Sheldon Richman, "'Unbounded Liberty, and Even Caprice': Why 'School Choice' Is Dangerous to Education," in *Freedom and School Choice*, pp. 91–107. See, in particular, pp. 91–92 and 98–106.

35. See Coulson, "On the Way to School" for more on this topic.

36. For more on the rights of children pertaining to education (and in general), see C. Bradley Thompson, "Do Children Have a 'Right' to an Education?," in *Freedom and School Choice*, pp. 129–51.

37. Siegan, *Drafting a Constitution*, p. 84.

38. Simpson, *Markets Don't Fail!*, pp. 91–92 and 181–88. Also, see Reisman, *Capitalism*, pp. 420–21.

39. Siegan, *Drafting a Constitution*, p. 91.

40. See my discussion of "privileges and immunities" in chapter 3 in the discussion of Article I, Section 6; in chapter 4 in the discussion of Article I, Section 9; and in chapter 5 in the discussion of Article IV, Section 2.

41. For a detailed discussion of the benefits of immigration, see Reisman, *Capitalism*, pp. 362–66.

42. On the potentially limitless amount of work to do, the causes of unemployment, and why free immigration does not cause unemployment, in addition to the previous reference, see ibid., pp. 59–61 and 580–89.

43. Radley Balko, "The El Paso Miracle," July 6, 2009, https://reason.com/2009/07/06/the-el-paso-miracle (accessed May 21, 2019).

44. Alex Nowrasteh, "The 14 Most Common Arguments Against Immigration and Why They Are Wrong," May 2, 2018, https://www.cato.org/blog/14-most-common-arguments-against-immigration-why-theyre-wrong (accessed May 19, 2019).

Chapter 9

Additional Amendments to the Constitution, Part 2

INTRODUCTION

This chapter completes the task of protecting rights not addressed, or only addressed in an abstract sense, in the Constitution. This chapter will focus on money, the freedom of speech in politics, further protections of property rights, and the right to life as it pertains to the military draft and jury duty.

THE LAST OF THE ADDITIONAL AMENDMENTS TO THE CONSTITUTION

Amendment LX

The freedom of speech and press include any contributions to political campaigns or to candidates for government office and shall extend to all mediums of communication. All mediums of communication shall be private property.

This amendment is based on Randy Barnett's fifth proposed amendment to the Constitution in his essay titled "A Bill of Federalism."[1] It protects fundamental freedoms that have been under attack recently and throughout most of the twentieth century. Recent attacks on the freedom of speech as it pertains to political donations include the McCain-Feingold Act, with its provision that limits direct contributions to political campaigns and bans corporations and unions from making direct contributions to campaigns. Donations to political campaigns and candidates are ways in which one can exercise one's freedom of speech. If one approves of the messages being offered by a candidate, one has the right to provide resources to the candidate (whether money, airtime, websites, etc.) to help that candidate disseminate his message.

Moreover, the right to free speech applies to both the candidate and the person who wants the candidate's message to be heard by more people. Donating money to a candidate does not initiate force against anyone. Hence, people have the right to give and receive donations.

In addition, it does not matter how much money one donates to a candidate or whether the donor is a person or organization (such as a union or corporation). The person or organization has the right to donate as much as he (or it) can afford, whether a few dollars or a few billion dollars. The claim that a candidate might win an election just because he outspends his opponent is irrelevant (and not valid anyways, since candidates who are outspent often win elections).

Those who want to limit political speech want to use political power to initiate force and violate the rights of those who want to participate in elections. In essence, they want to reach for a gun to dictate the resources people can use for political speech. This is a gross abuse of political power and should not be tolerated. If taken to its logical and consistent end, it will lead to further restrictions on political speech and greater restrictions of free speech in general.

Note that foreigners who are not citizens—even if they are residents of the United States—do not have the right to donate to political campaigns and candidates. The right to donate applies to those people the government will represent: citizens of the country. Limiting the right to donate to citizens of the United States also helps to protect the country from hostile foreign countries.

Some might think that an amendment to protect the freedom to make contributions to political campaigns and candidates is not needed because of the Supreme Court ruling in *Citizens United v. Federal Election Commission* (2010), which protected the right of corporations to engage in independent spending on political campaigns. However, even with this ruling there are still many restrictions on contributions that individuals and corporations can make to political campaigns and candidates (as I mention at the beginning of the discussion on this amendment). Further, opinion polls have shown significant opposition to this ruling, and some prominent individuals and state legislatures have expressed a desire for a constitutional amendment to overturn the ruling. Moreover, the ruling was a five-to-four decision and the Court could easily reverse itself in a future case. Hence, a constitutional amendment is needed to ensure free speech is protected in the political arena.

Some might be concerned that the elimination of restrictions on direct contributions to political campaigns and candidates could cause corruption, as candidates agree to provide political favors in trade for large contributions. While contributions in return for promises of, for example, government contracts would still need to be outlawed in a free society, what many people fail to realize is that political corruption is a problem that is inherent to statist forms of government, such as the mixed economy of the United States today, in which politicians have an enormous ability to grant favors to individuals and businesses due to the myriad laws that exist that violate rights (such as regulations and corporate welfare). The problem is statism, not free speech as it pertains to political contributions. The solution to this problem is to get the government out of the favor business. If the government is limited to only protecting rights, then the ability of politicians to dispense favors will be effectively eliminated. This is what my changes to the Constitution do.

Regarding mediums of communication, the users of airwaves (such as radio and television broadcasters) have had their rights violated since the creation of the Federal Radio Commission in 1927. That commission was created to regulate radio use "as the public interest, convenience, or necessity" requires. However, the airwaves are not public property. The "public" does not own them. The various frequencies used for communicating belong, as land does, to the first person who uses them to create a value. The proper role of the government is to protect the rights of users of the airwaves. This means preventing people from encroaching on the first users of a particular frequency, as the government would protect a landowner from trespassers.

Why does this amendment require an explicit statement that all mediums of communication are private property *and* a statement that says the freedom of speech and press apply to all mediums of communication? The answer: to make sure these rights—the right to property and the right to speak and publish—are protected in connection with all mediums of communication. It is obvious that the protections of free speech and a free press provided in the Bill of Rights have not been enough to protect broadcasting rights, since such rights have been routinely violated. So these rights need to be explicitly protected. This will ensure that existing regulations of the airwaves (and the regulatory agencies that enforce them, such as the Federal Communications Commission) will be abolished and no new ones will be enacted. For the same reason, I do not believe the amendment in chapter 8 that forbids the government from abridging the freedom of production and trade is enough to protect these rights either, even though the protection of these rights is implicit in that amendment.

Some claim that because there are only a limited number of frequencies, the government must control who uses the airwaves by giving out licenses to use them. However, all resources are limited in quantity, including land, oil, minerals, ores, and so on. A limited number of frequencies no more justifies the government handing out broadcasting licenses than does the limited amount of land justify the government handing out licenses to use land. Broadcasting frequencies, as land, should belong to the first people who use them to create values. The government's role with regard to broadcasting frequencies, as with land, is to develop a process for determining how owner-ship rights in them are acquired.[2]

Some might think that the government is justified in regulating the airwaves because if it does not, some broadcasters might broadcast offensive content or content inappropriate for children. The solution to offensive content is to change the channel. If parents do not want their children to be exposed to certain content, they can do what is possible to prevent their children from listening to or viewing such content and teach them to rationally assess the nature of such content. Pressure from the public, including boycotting, is also an option to persuade broadcasters either to not broadcast such content or to limit the means of gaining access to the content (such as through subscriber-based content). Devices for limiting access to material on the internet and cable television are widely available for parents to use as well. There are many means for parents to limit children's exposure to such content.

Amendment LXI

No federal, state, or local government shall create, issue, or coin money (including bills of credit) or regulate the value of money. Governments shall hold only standard money or money backed 100 percent by standard money. If the government receives money that is not fully backed by standard money, it must be exchanged as quickly as possible for standard money or money that is fully backed by standard money. Governments must store their money only in federal, state, or local government-owned banks. This amendment does not apply to the money of nations at war or in conflict with the United States.

No federal, state, or local government shall pass any law impairing the obligation of contracts.

As I state in chapter 4 in the discussion of the Coinage Clause, the govern-ment must be prevented from creating and regulating money. These activities are not a part of the proper functions of government. Preventing the gov-ernment from creating and regulating money will dramatically improve monetary stability in the economy. I discuss extensively why this will occur in both volumes of my book *Money, Banking, and the Business Cycle*. See the discussion in connection with the Coinage Clause and the Taxation and Spending Clauses in chapter 4 for relevant references to that book.

As a part of preventing the government from issuing money, it is also prevented in this amendment from issuing bills of credit. Bills of credit are forms of debt issued by the government that circulate as money. While the government is allowed to borrow money, it must be prevented from bor-rowing money and using the debt instruments to create a form of money. In addition, all levels of government must be prevented from borrowing in this manner. The federal government currently has the power to emit bills of credit and it has issued bills of credit in the past.[3] That is why the restriction on issuing bills of credit was removed from Article I, Section 10, where it applied only to the state governments, and is placed here, where it applies to all levels of government.

Government control of money leads to significant violations of rights. It makes it easier for the government to finance the welfare and regulatory state. It also makes it easier for the government to finance wars and conflicts that do not focus on the protection of the rights of Americans. The Korean and Vietnam Wars are two examples of these types of wars. Hence, this amendment will help prevent violations of rights.

I discuss in connection with the Coinage Clause why the government must be prevented from holding anything but standard money. This is necessary to prevent the government from lending money, at least implicitly. Lending money is not a part of the government's appropriate function. See the discussion on standard money and specific references to my book *Money, Banking, and the Business Cycle* cited in the Coinage Clause discussion for the details.

This amendment recognizes that the government may receive money that is not standard money or not backed 100 percent by standard money. That is why one clause requires the government to exchange partially backed money as quickly as possible for standard money or money fully backed by standard money. One might wonder what is meant by "as quickly as possible." It merely means that the government must exchange the money as soon as it is able to. It must not delay the exchange of money or attempt to hold onto partially backed money. I will give no specific amount of time because the actual amount of time such money is held may vary under differing circumstances. I will only say that the government should establish a procedure for ridding itself of such money, and as soon as it receives this type of money it must begin the process of exchanging the money.

This amendment also requires the government to keep its money only at government-owned banks. This restriction is necessary to prevent the government from potentially favoring particular private banks by keeping its money at those banks. This restriction will help maintain a separation of the government from the economy, which is necessary for the same reason we need a separation of the government from religion: to protect individual rights. For a detailed discussion of the arguments for the government keeping its money only at government-owned banks, see the references to *Money, Banking, and the Business Cycle* in the Coinage Clause discussion. In those references, I also discuss how the government-owned banks will interact with private banks.

The next clause focuses on the government being able to engage in some of the activities forbidden by this amendment during times of war. This is necessary to allow the government to properly fight a war. Fighting a war may require, for example, inflating the enemy's currency with counterfeit currency to devalue it and thus create chaos in the enemy's economy and undermine the enemy's ability to purchase goods. As another example, it may require using partially backed money during spy operations. To protect rights, the government must have all the appropriate tools to fight wars. "Conflicts" are added as well since war is not always formally declared against those nations who seek to violate the rights of Americans. The U.S. government must have all appropriate tools at its disposal to defeat its enemies in any war or conflict.

Finally, the prevention of all levels of government from interfering with legitimate contracts—contracts that respect the rights of individuals—is added to this amendment. This restriction had been placed only on the state governments in Article I, Section 10. I eliminated the provision there so that it could be applied here to all levels of government. The federal government must also be prevented from interfering in contracts. Of course, there is some redundancy with this amendment and Amendment LV, which prevents the government from infringing the freedom of production and trade, but that is acceptable.

Amendment LXII

Selective service, the military draft, and any other type of draft by the government are hereby prohibited.

Compulsory jury service is hereby prohibited.

The above amendment prohibits two related activities: the military draft and compulsory jury service. Since these are both forms of forced labor, it makes sense to include them in the same amendment.

The draft and Selective Service System (SSS) are obviously gross violations of individual rights. They initiate force against young adult males and send them to conflicts they may know nothing about and of which they may not approve. The draft and the SSS are immoral based on a rational code of morality—the morality of rational self-interest—because they sacrifice young men who are just starting out in life. While the draft has not been used since the early 1970s, under current law, male citizens of the United States and noncitizen male immigrants must register with the SSS within thirty days of their eighteenth birthday. This makes it very easy to reinstitute the draft should the federal government decide to do so.

Given the Constitution's prohibition of involuntary servitude (Amendment XIII), one would think that an amendment that explicitly bans the draft would not be necessary. Unfortunately, the Supreme Court ruled in *The Selective Draft Law Cases* (1918) that the draft is constitutional and that it does not violate the prohibition of involuntary servitude in Amendment XIII.[4] Therefore, an explicit amendment banning the draft is needed.

It also states in the ruling for *The Selective Draft Law Cases* that Article I, Section 8 of the Constitution, in which Congress is given the power to declare war, raise and support armies, make rules for the land and naval forces, and make all laws necessary and proper for carrying into execution the foregoing powers, provides the authority to Congress to enact the draft.[5] Nonetheless, these clauses of the Constitution do not provide justification for the draft. The purpose of the Constitution, and the only proper purpose of government, is to protect individual rights. While Congress does have a constitutional obligation to raise an army (and provide and maintain a navy), it also has a constitutional duty to protect individual rights. Because the latter is the fundamental purpose of government, it takes precedent over the former; the latter provides the guide to which the former must conform. Hence, the government must raise an army through voluntary means. Congress must provide the appropriate incentives (including sufficient pay) to get people to join the military voluntarily, as it does now.

This amendment not only states that the military draft is prohibited but that selective service and other forms of government drafts are prohibited. The SSS was established by the Selective Service Act of 1917. It includes the system and government agency that implements selective service and the draft. It implements a process for registering individuals and determining who is eligible to be drafted. This amendment makes it clear that not only is the draft itself prohibited, but the entire process that underlies and supports the draft is prohibited.

But the military draft is not the only type of draft that exists (or could exist). The government has also established a system for drafting medical personnel in times of emergency that is designated as the Health Care Personnel Delivery System (HCPDS). While the system is designed for drafting medical personnel into the military, it is stated by the SSS that the HCPDS would be used "If needed . . . to draft health care personnel in a crisis" and that the HCPDS is "designed to be implemented in connection with a national mobilization in an emergency."[6] The language describing the HCPDS could easily justify drafting medical personnel for purposes beyond military service because it is general enough to apply to any national "crisis" or "emergency."

In addition, the SSS has stated that it could expand the "special skills" draft to include not just medical personnel but linguists, environmental engineers, computer specialists, and other professionals.[7] If the government can expand the types of professionals that are subject to the draft, there is no reason to believe it could not expand the reasons that these professionals could be drafted beyond that of serving in the military. Hence, it is important that the amendment prohibit any form of government draft. If the government needs individuals of any profession to work in the military or elsewhere, it must provide the appropriate incentives to get them to work voluntarily. It should not be able to, in essence, reach for a gun to force people to work.

Furthermore, in *Butler v. Perry* (1916), the Supreme Court ruled that it was constitutional for local governments to compel individuals to work a short period of time each year to help maintain roads in the area near where they live. The Court stated that this did not violate Amendment XIII's prohibition of involuntary servitude. It compared the requirement to work on roads to the duty to serve in the military or on juries. It claimed that the "involuntary servitude" provision was meant to prohibit forced labor similar to slavery, not military service, working on roads or jury duty.[8] While this may be true, it does not deny that compulsory military service, jury duty, and requiring people to work on roads are types of forced labor. Moreover, while forcing people to work on roads or on juries is not generally considered to be a type of draft, one sees by the comparison to the requirement to serve in the military that it is, in essence, a type of draft. To ensure that other types of drafts are prohibited (or any forced labor that is imposed in a manner that is similar to a draft is prohibited), the provision in this amendment to ban any other form of government draft is necessary.

One might wonder how enough people will be obtained to fight a war without the draft. If it is a just war, the draft will not be needed to obtain enough soldiers. If it is not a just war, it should not be fought, and forcing people to fight in it would be a double injustice. It would be an injustice to force people to fight the war and, if that is not bad enough, it would be an injustice to force people to fight in an unjust war. Abolishing the draft will help prevent unjust wars from being waged because it will be difficult to find enough soldiers to fight in them. However, the United States will not have a problem finding enough volunteers to fight just wars without the draft. As evidence for this, one need only consider that there are currently a large number of troops in the U.S. military, and this is during a time of relative peace. In time of war, especially a just war, even more individuals will be willing to volunteer. If still more volunteers are needed, then the incentives to join the military should be increased. Better pay for military personnel would not only increase the number of people willing to join the military but reduce the amount of turnover and thus reduce the need for new recruits.[9] One must also consider, as I mention in chapter 6, the well-known fact that volunteer armies are generally superior to armies comprised of draftees. Hence, the draft is undesirable from a moral and a practical standpoint.

Regarding jury duty, it is obviously a violation of individual rights. Jury duty has been referred to as a type of draft.[10] Based on this, one might ask why the prohibition of other types of government drafts is not sufficient to ensure that compulsory jury service is prohibited. The answer lies in the fact that jury duty is widely used and has been used for a long time. Hence, implicitly banning it runs the risk of people rationalizing its continued existence by assuming that the ban on other types of drafts does not apply to jury duty. It needs to be explicitly banned in the new Constitution to ensure its abolition.

One might wonder how adequate numbers of jurors will be obtained if people are not forced to serve on juries. The answer is that they will be obtained in the same way that an adequate number of military personnel will be obtained: by providing strong enough incentives for people to become jurors voluntarily. People may actually be able to make a career out of being a juror because jurors will have to be paid enough to make it worth their time.

There are many ways that a voluntary jury system could be implemented; however, I envision the system looking much like the system today, except that individuals could potentially serve as jurors in a long-term capacity. Under a voluntary system, juries could still be selected from random pools of jurors. Furthermore, the present system of randomly selecting individuals for jury service could still be used (as either a supplement or alterative to people serving as jurors in a long-term capacity, depending on the need for jurors). Of course, the major differences would be that individuals could opt out of jury service and, if they chose to serve, they would be compensated at much higher rates than jurors are compensated at today.

In addition, since some individuals could be spending more time providing services as jurors and may have more frequent interactions with judges, prosecutors, and defense attorneys, precautions should be taken to minimize the chances of the latter attempting to influence the former. These precautions could include having a separate line of reporting for jurors so they do not report to judges or prosecutors. Precautions could be taken that are similar to those that are taken today to ensure that judges, prosecutors, and defense attorneys who may have more frequent interactions with each other do not behave inappropriately toward each other (such as precautions taken to ensure that judges do not engage in favoritism toward particular attorneys).

One might wonder where the government will obtain the money to pay the higher cost of attracting adequate numbers of jurors and military personnel voluntarily. It should not be difficult for the government to obtain the funds. As I discuss in chapter 4 in connection with the government's power to tax, in a free society government spending will be reduced dramatically. Probably 75 to 80 percent of all government spending that occurs today is inappropriate and will be eliminated. Given the radically reduced amount of spending, it should be much easier to obtain funds for the appropriate functions of government, including providing jurors for jury trials and personnel for the military. Citizens will not be overtaxed as they are today.

Finally, it must be made clear that while this amendment bans certain types of forced labor, it does not imply that forced labor imposed as a punishment for committing a crime should be banned. Amendment XIII makes it clear that forced labor as a punishment for being convicted of a crime is constitutional. This amendment is consistent with Amendment XIII. Forced labor as a punishment for committing a crime does not initiate physical force against the person required to engage in the labor. This represents a retaliatory use of force and can be an appropriate means of punishing convicted criminals.

Amendment LXIII

The freedom of individuals, and associations of individuals (including corporations), to use their property for all rights-respecting activities shall not be infringed.

This amendment is complementary to Amendment LVI, which protects the right of individuals to do what they want with their body and person. Individuals also have the right to do what they want with their property. Property includes any item that a person or a company, corporation, or other organization owns. It includes both real and personal property, as well as tangible and intangible assets.

This amendment also has some redundancy with Amendment LV. That amendment protects the freedom of production and trade. Production and trade obviously involve the use of property to produce and trade a good. The good is a piece of property, which one then has the freedom to sell to others. Even though protecting the freedom to use one's property also protects the freedom of production and trade, the freedom of production and trade needs to be explicitly protected because, as I have mentioned, this right has been routinely violated. The overlap between these two amendments will provide stronger protections of property rights and the right to liberty.

But the right to do what one wants with one's property can entail more than production and trade. It can involve the way in which one consumes or enjoys one's property. This amendment is also complementary to other portions of the Constitution that protect property rights, such as the Takings Clause (both in the original Fifth Amendment and, with even stronger protection of property rights, in the amended Fifth Amendment of the revised Constitution) and Amendment XIV, Section 1 (nor shall any state deprive any person of . . . property, without due process of law), as well as the amended version of Section 1 of Amendment XIV in the new Constitution.[11]

Of course, people are not free to violate the rights of others through the use of their property. That would be a violation of freedom. That is why it is stated in the amendment that individuals are free to use their property for all activities that respect individual rights.

Preventing someone from using his property in a way that does not initiate physical force against others initiates force against the property owner and thus violates the rights of the property owner. Uses of property that are currently forbidden by governments in some cases but that do not, by themselves, violate the rights of others and thus cannot be forbidden based on this amendment include leaving old vehicles on your front lawn that are an eyesore and in need of repair, painting your house a color that others might object to, erecting signs that people do not like, erecting houses or other buildings in coastal areas, erecting buildings above a maximum height or on lots that are smaller than a specific size, and many, many more. Of course, if one has agreed to not engage in any of these or other activities through a homeowners' agreement or restrictive covenant, one may be properly prevented from engaging in the offending activities. Note also that because these activities go beyond production and trade with one's property, Amendment LV does not apply to all forms of these activities. That is why this amendment is necessary.

Being able to do with one's property what one wants implies that zoning laws must be abolished. Zoning laws are also inconsistent with Amendment LV. The first citywide zoning laws were implemented in the United States in New York City in 1916. The Supreme Court upheld the constitutionality of zoning laws in the landmark case *Euclid v. Ambler Realty Co.* (1926). In its decision, the Court claimed the government can use zoning laws as a part of the use of its police power to prevent activities from taking place that violate rights. For instance, an implication of the Court's decision is that the government has the power to prevent the building of industrial buildings in residential areas when the productive activities that would take place in those buildings would create noxious gases in the surrounding atmosphere that would prevent the residents from enjoying the use of their property (or, in fact, harm residents). However, the Court also claimed the government can use zoning laws to prevent activities from taking place that do not violate rights. For example, the Court claimed that the government has the power to set maximum height restrictions on buildings.[12]

Creating noxious gases that harm people in surrounding areas, or just prevent them from enjoying their property (assuming people in the surrounding areas had settled on their property first), is a violation of rights that can be properly prevented by the government through nuisance laws. Hence, one does not need zoning laws to prevent this. However, imposing height restrictions on buildings does not protect rights, except in some exceptional cases (such as when applied to the construction of buildings at the end of an airport runway). Height restrictions generally violate the rights of property owners, and the government should therefore be prevented in virtually all cases from prohibiting buildings above a certain height. Because of the mixed basis for the decision in *Euclid*, it is not a decision that is completely consistent with the protection of individual rights. Hence, it does not provide a proper basis to evaluate the validity of zoning laws. The amendment being proposed in this section will help remedy the Court's decision in *Euclid.*

Some might think that eliminating zoning laws will lead to a chaotic use of property, including the above-mentioned construction of industrial buildings in residential areas. However, this will not happen. Houston provides a great example of a city with no zoning laws. It shows that the use of land is not chaotic. The use of land in Houston is as orderly as in cities with zoning laws.

However, while zoning laws do not lead to a more orderly use of land, they do lead to progressively greater and more minute government control over property (i.e., greater government violations of rights) and longer amounts of time being taken to make decisions with regard to the use of land. This, in turn, results in a lack of supply of housing, higher real estate prices, and a general lack of ability for land uses to be adapted to the needs and desires of people living in the area.[13]

Without zoning laws, restrictive covenants can be used to ensure that property in particular areas, such as residential areas, is limited to certain uses unless changes are approved by property owners in the areas. Restrictive covenants are voluntary agreements between buyers and sellers of property. They limit the activities that new buyers of property can engage in and are established by developers to ensure that purchasers of small parcels of land are provided with some long-term assurance of what surrounding land can be used for. They provide for stability in the use of land.

One might think that restrictive covenants are essentially the same as zoning laws. However, there are crucial differences between the two. For example, restrictive covenants do not affect areas as large as the areas that zoning laws affect. Restrictive covenants are generally confined to the subdivisions of the homeowners who agree to them. The covenants generally do not have any influence over adjacent land, including vacant land. The developer who owns vacant land would have the power to establish a new restrictive covenant for that area when it is developed. Homeowners of already developed adjacent land could control what happens in their area through their own covenants.

In contrast, homeowners can use zoning laws to restrict building outside their subdivision, including on vacant land. This gives them greater power to prevent people—including minorities and immigrants—from living in areas near them and makes it harder for developers to be responsive to the changing needs and desires for land use in surrounding areas. It also makes it harder for homeowners in surrounding areas to adapt their land use to their own needs and desires.

In addition, restrictive covenants are generally easier to change and are more limited in how long they are in force relative to zoning laws. Covenants often have expiration dates and can generally be changed with approval of only a majority of homeowners. Zoning laws typically do not have expiration dates and are generally more difficult to change because they must be changed through the political process. Changes could require approval of a supermajority of councilmembers, and homeowners in adjoining areas can influence the outcome. This means the changes might not reflect the wishes of the majority of voters in a specific area. Because of all these differences, restrictive covenants tend to be more adaptable to the changing needs and desires of people living in an area.

Most importantly, the government does not impose restrictive covenants through the initiation of physical force, as it does with zoning laws. Covenants protect the rights of property owners, whereas zoning laws violate the rights of property owners.[14]

The abolition of zoning will enable the uses of land to be better adapted to people's needs and desires. This is especially important when the needs and desires for land uses in an area change over time. People will not be restricted through zoning laws from establishing businesses, building residential or commercial structures, or building a particular type of residential or commercial structure (such as multifamily housing above a certain height that zoning laws might forbid). Zoning restrictions tend not to conform to what the market demands but to what politicians and their most powerful constituents demand, at the expense of the majority of people living or working in an area or other people who could potentially live or work in the area (such as, again, minorities and immigrants). The lack of housing and the higher priced housing to which zoning laws lead is one factor causing housing to be unaffordable in some large cities, such as San Francisco and New York. Cities with no zoning laws, such as Houston, have more affordable housing.[15] Abolishing zoning laws will lead to higher rates of economic progress and higher standards of living because it will eliminate unnecessary costs.[16]

The results are similar with regard to building code regulations and regulations in general. Building codes often raise the cost of construction by, for example, delaying the completion of construction projects, requiring unnecessary safety features, and requiring unnecessarily expensive building materials. The greater cost of construction has also contributed to the lesser supply and higher price of housing in many cities. This is particularly harmful to low-income individuals, since they can least afford to pay the higher prices.[17]

While the ostensible reason for building code regulations is to improve the safety and quality of housing and other buildings, the unstated reason why building code regulations and regulations in general are often imposed by the government is to appease pressure groups, such as existing producers in a field who want to keep new entrants out of the field to reduce competition. Building code regulations, in particular, are often desired to make housing more expensive and keep minorities and immigrants out of an area by making it too expensive for them to live in the area. We saw in chapter 1 that regulation of pharmaceutical drugs by the Food and Drug Administration makes drugs much more expensive, reduces the availability of drugs, and leads to more harm to individuals than it prevents. Chapter 4 highlighted how regulation in the financial industries leads to instability in those industries. In chapter 5 of my book *Markets Don't Fail!*, I discuss in detail why regulation of safety and quality in general leads to higher costs, a lower standard of living, and less safety and quality.

I also discuss in *Markets Don't Fail!* how improved safety and quality in products and working conditions are achieved through the free market. Markets lead to greater safety and quality by increasing the productive capability and standard of living. This is what makes possible the production of safer products and better worker conditions. Regulation does not magically bring into existence the ability to produce ventilation systems, indoor plumbing, water purification systems, safe electrical systems, fire retardant building materials, and so forth. This requires having a sufficiently productive economy so that these goods can be produced.

Imagine if U.S. building code regulations are imposed on Ethiopia. This will not magically make it so the Ethiopian economy can produce housing at the level of quality of that in the United States. All it will do is force many Ethiopians to live on the streets because much of the housing in Ethiopia will violate the building codes. The reason why higher quality housing can be built in the United States relative to Ethiopia is because of the greater productive capability in the United States relative to Ethiopia. It is not due to building code regulations.

The rational way to set standards for safety and quality is through the market. For instance, in the construction industry, insurance companies have an interest in making sure buildings are built to minimum standards to protect themselves from liability claims. Banks will require minimum standards as well to the extent the buildings are used as collateral on mortgage loans. For products more generally, as mentioned in chapter 4, private certification organizations, such as Consumer Reports and Underwriters Laboratories, would play a role. A company building and maintaining a good reputation and thus being viable as a business in the long-term would also play a role. The key difference between regulation and the market is that no one in the market can force their standards on others. In addition, the market takes safety, quality, *and* cost into account. Therefore, the interests of producers, insurers, lenders, *and* buyers are taken into account. Hence, the market not only leads to constantly rising levels of safety and quality, it leads to levels of safety and quality that people can afford.[18]

The importance of consistently protecting property rights cannot be stressed too strongly. Protecting the right of people to do what they want with their property is a fundamental aspect of protecting freedom. This includes protecting the right of property owners to do things with their property that others—even a majority of people—do not want them to do, such as develop land and build apartments, strip malls and high-rise buildings. Property rights are fundamental human rights. For example, in order to sustain and further one's life, one must produce material values and be able to keep and use the product of one's effort to further one's own life. If a person cannot keep and use the product of his effort, he is either enslaved to those who are able to take the product of his effort from him or he must be subjected to the whims of those who are able to forcibly prevent him from using the product of his effort for his own purposes. This is what protecting the freedom of people to use their property—and what this amendment—helps to prevent.

CONCLUSION

This chapter completes the amendments necessary to make the Constitution fully consistent with the protection of individual rights and freedom. It provides important protections of freedom by banning the draft, restricting how the government can use money, and further protecting property rights (among other protections of freedom). The revised Constitution is presented in its entirety without any intervening discussion in Appendix B.

This and the previous chapter focus on additional amendments that are needed to consistently protect rights. I have drawn on the works of others to identify appropriate amendments. However, other writers have also offered many amendments to the Constitution that allegedly protect rights but that do not, in fact, do so. Some writers have even offered whole constitutions that attempt to protect rights but that in some ways do not do so. The failure to protect rights in these cases is due either to the inclusion of provisions that are not necessary to protect rights or the inclusion of provisions that actually violate rights. In chapter 10, I provide a critique of many other attempts to protect rights that fail to do so.

NOTES

1. Randy E. Barnett, "A Bill of Federalism," *Forbes*, May 20, 2009, https://ww w.forbes.com/2009/05/20/bill-of-federalism-constitution-states-supreme-court-opi nions-contributors-randy-barnett.html (accessed July 2, 2017).

2. For more on the property status of airwaves, see Rand, *Capitalism*, pp. 122–29.

3. See Ali Khan, "The Evolution of Money: A Story of Constitutional Nullification," *University of Cincinnati Law Review* vol. 67 (Winter 1999), pp. 393–443. See, in particular, pp. 398–99 and 417–26. Also, see James B. Thayer, "Legal Tender," *Harvard Law Review* vol. 1, no. 2 (1887), pp. 73–97. See, in particular, pp. 76–80.

4. *The Selective Draft Law Cases*, 245 U.S. 366, p. 390 (1918).

5. Ibid., p. 377.

6. Selective Service System, "Medical Draft in Standby Mode," https://www.sss .gov/About/Medical-Draft-in-Standby-Mode (accessed June 9, 2018).

7. Roger A. Lalich, "Health Care Personnel Delivery System: Another Doctor Draft?," *Wisconsin Medical Journal* vol. 103, no. 1 (2004), pp. 21–24. See, in particular, p. 24.

8. *Butler v. Perry*, 240 U.S. 328, pp. 330–33 (1916).

9. Milton Friedman, "The Case for Abolishing the Draft—and Substituting for It an All-Volunteer Army," https://miltonfriedman.hoover.org/friedman_images/Colle ctions/2016c21/NYT_05_14_1967.pdf (accessed June 11, 2018). See, in particular, pp. 2 and 5 of this article.

10. See James A. Dorn, "Abolish the Jury 'Draft,'" https://www.cato.org/publicati ons/commentary/abolish-jury-draft (accessed June 10, 2018).

11. For a thorough discussion of the portions of the Constitution that protect property rights, see Bernard H. Siegan, *Property and Freedom: The Constitution, the Courts, and Land-Use Regulation* (New Brunswick, NJ: Transaction Publishers, 1997), pp. 13, 19–21, and 35–46.

12. *Euclid v. Ambler Realty Co.*, 272 U.S. 365, pp. 387–88 (1926).

13. See Siegan, *Property and Freedom*, pp. 181 and 189–201. Also, see Bernard H. Siegan, *Land Use Without Zoning* (Lexington, MA: Lexington Books, 1972), pp. 19–20, 59–65, 73–75, 77–84, and 152.

14. On the differences between zoning laws and restrictive covenants, see Siegan, *Land Use Without Zoning*, pp. 32–44 and 77–84.

15. Ibid., pp. 123–29; and Siegan, *Property and Freedom*, pp. 179–201. For another study on the effect of zoning regulations on housing affordability, see Joseph Gyourko and Raven Molloy, "Regulation and Housing Supply," NBER Working Paper 20536 (October 2014), http://www.nber.org/papers/w20536.pdf. See pp. 3–4, 6, 8–9, 40–42, and 50 in this document. In addition, see Sanford Ikeda and Emily Washington, "How Land-Use Regulation Undermines Affordable Housing," Mercatus Research (November 2015), https://www.mercatus.org/system/files/Ikeda-Land-U se-Regulation.pdf. See pp. 9–11, 12–14, and 18 in this document. Online content accessed August 26, 2018. For a study on the harmful effects of zoning on both housing and transportation availability, see Randal O'Toole, "Smart Growth and Housing," in *Housing America: Building Out of a Crisis*, edited by Randall G. Holcombe and Benjamin Powell (New Brunswick, NJ: Transaction Publishers, 2009), pp. 83–108.

16. See Chang-Tai Hsieh and Enrico Moretti, "Housing Constraints and Spatial Misallocation," *American Economic Journal: Macroeconomics* vol. 11, no. 2 (April 2019), pp. 1–39.

17. On the harmful nature of building code regulations and a rational alternative, see James D. Saltzman, "Building Code Blues," January 1, 1996, https://fee.org/arti cles/building-code-blues/ (accessed August 18, 2019). Also, see William Tucker, "Building Codes, Housing Prices, and the Poor," in *Housing America*, pp. 65–82.

18. See Simpson, *Markets Don't Fail!*, pp. 101–16 for more details.

Chapter 10

Addressing Other Proposals that Attempt to Protect Individual Rights and Freedom

INTRODUCTION

There have been many constitutional provisions offered by many writers that purport to protect rights and freedom but that fail to do so, such as the "right" of states to secede. The provisions fail to protect rights because those offering the provisions often do not have a proper understanding of what rights and freedom are and how to protect them. As a result, the provisions offered, in many cases, would actually lead to violations of rights and freedom. In addition, many provisions are offered that are not needed to protect freedom and may make it easier to violate freedom and rights, such as balanced-budget amendments and line-item veto power for the president. In this chapter, I address many constitutional provisions offered to protect freedom and describe why they do not, in fact, do so or why they are not needed. I also address the claim that the Constitution already protects rights adequately and therefore does not require any changes.

One of the constitutional provisions that other writers have put forward that is inconsistent with rights and freedom but that will not be addressed in this chapter is term limits.[1] I address the issue of term limits in chapter 7 in the discussion pertaining to Amendment XXII. So there is no need to address it here.

SECESSION

There is no general right for states, provinces, or political subunits to secede from a larger political unit. If a political subunit wishes to secede from a tyrannical government to form a free society, it has the right to do so. This is recognized in the Declaration of Independence (when a government "evinces a design to reduce them [the people] under absolute Despotism, it is their right . . . to throw off such Government"). However, there is no right of individuals, states, or provinces to secede for any reason whatsoever.[2] This implies the "right" to secede to violate rights. This is the case because if political subunits have a right to secede for any reason, then a subunit that wishes to violate rights would have the "right" to secede from a larger political unit that protects rights. That is a contradiction and stands in opposition to the appropriate function of government.

Even if a political subunit wants to secede from a free government to allegedly form another free government, it does not have the right to do so. The proper purpose of government is to protect individual rights. If a government performs its appropriate function, there is no moral or political justification to separate from it. It would be appropriate for the government one is trying to separate from to stop the secession in this case, by force if necessary, in the name of protecting rights because if one is trying to separate from a free government, one would have to question whether those who are seceding are really trying to separate to form another free government, given that they already live under freedom.

This applies to the Confederate States of America at the time of the Civil War. They seceded from a freer government to violate rights by preserving slavery. There may have been other issues that influenced the secession of the Southern States, such as states' rights, the expansion of the power of the federal government by President Lincoln, and the effect of tariffs on Southern States that were passed by Congress prior to the Civil War. However, none of these deny the overarching and growing conflict between the Union and the Confederacy that revolved around the legitimacy of slavery. For instance, one of the main issues underlying the states' rights debate was the right of a state to determine whether slavery should be legal within its borders. The fact that the Constitution of the Confederate States of America contained a number of provisions that significantly strengthened the institution of slavery also confirms that the issue of slavery was one of the central issues in the secession of the Southern States. If slavery was not a major issue to the South and the South was not concerned about preserving it, why did southerners take explicit action to preserve it in their founding document?

The Confederate Constitution was in large part a word-for-word copy of the U.S. Constitution, except for the replacement of "United" with "Confederate." However, many provisions were added to strengthen the protection of slavery. For example, Article I, Section 9, Clause 4 of the Confederate Constitution states, "No . . . law denying or impairing the right of property in negro slaves shall be passed." Article IV, Section 2, Clause 3 states, in part, "No slave . . . in any state . . . of the Confederate States, under the laws thereof, escaping or lawfully carried into another, shall, in consequence of any law or regulation therein, be discharged from such service . . . but shall be delivered up on claim of the party to whom such slave belongs . . . ." Next is Section 3, Clause 3 of that same article: "The institution of negro slavery as it now exists in the Confederate States, shall be recognized and protected by Congress, and by the territorial government." An obvious implication of these changes is that one of the major reasons for the secession of the Southern States was to preserve slavery.

While the Confederate Constitution also outlawed the importation of slaves in Article I, Section 9, this may have been done merely to placate border states and European powers. Many southern leaders were in favor of reopening the African slave trade, and it appears that if the Civil War had not broken out, the prohibition on the importation of slaves would have been repealed.[3] So the importation ban does not contradict the idea that the Confederate Constitution provides evidence that the preservation of slavery was one of the main drivers for secession.

The Confederate Constitution is not the only evidence that the Civil War and secession occurred due to slavery. Confederate and southern politicians made many speeches extolling the alleged virtues of slavery and stating that one of the important reasons for secession was slavery.[4] For example, John C. Calhoun, a Senator from South Carolina, made a speech on the floor of the Senate in 1837 stating that "the existing relation between the two races in the South . . . forms the most solid and durable foundation on which to rear free and stable political institutions."[5] While this does not directly show that slavery was the basis for secession, it certainly demonstrates the significance of slavery in southern culture, given that a very popular Senator from the south stated that slavery serves as the foundation for a stable political order.

If one thinks this does not serve as evidence at all for slavery being the basis for secession because it occurred too early in U.S. history, before the secession of the Southern States took place, consider this statement in an appeal for secession in the Georgia Assembly by one southern proponent of secession: "Our fathers made this government for the white man, rejecting the negro as an ignorant, inferior barbarian race, incapable of self-government, and not therefore, entitled to be associated with the white man upon terms of civil, political, and social equality."[6] Consider also the statement of the vice president of the Confederate States of America, Alexander Stephens, who made it clear after secession that "Our new government is founded . . . upon the great truth, that the negro is not equal to the white man; that slavery . . . is his natural and normal condition."[7] Consider also this statement of Robert H. Smith of Alabama, a member of the Constitutional Committee for the Confederacy, "We have dissolved the late Union chiefly because of the negro quarrel . . . . We have now placed our domestic institution, and secured its rights unmistakably, in the Constitution."[8]

If the above is not enough, consider that several Confederate states each stated in public declarations that maintaining slavery was at least one of the causes of secession. For example, the declaration for Mississippi states "Our position is thoroughly identified with the institution of slavery." The document for Texas states "We hold that the governments of the various states, and of the confederacy itself, were established by the white race, for themselves and their posterity." The declaration for South Carolina reads in part, "A geographical line has been drawn across the Union, and all the states north of that line have united in the election of a man to the high office of President of the United States, whose opinions and purposes are hostile to slavery."[9]

If one manages to ignore or evade this evidence for the idea that slavery was one, if not the only, main reason for secession, consider that all this evidence is irrelevant to the issue of whether the Southern States had a right to secede. They most certainly did not, given that they were slave states. The North had every right to free the slaves, whether through war or other means. States or other political units do not have the right to secede and, at the same time, preserve slavery, whether the preservation of slavery is given as a reason for the secession or not.

In addition, the position that individuals have a right to secede implicitly endorses anarchy. Individuals do not have the right to create "competing governments." Private security agencies are not a viable substitute for government. For one thing, who is to have a monopoly on the use of force and thus have the ultimate authority to end disputes? Such a situation would lead to chaos, endless conflicts, and the need to constantly negotiate agreements between individuals on how to handle disputes. It would not restrain the use of force but would lead to arbitrary uses of force. Violations of individual rights would be more frequent since rights-violating "governments" would be seen as legitimate options from the standpoint of individuals having the "right" to break away and form them.[10]

As long as a country has not descended into tyranny and there is still the possibility of changing it from within, there is still the chance of moving it toward a free society. Political subunits may have the right to secede from a mixed economy—given the violations of rights the government of a mixed economy engages in—but the best means to change such a society resides within the political process. This should be the first option pursued. This is also recognized in the Declaration of Independence ("Governments . . . should not be changed for light and transient causes"). However, if a society has descended into tyranny, then secession, revolution, or civil war may be the only options possible to establish a free government.

One must remember here that a proper constitution establishes and helps to maintain a free society. If a society has descended to the point where secession is necessary, a constitution that protects the right of people to secede from a rights-violating government will not help you. Why would those who violate your rights allow you to leave? They would not and have not throughout history. A constitution cannot provide a means to leave an unfree society.

Because of the nature of a rights-violating society, leaving it will have to be done either violently in the form of group secession or revolt, or secretly as an individual or individuals escaping to a better society, one that provides at least some protection of individual rights. For the above reasons, a provision to secede should not be included in the constitution of a free society. It is either unnecessary or useless and has the potential to lead to violations of individual rights by anarchists and political subunits that want to secede for the purpose of forming a government that violates rights.

AMENDMENTS FOR BALANCED BUDGETS, TAXING AND SPENDING LIMITS, AND LINE-ITEM VETO POWER FOR THE PRESIDENT

A balanced-budget amendment is not appropriate for the Constitution and will not help to protect individual rights. Many individuals have proposed such an amendment.[11] Some type of balanced-budget provision has been added to the constitutions of most states. Such an amendment in the Constitution would require that the government have a balanced budget in any given fiscal year. This is a bad idea, first, because it may be appropriate for the government to borrow money in particular years to increase its spending power, such as in times of war. Second, it would, at least partially, circumvent the separation of powers between the various branches of government.

How will a balanced-budget amendment circumvent the separation of powers? All the branches of government—the judicial, legislative, and executive branches—oversee each other to make sure no one branch engages in inappropriate activities. The Framers created the separate branches to ensure that the different branches keep each other in check, so that no one branch becomes too powerful and can violate rights on a large scale. There are, of course, flaws in the Constitution, which make it possible for the government to violate rights, but the separation of powers has been important in preventing rights from being violated to an even greater degree.

With a balanced-budget amendment, if the executive and legislative branches cannot balance the budget, the judicial branch will have to take action to ensure that the budget is balanced. Normally, the judicial branch determines whether legislation emanating from the other branches is constitutional or not. Since an unbalanced budget would be unconstitutional if we had a balanced-budget amendment, the judicial branch would, more than likely, have to appoint a committee to determine what stays in and what is cut from the budget. This would vastly increase the power of the judicial branch and allow it to grant favors with regard to spending and taxes. This, in turn, would generate lobbying of the judicial branch for favors. Furthermore, the judicial branch would be running the affairs of the legislative and executive branches, at least with regard to the budget. This unites the branches more, instead of separating them. To protect rights and limit their powers, we need to keep them as independent as possible.

Amendments that restrict spending and impose taxing limits to achieve a balanced budget or reduce the size of the government have similar problems.[12] The way to limit the power of the government is to require it to protect rights and nothing more. As a part of this, restricting the government to using only voluntary taxation in the Constitution is the one restriction that will severely limit the ability of the government to raise revenue. It will only be able to obtain revenue that is voluntarily donated to it by taxpayers or paid for services rendered (or paid for the right to such services, such as the right to have contractual disputes settled in a court of law). This will restrict the size of the government and its ability to spend. If the government is limited to obtaining funding through voluntary means, it will not be able to spend as much and it will be much harder for it to borrow to increase its spending as well. Preventing the government from being able to create money through the Federal Reserve, which would be abolished in a constitution that consistently protects freedom and individual rights, will also severely restrict the size and the ability of the government to borrow and spend. These are far more effective ways to limit the government's ability to tax and spend than an amendment that restricts spending and taxes but retains the government's ability to engage in confiscatory taxation and retains the Federal Reserve.

Line-item veto power for the president on appropriations bills runs into similar problems, as does line-item veto power for the president on any form of legislation.[13] Many states provide line-item veto power to their governors through their constitutions. In addition, a line-item veto law was enacted in 1996 at the federal level. This was declared unconstitutional by the Supreme Court in *Clinton v. City of New York* (1998), where it ruled that the law violated the Presentment Clause of Article I, Section 7. The problem with a line-item veto power amendment is that it would give the president implicit legislative powers. It would lead to him bargaining with members of Congress over when he will exercise the line-item veto or when he will not exercise it. For example, in exchange for not exercising the line-item veto power for the pet projects of Congressmen, the president can demand that his own pet projects be included in appropriations bills.[14] This unites, not separates, the executive and legislative branches of government.

We do not need gimmicks in the Constitution to limit spending and taxes, balance budgets, or give the president more specific veto power. We need provisions that protect rights, and none of these do that. In fact, they would probably lead to greater violations of rights.

THE ABILITY TO VOTE AND PREVENTING VOTER FRAUD

Protecting the ability of individuals to vote is addressed extensively in the current U.S. Constitution in Amendments XV, XIX, XXIII, XXIV, and XXVI. Amendments LIII and LIV of the revised Constitution strengthen protections of the ability to vote provided in Amendments XXIII and XXIV. At this point, an additional amendment that protects the ability to vote is not necessary. If an additional amendment is needed in the future to protect the ability to vote of a specific group (like Amendment XV does based on race and skin color or Amendment XIX does based on gender), such an amendment could be passed. However, I do not anticipate the need for such an amendment because of the extensive treatment the ability to vote already receives.

It is important that the ability to vote be protected in the Constitution because it is a part of achieving equality before the law. However, it must be understood that there is no right to vote. Different methods can legitimately be used to determine who can vote or who can hold political offices. Also, preserving the ability of everyone to vote is not fundamental to protecting rights. If the fundamental rights are protected (such as the rights to life, liberty, and property), restrictions on the ability to vote will not represent a threat to the rights of individuals because governments will still not be able to initiate physical force against people. In contrast, if the rights to life, liberty, and property are not protected but there are no restrictions on the ability to vote, what kind of protection would this afford? In this situation, your life would not belong to you. You may be able to participate in the voting process, but the majority of voters could vote to enslave you or worse. This could not happen under the first scenario.

In *Harper v. Virginia State Board of Elections* (1966), the Supreme Court reaffirmed its statement from an earlier case that the "right" to vote is "preservative of all rights" and is thus a fundamental right.[15] This is not true. Voting *can* protect other rights. However, the majority of voters *can violate* the rights of the minority of voters. For instance, the majority of voters can ban the use of plastic bags at grocery stores (as they have in California and elsewhere), thus violating the right to liberty of the minority of voters, who would obviously prefer to have the option to use plastic bags available. In addition, if voters approve of a confiscatory tax to finance the government, the majority of voters have violated the property rights of the minority, since confiscatory taxation initiates physical force to make people pay the tax. Hence, it is not necessarily true that the protection of the ability to vote protects other rights.

Voting fills a very narrow role in the mechanics of government, which mainly involves deciding who should fill certain positions. One does not define the proper function of government through the voting process.[16] Voting must exist within the context of a government limited solely to the function of protecting rights. Only then does it serve to protect rights. That is why the ability to vote is not fundamental to protecting rights.

On the issue of voter fraud, preventing such fraud is an important issue. Voter fraud is probably much more prevalent than is generally believed or than data indicate. However, I do not believe voter fraud rises to a high enough level of importance to justify passing a constitutional amendment. Although I have seen a proposed amendment that is supposed to help prevent voter fraud by, among other things, requiring photographic identification to vote and to register to vote,[17] at this point it is best handled through appropriate legislation.

HARMING OR THREATENING OTHERS
AND THE STATES OR PRESIDENT
BEING ABLE TO RESCIND LAWS

The constitutional lawyer Randy Barnett proposed an amendment that would allow the states to rescind specific federal regulations or particular pieces of federal legislation.[18] His amendment would require that a vote of three-quarters of the states would be necessary to rescind a law or regulation. This would provide another mechanism for abolishing a particular act of Congress and the president without modifying the Constitution. It would also provide another mechanism to put a check on Congress and the president.

While checks on government are good, there is a limit to how much protection they can provide. In the end, what is needed are provisions in the Constitution that limit the government to protecting rights. The problem with this type of amendment is that it could be used just as easily to prevent the federal government from protecting rights as it could be to prevent the federal government from violating rights. This would occur if the federal government passed a law that protected rights and at least three-quarters of the state legislatures voted to rescind the law. Hence, it does not add any additional protections to individual rights than are already provided by the Constitution.

This is another gimmick to limit what the federal government can do but whose purpose is not the protection of rights, since this power could be used just as easily to limit the federal government's ability to protect rights. This

gimmick is often put forward by those who believe that the state governments should have more power and the federal government should have less
(advocates of so-called states' rights). However, those who believe in "states'
rights" are not necessarily supporters of individual rights, as the issues of
slavery and the secession of the South demonstrate.

A modification of the Constitution put forward by Objectivists at the
Objectivism Wiki website states that "The President shall be obliged to veto
any bill and negate any law which is in violation of this Constitution."[19] Such
a clause is unnecessary for a couple of reasons. First, the president already
has veto power as stated in Article I, Section 7 of the Constitution, so there is
no reason to add this power in another section of the Constitution.

Of course, the focus of the veto power here is vetoing bills that violate the
Constitution. One would hope that both the president *and* Congress do not
pass or sign into law legislation that violates the Constitution, but putting a
clause in the Constitution stating that the president must veto bills that violate
the Constitution will not help prevent this because the president and every
member of Congress already take an oath to uphold the Constitution. If that
does not prevent the president from violating the Constitution, stating in the
Constitution that he must veto bills that violate the Constitution will not make
him do it. The same is true of negating laws that violate the Constitution.
Hence, this provision is not necessary.

Another modification put forward by Objectivists at the Objectivism Wiki
website states that the government shall not abridge any action that does
not harm or threaten another person.[20] The problem here is that the terms
"threaten" and "harm" are too broad. If a rival business opens next door and
financially harms its competitors by selling superior products and thus threatens the livelihood of the owners of the competing stores, does this mean the
government can shut the new business down? Of course not.

It is threats to individual rights or harms caused through violations of
rights that the government is to prevent or punish. This is what the new
Constitution does. I have added many provisions that help prevent violations of rights in specific situations (such as those pertaining to trade and
production), and I have already stated in the preamble that the purpose of the
Constitution is to protect rights. Therefore, no additional general statement
about the government not being able to abridge activities that do not violate
rights is needed.

RESTITUTION FOR GOVERNMENT WRONGS

A number of constitutional provisions have been put forward that call for
restitution from the government for wrongful actions by the government.
These pertain mainly, but are not limited, to criminal proceedings. For

example, Bernard Siegan in his book *Drafting a Constitution for a Nation or Republic Emerging into Freedom* states in his model constitution, Article VII, Section 8, that "A person who has been illegally arrested, detained, or imprisoned may receive indemnity for physical injury or material losses suffered thereby."[21]

Roderick T. Long provides additional examples in a constitution he developed. They exist in Part One, Sections 1.4.9 and 1.4.12 of his constitution. Section 1.4.9 states, in part, "A person who has been arrested, detained, imprisoned, tried, or sentenced either illegally or in error shall receive restitution." Section 1.4.12 states, in part:

> The government . . . shall as far as possible make full restitution for all loss suffered by persons arrested, indicted, restrained, imprisoned, expropriated, or otherwise injured in the course of criminal proceedings that do not result in their conviction. When they are responsible, government employees or agents shall be liable for this restitution.[22]

The last example comes from the Charter of Fundamental Rights of the European Union (EU). Article 41, Section 2.3 states "Every person has the right to have the Union make good any damage caused by its institutions or by its servants in the performance of their duties, in accordance with the general principles common to the laws of the Member States."[23]

The provisions from Siegan and Long focus on restitution for wrongful arrest, detainment, imprisonment, and so on. The EU Charter is much broader in scope. It provides restitution for *any* damages caused by the government or its servants, although it is qualified by the clause "in accordance with the general principles common to the laws of the Member States."

I address the responsibility of the government for wrongful acts in my discussion on sovereign immunity in chapter 5 that pertains to Article III, Section 2 of the Constitution. In that chapter, I state that the government must obey its own laws, be held liable for certain types of harm to individuals in the process of protecting rights, and be held responsible for meeting its contractual obligations. I also state that the possible scenarios in which the government should be held responsible are too numerous to identify. Where general rules can be identified, the government should enact statutes that determine when the government should and should not be held responsible. Otherwise, the courts must be relied upon in cases that do not fall under any general rule.

A provision stating that the government should provide restitution for government wrongs should not be included in the constitution of a government that consistently protects rights (at least not at this point). It would probably lead to many invalid lawsuits. As an example, consider restitution for arrests that do not lead to a conviction. There are many reasons, besides arresting the wrong person, why a conviction might not be obtained, even if the person on trial is, in fact, guilty. It could be due to a lack of evidence, incompetent prosecution, incompetent crime investigation, jury nullification, and many more reasons. You could end up with restitution being provided in many cases in which it is not justified. If restitution for any type of government wrong is incorporated into the Constitution, it could hamstring the government's ability to perform its proper functions by getting it tied up in many invalid lawsuits. It is best to leave the determination of when restitution by the government is appropriate to the courts and statutes.

If it turns out that the courts and statutes do not adequately provide for proper restitution to those individuals who have had wrongs committed against them by the government, it might be appropriate to amend the Constitution to address the issue. However, I would first want to see evidence that injustices are routinely committed by the government and proper restitution is not provided.

I do not believe that such an amendment will be necessary. One must remember that in a free society the government will be severely restricted regarding what it can do relative to today, where the government is able to violate rights on a significant scale. It will therefore be more difficult in a free society for the government to commit wrongful acts.

Such an amendment would be more appropriate in a society like we have today. Many wrongful acts by the government have their source in laws that violate rights, such as laws that make the use of certain drugs illegal (for example, cocaine) and laws enabling civil asset forfeiture under certain circumstances, as well as affirmative action (and antidiscrimination laws more generally). Affirmative action and antidiscrimination laws can lead to, among other things, fines being imposed on businesses for refusing to do business with people against which the laws forbid discrimination. In addition, laws forbidding the use of certain drugs, in combination with civil asset forfeiture laws, can lead to the confiscation of property from people for merely suspecting them of using or selling drugs (or suspecting the use or sale of drugs on their property). This latter, of course, is a violation of the current Constitution, namely, the Due Process Clause in Amendments V and XIV. These types of government wrongs are probably far more numerous than any government wrongs that would occur in a free society. Restitution for these wrongs should be provided and the laws making these wrongful acts possible should be abolished. Of course, abolishing these types of laws will prevent these types of wrongs from occurring in the first place, which is exactly what my changes to the Constitution are intended to do.

Related to the issue of the government providing restitution for wrongful acts it commits is the idea of incorporating provisions into the Constitution that require restitution from convicted individuals to their victims as a part of the punishment for committing a crime. One proposed provision of this type comes from Bernard Siegan's constitution. Article VII, Section 9 of his constitution states, in part, "As part of the sentence imposed for criminal wrongdoing, judges shall require restitution from the convicted person to a crime victim who suffers a loss."[24] One must first recognize that in many cases, especially when the perpetrators are poor or victims are murdered, restitution would not be possible. Nonetheless, where possible, restitution can already be provided through statutes, which give judges the power to impose such penalties. In addition, crime victims could bring civil suits for damages, if necessary, to obtain restitution. Furthermore, statutes could easily be passed to make further provision for such penalties, if it becomes necessary.

Such a constitutional amendment is not necessary, but the Constitution could be modified to make such penalties possible. I would want to see evidence that providing for such penalties in the Constitution is necessary before making the necessary modifications. Only if appropriate restitution cannot be provided (or can only be provided with great difficulty) through current means would it be appropriate to amend the Constitution with such provisions.

In another related provision from another constitution, the constitution developed by Roderick Long, law enforcement officers could be held criminally responsible for obtaining evidence illegally. The provision states, in part, "Where illegally obtained evidence is judged to be admissible in court, those who obtained it remain subject to criminal prosecution."[25] The provision allows illegally obtained evidence to be admissible in court but allows for criminal prosecution of those who obtained the evidence. This makes it possible to use relevant evidence in the prosecution of a criminal but also makes it possible to punish the government agent who illegally obtained the evidence. Under the current system, illegally obtained evidence may lead to a guilty defendant going free, since the evidence is inadmissible, and no punishment for the person who obtained the evidence. Thus, neither wrongdoer may be punished.

This provision could be consistent with the protection of individual rights. As Long states, this provision offers an alternative to the rules of evidence followed today.[26] It might be a better way of treating illegally obtained evidence than the current method, although it might also lead to more violations of rights due to illegal methods being used more often to obtain evidence. Because the current method consistently protects rights and appears to do an acceptable job, I see no reason to add a provision like this to the modified Constitution.

SUNSET CLAUSES, OMNIBUS BILLS, AND
UNAMENDABLE OR UNREPEALABLE CLAUSES

Some writers have advocated that sunset clauses be included in the Constitution. This type of clause would apply to all laws and/or federal agencies and departments.[27] The belief is that it will reduce the number of bad laws that are in force because laws will expire if they are not explicitly renewed by the legislature.

This is another gimmick that does not protect rights. In fact, it could make it harder to protect rights. This is the case because the clause would apply equally to laws that protect rights and laws that violate rights. If laws that protect rights expire and the legislature does not renew them, rights will not be protected as strongly. Of course, laws that violate rights will expire as well. Based on this consideration, sunset clauses are to our advantage in a political environment in which laws are routinely passed that violate rights. However, in such an environment, since the government and the people obviously want such laws—that's why rights-violating politicians are routinely voted into office in such an environment and why they routinely pass laws that violate rights—there is no reason why new laws would not continuously be passed that violate rights.

The same, of course, could be said of an environment in which laws are passed that protect rights. If they expire, new laws that protect rights could be continuously passed. However, identifying and passing laws that protect rights is a much more difficult task, as the history of the U.S. government, and governments in general, demonstrate. Protecting rights requires gaining knowledge and acting on it consistently. Violating rights requires ignorance, which is the default position for mankind. Gaining knowledge, disseminating it, passing it on from generation to generation, and acting on it consistently require enormous effort. As a result, the protection of rights is much more difficult and can be fleeting. Hence, I would much rather have laws remain permanently in place until explicitly repealed. This ultimately favors the protection of rights.

Despite the fact that sunset clauses tip the balance in favor of laws that violate rights and that I therefore favor laws remaining permanently in place until explicitly repealed, I do not consider sunset clauses fundamentally opposed to the protection of rights. They are a procedural gimmick that makes it mildly more difficult to keep laws in place that protect rights. However, the fundamental problem is the invalid ideas that are embraced in a nation that lead to laws being passed that violate individual rights in the first place (see chapter 1 for these ideas). Hence, I do not consider sunset clauses incompatible with the protection of individual rights. They are an optional procedural method that could be used in the context of protecting rights. However, because they are a mere procedural method and do not focus on the creation and maintenance of laws that protect rights, when sunset clauses are proposed as laws that can help protect rights (or limit government power or reduce the size of government), it is obvious that the people proposing such laws do not understand what rights are or how to protect them (or, likewise, how to reduce the size and power of government).

The next issue to address is omnibus bills. Some writers want to limit the number of subjects a bill or constitutional amendment can embrace to only one subject. They also want to limit appropriations bills to the spending of money.[28] These rules are often wanted because it is sometimes easier to incorporate controversial legislation in omnibus bills or in appropriations bills. Legislators who may not vote for specific provisions if they were proposed in a bill by themselves may vote for the legislation if it is part of a number of other provisions. Legislators may vote for an omnibus bill, even if it has legislation they do not like, as long as it has legislation they want to pass. The same is true with regard to the president signing a bill into law. Those people who oppose the use of omnibus bills generally believe this will prevent what they consider to be bad legislation from being passed.

The problem with this argument is that controversial legislation can go both ways. It can violate rights and it can protect rights. Hence, in some cases, controversial legislation that protects rights might be more likely to pass if it is incorporated into an omnibus bill or within an appropriations bill. In a society that leans to the left (more toward socialism and the welfare state, such as the United States today), it might be the case that controversial bills that violate rights will more likely pass if incorporated into omnibus or appropriations bills. However, in a society that leans to the right (toward capitalism), bills that protect rights might be more likely to pass.

The desire to restrict the number of subjects a bill can embrace or limit appropriations bills to the spending of money is another gimmick that does not focus on protecting rights. It is an optional procedural method that is consistent with the protection of rights. However, to protect rights, laws must focus on banning the initiation of physical force. Banning omnibus bills does not do that. Hence, I do not include such a ban in the revised Constitution.

The last topic to address in this section is unamendable or unrepealable provisions in a constitution. Such provisions are seen as desirable to prevent the most important provisions of a constitution from being repealed or modified. Roderick Long uses such a provision in his proposed constitution to guarantee that constitutional provisions that protect the rights of the people cannot be repealed or modified.[29] While I would love to be able to guarantee that the most important provisions—the parts that are absolutely necessary to protect rights—cannot be repealed or amended, that is an unrealistic desire.

A mechanism to modify a constitution is needed. This includes all parts of the constitution. This recognizes the fact that human beings have free will and the ideas generally embraced in an entire country or culture can change. Hence, if a portion of a constitution is unamendable or unrepealable and it falls out of favor on a large enough scale, it will be ignored, amended, or repealed anyway. People will rationalize ignoring or repealing the undesirable clause by saying that it does not work for our particular situation or in "our times" or under "our circumstances." They will claim that "we need to start over."

Essentially just this occurred with the Articles of Confederation. Article XIII of the Articles of Confederation required that the legislatures of all thirteen states confirm any changes to the Articles. However, based on Article VII of the Constitution, the establishment of the Constitution required ratification of the conventions of only nine states. Even though all thirteen states eventually ratified the Constitution, all thirteen would have first had to confirm changes to the ratification process in the Articles if the states were to follow the process for making changes to the Articles. This was never done. In fact, only twelve of the states sent representatives to the Constitutional Convention. Rhode Island did not send any delegates, although even if it did, the change would still have been required to be confirmed by all state legislatures if the states were to follow the Articles of Confederation. The provision in the Articles that dictated the procedures for changing the Articles was ignored because the Articles were not working. It was the right decision to make to abandon the Articles and create the Constitution, but my point here is that if certain provisions fall out of favor on a wide enough scale, they will simply be ignored and/or changed, as the abandonment of the Articles demonstrates.[30]

Hence, provisions that call for certain portions of a constitution to be unre-pealable or unamendable are pointless. This is another gimmick that focuses not on protecting rights but on attempting to lock into place—forever—certain constitutional provisions, even if there are overwhelming political forces opposing such provisions. This is impossible and useless to attempt to do. Therefore, I do not include it in the revised Constitution.

THE CONSTITUTION ALREADY PROTECTS RIGHTS AND DOES NOT NEED TO BE CHANGED

While this chapter focuses on proposed changes to the Constitution that attempt to protect rights and freedom but, in fact, do not, there are some lawyers who believe no changes to the Constitution are necessary in order to protect rights consistently. The problem with the Constitution, according to these lawyers, is not what the Constitution says but the way it is interpreted (or the fact that it is ignored).[31] A response to this claim is needed to show why changes to the Constitution are, in fact, needed.

According to Stephen Plafker, the Constitution is interpreted improperly because of the invalid philosophical ideas that people generally embrace today in the United States.[32] When individuals embrace philosophical ideas based on mysticism, altruism, and collectivism, and therefore abandon reason and reject egoism and individualism, it does not matter if the Constitution clearly protects individual rights and freedom. People will interpret the Constitution improperly and reject the protection of rights that the Constitution affords. So, the key to enabling the Constitution to protect rights, as the language currently in it is intended to do, is to ensure that a rational philosophy is widely embraced throughout the culture.

Plafker also states that the Constitution should not list rights, including the Bill of Rights, because rights are an integrated unity and when you list rights you disintegrate them.[33] While I agree that rights are an integrated unity, Plafker does not provide an explanation for why listing some rights disintegrates them. Others have also stated that specific rights should not be listed in the Constitution because it may imply that individuals possess only the rights that are listed. Hence, any rights not listed may not be recognized and protected.

Plafker is an Objectivist and argues that what is necessary to achieve a society in which rights are consistently protected is to have the widespread acceptance of Objectivist philosophy. This is the philosophy that states that the only proper purpose of government is to protect rights and that the protection of rights depends on the acceptance of the validity of the fundamental philosophical ideas of reason, egoism, and individualism. I agree with this and have discussed in detail in chapter 1 how Objectivist philosophy is the only philosophical system that provides a complete philosophical defense for the protection of rights. However, that does not mean that it is not useful to enumerate rights and that it would not be helpful in protecting rights to change the Constitution so that it consistently protects them.

In responding to Plafker's arguments, one must first recognize that it will be very unlikely that an entire nation or culture will embrace one philosophical viewpoint, even if one philosophical viewpoint is widely accepted. Many philosophical viewpoints will more than likely exist in one nation. Moreover, one does not want to write a constitution for the most rational individuals within the culture. Since it is the irrational who violate rights, one needs to write a constitution to stop them, as much as possible, from doing so. In essence, the rational, rights-respecting individuals must be able to use the Constitution as a weapon to protect themselves from the irrational.

In addition, while the establishment of a constitution that consistently protects rights will require that Objectivism have significant influence within the culture, one must also remember that individuals have free will and the ideas accepted in a culture can change. Cultures can shift from being more rational to more irrational and vice versa. To ensure that the protection of rights is as strong as possible throughout time, especially when changes move a culture toward the irrational end of the philosophical spectrum, it is best to have a constitution that consistently protects rights. Of course, such a constitution will not guarantee the protection of rights, and if a culture becomes irrational enough it will lead to improper interpretations of, and people ignoring, the constitution. However, a constitution that consistently protects rights will erect the most significant political and legal barriers that are possible in the way of those who want to violate rights. Moreover, explicit statements of which rights are protected will help to prevent misinterpretations. This is how it will help to protect rights and why such a constitution is necessary.

For the same reasons, it is also crucial to enumerate fundamental and important rights—or rights that are routinely violated—in a constitution. Enumerating rights can help people learn by example what rights are and how to protect them. It will help prevent rights from being floating abstractions—abstract ideas not grounded in the facts of reality.[34]

In addition, enumerating rights can make it more difficult to evade or ignore what the constitution says and what rights it protects. For example, it is much more difficult to violate the right to produce and trade and the right to choose not to trade with others if the constitution explicitly states that these rights are to be protected. I will grant that these rights are already protected (at least to some extent) by the right to property and liberty that the current Constitution upholds. However, the rights to property and liberty are much more abstract. The right to produce and trade is a specific example of the rights to liberty and property. There is a much clearer link, and thus a much easier connection to make, between protecting the right to produce and trade and the actions of producing and trading goods with others than there is between the rights to liberty and property and the actions of producing and trading with others.

Furthermore, as I have said, redundancy is a good thing when protecting rights. Here it helps to have redundancy in the form of specific examples of abstract rights for the purpose of making sure those specific, concrete rights are protected and to help people understand the nature of the abstract rights. This will enable better protection of the abstract rights.

Additionally, it would be suicidal for freedom if the Bill of Rights was eliminated. Imagine the violations of rights that would take place today without it. There would be much less protection of the freedom of the press, the right to bear arms, the right to be secure against unreasonable searches and seizures, and so forth. In many cases, those who have their rights violated would not have a clause in the Constitution to refer to in defense of their rights if the Bill of Rights did not exist.

Moreover, while it is true that all rights cannot be listed in the Constitution, Amendment IX can be used to protect the rights not listed.[35] The much clearer focus of the modified Constitution on the protection of rights will also help to protect the rights not listed. If more rights had been listed by the Framers (such as the freedom of production and trade), our rights would be much better protected today because more rights would be explicitly protected and they could serve as a better guide in the protection of unenumerated rights. Furthermore, for my purposes, and more generally in a culture in which rights are not understood (as in America today), listing specific rights is extremely useful as a pedagogical device. Discussion of these rights can help people learn about rights and thus move a society toward freedom, or possibly slow its dissent into tyranny.

CONCLUSION

There are many other proposals that have been put forward in an attempt to protect rights which I do not address here. They include a proposal that says that those who are impeached be subject to criminal punishment.[36] They also include a provision that prevents the legislature from being able to delegate its legislative power to any other person, body, or bureau.[37] In addition, they include a proposal to return voting for senators to the pre–Seventeenth Amendment procedure where state legislatures chose their senators according to Article I.[38] Furthermore, they include proposals to limit the power that treaties can confer on Congress.[39] They include many more proposals as well. The proposals not included in this chapter have not been included for a variety of reasons. One basis for choosing provisions to include in this chapter was that they were raised by many individuals. In addition, some have been addressed adequately by others and thus I did not discuss them in this chapter. Some I did not consider important enough to address.

Some provisions were included in this chapter because of their importance. That is, the discussion of certain proposals could be used to help readers understand the nature of rights and how to protect them (or how not to protect them). In the end, the page limits of a book come into play as well. However, what I have included is diverse enough to provide indications of why other proposals that are not included in the chapter should not be included (or necessarily included) in a constitution that consistently protects individual rights.

The revised Constitution does not (and should not) enumerate all rights. The purpose of a constitution is to define the basic structure of a government, protect fundamental rights, and ensure that the power of the government is restricted to only protecting individual rights. One does not need to enumerate all rights in a constitution to do this. One does not need to be able to point to a right in a constitution to be able to claim that he has had his rights violated. As already mentioned, Amendment IX tells us that there are rights that the people possess that are not enumerated in the Constitution. What is crucial is that the fundamental rights be listed in the Constitution and enough limitations on the power of the government be provided in the Constitution so that rights and freedom can be consistently protected. This is what the revised Constitution does.

NOTES

1. For some examples of those who have offered proposals on term limits, see Levin, *The Liberty Amendments*, p. 19; and Barnett, "A Bill of Federalism," Article 7.

2. For one writer who puts forward such a view, see Robert W. McGee, "Secession Reconsidered," *The Journal of Libertarian Studies* vol. 11, no. 1 (Fall 1994), pp. 11–33. See pp. 21–26.

3. Richard Shedenhelm, "The Cause of the Civil War According to Confederate Leaders," *The Objective Standard* vol. 10, no. 3 (Fall 2015), pp. 51–56. See p. 53.

4. For examples, see Alexander V. Marriott, "Getting Lincoln Right," *The Objective Standard* vol. 9, no. 2 (Summer 2014), pp. 11–38. See pp. 20–23. Also, see Shedenhelm, "The Cause of the Civil War," pp. 53–55.

5. Marriott, "Getting Lincoln Right," p. 22.

6. Ibid., p. 23.

7. Shedenhelm, "The Cause of the Civil War," p. 54.

8. Ibid., pp. 53–54.

9. Ibid., pp. 51–53.

10. For an excellent essay on the destructive nature of anarchy and its inconsistency with the protection of individual rights, see Harry Binswanger, "Sorry Libertarian Anarchists, Capitalism Requires Government," *Forbes*, January 24, 2014, https://www.forbes.com/sites/harrybinswanger/2014/01/24/sorry-libertarian-anarchists-capitalism-requires-government-2/#f3def8a7d89b (accessed September 4, 2018).

11. For one example, see Steven G. Calabresi, "An Agenda for Constitutional Reform," in *Constitutional Stupidities, Constitutional Tragedies*, edited by William N. Eskridge, Jr. and Sanford Levinson (New York: New York University Press, 1998), pp. 22–27. See p. 24. For another example, see Barnett, "A Bill of Federalism," Article 8.

12. For an example of such an amendment, see Levin, *The Liberty Amendments*, p. 73.

13. See Calabresi, "An Agenda for Constitutional Reform," p. 24; and Barnett, "A Bill of Federalism," Article 8 for examples where authors have supported such an amendment.

14. On the line-item veto power, see George Reisman, "The Line-Item Veto is a Bad Idea," February 14, 1998, http://capitalism.net/articles/li_veto.htm (accessed August 13, 2017).

15. *Harper v. Virginia State Board of Elections*, 383 U.S. 663, p. 667 (1966).

16. Tara Smith, "The Politics of Pretend—and Its Impact on the Legal System," audio recording (Irvine, CA: The Ayn Rand Institute, 2013).

17. See Levin, *The Liberty Amendments*, pp. 183–84.

18. Barnett, "A Bill of Federalism," Article 6.

19. See Article II, Clause 9 of the new constitution at the Objectivism Wiki website, http://wiki.objectivismonline.net/New_constitution (accessed August 21, 2017).

20. See Amendment I of the new constitution at the Objectivism Wiki website, http://wiki.objectivismonline.net/Existing_Amendments#Amendment_1 (accessed August 21, 2017).

21. Siegan, *Drafting a Constitution*, p. 93.

22. Roderick T. Long, "Imagineering Freedom: A Constitution of Liberty, Part II: Defining Federal Powers," *Formulations* vol. 2, no. 2 (Winter 1994–1995), http://www.freenation.org/a/f22l2.html (accessed September 4, 2017).

23. "Charter of Fundamental Rights of the European Union," *Official Journal of the European Union* vol. 50 (December 14, 2007), pp. 1–17. See p. 11.

24. Siegan, *Drafting a Constitution*, p. 93.

25. Long, "Defining Federal Powers," Part 1, Section 1.4.10 of his constitution.

26. Ibid. See the discussion on Section 1.4.10.

27. For one example, see Levin, *The Liberty Amendments*, p. 99.

28. For an example, see Siegan, *Drafting a Constitution*, p. 83.

29. Long, "The Rights of the People."

30. See Akhil Reed Amar, *America's Constitution: A Biography* (New York: Random House, 2005), pp. 30 and 517, note 65 for a perspective on how the transition to the Constitution from the Articles might have taken place without violating the Articles even if all states did not confirm a change to the ratification process in the Articles, although it is admitted by Amar that at the time of the creation of the Constitution there is no evidence that anyone ever invoked this method of transition. James Madison, in *The Federalist* No. 43, puts forward a perspective on the transition closer to my view of how it took place. See Madison, Hamilton, and Jay, *The Federalist Papers*, pp. 285–86.

31. For examples, see Randy E. Barnett, *Restoring the Lost Constitution: The Presumption of Liberty* (Princeton, NJ: Princeton University Press, 2004), pp. 354–57; and hear Plafker, "Structure of the American Constitution." In the latter, hear Lectures 2 and 3.

32. Plafker, "Structure of the American Constitution," Lectures 2 and 3.

33. Ibid., Lecture 3.

34. On floating abstractions, see Peikoff, *Objectivism*, p. 96.

35. On the Ninth Amendment's ability to protect unenumerated rights, despite the fact that it is seen as largely irrelevant today, see Randy E. Barnett, "The Ninth Amendment: It Means What It Says," *Texas Law Review* vol. 85, no. 1 (November 2006), pp. 1–82.

36. Seigan, *Drafting a Constitution*, p. 87.

37. See Long, "Defining Federal Powers," Part 1, Section 1.2.16 of his constitution.

38. Levin, *The Liberty Amendments*, p. 33.

39. Barnett, "A Bill of Federalism," Article 4.

Epilogue

One of the main tasks I perform in this book is to provide a constitution that can help to create and maintain a free society. This constitution is based on the U.S. Constitution. The U.S. Constitution is close enough to consistently protecting individual rights to be able to use it as the starting point for creating the constitution of a free society.

The main changes to the Constitution that are proposed include preventing the government from regulating commerce and interfering in general with the freedom to trade, as well as preventing the government from engaging in confiscatory taxation and taking private property. The changes also include preventing the government from coining and regulating money, paying for the attorneys of poor individuals beyond the minimum representation necessary to protect rights in criminal cases, and violating the freedom of thought, the latter of which includes better protections of the freedom of speech. In addition, the changes include eliminating the government's ability to establish post offices and post roads and preventing it from providing assistance to individuals and organizations that does not involve protecting rights. Moreover, they include restricting the type of property the government can own and protecting the right of individuals to do what they want with their property, so long as individuals do not violate the rights of others. Finally, they include abolishing Selective Service and the draft, as well as protecting the right of individuals to the control of their own bodies and the right to do with their own persons what they want (again, of course, so long as they do not violate the rights of others).

Some of these main changes might seem trivial. For instance, eliminating the government's ability to establish post offices and post roads may seem like a minor change, since the business the Post Office engages in represents only a small portion of all economic activity in the nation. However, this, in fact, represents a significant change because it is widely accepted that the government should provide postal services. To make such a change requires a fundamental shift in the thinking of individuals. If enough people embrace this change to make it possible to prevent the government from engaging in this activity, it will signify that a large number of people now understand the proper functions of government. It will mean, more broadly, that not only has the culture shifted enough to make this one, concrete change possible, but that radical cultural change has taken place to make the achievement of a capitalist society possible.

It is important to emphasize that the new Constitution does not focus on explicitly protecting all rights. A constitution, being the fundamental law of the land, is purposely general in nature. As I state in previous chapters, it provides the basic structure of government, protects fundamental rights, and restricts the power of government sufficiently so that it is limited to only protecting rights. The revised Constitution performs this latter function, in part, by protecting rights that tend to be more frequently violated, such as the right to donate to political campaigns and the right to do with one's own person what one wants.

In addition, a constitution must be general enough to apply throughout time. It is impossible to anticipate all scenarios with regard to which rights need to be protected, including changing technologies and new discoveries of natural resources. Any laws needed to protect rights in a more detailed fashion based on new discoveries or because of other changes can be supplied by Congress passing the necessary legislation. The Constitution, of course, will serve as the guide that must be adhered to in these situations.

There are a number of radical features of the new Constitution. Radical change is what is needed to make our society fully consistent with the requirements of human life. Extreme change should not be seen as something negative. These changes will lead to extreme peace, prosperity, and good will among human beings.

One might ask, how is the United States to transition to the new Constitution given that some of the amendments require radical changes in the government and the nation? This is particularly true of the amendments that will require voluntary taxation to be used to finance the government, but it is true for other amendments as well. Given what I said in the discussion of the amendments on taxation, it obviously makes sense to first ratify the amendments that do *not* impose voluntary taxation. The taxation amendments should be implemented last. The most important amendments to ratify are those that achieve the greatest increases in freedom and the rate of economic progress. These include the amendments that focus on regulation, the freedom of trade, welfare, and the type of property the government can own and operate. These should be ratified first. This will help to decrease the size and scope of government and also help to reduce in the quickest fashion possible the funding needed to finance the government. Some of the constitutional provisions, once ratified, may require several years to implement, such as those pertaining to eliminating government assistance and disposing of organizations and other property the government should not own. This can be achieved by including clauses that provide the government a specific period of time to implement the provisions. Once the government has been largely or completely reduced to its appropriate size, the amendments focusing on taxation can then be ratified. Other amendments, that will not reduce the size of government (such as amendments focusing on the age of politicians), can be ratified either before or after the amendments focusing on taxation. From the existing starting point of the U.S. Constitution, there are many optional (and some nonoptional) orders that can be followed to create and implement a constitution that consistently protects rights.

One issue that must be addressed is the large number of amendments I propose to the Constitution: thirty-six in total. One might think that the Constitution must not do a very good job of protecting rights if thirty-six amendments are required to make it fully consistent with rights. One would be wrong if one came to this conclusion.

The proposed changes are necessary to make the Constitution *completely* consistent with the protection of freedom and rights. Many issues must be addressed to do this, including regulation, taxation, stronger protection of the freedom of speech and thought, stronger protection of property rights, the age of representatives, senators and the president, the ability to vote, and many, many more. Some issues are more important than others. For example, reducing how old people must be to become a representative, senator or the president is a minor issue. If no amendment is ratified reducing these ages, it would be a very minor inconsistency with the protection of individual rights that remains. A society with all the changes to the Constitution that I describe, except for the amendments pertaining to the age of politicians, would still be a free society. In fact, if the most important amendments I propose are ratified, for all practical purposes, the United States would be a free society.[1] I chose to write a book that presents the changes necessary to make the Constitution completely consistent with the protection of rights and freedom because that helps to provide the best exposition of the nature of rights and freedom, which is something the world desperately needs to learn about.

Many of the changes made to the Constitution are necessary due to the philosophical corruption that exists in today's culture. These changes include modifications to provisions that call for the government to provide for the general welfare, qualifications on privileges and immunities, modifications to the Second Amendment, among other changes. These kinds of changes should not be seen as necessary due to deficiencies of the Constitution.

Detailed changes are needed to counter the philosophical corruption (i.e., the abandonment of reason) that exists in the United States today and the rights-violating laws and interpretations of the Constitution such corruption spawns. The changes to the Constitution will ultimately need to be made in more philosophically sound times, when the efficacy of reason is more widely embraced. However, once written into the Constitution, these changes can protect rights even if a society moves significantly in an irrational direction. One can get an idea of the corruption I am referring to from chapter 1 of this book. The opposing philosophical ideas—namely, variants of mysticism, altruism, and collectivism—that I discuss in chapter 1 are a part of the philosophical corruption that exists. They either underlie the rejection of rights or provide invalid justifications for rights.

Some might think that the changes I propose are impractical because they are so radical. The changes are radical because they are far removed from the type of political ideas and policies that are generally accepted today. But the changes are needed to move us toward a capitalist society. A capitalist society is, in fact, the most practical form of society because it is the only society that is fully consistent with the requirements of human life. It is statism that is impractical. This has been seen in the disasters created by socialism in Cuba, the former USSR, North Korea, and Venezuela (among others). It has also been seen through the disasters created by the welfare state, such as, recently, in Greece. Let us also not forget the first welfare state created in Germany in the 1880s under Otto von Bismarck and what it eventually led to: the rise of Hitler and the Nazi form of socialism in the 1930s. The welfare state that exists today in the United States is headed down a similar path. If the practical is that which helps to accomplish some useful result, then what I propose in this book is immensely practical because of the flourishing of human life that it can help to achieve. Based on this standard, socialism and the welfare state are undeniably impractical.[2] The key, as mentioned previously, is to implement the changes in the proper order to ensure the government will always be adequately funded at each stage of the movement toward a capitalist society.

It is important to note that my modifications to the Constitution are consistent with the original Constitution and the intent of the Founding Fathers to protect individual rights. The founders made huge strides toward this end. However, in some ways, they were inconsistent with this goal and in other ways they only made partial progress in achieving this goal. I have worked out the inconsistencies. In essence, the changes I propose to the Constitution complete the project, started at the founding of the nation, of creating a free society. They create a free society *without contradictions*.

There are no gaps in the new Constitution that can be used to violate freedom. Violations of freedom could only occur by ignoring the new Constitution. This is often how violations of freedom occur today, but today there is the added problem of the portions of the Constitution that are inconsistent with freedom and the protection of individual rights. This latter would no longer be a potential with the Constitution created by my proposed changes.

In addition, a revised Declaration of Independence is provided that eliminates the inconsistencies in the defense of freedom and individual rights provided in that document. The Declaration of Independence, as it is currently written, is a great document. Only a few changes are needed to make it fully consistent with the protection of rights. These include changing references to God that attribute causal significance to God. As I have shown, God does not exist and thus is not the source of anything, including individual rights. I recognize, instead, the secular source of rights. Moreover, property rights are added to the list of inalienable rights. The epistemological status of the truths that the Founding Fathers considered self-evident is corrected as well. Finally, "all men are created equal" is changed to "all men are born equally free." The changes to the Declaration and the supporting discussion in chapter 2 provide further understanding of the nature of rights and will help to strengthen the overall protection of rights.

One virtue of this book is that it not only provides a new Constitution that consistently protects individual rights, but it provides its own "federalist papers" as well. In the book, one can see not only what provisions are necessary to consistently protect rights in a constitution, but one can see why these provisions are necessary and what alternatives were considered. This will help future generations of judges, legislators, and presidents interpret the law and create laws in ways that best protects rights.

The knowledge that readers can gain about what is required to protect rights is an especially important take away from reading this book given that it will be a long time before the Constitution can be changed to consistently protect rights. Nonetheless, the ultimate goal should be to create a government that consistently protects rights; it must be the ideal for which we strive. But even if one cannot achieve the ideal of fully implementing the changes I have outlined in this book, the book can help move the country incrementally in the direction of protecting rights if some of the changes are implemented. The important practical consequences of every step the country moves in the direction of consistently protecting rights will be to achieve a more civilized, peaceful, and prosperous society.

Even in a society in which no amendment to a constitution can be ratified to more consistently protect rights, this book can help move that society forward to protect rights. By helping people understand the nature and proper application of rights, this book can help lawmakers understand the legislation that needs to be enacted to protect rights. While there may be limits to what rights-protecting laws can be passed if the constitution does not consistently protect rights, it may be possible to pass some laws that more consistently protect rights even without a constitution that consistently does so. Moreover, it is generally easier to pass legislation than make constitutional changes. So if constitutional changes are impossible, passing legislation that protects rights may still be achievable.

In addition, the greater understanding of rights that this book can help individuals achieve can help courts provide judicial review that is more consistent with the protection of rights. While judicial review must necessarily be based on the laws that exist, to the extent that a review based on the protection of rights is consistent with a country's constitution, this book will be useful to the courts in such a country. The courts should move the review of the laws in the direction of protecting rights to the extent the constitution allows. Further movement will, of course, require modifications to the constitution itself.

Even if a society has declined to the point that the constitution, laws, and judicial review cannot be changed in ways to better protect rights, by understanding what is necessary to protect rights in practice, one can achieve a greater understanding of the nature of rights and help spread that knowledge throughout society. Such knowledge is crucial to ultimately understand how to protect rights consistently. This is the first step that must be taken if rights are to be protected more consistently, or at all, in a society. It is the lack of knowledge of what rights are and the lack of knowledge of the philosophical foundations of rights, including the lack of understanding of the fundamental importance of the protection of individual rights to human life, that ultimately prevents countries from more consistently protecting them (or protecting them at all).

Finally, some might think that the constitution about which I write is impossible to achieve because too many people would oppose such a constitution. That is true in today's philosophically corrupt world in which reason and the morality of rational self-interest are rejected and denounced. However, an enormous achievement such as the creation of a constitution that rigorously adheres to the requirements of a free society is possible. To paraphrase the philosopher whose ideas—more than anyone else's ideas—will make it possible, Ayn Rand, this world is real, it exists, and it can be won. But achieving this world requires a total break from the past.[3] It requires a revolution, both philosophically and politically. This book is part of helping to create such a revolution.

NOTES

1. The most important amendments are Amendments XXXI (requiring voluntary taxation), XXXII (eliminating the Commerce Clause), XXXIII (eliminating the

coining and regulating of money), XXXV (eliminating government provision of postal services), XLIV (protecting the freedom of thought, freedom of association, and freedom from religion), XLVII (eliminating eminent domain), XLVIII (limiting the provision of counsel by the government), L (eliminating the income tax), LV (protecting the freedom of production and trade), LVI (protecting the control over our own bodies and persons), LVII (preventing government ownership and assistance of private organizations and government assistance to individuals and other governments, unless necessary for the protection of rights), LVIII (restricting government ownership of property), LX (strengthening freedom of speech), LXI (preventing the coining and regulating of money and imposing other restrictions on the government's use of money), LXII (eliminating Selective Service, the draft, and compulsory jury service), and LXIII (providing stronger protection of property rights).

2. See Simpson, *Markets Don't Fail!* for a detailed discussion of the practicality of capitalism and the impracticality of socialism and the mixed economy or welfare state. See especially chapter 1 and the epilogue. On the first welfare state created in Germany under Bismarck in the 1880s, its connection to the rise of socialism in Germany in the 1930s, and the similar path down which the United States is headed, see Peikoff, *Ominous Parallels*.

3. For the paraphrased material, see Rand, *Atlas Shrugged*, p. 1069.

Appendix A

The Revised Declaration of Independence

In Congress, July 4, 1776.

The unanimous Declaration of the thirteen united States of America,

When in the Course of human events, it becomes necessary for one people to dissolve the political bands which have connected them with another, and to assume among the powers of the earth, the separate and equal station to which the Laws of Nature entitle them, a decent respect to the opinions of mankind requires that they should declare the causes which impel them to the separation.

We hold these truths to be undeniable, that all men are born equally free, that they possess based on their nature as rational beings certain unalienable Rights, that among these are Life, Liberty, Property and the pursuit of Happiness.—That to secure these rights, Governments are instituted among Men, deriving their just powers from the consent of the governed,—That whenever any Form of Government becomes destructive of these ends, it is the Right of the People to alter or to abolish it, and to institute new Government, laying its foundation on such principles and organizing its powers in such form, as to them shall seem most likely to effect their Safety and Happiness. Prudence, indeed, will dictate that Governments long established should not be changed for light and transient causes; and accordingly all experience hath shewn, that mankind are more disposed to suffer, while evils are sufferable, than to right themselves by abolishing the forms to which they are accustomed. But when a long train of abuses and usurpations, pursuing invariably the same Object evinces a design to reduce them under absolute Despotism, it is their right, it is their duty, to throw off such Government, and to provide new Guards for their future security.—Such has been the patient sufferance of these Colonies; and such is now the necessity which constrains them to alter their former Systems of Government. The history of the present King of Great Britain is a history of repeated injuries and usurpations, all having in direct object the establishment of an absolute Tyranny over these States. To prove this, let Facts be submitted to a candid world.

He has refused his Assent to Laws, the most wholesome and necessary for the public good.

He has forbidden his Governors to pass Laws of immediate and pressing importance, unless suspended in their operation till his Assent should be obtained; and when so suspended, he has utterly neglected to attend to them.

He has refused to pass other Laws for the accommodation of large districts of people, unless those people would relinquish the right of Representation in the Legislature, a right inestimable to them and formidable to tyrants only.

He has called together legislative bodies at places unusual, uncomfortable, and distant from the depository of their public Records, for the sole purpose of fatiguing them into compliance with his measures.

He has dissolved Representative Houses repeatedly, for opposing with manly firmness his invasions on the rights of the people.

He has refused for a long time, after such dissolutions, to cause others to be elected; whereby the Legislative powers, incapable of Annihilation, have returned to the People at large for their exercise; the State remaining in the mean time exposed to all the dangers of invasion from without, and convulsions within.

He has endeavoured to prevent the population of these States; for that purpose obstructing the Laws for Naturalization of Foreigners; refusing to pass others to encourage their migrations hither, and raising the conditions of new Appropriations of Lands.

He has obstructed the Administration of Justice, by refusing his Assent to Laws for establishing Judiciary powers.

He has made Judges dependent on his Will alone, for the tenure of their offices, and the amount and payment of their salaries.

He has erected a multitude of New Offices, and sent hither swarms of Officers to harrass our people, and eat out their substance.

He has kept among us, in times of peace, Standing Armies without the Consent of our legislatures.

He has affected to render the Military independent of and superior to the Civil power.

He has combined with others to subject us to a jurisdiction foreign to our constitution, and unacknowledged by our laws; giving his Assent to their Acts of pretended Legislation:

For Quartering large bodies of armed troops among us:

For protecting them, by a mock Trial, from punishment for any Murders which they should commit on the Inhabitants of these States:

For cutting off our Trade with all parts of the world:

For imposing Taxes on us without our Consent:

For depriving us in many cases, of the benefits of Trial by Jury:

For transporting us beyond Seas to be tried for pretended offences:

For abolishing the free System of English Laws in a neighbouring Province, establishing therein an Arbitrary government, and enlarging its Boundaries so as to render it at once an example and fit instrument for introducing the same absolute rule into these Colonies:

For taking away our Charters, abolishing our most valuable Laws, and altering fundamentally the Forms of our Governments:

For suspending our own Legislatures, and declaring themselves invested with power to legislate for us in all cases whatsoever.

He has abdicated Government here, by declaring us out of his Protection and waging War against us.

He has plundered our seas, ravaged our Coasts, burnt our towns, and destroyed the lives of our people.

He is at this time transporting large Armies of foreign Mercenaries to compleat the works of death, desolation and tyranny, already begun with circumstances of Cruelty & perfidy scarcely paralleled in the most barbarous ages, and totally unworthy the Head of a civilized nation.

He has constrained our fellow Citizens taken Captive on the high Seas to bear Arms against their Country, to become the executioners of their friends and Brethren, or to fall themselves by their Hands.

He has excited domestic insurrections amongst us, and has endeavoured to bring on the inhabitants of our frontiers, the merciless Indian Savages, whose known rule of warfare, is an undistinguished destruction of all ages, sexes and conditions.

In every stage of these Oppressions We have Petitioned for Redress in the most humble terms: Our repeated Petitions have been answered only by repeated injury. A Prince whose character is thus marked by every act which may define a Tyrant, is unfit to be the ruler of a free people.

Nor have We been wanting in attentions to our British brethren. We have warned them from time to time of attempts by their legislature to extend an unwarrantable jurisdiction over us. We have reminded them of the circumstances of our emigration and settlement here. We have appealed to their native justice and magnanimity, and we have conjured them by the ties of our common kindred to disavow these usurpations, which, would inevitably interrupt our connections and correspondence. They too have been deaf to the voice of justice and of consanguinity. We must, therefore, acquiesce in the necessity, which denounces our Separation, and hold them, as we hold the rest of mankind, Enemies in War, in Peace Friends.

We, therefore, the Representatives of the united States of America, in General Congress, Assembled, appealing to the ultimate arbiters of truth—Reason and Reality—for the rectitude of our intentions, do, in the Name, and by Authority of the good People of these Colonies, solemnly publish and declare, That these United Colonies are, and of Right ought to be Free and Independent States; that they are Absolved from all Allegiance to the British Crown, and that all political connection between them and the State of Great Britain, is and ought to be totally dissolved; and that as Free and Independent States, they have full Power to levy War, conclude Peace, contract Alliances, establish Commerce, and to do all other Acts and Things which Independent States may of right do. And for the support of this Declaration, with a firm reliance on the righteousness of our cause, we mutually pledge to each other our Lives, our Fortunes and our sacred Honor.[1]

NOTE

1. I do not include the signature block at the end of the original Declaration.

Appendix B

The Revised U.S. Constitution

PREAMBLE[1]

We the People of the United States, in Order to form a more perfect Union, establish Justice, insure domestic Tranquility, provide for the common defence, promote the general Welfare, and secure the Blessings of Liberty to ourselves and our Posterity, do ordain and establish this Constitution for the United States of America.

ARTICLE I

Section 1

All legislative Powers herein granted shall be vested in a Congress of the United States, which shall consist of a Senate and House of Representatives.

Section 2

The House of Representatives shall be composed of Members chosen every second Year by the People of the several States, and the Electors in each State shall have the Qualifications requisite for Electors of the most numerous Branch of the State Legislature.

[No Person shall be a Representative who shall not have attained the Age of twenty-five Years, and been seven Years a Citizen of the United States,][2] and who shall not, when elected, be an Inhabitant of that State in which he shall be chosen.

[Representatives and direct Taxes shall be apportioned among the several States which may be included within this Union, according to their respective Numbers, which shall be determined by adding to the whole Number of free Persons, including those bound to Service for a Term of Years, and excluding Indians not taxed, three-fifths of all other Persons.][3] The actual Enumeration shall be made within three Years after the first Meeting of the Congress of the United States, and within every subsequent Term of ten Years, in such Manner as they shall by Law direct. The Number of Representatives shall not exceed one for every thirty Thousand, but each State shall have at Least one Representative; and until such enumeration shall be made, the State of New Hampshire shall be entitled to chuse three, Massachusetts eight, Rhode-Island and Providence Plantations one, Connecticut five, New-York six, New Jersey four, Pennsylvania eight, Delaware one, Maryland six, Virginia ten, North Carolina five, South Carolina five, and Georgia three.

When vacancies happen in the Representation from any State, the Executive Authority thereof shall issue Writs of Election to fill such Vacancies.

The House of Representatives shall chuse their Speaker and other Officers and shall have the sole Power of Impeachment.

Section 3

The Senate of the United States shall be composed of two Senators from each State, [chosen by the Legislature][4] thereof, for six Years; and each Senator shall have one Vote.

Immediately after they shall be assembled in Consequence of the first Election, they shall be divided as equally as may be into three Classes. The Seats of the Senators of the first Class shall be vacated at the Expiration of the second Year, of the second Class at the Expiration of the fourth Year, and of the third Class at the Expiration of the sixth Year, so that one-third may be chosen every second Year; [and if Vacancies happen by Resignation, or otherwise, during the Recess of the Legislature of any State, the Executive thereof may make temporary Appointments until the next Meeting of the Legislature, which shall then fill such Vacancies.][5]

[No Person shall be a Senator who shall not have attained to the Age of thirty Years, and been nine Years a Citizen of the United States,][6] and who shall not, when elected, be an Inhabitant of that State for which he shall be chosen.

The Vice President of the United States shall be President of the Senate, but shall have no Vote, unless they be equally divided.

The Senate shall chuse their other Officers, and also a President pro tempore, in the Absence of the Vice President, or when he shall exercise the Office of President of the United States.

The Senate shall have the sole Power to try all Impeachments. When sitting for that Purpose, they shall be on Oath or Affirmation. When the President of the United States is tried, the Chief Justice shall preside: And no Person shall be convicted without the Concurrence of two-thirds of the Members present.

Judgment in Cases of Impeachment shall not extend further than to removal from Office, and disqualification to hold and enjoy any Office of honor, Trust or Profit under the United States: but the Party convicted shall nevertheless be liable and subject to Indictment, Trial, Judgment and Punishment, according to Law.

Section 4

The Times, Places and Manner of holding Elections for Senators and Representatives, shall be prescribed in each State by the Legislature thereof; but the Congress may at any time by Law make or alter such Regulations, except as to the Places of chusing Senators.

The Congress shall assemble at least once in every Year, and such Meeting shall [be on the first Monday in December,][7] unless they shall by Law appoint a different Day.

Section 5

Each House shall be the Judge of the Elections, Returns and Qualifications of its own Members, and a Majority of each shall constitute a Quorum to do Business; but a smaller Number may adjourn from day to day, and may be authorized to compel the Attendance of absent Members, in such Manner, and under such Penalties as each House may provide.

Each House may determine the Rules of its Proceedings, punish its Members for disorderly Behaviour, and, with the Concurrence of two-thirds, expel a Member.

Each House shall keep a Journal of its Proceedings, and from time to time publish the same, excepting such Parts as may in their Judgment require Secrecy; and the Yeas and Nays of the Members of either House on any question shall, at the Desire of one-fifth of those Present, be entered on the Journal.

Neither House, during the Session of Congress, shall, without the Consent of the other, adjourn for more than three days, nor to any other Place than that in which the two Houses shall be sitting.

Section 6

The Senators and Representatives shall receive a Compensation for their Services, to be ascertained by Law, and paid out of the Treasury of the United

States. They shall in all Cases, except Treason, Felony and Breach of the Peace, be privileged from Arrest during their Attendance at the Session of their respective Houses, and in going to and returning from the same; and for any Speech or Debate in either House, they shall not be questioned in any other Place.

No Senator or Representative shall, during the Time for which he was elected, be appointed to any civil Office under the Authority of the United States, which shall have been created, or the Emoluments whereof shall have been encreased during such time; and no Person holding any Office under the United States, shall be a Member of either House during his Continuance in Office.

Section 7

All Bills for raising Revenue shall originate in the House of Representatives; but the Senate may propose or concur with Amendments as on other Bills.

Every Bill which shall have passed the House of Representatives and the Senate, shall, before it become a Law, be presented to the President of the United States; If he approve he shall sign it, but if not he shall return it, with his Objections to that House in which it shall have originated, who shall enter the Objections at large on their Journal, and proceed to reconsider it. If after such Reconsideration two-thirds of that House shall agree to pass the Bill, it shall be sent, together with the Objections, to the other House, by which it shall likewise be reconsidered, and if approved by two-thirds of that House, it shall become a Law. But in all such Cases, the Votes of both Houses shall be determined by yeas and Nays, and the Names of the Persons voting for and against the Bill shall be entered on the Journal of each House, respectively. If any Bill shall not be returned by the President within ten Days (Sundays excepted) after it shall have been presented to him, the Same shall be a Law, in like Manner as if he had signed it, unless the Congress by their Adjournment prevent its Return, in which Case it shall not be a Law.

Every Order, Resolution, or Vote to which the Concurrence of the Senate and House of Representatives may be necessary (except on a question of Adjournment) shall be presented to the President of the United States; and before the Same shall take Effect, shall be approved by him, or being disapproved by him, shall be repassed by two-thirds of the Senate and House of Representatives, according to the Rules and Limitations prescribed in the Case of a Bill.

Section 8

[The Congress shall have Power To lay and collect Taxes, Duties, Imposts and Excises, to pay the Debts and provide for the common Defence and general Welfare of the United States; but all Duties, Imposts and Excises shall be uniform throughout the United States;][8]

To borrow Money on the credit of the United States;

[To regulate Commerce with foreign Nations, and among the several States, and with the Indian Tribes;][9]

To establish an uniform Rule of Naturalization, and uniform Laws on the subject of Bankruptcies throughout the United States;

[To coin Money, regulate the Value thereof, and of foreign Coin, and fix the Standard of Weights and Measures;][10]

[To provide for the Punishment of counterfeiting the Securities and current Coin of the United States;][11]

[To establish Post Offices and post Roads;][12]

To promote the Progress of Science and useful Arts, by securing for limited Times to Authors and Inventors the exclusive Right to their respective Writings and Discoveries;

To constitute Tribunals inferior to the supreme Court;

To define and punish Piracies and Felonies committed on the high Seas, and Offences against the Law of Nations;

To declare War, grant Letters of Marque and Reprisal, and make Rules concerning Captures on Land and Water;

To raise and support Armies, but no Appropriation of Money to that Use shall be for a longer Term than two Years;

To provide and maintain a Navy;

To make Rules for the Government and Regulation of the land and naval Forces;

To provide for calling forth the Militia to execute the Laws of the Union, suppress Insurrections and repel Invasions;

To provide for organizing, arming, and disciplining, the Militia, and for governing such Part of them as may be employed in the Service of the United States, reserving to the States, respectively, the Appointment of the Officers, and the Authority of training the Militia according to the discipline prescribed by Congress;

To exercise exclusive Legislation in all Cases whatsoever, over such District (not exceeding ten Miles square) as may, by Cession of particular States, and the Acceptance of Congress, become the Seat of the Government of the United States, and to exercise like Authority over all Places purchased by the Consent of the Legislature of the State in which the Same shall be, for the Erection of Forts, Magazines, Arsenals, dock-Yards, and other needful Buildings;—And

To make all Laws which shall be necessary and proper for carrying into Execution the foregoing Powers, and all other Powers vested by this Constitution in the Government of the United States, or in any Department or Officer thereof.

Section 9

The Migration or Importation of such Persons as any of the States now existing shall think proper to admit, shall not be prohibited by the Congress prior to the Year one thousand eight hundred and eight, but a Tax or duty may be imposed on such Importation, not exceeding ten dollars for each Person.

The Privilege of the Writ of Habeas Corpus shall not be suspended, unless when in Cases of Rebellion or Invasion the public Safety may require it.

No Bill of Attainder or ex post facto Law shall be passed.

No Capitation, or other direct, Tax shall be laid, [unless in Proportion to the Census or enumeration herein before directed to be taken.][13]

No Tax or Duty shall be laid on Articles exported from any State.

[No Preference shall be given by any Regulation of Commerce or Revenue to the Ports of one State over those of another:][14] nor shall Vessels bound to, or from, one State, be obliged to enter, clear, or pay Duties in another.

No Money shall be drawn from the Treasury, but in Consequence of Appropriations made by Law; and a regular Statement and Account of the Receipts and Expenditures of all public Money shall be published from time to time.

No Title of Nobility shall be granted by the United States: And no Person holding any Office of Profit or Trust under them, shall, without the Consent of the Congress, accept of any present, Emolument, Office, or Title, of any kind whatever, from any King, Prince, or foreign State.

Section 10

[No State shall enter into any Treaty, Alliance, or Confederation; grant Letters of Marque and Reprisal; coin Money; emit Bills of Credit; make any Thing but gold and silver Coin a Tender in Payment of Debts; pass any Bill of Attainder, ex post facto Law, or Law impairing the Obligation of Contracts, or grant any Title of Nobility.][15]

[No State shall, without the Consent of the Congress, lay any Imposts or Duties on Imports or Exports, except what may be absolutely necessary for executing it's inspection Laws: and the net Produce of all Duties and Imposts, laid by any State on Imports or Exports, shall be for the Use of the Treasury of the United States; and all such Laws shall be subject to the Revision and Controul of the Congress.][16]

[No State shall, without the Consent of Congress, lay any Duty of Tonnage,][17] keep Troops, or Ships of War in time of Peace, enter into any Agreement or Compact with another State, or with a foreign Power, or engage in War, unless actually invaded, or in such imminent Danger as will not admit of delay.

ARTICLE II

Section 1

The executive Power shall be vested in a President of the United States of America. He shall hold his Office during the Term of four Years, and, together with the Vice President, chosen for the same Term, be elected, as follows

Each State shall appoint, in such Manner as the Legislature thereof may direct, a Number of Electors, equal to the whole Number of Senators and Representatives to which the State may be entitled in the Congress: but no Senator or Representative, or Person holding an Office of Trust or Profit under the United States, shall be appointed an Elector.

[The Electors shall meet in their respective States, and vote by Ballot for two Persons, of whom one at least shall not be an Inhabitant of the same State with themselves. And they shall make a List of all the Persons voted for, and of the Number of Votes for each; which List they shall sign and certify, and transmit sealed to the Seat of the Government of the United States, directed to the President of the Senate. The President of the Senate shall, in the Presence of the Senate and House of Representatives, open all the Certificates, and the Votes shall then be counted. The Person having the greatest Number of Votes shall be the President, if such Number be a Majority of the whole Number of Electors appointed; and if there be more than one who have such Majority, and have an equal Number of Votes, then the House of Representatives shall immediately chuse by Ballot one of them for President; and if no Person have a Majority, then from the five highest on the List the said House shall in like Manner chuse the President. But in chusing the President, the Votes shall be taken by States, the Representation from each State having one Vote; A quorum for this Purpose shall consist of a Member or Members from two-thirds of the States, and a Majority of all the States shall be necessary to a Choice. In every Case, after the Choice of the President, the Person having the greatest Number of Votes of the Electors shall be the Vice President. But if there should remain two or more who have equal Votes, the Senate shall chuse from them by Ballot the Vice President.][18]

The Congress may determine the Time of chusing the Electors, and the Day on which they shall give their Votes; which Day shall be the same throughout the United States.

[No Person except a natural born Citizen, or a Citizen of the United States, at the time of the Adoption of this Constitution, shall be eligible to the Office of President; neither shall any Person be eligible to that Office who shall not have attained to the Age of thirty-five Years, and been fourteen Years a Resident within the United States.][19]

[In Case of the Removal of the President from Office, or of his Death, Resignation, or Inability to discharge the Powers and Duties of the said Office, the Same shall devolve on the Vice President, and the Congress may by Law provide for the Case of Removal, Death, Resignation or Inability, both of the President and Vice President, declaring what Officer shall then act as President, and such Officer shall act accordingly, until the Disability be removed, or a President shall be elected.][20]

The President shall, at stated Times, receive for his Services, a Compensation, which shall neither be encreased nor diminished during the Period for which he shall have been elected, and he shall not receive within that Period any other Emolument from the United States, or any of them.

Before he enter on the Execution of his Office, he shall take the following Oath or Affirmation:—"I do solemnly swear (or affirm) that I will faithfully execute the Office of President of the United States, and will to the best of my Ability, preserve, protect and defend the Constitution of the United States."

Section 2

The President shall be Commander-in-Chief of the Army and Navy of the United States, and of the Militia of the several States, when called into the actual Service of the United States; he may require the Opinion, in writing, of the principal Officer in each of the executive Departments, upon any Subject relating to the Duties of their respective Offices, and he shall have Power to grant Reprieves and Pardons for Offences against the United States, except in Cases of Impeachment.

He shall have Power, by and with the Advice and Consent of the Senate, to make Treaties, provided two-thirds of the Senators present concur; and he shall nominate, and by and with the Advice and Consent of the Senate, shall appoint Ambassadors, other public Ministers and Consuls, Judges of the supreme Court, and all other Officers of the United States, whose Appointments are not herein otherwise provided for, and which shall be established by Law: but the Congress may by Law vest the Appointment of such inferior Officers, as they think proper, in the President alone, in the Courts of Law, or in the Heads of Departments.

The President shall have Power to fill up all Vacancies that may happen during the Recess of the Senate, by granting Commissions which shall expire at the End of their next Session.

Section 3

He shall from time to time give to the Congress Information of the State of the Union, and recommend to their Consideration such Measures as he shall judge necessary and expedient; he may, on extraordinary Occasions, convene both Houses, or either of them, and in Case of Disagreement between them, with Respect to the Time of Adjournment, he may adjourn them to such Time as he shall think proper; he shall receive Ambassadors and other public Ministers; he shall take Care that the Laws be faithfully executed, and shall Commission all the Officers of the United States.

Section 4

The President, Vice President and all civil Officers of the United States, shall be removed from Office on Impeachment for, and Conviction of, Treason, Bribery, or other high Crimes and Misdemeanors.

ARTICLE III

Section 1

The judicial Power of the United States, shall be vested in one supreme Court, and in such inferior Courts as the Congress may from time to time ordain and establish. The Judges, both of the supreme and inferior Courts, shall hold their Offices during good Behaviour, and shall, at stated Times, receive for their Services, a Compensation, which shall not be diminished during their Continuance in Office.

Section 2

The judicial Power shall extend to all Cases, in Law and Equity, arising under this Constitution, the Laws of the United States, and Treaties made, or which shall be made, under their Authority;—to all Cases affecting Ambassadors, other public Ministers and Consuls;—to all Cases of admiralty and maritime Jurisdiction;—to Controversies to which the United States shall be a Party;—to Controversies between two or more States;— [between a State and Citizens of another State,]²¹—between Citizens of different States,—between Citizens of the same State claiming Lands under Grants of different States, [and between a State, or the Citizens thereof, and foreign States, Citizens or Subjects.]²²

In all Cases affecting Ambassadors, other public Ministers and Consuls, and those in which a State shall be Party, the supreme Court shall have original Jurisdiction. In all the other Cases before mentioned, the supreme Court shall have appellate Jurisdiction, both as to Law and Fact, with such Exceptions, and under such Regulations as the Congress shall make.

The Trial of all Crimes, except in Cases of Impeachment, shall be by Jury; and such Trial shall be held in the State where the said Crimes shall have been committed; but when not committed within any State, the Trial shall be at such Place or Places as the Congress may by Law have directed.

Section 3

Treason against the United States, shall consist only in levying War against them, or in adhering to their Enemies, giving them Aid and Comfort. No Person shall be convicted of Treason unless on the Testimony of two Witnesses to the same overt Act, or on Confession in open Court.

The Congress shall have Power to declare the Punishment of Treason, but no Attainder of Treason shall work Corruption of Blood, or Forfeiture except during the Life of the Person attainted.

ARTICLE IV

Section 1

Full Faith and Credit shall be given in each State to the public Acts, Records, and judicial Proceedings of every other State. And the Congress may by general Laws prescribe the Manner in which such Acts, Records and Proceedings shall be proved, and the Effect thereof.

Section 2

[The Citizens of each State shall be entitled to all Privileges and Immunities of Citizens in the several States.]23

A Person charged in any State with Treason, Felony, or other Crime, who shall flee from Justice, and be found in another State, shall on Demand of the executive Authority of the State from which he fled, be delivered up, to be removed to the State having Jurisdiction of the Crime.

[No Person held to Service or Labour in one State, under the Laws thereof, escaping into another, shall, in Consequence of any Law or Regulation therein, be discharged from such Service or Labour, but shall be delivered up on Claim of the Party to whom such Service or Labour may be due.]24

Section 3

New States may be admitted by the Congress into this Union; but no new State shall be formed or erected within the Jurisdiction of any other State; nor any State be formed by the Junction of two or more States, or Parts of States, without the Consent of the Legislatures of the States concerned as well as of the Congress.

The Congress shall have Power to dispose of and make all needful Rules [and Regulations]²⁵ respecting the Territory or other Property belonging to the United States; and nothing in this Constitution shall be so construed as to Prejudice any Claims of the United States, or of any particular State.

Section 4

The United States shall guarantee to every State in this Union a Republican Form of Government, and shall protect each of them against Invasion; and on Application of the Legislature, or of the Executive (when the Legislature cannot be convened), against domestic Violence.

ARTICLE V

The Congress, whenever two-thirds of both Houses shall deem it necessary, shall propose Amendments to this Constitution, or, on the Application of the Legislatures of two-thirds of the several States, shall call a Convention for proposing Amendments, which, in either Case, shall be valid to all Intents and Purposes, as Part of this Constitution, when ratified by the Legislatures of three-fourths of the several States, or by Conventions in three-fourths thereof, as the one or the other Mode of Ratification may be proposed by the Congress; Provided that no Amendment which may be made prior to the Year One thousand eight hundred and eight shall in any Manner affect the first and fourth Clauses in the Ninth Section of the first Article; and that no State, without its Consent, shall be deprived of its equal Suffrage in the Senate.

ARTICLE VI

All Debts contracted and Engagements entered into, before the Adoption of this Constitution, shall be as valid against the United States under this Constitution, as under the Confederation.

This Constitution, and the Laws of the United States which shall be made in Pursuance thereof; and all Treaties made, or which shall be made, under the Authority of the United States, shall be the supreme Law of the Land; and the Judges in every State shall be bound thereby, any Thing in the Constitution or Laws of any State to the Contrary notwithstanding.

The Senators and Representatives before mentioned, and the Members of the several State Legislatures, and all executive and judicial Officers, both of the United States and of the several States, shall be bound by Oath or Affirmation, to support this Constitution; but no religious Test shall ever be required as a Qualification to any Office or public Trust under the United States.

ARTICLE VII

The Ratification of the Conventions of nine States, shall be sufficient for the Establishment of this Constitution between the States so ratifying the Same.

The Word, "the," being interlined between the seventh and eighth Lines of the first Page, The Word "Thirty" being partly written on an Erazure in the fifteenth Line of the first Page, The Words "is tried" being interlined between the thirty second and thirty third Lines of the first Page and the Word "the" being interlined between the forty third and forty fourth Lines of the second Page.

Attest William Jackson Secretary

done in Convention by the Unanimous Consent of the States present the Seventeenth Day of September in the Year of our Lord one thousand seven hundred and Eighty-seven and of the Independance of the United States of America the Twelfth In witness whereof We have hereunto subscribed our Names.[26]

AMENDMENT I[27]

Congress shall make no law respecting an establishment of religion, or prohibiting the free exercise thereof; or abridging the freedom of speech, or of the press; or the right of the people peaceably to assemble, and to petition the Government for a redress of grievances.

AMENDMENT II[28]

A well regulated Militia, being necessary to the security of a free State, the right of the people to keep and bear Arms, shall not be infringed.

AMENDMENT III[29]

No Soldier shall, in time of peace be quartered in any house, without the consent of the Owner, nor in time of war, but in a manner to be prescribed by law.

AMENDMENT IV

The right of the people to be secure in their persons, houses, papers, and effects, against unreasonable searches and seizures, shall not be violated, and no Warrants shall issue, but upon probable cause, supported by Oath or affirmation, and particularly describing the place to be searched, and the persons or things to be seized.

AMENDMENT V

No person shall be held to answer for a capital, or otherwise infamous crime, unless on a presentment or indictment of a Grand Jury, except in cases arising in the land or naval forces, or in the Militia, when in actual service in time of War or public danger; nor shall any person be subject for the same offence to be twice put in jeopardy of life or limb; nor shall be compelled in any criminal case to be a witness against himself, nor be deprived of life, liberty, or property, without due process of law; [nor shall private property be taken for public use, without just compensation.][30]

AMENDMENT VI

In all criminal prosecutions, the accused shall enjoy the right to a speedy and public trial, by an impartial jury of the State and district wherein the crime shall have been committed, which district shall have been previously ascertained by law, and to be informed of the nature and cause of the accusation; to be confronted with the witnesses against him; to have compulsory process for obtaining witnesses in his favor, [and to have the Assistance of Counsel for his defence.][31]

AMENDMENT VII

In Suits at common law, where the value in controversy shall exceed twenty dollars, the right of trial by jury shall be preserved, and no fact tried by a jury, shall be otherwise re-examined in any Court of the United States, than according to the rules of the common law.

AMENDMENT VIII

Excessive bail shall not be required, nor excessive fines imposed, nor cruel and unusual punishments inflicted.

AMENDMENT IX

The enumeration in the Constitution, of certain rights, shall not be construed to deny or disparage others retained by the people.

AMENDMENT X

The powers not delegated to the United States by the Constitution, nor prohibited by it to the States, are reserved to the States, respectively, or to the people.

AMENDMENT XI[32]

The Judicial power of the United States shall not be construed to extend to any suit in law or equity, commenced or prosecuted against one of the United States by Citizens of another State, or by Citizens or Subjects of any Foreign State.

AMENDMENT XII[33]

The Electors shall meet in their respective states and vote by ballot for President and Vice-President, one of whom, at least, shall not be an inhabitant of the same state with themselves; they shall name in their ballots the person voted for as President, and in distinct ballots the person voted for as Vice-President, and they shall make distinct lists of all persons voted for as President, and of all persons voted for as Vice-President, and of the number of votes for each, which lists they shall sign and certify, and transmit sealed to the seat of the government of the United States, directed to the President of the Senate;—the President of the Senate shall, in the presence of the Senate and House of Representatives, open all the certificates and the votes shall then be counted;—The person having the greatest number of votes for President, shall be the President, if such number be a majority of the whole number of Electors appointed; and if no person have such majority, then from the persons having the highest numbers not exceeding three on the list of those voted for as President, the House of Representatives shall choose immediately, by ballot, the President. But in choosing the President, the votes shall be taken by states, the representation from each state having one vote; a quorum for this purpose shall consist of a member or members from two-thirds of the states, and a majority of all the states shall be necessary to a choice. [And if the House of Representatives shall not choose a President whenever the right of choice shall devolve upon them, before the fourth day of March next following, then the Vice-President shall act as President, as in case of the death or other constitutional disability of the President.—][34] The person having the greatest number of votes as Vice-President, shall be the Vice-President, if such number be a majority of the whole number of Electors appointed, and if no person have a majority, then from the two highest numbers on the list, the Senate shall choose the Vice-President; a quorum for the purpose shall consist of two-thirds of the whole number of Senators, and a majority of the whole number shall be necessary to a choice. But no person constitutionally ineligible to the office of President shall be eligible to that of Vice-President of the United States.

AMENDMENT XIII[35]

Section 1

Neither slavery nor involuntary servitude, except as a punishment for crime whereof the party shall have been duly convicted, shall exist within the United States, or any place subject to their jurisdiction.

Section 2

Congress shall have power to enforce this article by appropriate legislation.

AMENDMENT XIV[36]

Section 1

All persons born or naturalized in the United States, and subject to the jurisdiction thereof, are citizens of the United States and of the State wherein they reside. [No State shall make or enforce any law which shall abridge the privileges or immunities of citizens of the United States; nor shall any State deprive any person of life, liberty, or property, without due process of law; nor deny to any person within its jurisdiction the equal protection of the laws.][37]

Section 2

Representatives shall be apportioned among the several States according to their respective numbers, counting the whole number of persons in each State, excluding Indians not taxed. But when the right to vote at any election for the choice of electors for President and Vice-President of the United States, Representatives in Congress, the Executive and Judicial officers of a State, or the members of the Legislature thereof, is denied to any of the male inhabitants of such State, [being twenty-one years of age,][38] and citizens of the United States, or in any way abridged, except for participation in rebellion, or other crime, the basis of representation therein shall be reduced in the proportion which the number of such male citizens shall bear to the whole number of male citizens twenty-one years of age in such State.

Section 3

No person shall be a Senator or Representative in Congress, or elector of President and Vice-President, or hold any office, civil or military, under the United States, or under any State, who, having previously taken an oath, as a member of Congress, or as an officer of the United States, or as a member of any State legislature, or as an executive or judicial officer of any State, to support the Constitution of the United States, shall have engaged in insurrection or rebellion against the same, or given aid or comfort to the enemies thereof. But Congress may by a vote of two-thirds of each House, remove such disability.

Section 4

The validity of the public debt of the United States, authorized by law, including debts incurred for payment of pensions and bounties for services in suppressing insurrection or rebellion, shall not be questioned. But neither the United States nor any State shall assume or pay any debt or obligation incurred in aid of insurrection or rebellion against the United States, or any claim for the loss or emancipation of any slave; but all such debts, obligations and claims shall be held illegal and void.

Section 5

The Congress shall have the power to enforce, by appropriate legislation, the provisions of this article.

AMENDMENT XV[39]

Section 1

The right of citizens of the United States to vote shall not be denied or abridged by the United States or by any State on account of race, color, or previous condition of servitude—

Section 2

The Congress shall have the power to enforce this article by appropriate legislation.

AMENDMENT XVI[40]

The Congress shall have power to lay and collect taxes on incomes, from whatever source derived, without apportionment among the several States, and without regard to any census or enumeration.

AMENDMENT XVII[41]

The Senate of the United States shall be composed of two Senators from each State, elected by the people thereof, for six years; and each Senator shall have one vote. The electors in each State shall have the qualifications requisite for electors of the most numerous branch of the State legislatures.

When vacancies happen in the representation of any State in the Senate, the executive authority of such State shall issue writs of election to fill such vacancies: *Provided*, That the legislature of any State may empower the executive thereof to make temporary appointments until the people fill the vacancies by election as the legislature may direct.

This amendment shall not be so construed as to affect the election or term of any Senator chosen before it becomes valid as part of the Constitution.

AMENDMENT XVIII[42]

Section 1

After one year from the ratification of this article the manufacture, sale, or transportation of intoxicating liquors within, the importation thereof into, or the exportation thereof from the United States and all territory subject to the jurisdiction thereof for beverage purposes is hereby prohibited.

Section 2

The Congress and the several States shall have concurrent power to enforce this article by appropriate legislation.

Section 3

This article shall be inoperative unless it shall have been ratified as an amendment to the Constitution by the legislatures of the several States, as provided in the Constitution, within seven years from the date of the submission hereof to the States by the Congress.

AMENDMENT XIX[43]

The right of citizens of the United States to vote shall not be denied or abridged by the United States or by any State on account of sex.

Congress shall have power to enforce this article by appropriate legislation.

AMENDMENT XX[44]

Section 1

The terms of the President and the Vice President shall end at noon on the 20th day of January, and the terms of Senators and Representatives at noon on the 3d day of January, of the years in which such terms would have ended if this article had not been ratified; and the terms of their successors shall then begin.

Section 2

The Congress shall assemble at least once in every year, and such meeting shall begin at noon on the 3d day of January, unless they shall by law appoint a different day.

Section 3

If, at the time fixed for the beginning of the term of the President, the President elect shall have died, the Vice President elect shall become President. If a President shall not have been chosen before the time fixed for the beginning of his term, or if the President elect shall have failed to qualify, then the Vice President elect shall act as President until a President shall have qualified; and the Congress may by law provide for the case wherein neither a President elect nor a Vice President elect shall have qualified, declaring who shall then act as President, or the manner in which one who is to act shall be selected, and such person shall act accordingly until a President or Vice President shall have qualified.

Section 4

The Congress may by law provide for the case of the death of any of the persons from whom the House of Representatives may choose a President whenever the right of choice shall have devolved upon them, and for the case of the death of any of the persons from whom the Senate may choose a Vice President whenever the right of choice shall have devolved upon them.

Section 5

Sections 1 and 2 shall take effect on the 15th day of October following the ratification of this article.

Section 6

This article shall be inoperative unless it shall have been ratified as an amendment to the Constitution by the legislatures of three-fourths of the several States within seven years from the date of its submission.

AMENDMENT XXI[45]

Section 1

The eighteenth article of amendment to the Constitution of the United States is hereby repealed.

Section 2[46]

The transportation or importation into any State, Territory, or possession of the United States for delivery or use therein of intoxicating liquors, in violation of the laws thereof, is hereby prohibited.

Section 3

This article shall be inoperative unless it shall have been ratified as an amendment to the Constitution by conventions in the several States, as provided in the Constitution, within seven years from the date of the submission hereof to the States by the Congress.

AMENDMENT XXII[47]

Section 1

No person shall be elected to the office of the President more than twice, and no person who has held the office of President, or acted as President, for more than two years of a term to which some other person was elected President shall be elected to the office of the President more than once. But this Article shall not apply to any person holding the office of President when this Article was proposed by the Congress, and shall not prevent any person who may be holding the office of President, or acting as President, during the term within which this Article becomes operative from holding the office of President or acting as President during the remainder of such term.

Section 2

This article shall be inoperative unless it shall have been ratified as an amendment to the Constitution by the legislatures of three-fourths of the several States within seven years from the date of its submission to the States by the Congress.

AMENDMENT XXIII[48]

Section 1

The District constituting the seat of Government of the United States shall appoint in such manner as the Congress may direct:

A number of electors of President and Vice President equal to the whole number of Senators and Representatives in Congress to which the District would be entitled if it were a State, but in no event more than the least populous State; they shall be in addition to those appointed by the States, but they shall be considered, for the purposes of the election of President and Vice President, to be electors appointed by a State; and they shall meet in the District and perform such duties as provided by the twelfth article of amendment.

Section 2

The Congress shall have power to enforce this article by appropriate legislation.

AMENDMENT XXIV[49]

Section 1[50]

The right of citizens of the United States to vote in any primary or other election for President or Vice President, for electors for President or Vice President, or for Senator or Representative in Congress, shall not be denied or abridged by the United States or any State by reason of failure to pay any poll tax or other tax.

Section 2

The Congress shall have power to enforce this article by appropriate legislation.

AMENDMENT XXV[51]

Section 1

In case of the removal of the President from office or of his death or resignation, the Vice President shall become President.

Section 2

Whenever there is a vacancy in the office of the Vice President, the President shall nominate a Vice President who shall take office upon confirmation by a majority vote of both Houses of Congress.

Section 3

Whenever the President transmits to the President pro tempore of the Senate and the Speaker of the House of Representatives his written declaration that he is unable to discharge the powers and duties of his office, and until he transmits to them a written declaration to the contrary, such powers and duties shall be discharged by the Vice President as Acting President.

Section 4

Whenever the Vice President and a majority of either the principal officers of the executive departments or of such other body as Congress may by law provide, transmit to the President pro tempore of the Senate and the Speaker of the House of Representatives their written declaration that the President is unable to discharge the powers and duties of his office, the Vice President shall immediately assume the powers and duties of the office as Acting President.

Thereafter, when the President transmits to the President pro tempore of the Senate and the Speaker of the House of Representatives his written declaration that no inability exists, he shall resume the powers and duties of his office unless the Vice President and a majority of either the principal officers of the executive department or of such other body as Congress may by law provide, transmit within four days to the President pro tempore of the Senate and the Speaker of the House of Representatives their written declaration that the President is unable to discharge the powers and duties of his office. Thereupon Congress shall decide the issue, assembling within forty-eight hours for that purpose if not in session. If the Congress, within twenty-one days after receipt of the latter written declaration, or, if Congress is not in session, within twenty-one days after Congress is required to assemble, determines by two-thirds vote of both Houses that the President is unable to discharge the powers and duties of his office, the Vice President shall continue to discharge the same as Acting President; otherwise, the President shall resume the powers and duties of his office.

AMENDMENT XXVI[52]

Section 1

The right of citizens of the United States, who are eighteen years of age or older, to vote shall not be denied or abridged by the United States or by any State on account of age.

Section 2

The Congress shall have power to enforce this article by appropriate legislation.

AMENDMENT XXVII[53]

No law, varying the compensation for the services of the Senators and Representatives, shall take effect, until an election of Representatives shall have intervened.

AMENDMENT XXVIII

The Preamble to the Constitution of the United States shall be repealed and replaced with the following: Given that the only proper purpose of government is to protect Freedom and Individual Rights, and that the only way to violate Freedom and Individual Rights is by initiating physical force, we the People of the United States, in Order to form a more perfect Union, establish Justice, insure domestic Tranquility, provide for the common defence, and secure the Blessings of Liberty to ourselves and our Posterity, do ordain and establish this Constitution for the United States of America.

AMENDMENT XXIX

In Article I, Section 2 of the Constitution of the United States, the minimum age requirement for representatives shall be changed from twenty-five years to eighteen years and the citizenship requirement for representatives shall be changed from a minimum of seven years to only requiring individuals to be United States citizens before being eligible to become a representative.

AMENDMENT XXX

In Article I, Section 3 of the Constitution of the United States, the minimum age requirement for senators shall be changed from thirty years to eighteen years and the citizenship requirement for senators shall be changed from a minimum of nine years to only requiring individuals to be United States citizens before being eligible to become a senator.

AMENDMENT XXXI

The following portion of Article I, Section 8 of the Constitution of the United States shall be repealed: The Congress shall have Power To lay and collect Taxes, Duties, Imposts and Excises, to pay the Debts and provide for the common Defence and general Welfare of the United States; but all Duties, Imposts and Excises shall be uniform throughout the United States. It shall be replaced with the following: The Congress shall have Power To lay and collect Duties on imports, to collect voluntary Taxes and Fees and use other voluntary methods to raise revenue, to pay the Debts and provide for the common Defence and protection of Individual rights of citizens of the United States; but all Duties, Fees and other methods of raising revenue, besides Taxes, shall be uniform throughout the United States.

AMENDMENT XXXII

The following clause in Article I, Section 8 of the Constitution of the United States shall be repealed: To regulate Commerce with foreign Nations, and among the several States, and with the Indian Tribes.

AMENDMENT XXXIII

The following portion of Article I, Section 8 of the Constitution of the United States shall be repealed: To coin Money, regulate the Value thereof, and of foreign Coin, and fix the Standard of Weights and Measures. It shall be replaced with the following: To make Money that has been widely accepted in the marketplace a Tender in Payment of Debts and fix the Standard of

Weights and Measures based on what has been widely accepted in the marketplace, but individuals may use alternative Money or Standards of Weights and Measures if agreed upon.

AMENDMENT XXXIV

The following clause in Article I, Section 8 of the Constitution of the United States shall be repealed: To provide for the Punishment of counterfeiting the Securities and current Coin of the United States. It shall be replaced with the following: To provide for the Punishment of counterfeiting the Securities of, and Money used in, the United States.

AMENDMENT XXXV

The following clause in Article I, Section 8 of the Constitution of the United States shall be repealed: To establish Post Offices and post Roads.

AMENDMENT XXXVI

The following clause in Article I, Section 9 of the Constitution of the United States shall be repealed: No Capitation, or other direct, Tax shall be laid, unless in Proportion to the Census or enumeration herein before directed to be taken. It shall be replaced with the following: No confiscatory Tax shall be laid.

AMENDMENT XXXVII

The following clause in Article I, Section 9 of the Constitution of the United States shall be repealed: No Preference shall be given by any Regulation of Commerce or Revenue to the Ports of one State over those of another. It shall be replaced with the following: No Preference shall be given to the Ports of one State over those of another, except for the purpose of protecting the rights of United States citizens in the best manner possible.

AMENDMENT XXXVIII

The following clauses in Article I, Section 10 of the Constitution of the United States shall be repealed: No State shall . . . coin Money; emit Bills of Credit; make any Thing but gold and silver Coin a Tender in Payment of Debts; pass any . . . Law impairing the Obligation of Contracts, ... They shall be replaced with the following: No State shall . . . make any Thing but Money widely accepted in the marketplace a Tender in Payment of Debts, but individuals may use alternative Money if agreed upon; . . . .

AMENDMENT XXXIX

The following portion of Article I, Section 10 of the Constitution of the United States shall be repealed: No State shall, without the Consent of the Congress, lay any Imposts or Duties on Imports or Exports, except what may be absolutely necessary for executing it's inspection Laws: and the net Produce of all Duties and Imposts, laid by any State on Imports or Exports, shall be for the Use of the Treasury of the United States; and all such Laws shall be subject to the Revision and Controul of the Congress. It shall be replaced with the following: No State shall lay any Duties on Exports; and No State shall lay any Duties on Imports, except what may be necessary for the protection of individual rights; and all such Duties on Imports shall require the Consent of Congress and be subject to the Revision and Control of Congress.

AMENDMENT XL

The following portion of Article I, Section 10 of the Constitution of the United States shall be repealed: No State shall, without the Consent of Congress, lay any Duty of Tonnage, ... It shall be replaced with the following: No State shall lay any Duty of Tonnage and, without the Consent of Congress, ...

AMENDMENT XLI

The citizenship requirement for the Office of the President shall be changed from being a natural born citizen of the United States to only requiring individuals to be a citizen of the United States. The minimum age requirement for the Office of the President shall be changed from thirty-five years to eighteen years. The residency requirement for the Office of the President shall be changed from a minimum of fourteen years to only requiring individuals to be a resident of the United States.

AMENDMENT XLII

The following clause of Article IV, Section 2 of the Constitution of the United States shall be modified: The Citizens of each State shall be entitled to all Privileges and Immunities of Citizens in the several States. The modified clause is as follows: The Citizens of each State shall be entitled to all Privileges and Immunities of Citizens in the several States, but all Privileges and Immunities shall be consistent with the protection of Individual Rights.

AMENDMENT XLIII

The reference to "Regulations" in Article IV, Section 3 of the Constitution of the United States shall be eliminated. Henceforth, the clause in this section of the Constitution that previously referred to regulations shall state: The Congress shall have Power to dispose of and make all needful Rules respecting the Territory or other Property belonging to the United States.

AMENDMENT XLIV

The first article of amendment to the Constitution of the United States is hereby repealed and shall be replaced with the following: Congress shall make no law respecting an establishment of religion, or prohibiting the free exercise or rejection thereof, or approving or disapproving of religion or religious sayings, ceremonies, or symbols; or abridging the freedom of thought, of association, of speech, or of the press; or the freedom to not associate with others; or the right of the people peaceably to assemble, and to petition the Government for a redress of grievances.

AMENDMENT XLV

The second article of amendment to the Constitution of the United States is hereby repealed and shall be replaced with the following: While it is acknowledged that the use of force to protect rights has been delegated by the people to the government, the right of individuals to keep and bear arms for self-defense, hunting, and other purposes that respect individual rights shall not be infringed.

AMENDMENT XLVI

The third article of amendment to the Constitution of the United States shall be repealed and replaced with the following: No Soldier shall, at any time, be quartered in any house, without the consent of the Owner.

AMENDMENT XLVII

In the fifth article of amendment to the Constitution of the United States, the following clause shall be repealed: nor shall private property be taken for public use, without just compensation. It shall be replaced with the following: nor shall private property be taken for public or private use or purpose.

AMENDMENT XLVIII

The phrase "but any counsel provided by the government shall be limited to no more than the minimum necessary to achieve justice and counsel shall not be provided by the government in civil trials" shall be added after "defence" in the sixth article of amendment to the Constitution of the United States. Henceforth, the last clause shall read as follows: and to have the Assistance of Counsel for his defence but any counsel provided by the government shall be limited to no more than the minimum necessary to achieve justice and counsel shall not be provided by the government in civil trials.

AMENDMENT XLIX

The clause in Section 1 of the fourteenth article of amendment to the Constitution of the United States that says "No State shall make or enforce any law which shall abridge the privileges or immunities of citizens of the United States" shall be repealed and replaced with the following: No State shall make or enforce any law which shall abridge the rights of citizens of the United States or its own citizens. In addition, the following clause shall be added to the end of Section 1 of the fourteenth article of amendment to the Constitution of the United States: nor shall any local government make or enforce any law which shall abridge the rights of citizens of the United States or the several states, deprive any person of life, liberty or property without due process of law, or deny to any person the equal protection of the law. Henceforth, the last sentence of Section 1 of the fourteenth article of amendment shall read: No State shall make or enforce any law which shall abridge the rights of citizens of the United States or its own citizens; nor shall any State deprive any person of life, liberty, or property, without due process of law; nor deny to any person within its jurisdiction the equal protection of the laws; nor shall any local government make or enforce any law which shall abridge the rights of citizens of the United States or the several states, deprive any person of life, liberty or property without due process of law, or deny to any person the equal protection of the law.

AMENDMENT L

The sixteenth article of amendment to the Constitution of the United States is hereby repealed.

AMENDMENT LI

Section 2 of the twenty-first article of amendment to the Constitution of the United States is hereby repealed.

AMENDMENT LII

The twenty-second article of amendment to the Constitution of the United States is hereby repealed.

AMENDMENT LIII

Section 1: For purposes of representation in the Congress, election of the President and Vice President, and article V of this Constitution, the District constituting the seat of government of the United States shall be treated as though it were a State. Section 2: The exercise of the rights and powers conferred under this article shall be by the people of the District constituting the seat of government, and as shall be provided by the Congress. Section 3: The twenty-third article of amendment to the Constitution of the United States is hereby repealed.

AMENDMENT LIV

Section 1 of the twenty-fourth article of amendment to the Constitution of the United States shall be repealed and replaced with the following: The right of citizens of the United States to vote in any primary or other election for President or Vice President, for electors for President or Vice President, for Senator or Representative in Congress, or in any State or Local primary or election, shall not be denied or abridged by the United States or any State or Local Government by reason of failure to pay any poll tax or other tax.

AMENDMENT LV

No law shall be made abridging the freedom of production and trade. No law shall also be made abridging the freedom to choose to not trade with others.

AMENDMENT LVI

The right of each individual to the control of his or her own body shall not be infringed, and the right to do as he or she chooses with his or her own person, including engaging in voluntary, consensual, or contractual relationships with others, shall not be infringed.

AMENDMENT LVII

No federal, state, or local government shall own, operate, or provide financial assistance or any other type of assistance to any commercial enterprise, educational enterprise, or private organization; nor shall it provide financial assistance or any other type of assistance to any individual or other government, unless such ownership, operation, or assistance is directly necessary for the protection of individual rights of citizens of the United States.

No federal, state, or local government shall provide assistance to individuals and organizations in the form of loans.

AMENDMENT LVIII

No federal, state, or local government shall purchase or own any property, except that which is directly necessary to protect individual rights.

AMENDMENT LIX

Foreign nationals shall have the right to immigrate to and become citizens of the United Sates and the several states. Foreign nationals in the United States who are not citizens shall be entitled to all the privileges and immunities of citizens of the United States and the several states, but all privileges and immunities shall be consistent with the protection of individual rights.

AMENDMENT LX

The freedom of speech and press include any contributions to political campaigns or to candidates for government office and shall extend to all mediums of communication. All mediums of communication shall be private property.

AMENDMENT LXI

No federal, state, or local government shall create, issue, or coin money (including bills of credit) or regulate the value of money. Governments shall hold only standard money or money backed 100 percent by standard money. If the government receives money that is not fully backed by standard money, it must be exchanged as quickly as possible for standard money or money that is fully backed by standard money. Governments must store their money only in federal, state, or local government-owned banks. This amendment does not apply to the money of nations at war or in conflict with the United States.

No federal, state, or local government shall pass any law impairing the obligation of contracts.

AMENDMENT LXII

Selective service, the military draft, and any other type of draft by the government are hereby prohibited.

Compulsory jury service is hereby prohibited.

AMENDMENT LXIII

The freedom of individuals, and associations of individuals (including corporations), to use their property for all rights-respecting activities shall not be infringed.

NOTES

1. Repealed and replaced by Amendment XXVIII.
2. The minimum age for representatives and the minimum number of years representatives must be a citizen were changed by Amendment XXIX.
3. Modified by Amendment XIV, Section 2, as well as Amendments XXXI, XXXVI, and L.

4. Changed by Amendment XVII.

5. Changed by Amendment XVII.

6. The minimum age for senators and the minimum number of years senators must be a citizen were changed by Amendment XXX.

7. Changed by Amendment XX, Section 2.

8. Repealed and replaced by Amendment XXXI.

9. Repealed by Amendment XXXII.

10. Repealed and replaced by Amendment XXXIII.

11. Repealed and replaced by Amendment XXXIV.

12. Repealed by Amendment XXXV.

13. The portion in brackets was changed by Amendment XVI. However, the entire clause was repealed and replaced by Amendment XXXVI.

14. Repealed and replaced by Amendment XXXVII.

15. Modified by Amendment XXXVIII.

16. Repealed and replaced by Amendment XXXIX.

17. Repealed and replaced by Amendment XL.

18. Superseded by Amendment XII.

19. The citizenship, age, and residency requirements for the president were changed by Amendment XLI.

20. Changed by Amendment XXV.

21. Superseded by Amendment XI.

22. Modified by Amendment XI.

23. Modified by Amendment XLII.

24. Superseded by Amendment XIII.

25. Eliminated by Amendment XLIII.

26. I do not include the signature block at the end of the original Constitution.

27. The first ten amendments to the Constitution, known as the Bill of Rights, were proposed by Congress September 25, 1789 and ratified December 15, 1791. Amendment I was repealed and replaced by Amendment XLIV.

28. Repealed and replaced by Amendment XLV.

29. Repealed and replaced by Amendment XLVI.

30. Repealed and replaced by Amendment XLVII.

31. Modified by Amendment XLVIII.

32. Passed by Congress March 4, 1794. Ratified February 7, 1795. Article III, Section 2 of the Constitution was modified by Amendment XI.

33. Passed by Congress December 9, 1803. Ratified June 15, 1804. A portion of Article II, Section 1 of the Constitution was superseded by Amendment XII.

34. Superseded by Section 3 of Amendment XX.

35. Passed by Congress January 31, 1865. Ratified December 6, 1865. A portion of Article IV, Section 2 of the Constitution was superseded by Amendment XIII.

36. Passed by Congress June 13, 1866. Ratified July 9, 1868. Article I, Section 2 of the Constitution was modified by Section 2 of Amendment XIV.

37. Modified by Amendment XLIX.

38. Changed by Section 1 of Amendment XXVI.

39. Passed by Congress February 26, 1869. Ratified February 3, 1870.

40. Passed by Congress July 2, 1909. Ratified February 3, 1913. Article I, Section 9 of the Constitution was modified by Amendment XVI. Amendment XVI was repealed by Amendment L.

41. Passed by Congress May 13, 1912. Ratified April 8, 1913. Article I, Section 3 of the Constitution was modified by Amendment XVII.

42. Passed by Congress December 18, 1917. Ratified January 16, 1919. Repealed by Amendment XXI.

43. Passed by Congress June 4, 1919. Ratified August 18, 1920.

44. Passed by Congress March 2, 1932. Ratified January 23, 1933. Article I, Section 4 of the Constitution was modified by Section 2 of this amendment. In addition, a portion of Amendment XII was superseded by Section 3.

45. Passed by Congress February 20, 1933. Ratified December 5, 1933.

46. Repealed by Amendment LI.

47. Passed by Congress March 21, 1947. Ratified February 27, 1951. Repealed by Amendment LII.

48. Passed by Congress June 16, 1960. Ratified March 29, 1961. Repealed by Amendment LIII.

49. Passed by Congress August 27, 1962. Ratified January 23, 1964.

50. Repealed and replaced by Amendment LIV.

51. Passed by Congress July 6, 1965. Ratified February 10, 1967. Article II, Section 1 of the Constitution was affected by Amendment XXV.

52. Passed by Congress March 23, 1971. Ratified July 1, 1971. Amendment XIV, Section 2 of the Constitution was modified by Section 1 of Amendment XXVI.

53. Originally proposed September 25, 1789. Ratified May 7, 1992.

List of Supreme Court
Cases Referenced

Alabama v. Shelton, 535 U.S. 654 (2002)
Argersinger v. Hamlin, 407 U.S. 25 (1972)
Butler v. Perry, 240 U.S. 328 (1916)
Calder v. Bull, 3 U.S. 386 (1798)
Citizens United v. Federal Election Commission, 558 U.S. 310 (2010)
Clinton v. City of New York, 524 U.S. 417 (1998)
District of Columbia v. Heller, 554 U.S. 570 (2008)
Dobbert v. Florida, 432 U.S. 282 (1977)
Everson v. Board of Education of Ewing Township, 330 U.S. 1 (1947)
Gibbons v. Ogden, 22 U.S. 1 (1824)
Gideon v. Wainwright, 372 U.S. 335 (1963)
Harper v. Virginia State Board of Elections, 383 U.S. 663 (1966)
Hawaii Housing Authority v. Midkiff, 467 U.S. 229 (1984)
Heart of Atlanta Motel, Inc. v. United States, 379 U.S. 241 (1964)
Helvering v. Davis, 301 U.S. 619 (1937)
Kelo v. City of New London, 545 U.S. 469 (2005)
Marbury v. Madison, 5 U.S. 137 (1803)
NAACP v. Alabama, 357 U.S. 449 (1958)
Roberts v. United States Jaycees, 468 U.S. 609 (1984)
Roe v. Wade, 410 U.S. 113 (1973)
Runyon v. McCrary, 427 U.S. 160 (1976)
The Selective Draft Law Cases, 245 U.S. 366 (1918)
The Slaughter-House Cases, 83 U.S. 36 (1873)
Steward Machine Co. v. Collector of Internal Revenue, 301 U.S. 548 (1937)
Thompson v. Missouri, 171 U.S. 380 (1898)
Thompson v. Utah, 170 U.S. 343 (1898)
United States v. Miller, 307 U.S. 174 (1939)
Village of Euclid, Ohio v. Ambler Realty Co., 272 U.S. 365 (1926)

Bibliography

Abel, Laura K., "A Right to Counsel in Civil Cases: Lessons from *Gideon v. Wainwright,*" *Temple Political & Civil Rights Law Review* vol. 15 (2006), pp. 527–55.

Ackerman, Bruce, "Post by Bruce Ackerman," *The Constitution in 2020,* March 11, 2005, http://constitutionin2020.blogspot.com/2005/03/post-by-bruce-ackerman.html (accessed April 17, 2016).

Amar, Akhil Reed, *America's Unwritten Constitution: The Precedents and Principles We Live By* (New York: Basic Books, 2012).

———, *America's Constitution: A Biography* (New York: Random House, 2005).

The Association of Objective Law, "Highlights of TAFOL Panel Presentation at The Jefferson School: Subpoena Power," *Bulletin #3* (Spring 1989), pp. 2–3, http://www.tafol.org/bulletinsindex.html (accessed November 19, 2016).

Balko, Radley, "The El Paso Miracle," July 6, 2009, https://reason.com/2009/07/06/the-el-paso-miracle (accessed May 21, 2019).

Barnett, Randy E., "A Bill of Federalism," *Forbes,* May 20, 2009, https://www.forbes.com/2009/05/20/bill-of-federalism-constitution-states-supreme-court-opinions-contributors-randy-barnett.html (accessed July 2, 2017).

———, "The Ninth Amendment: It Means What It Says," *Texas Law Review* vol. 85, no. 1 (November 2006), pp. 1–82.

———, *Restoring the Lost Constitution: The Presumption of Liberty* (Princeton, NJ: Princeton University Press, 2004).

Bernstein, Andrew, *Capitalist Solutions: A Philosophy of American Moral Dilemmas* (New Brunswick, NJ: Transaction Publishers, 2012).

———, "The Welfare State Versus the Mind," *The Intellectual Activist: An Objectivist Review* vol. 15, no. 10 (October 2001), pp. 11–24.

Biddle, Craig, "Freedom of Speech is Freedom to Think," September 19, 2017, https://www.theobjectivestandard.com/2017/09/freedom-of-speech-is-freedom-to-think/ (accessed March 4, 2018).

————, "Weighing Gary Johnson for President," August 29, 2016, https://www.the objectivestandard.com/2016/08/weighing-gary-johnson-for-president/ (accessed March 3, 2018).

Binswanger, Harry, *How We Know: Epistemology on an Objectivist Foundation* (New York: TOF Publications, Inc., 2014).

————, "Sorry Libertarian Anarchists, Capitalism Requires Government," *Forbes*, January 24, 2014, https://www.forbes.com/sites/harrybinswanger/2014/01/24/sorry -libertarian-anarchists-capitalism-requires-government-2/#f3def8a7d89b (accessed September 4, 2018).

Binswanger, Harry, editor, *The Ayn Rand Lexicon: Objectivism from A to Z* (New York: Penguin Books, 1986).

Bogen, David S., "The Individual Liberties within the Body of the Constitution: A Symposium: The Privileges and Immunities Clause of Article IV," *Case Western Reserve Law Review* vol. 37 (1987), pp. 794–861.

Boyd, Julian P., editor, *The Papers of Thomas Jefferson: Vol. 1, 1760–1776* (Princeton, NJ: Princeton University Press, 1950).

Burrell, Thomas H., "A Story of Privileges and Immunities: From Medieval Concept to the Colonies and United States Constitution," *Campbell Law Review* vol. 34, no. 1 (Fall 2011), pp. 7–120.

Calabresi, Steven G., "An Agenda for Constitutional Reform," in *Constitutional Stupidities, Constitutional Tragedies*, edited by William N. Eskridge, Jr. and Sanford Levinson (New York: New York University Press, 1998), pp. 22–27.

Cochrane, John, "Trump's Tariffs Will Hurt Trade, and Trade Is a Good Thing – Really," March 5, 2018, https://www.foxnews.com/opinion/trumps-tariffs-will-hur t-trade-and-trade-is-a-good-thing-really (accessed May 10, 2019).

Coghan, Neil H., editor, *The Complete Bill of Rights: The Drafts, Debates, Sources, & Origins*, 2nd edition (New York: Oxford University Press, 2015).

Coulson, Andrew J., "On the Way to School: Why and How to Make a Market in Education," in *Freedom and School Choice in American Education*, edited by Greg Forster and C. Bradley Thompson (New York: Palgrave Macmillan, 2011), pp. 17–29.

Dorn, James A., "Abolish the Jury 'Draft'," https://www.cato.org/publications/c ommentary/abolish-jury-draft (accessed June 10, 2018).

Duker, William F., "The President's Power to Pardon: A Constitutional History," *William & Mary Law Review* vol. 18, no. 3 (Spring 1977), pp. 475–538.

Durchslag, Melvyn R., *State Sovereign Immunity: A Reference Guide to the United States Constitution* (Westport, CT: Praeger, 2002).

Epstein, Richard A., *Supreme Neglect: How to Revive Constitutional Protection for Private Property* (Oxford: Oxford University Press, 2008).

Farrand, Max, editor, *The Records of the Federal Convention of 1787*, Vol. II (New Haven, CT: Yale University Press, 1911).

Forte, David F. and Matthew Spalding, editors, *The Heritage Guide to the Constitution*, 2nd edition (Washington, DC: Regnery Publishing, 2014).

Foust, John, "State Power to Regulate Alcohol Under the Twenty-First Amendment: The Constitutional Implications of the Twenty-First Amendment Enforcement Act," *Boston College Law Review* vol. 41, no. 3 (2000), pp. 659–97.

Friedman, Milton, "The Case for Abolishing the Draft—and Substituting for It an All-Volunteer Army," https://miltonfriedman.hoover.org/friedman_images/Colle ctions/2016c21/NYT_05_14_1967 (accessed June 11, 2018).

Gerber, Scott Douglas, *To Secure These Rights: The Declaration of Independence and Constitutional Interpretation* (New York: New York University Press, 1995).

Gotthelf, Allan and Gregory Salmieri, editors, *A Companion to Ayn Rand* (Chichester, UK: Wiley Blackwell, 2016).

Graber, Mark, "The Declaration of Independence and Contemporary Constitutional Pedagogy," *Southern California Law Review* vol. 89, no. 3 (March 2016), pp. 509–39.

Guardiano, John R., David Haarmeyer, and Robert W. Poole, Jr., "Fire Protection Privatization: A Cost-Effective Approach to Public Safety" (October 1992), https ://reason.org/wp-content/uploads/files/c2bbfe415eccfdff424a2bf7c8a20585.pdf (accessed August 16, 2019).

Gwartney, James D., Richard L. Stroup, Russell S. Sobel, and David A. Macpherson, *Macroeconomics: Private and Public Choice*, 15th edition (Stamford, CT: Cengage Learning, 2015).

Gwartney, James, Robert Lawson, Joshua Hall, and Ryan Murphy, *Economic Freedom of the World: 2019 Annual Report* (Vancouver, BC, Canada: Fraser Institute, 2019).

Gyourko, Joseph and Raven Molloy, "Regulation and Housing Supply," NBER Working Paper 20536 (October 2014), http://www.nber.org/papers/w20536.pdf (accessed August 26, 2018).

Hamilton, Alexander, *Report on Manufactures*, December 5, 1791, http://www.cons titution.org/ah/rpt_manufactures.pdf (accessed November 10, 2017).

Holy Bible, Revised standard version (Nashville, TN: Thomas Nelson, Inc., 1972).

Hsieh, Chang-Tai and Enrico Moretti, "Housing Constraints and Spatial Misallocation," *American Economic Journal: Macroeconomics* vol. 11, no. 2 (April 2019), pp. 1–39.

Ikeda, Sanford and Emily Washington, "How Land-Use Regulation Undermines Affordable Housing," Mercatus Research (November 2015), https://www.mer catus.org/system/files/Ikeda-Land-Use-Regulation.pdf (accessed August 26, 2018).

Institute for Justice, "Myths and Realities of Eminent Domain Abuse" (June 2006), https://ij.org/wp-content/uploads/2015/03/CC_Myths_Reality-Final.pdf (accessed July 25, 2020).

Itani, Talal, translator, *Quran in English*, https://www.clearquran.com/downloads/qur an-in-english-clearquran.pdf (accessed April 24, 2019).

Jaffe, Louis L., "Suits against Governments and Officers: Damage Actions," *Harvard Law Review* vol. 77, no. 2 (December 1963), pp. 209–39.

Kalt, Brian C., "Pardon Me?: The Constitutional Case against Presidential Self-Pardons," *The Yale Law Journal* vol. 106, no. 3 (December 1996), pp. 779–809.

Kates, Don B., Jr., "Handgun Prohibition and the Original Meaning of the Second Amendment," *Michigan Law Review* vol. 82, no. 2 (November 1983), pp. 204–73.

Katz, Martin J., "Guantanamo, *Boumediene*, and Jurisdiction-Stripping: The Imperial President Meets the Imperial Court," *Constitutional Commentary* vol. 25 (2009), pp. 377–423.

Khan, Ali, "The Evolution of Money: A Story of Constitutional Nullification," *University of Cincinnati Law Review* vol. 67 (Winter 1999), pp. 393–443.

Koch, Adrienne and William Peden, editors, *The Life and Selected Writings of Thomas Jefferson* (New York: The Modern Library, 1998).

Lalich, Roger A., "Health Care Personnel Delivery System: Another Doctor Draft?," *Wisconsin Medical Journal* vol. 103, no. 1 (2004), pp. 21–24.

Levin, Mark R., *The Liberty Amendments: Restoring the American Republic* (New York: Threshold Editions, 2013).

Levinson, Sanford, "The Embarrassing Second Amendment," *The Yale Law Journal* vol. 99, no. 3 (December 1989), pp. 637–59.

Locke, John, *The Second Treatise on Civil Government* (Amherst, NY: Prometheus Books, 1986 [1689]).

Long, Roderick T., "Imagineering Freedom: A Constitution of Liberty, Part IV: The Rights of the People," *Formulations* vol. 2, no. 4 (Summer 1995), http://www.freenation.org/a/f24l2.html (accessed February 26, 2017).

———, "Imagineering Freedom: A Constitution of Liberty, Part II: Defining Federal Powers," *Formulations* vol. 2, no. 2 (Winter 1994–1995), http://www.freenation.org/a/f22l2.html (accessed September 4, 2017).

Lott, Jr., John R., *More Guns, Less Crime: Understanding Crime and Gun-Control Laws*, 3rd edition (Chicago, IL: The University of Chicago Press, 2010).

Lund, Nelson, "The Second Amendment, Political Liberty, and the Right to Self-Preservation," *Alabama Law Review* vol. 39 (1987), pp. 103–30.

Madison, James, Alexander Hamilton, and John Jay, *The Federalist Papers*, edited by Isaac Kramnick (London: Penguin Books, 1987).

Marriott, Alexander V., "Getting Lincoln Right," *The Objective Standard* vol. 9, no. 2 (Summer 2014), pp. 11–38.

McGee, Robert W., "Secession Reconsidered," *The Journal of Libertarian Studies* vol. 11, no. 1 (Fall 1994), pp. 11–33.

Mickenberg, Ira, "Abusing the Exceptions and Regulations Clause: Legislative Attempts to Divest the Supreme Court of Appellate Jurisdiction," *The American University Law Review* vol. 32, no. 2 (1983), pp. 497–542.

Miller, Fred D., Jr. and Adam Mossoff, "Political Theory: A Radical for Capitalism," in *A Companion to Ayn Rand*, edited by Allan Gotthelf and Gregory Salmieri (Malden, MA: Wiley Blackwell, 2016), pp. 187–202.

Miron, Jeffrey A., "Violence and U.S Prohibitions of Drugs and Alcohol," NBER Working Paper 6950 (February 1999), https://www.nber.org/papers/w6950.pdf (accessed May 12, 2019).

Miron, Jeffrey A. and Jeffrey Zwiebel, "The Economic Case Against Drug Prohibition," *Journal of Economic Perspectives* vol. 9, no. 4 (Fall 1995), pp. 175–92.

Mises, Ludwig von, *Socialism* (Indianapolis, IN: LibertyClassics [sic], 1981 [1951]).

Monroe, James, "Special Message to the House of Representatives Containing the Views of the President of the United States on the Subject of Internal Improvements," May 4, 1822, published online by Gerhard Peters and John T. Woolley, *The American Presidency Project*, https://www.presidency.ucsb.edu/documents/special-message-the-house-representatives-containing-the-views-the-president-the-united (accessed June 27, 2020).

———, "Veto Message," May 4, 1822, published online by Gerhard Peters and John T. Woolley, *The American Presidency Project*, https://www.presidency.ucsb.edu/documents/veto-message (accessed June 27, 2020).

Mossoff, Adam, "What Is Property? Putting the Pieces Back Together," *Arizona Law Review* vol. 45 (Summer 2003), pp. 371–443.

Natelson, Robert G., "The Original Meaning of the Privileges and Immunities Clause," *Georgia Law Review* vol. 43 (Summer 2009), pp. 1117–93.

———, "Statutory Retroactivity: The Founders' View," *Idaho Law Review* vol. 39 (2003), pp. 489–529.

Nowrasteh, Alex, "The 14 Most Common Arguments Against Immigration and Why They Are Wrong," May 2, 2018, https://www.cato.org/blog/14-most-common-arguments-against-immigration-why-theyre-wrong (accessed May 19, 2019).

Osili, Una and Sasha Zarins, "American Giving Lost Some Ground in 2018 Amid Tax Changes and Stock Market Losses," *The Conversation*, June 18, 2019, https://theconversation.com/american-giving-lost-some-ground-in-2018-amid-tax-changes-and-stock-market-losses-118892 (accessed September 6, 2020).

O'Toole, Randal, "Smart Growth and Housing," in *Housing America: Building Out of a Crisis*, edited by Randall G. Holcombe and Benjamin Powell (New Brunswick, NJ: Transaction Publishers, 2009), pp. 83–108.

Palmer, Tom G., editor, *After the Welfare State* (Ottawa, IL: Jameson Books, 2012).

Peikoff, Amy L., "Beyond Reductionism: Reconsidering the Right to Privacy," *New York University Journal of Law & Liberty* vol. 3, no. 1 (2008), pp. 1–47.

Peikoff, Leonard, *Objectivism: The Philosophy of Ayn Rand* (New York: Meridian, 1991).

———, *The Ominous Parallels* (New York: Stein and Day, 1982).

Peikoff, Leonard, editor, *The Voice of Reason: Essays in Objectivist Thought* (New York: Meridian, 1989).

Plafker, Stephen, "Structure of the American Constitution," audio recording (Irvine, CA: The Ayn Rand Institute, 2006).

Poe, Richard, *The Seven Myths of Gun Control: Reclaiming the Truth About Guns, Crime, and the Second Amendment* (Roseville, CA: FORUM, 2001).

Poole, Jr., Robert W., "Leisure and Recreational Services," in *The Theory of Market Failure: A Critical Examination*, edited by Tyler Cowen (Fairfax, VA: George Mason University Press, 1988), pp. 327–39.

Powell, Benjamin, "The Trump Policy that Will 'Shrink the Economy and Make the U.S. Poorer'," November 18, 2016, http://www.independent.org/news/article.asp?id=8929 (accessed May 10, 2019).

Rakove, Jack N., *The Annotated U.S. Constitution and Declaration of Independence* (Cambridge, MA: The Belknap Press, 2009).

Rand, Ayn, *Atlas Shrugged*, 35th anniversary edition (New York: Signet, 1992 [1957]).

———, *Philosophy: Who Needs It* (New York: Signet, 1982).

———, *The New Left: The Anti-Industrial Revolution*, Revised edition (New York: Signet, 1975).

———, *Capitalism: The Unknown Ideal* (New York: Signet, 1967).

———, "Politics of a Free Society," Radio Interview of Ayn Rand (1965), https://campus.aynrand.org/works/1965/01/01/politics-of-a-free-society (accessed December 21, 2016).

———, *The Virtue of Selfishness* (New York: Signet, 1964).

———, *For the New Intellectual* (New York: Signet, 1961).

Ratner, Leonard G., "Majoritarian Constraints on Judicial Review: Congressional Control of Supreme Court Jurisdiction," *Villanova Law Review* vol. 27, no. 5 (1982), pp. 929–58.

Rawle, William, *A View of the Constitution of the United States of America*, 2nd edition (Colorado Springs, CO: Portage Publications, 2011 [1829]).

Rector, Robert and Rachel Sheffield, "Understanding Poverty in the United States: Surprising Facts About America's Poor," *Backgrounder* no. 2607, September 13, 2011, http://thf_media.s3.amazonaws.com/2011/pdf/bg2607.pdf (accessed November 17, 2017).

Reisman, George, "Globalization: The Long-Run Big Picture," November 17, 2006, http://capitalism.net/articles/Globalization.htm (accessed May 11, 2019).

———, "The Line-Item Veto is a Bad Idea," February 14, 1998, http://capitalism.net/articles/li_veto.htm (accessed August 13, 2017).

———, *Capitalism: A Treatise on Economics* (Ottawa, IL: Jameson Books, 1996).

———, "The Real Right to Medical Care Versus Socialized Medicine" (1994), http://capitalism.net/articles/SOC_MED_files/The%20Real%20Right%20to%20Medical%20Care%20Versus%20Socialized%20Medicine.html (accessed August 16, 2019).

Richman, Sheldon, "'Unbounded Liberty, and Even Caprice': Why 'School Choice' Is Dangerous to Education," in *Freedom and School Choice*, edited by Greg Forster and C. Bradley Thompson (New York: Palgrave Macmillan, 2011), pp. 91–107.

Robbins, Gary, "What You Need to Know about Buying Recreational Marijuana in San Diego," *The San Diego Union-Tribune*, November 10, 2017, https://www.sandiegouniontribune.com/news/science/sd-me-marijuana-qanda-20171108-story.html (accessed July 27, 2019).

Rotter, Jonathan M. and Joshua S. Stambaugh, "What's Left of the Twenty-First Amendment?," *Cardozo Public Law, Policy & Ethics Journal* vol. 6, no. 3 (Summer 2008), pp. 601–49.

Ruwart, Mary J., *Death by Regulation: How We Were Robbed of a Golden Age of Health and How We Can Reclaim It* (Kalamazoo, MI and San Francisco, CA: SunStar Press and Liberty International, 2018).

Saltzman, James D., "Building Code Blues," January 1, 1996, https://fee.org/articles/building-code-blues/ (accessed August 18, 2019).

Sandefur, Timothy, *The Conscience of the Constitution: The Declaration of Independence and the Right to Liberty* (Washington, DC: Cato Institute, 2014).

Selective Service System, "Medical Draft in Standby Mode," https://www.sss.gov/About/Medical-Draft-in-Standby-Mode (accessed June 9, 2018).

Shedenhelm, Richard, "The Cause of the Civil War According to Confederate Leaders," *The Objective Standard* vol. 10, no. 3 (Fall 2015), pp. 51–56.

Shortell, Christopher, *Rights, Remedies, and the Impact of State Sovereign Immunity* (Albany, NY: State University of New York Press, 2008).

Siegan, Bernard H., *Property and Freedom: The Constitution, the Courts, and Land-Use Regulation* (New Brunswick, NJ: Transaction Publishers, 1997).

———, *Drafting a Constitution for a Nation or Republic Emerging into Freedom*, 2nd edition (Fairfax, VA: George Mason University Press, 1994).

———, *Land Use Without Zoning* (Lexington, MA: Lexington Books, 1972).

Simpson, Brian P., *Money, Banking, and the Business Cycle, Vol. 2: Remedies and Alternative Theories* (New York: Palgrave Macmillan, 2014).

———, *Money, Banking, and the Business Cycle, Vol. 1: Integrating Theory and Practice* (New York: Palgrave Macmillan, 2014).

———, *Markets Don't Fail!* (Lanham, MD: Lexington Books, 2005).

Smith, Noah, "Companies That Discriminate Fail (Eventually)," September 23, 2016, https://www.bloomberg.com/opinion/articles/2016-09-23/companies-that-discriminate-fail-eventually (accessed December 26, 2019).

Smith, Tara, *Judicial Review in an Objective Legal System* (New York: Cambridge University Press, 2015).

———, "The Politics of Pretend—and Its Impact on the Legal System," audio recording (Irvine, CA: The Ayn Rand Institute, 2013).

———, *Viable Values: A Study of Life as the Root and Reward of Morality* (Lanham, MD: Rowman & Littlefield Publishers, Inc., 2000).

Starr, Kenneth W., "Testimony of the Hon. Kenneth W. Starr Before the House Government Reform Committee," *DC Vote*, June 23, 2004, http://www.dcvote.org/sites/default/files/kstarr062304_0.pdf (accessed December 17, 2016).

Stevens, John Paul, *Six Amendments: How and Why We Should Change the Constitution* (New York: Little, Brown and Company, 2014).

Strasser, Mark, "Taking Exception to Traditional Exceptions Clause Jurisprudence: On Congress's Power to Limit the Court's Jurisdiction," *Utah Law Review* vol. 1 (2001), pp. 125–87.

Thayer, James B., "Legal Tender," *Harvard Law Review* vol. 1, no. 2 (1887), pp. 73–97.

Thierer, Adam, "Advertising, Commercial Speech, and First Amendment Parity," *Charleston Law Review* vol. 5, no. 3 (2011), pp. 503–19.

Thompson, C. Bradley, "Do Children Have a 'Right' to an Education?," in *Freedom and School Choice*, edited by Greg Forster and C. Bradley Thompson (New York: Palgrave Macmillan, 2011), pp. 129–51.

Tracinski, Robert, "America's 'Field of Blackbirds': How the Campaign for Reparations for Slavery Perpetuates Racism," *The Intellectual Activist: An Objectivist Review* vol. 15, no. 6 (June 2001), pp. 21–31.

Transform Drug Policy Foundation, "The War on Drugs: Creating Crime, Enriching Criminals," http://www.countthecosts.org/sites/default/files/Crime-briefing.pdf (accessed May 12, 2019).

Troy, Daniel E., "Toward a Definition and Critique of Retroactivity," *Alabama Law Review* vol. 51, no. 3 (2000), pp. 1329–53.

Tucker, William, "Building Codes, Housing Prices, and the Poor," in *Housing America: Building Out of a Crisis*, edited by Randall G. Holcombe and Benjamin Powell (New Brunswick, NJ: Transaction Publishers, 2009), pp. 65–82.

United States General Accounting Office, *Report to the Chairman, Committee on Resources, House of Representatives – U.S. Insular Areas: Application of the U.S. Constitution* (November 1997), https://www.gao.gov/archive/1998/og98005.pdf (accessed May 6, 2018).

Upham, David R., "*Corfield v. Coryell* and the Privileges and Immunities of American Citizenship," *Texas Law Review* vol. 83, no. 5 (April 2005), pp. 1483–534.

Van Alstyne, William W., "A Critical Guide to *Ex Parte McCardle*," *Arizona Law Review* vol. 15 (1973), pp. 229–69.

Vedder, Richard K., *Restoring the Promise: Higher Education in America* (Oakland, CA: Independent Institute, 2019).

Vile, John R., *Re-Framers: 170 Eccentric, Visionary, and Patriotic Proposals to Rewrite the U.S. Constitution* (Santa Barbara, CA: ABC-CLIO, LLC, 2014).

Young, Gordon G., "Congressional Regulation of Federal Courts' Jurisdiction and Processes: *United States v. Klein* Revisited," *Wisconsin Law Review* (1981), pp. 1189–262.

Index

Note: I do not reference specific clauses or parts of the Declaration and Constitution in the index in connection with the main discussion of those clauses or parts, although there are some exceptions to this rule. I mainly reference specific clauses or parts of these documents only if they are mentioned outside the main discussion of them. For example, the main discussion of Amendment VI is in chapter 6, where the Bill of Rights is addressed. No reference to Amendment VI is made in the index in connection with the main discussion of Amendment VI. However, mention of Amendment VI in chapter 5 in connection with the Exceptions and Regulations Clause is referenced in the index. I make exceptions to this rule when I think it is important to reference the main discussion of clauses and parts of these documents in the index.

Also by the Author

Money, Banking, and the Business Cycle, Volume 2: Remedies and Alternative Theories (New York: Palgrave Macmillan, 2014)

Money, Banking, and the Business Cycle, Volume 1: Integrating Theory and Practice (New York: Palgrave Macmillan, 2014)

Markets Don't Fail! (Lanham, MD: Lexington Books, 2005)

About the Author

Brian P. Simpson is professor and chair in the Department of Accounting, Finance, and Economics in the College of Professional Studies at National University in La Jolla, California. He is author of the two-volume book on Austrian business cycle theory titled *Money, Banking, and the Business Cycle*. The book provides a comprehensive analysis of the business cycle. Volume 1 explains the business cycle using Austrian business cycle theory. It also presents empirical evidence in support of Austrian business cycle theory and defends the theory from criticisms. Volume 2 critiques alternative theories of the cycle, including real business cycle theory and Keynesian business cycle theory. Volume 2 also offers policy solutions to solve the problem of the business cycle. Both volumes of *Money, Banking, and the Business Cycle* were published in 2014. Dr. Simpson is also author of *Markets Don't Fail!*, a book that demonstrates that the standard claims of economists of market failure, such as those pertaining to monopoly, externalities, inequality, and environmental issues, are not valid. *Markets Don't Fail!* was published in 2005. A Chinese translation of *Markets Don't Fail!* was published in 2012. Before pursuing a career in economics, Dr. Simpson was an aerospace engineer performing rigid body dynamic separation analyses in the Delta Launch Vehicle Division of McDonnell Douglas Space Systems Company in Huntington Beach, California. He holds a Ph.D. and M.A. in economics from George Mason University, an M.B.A. from Pepperdine University, and a B.S. in aerospace engineering from Syracuse University.

Lightning Source UK Ltd.
Milton Keynes UK
UKHW011320130722
405800UK00002B/5